Social Anthropology

Social Anthropology

S.L. Doshi
P.C. Jain

RAWAT PUBLICATIONS
Jaipur • New Delhi • Bangalore • Guwahati • Kolkata

ISBN 978-81-7033-646-4 (HB)
ISBN 978-81-7033-647-1 (PB)

Reprinted, 2022

Published by
Prem Rawat for Rawat Publications
Satyam Apts., Sector 3, Jawahar Nagar, Jaipur - 302 004 (India)
Phones: 0141 265 1748 / 265 7006
E-mail : info@rawatbooks.com
Website: rawatbooks.com

Delhi Office
4858/24, Ansari Road, Daryaganj, New Delhi 110 002
Phone: 011-23263290

Also at *Bangalore, Guwahati* and *Kolkata*

Typeset by Rawat Computers, Jaipur
Printed at Nice Printing Press, New Delhi

Contents

Preface

The present work is a revisit to social anthropology. Indian social anthropology is basically an image of British social anthropology. This image has, in course of time, evolved because of the relationship between social anthropology and sociology. In Britain, one can easily differentiate social anthropology from sociology. But, in India, the freedom struggle, the British rule, and historical forces have created a situation in which it is difficult to isolate social anthropology from sociology. During the course of its development social anthropology in India has not been able to construct its own theoretical, conceptual and ideological systems. As a result of such a 'lag' in social anthropology its presentation to scholars and students has always been of a stereotype. Even today, the tribals of India are presented as savages, backward and illiterate.

We find that much change has come among the primitives in the world. Evans-Pritchard's Azande and Nuer, Fortes' Tallensi, Gluckman's Barotse and Malinowski's Trobriand islanders have undergone a tremendous change. They have accepted modernization and a few of them have embraced postmodernism. If this has happened with the isolated tribals of Africa, we should not think that Indian tribes—Gond, Bhil, Oroan and others---have remained static, quite unchanging. This warrants us to take stock of the changing situation of Indian tribes. If we do that, naturally, some of our old anthropological categories would lose their relevance. As a matter of fact, in India, the tribal situation, including their culture, has been politicized. This must be argued.

The forces of fundamentalism have been so strong in India that the tribals are identified either as Hindus or Christians. If we look from the scientific perspectives of social anthropology and also racial and ethnic standpoint, we find that tribals constitute a distinct society. Even historically, they constitute a type of society. They are located at an evolutionary stage of development. Thus, it is held by social anthropologists that a tribal society is neither a Hindu society, nor any other society. It is a particular distinct ethnic society. Such a perspective of tribal society is clear from the social evidence given by the *People of India* project that the tribals might adopt the Hindu gods and goddesses, Christian church and rituals, but basically they remain tribal. In any hierarchy of gods, the local village deity occupies the apex position. And this makes them indigenous. The present work is characterized by such perspectives. We argue that the mode of production and the social organization have positive relations. Let it be worked out in the case of tribals. For instance, if the tribals have their own indigenous identity, why should we make them Hindus or Christians.

We have discussed aspects of political anthropology also. The tribal social movements have been analyzed thoroughly. In course of our discussion, we find a strange behaviour on the part of tribals. History provides evidence. The Munda, Ho, Bhil and Gond tribes have revolted against the British raj or princely rulers during the British period. The tribals have waged guerrilla wars against their adversaries and have followed the tactic of hit and run. But how is it that such a vibrant tribal folk is not committing any serious revolt? Naxalism has remained restricted to very few pockets only. The tribals know that a large part of money spent on their development has been cornered by groups of vested interests. This is a case of injustice. Why do the tribals not rise against this kind of false investment in their development? Perhaps, a thorough study of their social structure might help us understand the 'culture of silence' that we find among them.

It is a textbook that gives a fresh, updated recipe to the students of social anthropology. The work abandons biases and stereotypes which characterize our tribal people. It gives new theoretical and conceptual categories to analyze the current tribal situation. Apart from being a textbook, it also reviews the whole mass of data generated by the researchers in post-independence India. It is a stock-taking of the current trends in the world of social anthropology. This makes the work useful for the researchers and academicians. Thus, its status is both that of a research work and of a textbook.

S.L. Doshi
P.C. Jain

1

What Anthropology is About: The Culture of Anthropology

It is amazing but true that social anthropology does not enjoy a respectable status in India and other Third World countries. Among the social sciences it was social anthropology which became a tool by providing a tacit fund of knowledge to the colonial powers for the suppression of the people. The British had their colonial rule in India and many parts of Africa. They ruled over the masses of people without doing any substantial good to the common man. This historically made the colonial people quite unfriendly to the general public. The British administrators-turned-social anthropologists, such as Risley and Russell, provided clues to the British empire for doing all kinds of injustice. It happened in South Africa and other parts of the world. Historically, all this ended in the erosion of the public trust towards social anthropology.

Interestingly enough, the hangover of the bruised reputation of social anthropology was witnessed in post-independence India also. In the decades of forties and fifties and afterwards, sociology became a popular discipline in universities and colleges, whereas the chair of social anthropology in a large number of universities was wanted. Even today, the universities and colleges are quite eager to open up new departments of sociology but at the same time are quite hesitant to start departments of social anthropology. The colonial hatred persists. However, it must be said that social anthropology is rich in its skills to study the indigenous knowledge of the masses of people living in hills, forests and villages. The argument is simple—if social anthropology has the guts to help the colonial regime to settle in India and consolidate its power, it also has the potential to carry the people to the road of progress and development. It is an academic tool, a weapon which leaves us to decide how to use it.

But it is difficult to win over the prejudices against social anthropology. There is enough evidence to support our argument. Some of our sociologists are basically, in terms of holding the university degree, social anthropologists. But, in their formal status of sociologists, they have contributed substantially to the knowledge of social anthropology. Our sociological fund of knowledge owes much to social anthropology. The contributions of sociologists like M.N. Srinivas, S.C. Dube and G.S. Ghurye are basically anthropological in their content but are included in the field of sociology. As a matter of fact, in countries like India, Pakistan, Bangladesh and South Africa, it is difficult to separate social anthropology from sociology. Simply, they are inseparable. Despite this understanding social anthropology would require several decades to establish itself in the popular framework of the intellectual society.

Ideologically, social anthropology is considered to be an active partner with the religiosity and capitalism dominating the society. The anthropological studies conducted in the southern part of Africa very convincingly show that after independence the clergymen and the businessmen had to flee with a copy of the Bible under the arm and a briefcase in hand. The history of colonial and feudal regimes in the South African countries shows that social anthropology had a dirty relationship with imperialism, capitalism and religious conversion. It is with this historical background in view that we analyze the new horizons which social anthropology has opened up for the development of the indigenous people, weaker sections and rural people. Now is the time when we should employ social anthropological potential for the new goals charted out by different developing countries. We believe that if the sociological knowledge and researches are properly utilized, the discipline itself would be enriched in theory, methods and data and would also help the society and state to attain new future.

How Do We Look at Social Anthropology?

Social anthropology is a social science and, therefore, it enjoys a tall status in the realm of social sciences. Despite its long history many of its concepts are still not clear. Long back in 1950 when E.E. Evans-Pritchard delivered the memorable Marett Lecture at Oxford he lamented on the ambiguities which prevailed in social anthropology.

For instance, he said:

> Social anthropology has a very limited technical vocabulary, so that it has to use everyday language and this, as we all know, is not very precise. Such words as 'society', 'culture', 'custom', 'religion', 'sanction', 'structure', 'function', 'political' and 'democratic' do not always convey the same meaning either to different people or in different contexts.

The use of non-technical words has obscured its precise meaning. Yet at another place Evans-Pritchard observes in his lecture by saying that even among the well-read laymen there is a good deal of haziness about the subject. He writes:

> I must assume that some of you are frankly ignorant of what social anthropology is and what others believe it to be what it is not.

The haziness that social anthropology contains is obvious in USA, England, and other countries of the European continent. In all these countries the understanding of social anthropology is diverse. In other words, it means differently in different countries.

Quickly, let us look at the understanding of social anthropology in USA, England and the rest of the European countries. In England and also in USA, to some extent, social anthropology is regarded as a larger and comprehensive discipline. It studies man from a number of aspects. It concerns itself with human cultures and societies. However, in other countries of Europe a different terminology is used. There, when people speak of anthropology, they mean physical anthropology. In a broader way physical anthropology studies the biological aspects of man. In England, on the other hand, what they call social anthropology is understood as ethnology or sociology in the continent. In short, in Europe itself, social anthropology has two definite understandings. Viewed from such a prevalence of the approach to social anthropology, it is felt that the discipline is mainly concerned with the study of social structure. In other words, social anthropology is oriented to the inquiry about social structure and social organization.

In USA, the traditional use of social anthropology is quite different from that in England and the European continent. Here, anthropology concerns itself with the study of culture. In England, the meaning of social anthropology is drawn from the works of A.R.

Radcliffe-Brown and Bronislaw Malinowski. According to these giant social anthropologists, the subject "is said to study social relations rather than culture, social systems rather than isolated customs and cultural traits". In USA, social anthropology has been shaped by A.L. Kroeber and Melville Herskovits. G.P. Murdock who has made a classical study of social structure also claims to be a culturologist. He says: "The special province of anthropology in relation to its sister disciplines is the study of culture." Herskovits, the noted American cultural anthropologist, also pleads for cultural orientation of social anthropology.

In India, the discipline of social anthropology is seen from a different perspective. Here, in some cases, social anthropology is a part of sociology; in other cases it is considered as a branch of anthropology. History has shaped the tradition of social anthropology in a different way. Whereas in USA the study of 'other cultures' is considered to be social anthropology, in our country a concern for caste, village and religion is said to be social anthropology.

As a matter of fact, the domain of the social anthropology all over the world is passing through a process of discipline formation. Each country, and for that matter, each society has given a specific shape to social anthropology. Indian society looks at it with a mixed orientation of culture and social structure. In the European continent, the discipline is concerned with the study of social system. Quite opposite to it, the approach to social anthropology is culture specific. These are a few of the ambiguities specifically spelt out by Evans-Pritchard which a student of social anthropology will have to combat for some time to come.

Why Study Social Anthropology in India?

Admittedly, social anthropology was used as a tool or weapon for subjugating the masses of people in the Third World countries. But, it has a very bright record in promoting the vital concerns of the weaker segments of society, namely, Scheduled Castes and Scheduled Tribes, bringing to light gender discrimination and exploitation of villages in India and the domination of white people over the native masses. This new orientation of social anthropology was witnessed by the middle of the 20th century.

The need for studying social anthropology in developing countries and particularly in India is urgent. Developing societies are confronted with the problems of poverty, illiteracy, lack of availability of funds, and general backwardness. These wretched of the earth or the subalterns cannot be led to the road of progress unless social anthropology makes a thorough study to identify their problems and suggest some prescriptions. Our question is simple: if the colonial regime, and for that matter, the British administrators-turned-social anthropologists could retain their power for a number of years with the insights gained with social anthropology, can we not use this discipline or apply its stock of knowledge for the betterment of the disadvantaged people? This is the prime use of social anthropology in India and elsewhere in the world. Some have worked towards the development of an urgent social anthropology or applied social anthropology.

John Beattie and others, in their study of 'other cultures', have suggested some reasons for the study of social anthropology in India and South Africa. These are listed below:

(i) Understanding the primitives and tribals

Social anthropology makes for a sympathetic understanding of other peoples, and especially the primitives and the tribals who reside in isolation. In the developing countries, planned and massive development programmes are implemented in the societies of these people. If proper research is done among these people, the implementation of these development programmes would yield fruitful results.

(ii) Easy to study simple and small-size societies

Social anthropology is concerned with the study of tribals, villagers and backward people. These groups are small in size and simple in lifestyle. It is easy for social anthropologists to study such an integrated and composite social group. Stressing the importance of social anthropology in the study of simple and indigenous people, John Lewis very rightly observes:

> To get to know a whole people intimately, to learn to recognize the common sense meaning of behaviour, beliefs, strict rules of living, alien to what we feel to be normal is a fascinating study. It is because these societies are simple compared with others and small, so that we can grasp the whole pattern in all its interacting parts, that we study primitive societies. The range of social contacts, lack of developed

technology, the relatively small scale of numbers and territory give us a chance to learn a great deal about a complete self-sustaining community.

In other words, the study of indigenous people, who are simple in lifestyle, small in size, and limited to a territory, helps enough to plan and construct theories of welfare for the society as a whole.

(iii) Findings applicable to other cultures also

Social anthropology needs to be emphasized because the progressive and developed segments of society today are also encountering crises which are threatening their very survival. The findings of anthropological studies can also be utilized for the urban, industrial, progressive groups. The theoretical formulations constructed from the study of simple societies also apply to complex societies. Radcliffe-Brown and Malinowski have demonstrated such uses of social anthropology.

(iv) Knowledge of uniformities and regularities of social life

Whatever may be the structure of a society—primitive or modern—social anthropology endeavours to find out some kind of order in the social structure. It is this order which is required to be possessed by all the societies. With the identification of this order in simple societies we can find out some uniformities and regularities in complex societies also. John Lewis stresses this point much and says that social anthropology has great potential for the non-primitive indigenous society. He writes:

> Finally, let us come back to the importance of anthropology for ourselves. The study of these societies which, while primitive, are not necessarily simpler than our own in that their kinship rules throws into relief certain general features of social life which concern all of us. *We can learn something applicable to the whole of human evolution from the first true man to the races of today; we can perhaps reach conclusions that are valid for all human societies* (emphasis added).

(v) Mitigation or removal of racial and caste bias

One of the important contributions of social anthropology is to mitigate and reduce our prejudices about races and castes. For instance, in India, the twice-born castes were considered to be an intellectual and sacred category of people. This prejudice imposed certain social, cultural and educational disabilities on the subaltern people of the society. Social anthropology has done something to do away with such prejudices.

Ruth Benedict has contributed much in this respect. She denied any social and cultural achievement of a race as hereditary. Advocating the theory of racism, she opposed the racial prejudices found prevalent in the European continent. In 1951, the UNESCO appointed an expert committee which, in its recommendations, observed that all humans in the world have evolved from *homo sapiens* and hence racial prejudice has no scientific standing. Our argument is that social anthropology has made substantial contributions which help us to shed some of our biases. In the Indian context, the 'caste war' which has become vital in our social fabric can be scientifically tackled with the popularization of social anthropological studies.

(vi) Strengthening the development programmes

Social anthropology also helps to strengthen the development programmes among the tribals and weaker sections of society. Village development programmes can be made much more fruitful with the help of the researches done in this field. Verrier Elvin, being an anthropologist, was appointed advisor to the Government of India to study the tribals of the north-east. It was on the basis of the briefs given by him that Jawaharlal Nehru expounded the concept of *Panchsheel* for framing the policy for tribal development.

There are several reasons for promoting and teaching social anthropology in the Third World countries. At present, the growth of the discipline is restricted to a few pockets of the country. It needs to be encouraged among the social workers, development administrators and university students so that the social anthropologist becomes a dependable agent for social change among the weaker segments of society. Recently, Satish Sabbarwal has advocated for the emergence of urgent social anthropology in India.

Early Approach to Anthropology

In Europe, including England, the earlier meaning of anthropology was quite comprehensive. A.C. Haddon has traced the origin of the earlier meaning and definition of anthropology. He informs that the credit of coining the word 'anthropologist' goes to Aristotle. But his use of the word was quite rudimentary. It did not appear in the Latin language vocabulary. Aristotle took it from the folk use of the word. For him, an anthropologist was a "lofty-minded man in his book ethics". This man did not talk about himself. But, the word does not seem to have occupied a paramount place in the Greek language, and we next meet it in a Latin form in the 16th century. During this period, *anthropologium* was used in a restricted sense, relating to man's bodily structure. In the year 1501, the word was precisely used for anatomy and physiology.

The meaning of the word 'anthropology' was scarcely defined in the beginning of the 19th century, when we find it in the *British Encyclopaedia* of 1822. It was defined as under:

> Anthropology is a discourse upon human nature and among divines that manner of expression by which the inspired writers attribute human parts and passions to god.

The earliest definition of anthropology belonged to the last quarter of the 19th century. Topinard (1876), a renowned British anthropologist, defined it as below:

> Anthropology is the branch of natural history which treats of man and the races of man.

Thus, these earlier definitions of anthropology dwell on the understanding of: (i) the nature of man, and (ii) the physiology of man. Haddon had summarized the early meaning of anthropology by saying that it is the science of man which comprises two main divisions: the one which deals with the natural man, and the other which is concerned with man in relation to his fellows, or in other words, with social man. According to Haddon again, physical anthropology, as we call it today, was the only form of anthropology in the European continent. In other words, anthropology is composed of two words: *anthropos*, that is, man, and *ology*, that is, science. Thus, anthropology is the science of man. But, man is not only biological, he is also social and cultural, and thus, when anthropology studies man, it studies him in all his multiple aspects.

Current Approach to Anthropology

The present-day anthropology, which is practised in USA and the European continent, has received some refinement and modification.

Herskovits has defined it in a very precise way when he says that "it is a social science concerned with the study of man and his works". He says:

> A comprehensive definition of anthropology is the study of man and his works; because anthropology centers its attention on man, whether the focus of concern is broad or narrow. The great range of its subject matter has made it necessary for anthropology to develop special techniques and objectives to give unity to its aims and methods. At the same time, this vary range brings anthropology into relation with many other subjects.

In Europe, and particularly in England, as stated earlier, anthropology invariably means physical anthropology. However, the approach to anthropology in USA is culture-oriented. A.L. Kroeber makes the focus of anthropology in USA very clear:

> Of all the social sciences, anthropology is perhaps the most distinctively culture-conscious. It aims to investigate human culture as such, at all times, everywhere, in all its parts and aspects and workings. It looks for generalized findings as to how culture operates—literally, how human beings behave under given cultural conditions—and for the major developments of the history of culture.

Recently, David Bidney has tried to integrate the European social system approach to anthropology and the cultural approach to it in USA. He argues that culture stems from social system and that it gives formation to social system. In reality, social system and culture are inseparable. He suggests that anthropology should study both culture and social system along with the biology of man.

The current approach to the meaning and definition of anthropology is perhaps best exemplified by the definition given by John Lewis:

> Anthropology is the general term for the science of man: the cultural, social, physical development and behaviour of man throughout his history. The general term includes the special term, physical anthropology, human evolution, archaeology, (prehistory), cultural anthropology, social anthropology and linguistic anthropology.

Thus, according to Lewis, anthropology is very comprehensive in its scope and includes an elaborate classification of it. It also integrates system approach and cultural focus.

In his recent publication, Thomas Hylland Eriksen (*Small Places, Large Issues*, London, 1995) has defined anthropology in a wider context. He writes:

> Anthropology tries to account for the social and cultural variation in world, but a crucial part of the anthropological project also consists in conceptualizing and understanding similarities between social systems and human relations.

One very important aspect of anthropology is that it is not concerned with the individual man. The investigation of an individual man is the job of a physician. Anthropology is concerned with men in groups, with races and peoples and their happenings and doings. Anthropologists focus on the composition of races, their biology or organism. Besides biology, they also study the social and cultural aspects of man and groups. In other words, they try to find out what is biological in man and what is sociological and historical in him. This can be illustrated by a simple example.

We find a Bhil in a village in western India. We see that he has a complexion of olive to copper and dusky brown, he possesses a fine nose. He has an average Indian height. His eyes are full, expressive and dark. How do we explain these physical features of a Bhil? The answer is ready: He was born so. Cows produce calves, and lions cubs, so a Bhil springs from Bhil and a Gond springs from Gond. Our Bhil, as we also find, occasionally plays on the flute and sings his folk songs. He also takes a fancy to singing film songs. How do we answer this behaviour of a Bhil? Is it because of his heredity? No. He has acquired the habit of singing from his containing society. His father surely did not sing. And, definitely he did not have any knowledge of the film song which was alien to him. As for the specific song, heredity can obviously no longer be the cause. It shows that heredity is displaced by tradition, nature by nurture. The efficient forces now are quite different from those which made his skin black and gave him a fine nose.

"Here then is one distinctive task for anthropology. The interpretation of those phenomena into which both innate organic factors and social or acquired factors enter or may enter." For instance, the physical characteristics of a Bhil are based on heredity and the tradition or culture as singing folk and film music is acquired—socially and culturally. Anthropology, therefore, studies both biological or organic and socio-cultural factors.

Anthropology has its kit of methods also. For organic or physical anthropology, there is always need for a laboratory. If not laboratory at least investigations have to be made under experimental conditions. Socio-cultural phenomena have to be taken as they come and laboriously sifted and resifted afterwards. For this, hard fieldwork is the usual mode to be used by an anthropologist.

Evans-Pritchard has further elaborated the meaning and definition of the general term 'anthropology'. He very clearly states:

> Physical anthropology is that branch of human biology that comprises such interests as heredity, nutrition, sex differences, the comparative anatomy and physiology of races and the theory of human evolution.

What is important in the above definition is that the study of human biology or heredity is not made at the level of the individual. It focuses on the group and, therefore, Evans-Pritchard talks about comparative anatomy. For instance, the study of a Bhil in his biology is meaningless for anthropology. What is meaningful is that the whole racial composition of the Bhil tribe (not individual) constitutes the theme of anthropology. This emphasis on physiology at the group level was also stressed by Kroeber.

Stress on the study of comparative anatomy has also been made by Herskovits when he says:

> Physical anthropologists study such matters as the nature of racial differences, the inheritance of bodily traits, the growth, the development and decay of the human organism, and the influences of the natural environment on man.

Herskovits argues that all human beings spring from *homo sapiens.* This is the core unity of mankind. But, with the organic, social and cultural processes that men have acquired are of varying characteristics. Anthropology studies these variations. Comparison is the supreme methodological idiom of anthropology. One very important aspect of physical anthropology is the realm of somatology. A.C. Haddon, in his earlier work on anthropology, has discussed the importance of somatology. Actually, the first branch to attract anthropologists was somatology, that is, the physical aspect of man. Perhaps, Blumenbach was first to strike a keynote by recording the shape of the skull and of the face. Later on, somatology became a sub-specialization of physical anthropology and studied the bodily characteristics of man. Actually, somatology is the biological science of skulls.

At this stage of our discussion and analysis we observe that anthropology is quite comprehensive in its meaning and has a detailed classification. We will dwell on the classification in the following section. But before we do that, let us close our earlier discussion on the definition and meaning of anthropology with the following broad observations:

(1) Anthropology is a broad social science which includes biology, organicism and social and cultural systems.
(2) It is, therefore, both a biological science and a social-historical science.
(3) As a biological science it studies physical anthropology, human evolution (the science of fossilman). And, as a social science, it studies social system and culture.
(4) The approach to anthropology in the European continent is oriented to human biology. In England, which is a part of the continent, anthropology is generally termed as social anthropology or ethnology. In USA, however, the approach to anthropology is culture-specific. People there understand anthropology by the term 'cultural anthropology'.
(5) Broadly, anthropology is the science of the study of man. Man is studied in his totality, that is, in his biological, social, cultural aspects.
(6) Laboratory, fieldwork and comparative methods are the basic tools of an anthropological study.

Branches of Anthropology

The discipline of anthropology, as we find it today, is the result of several historical, biological and socio-cultural forces. There have also been efforts to improve, refine and redefine the discipline. The broader aspects of anthropology have now been divided into several branches. Each branch has a speciality. Some anthropologists have also tried to specify the special branches of anthropology. Among these are included Ralph Piddington, E.A. Hoebel and Ralph Linton. The anthropological specialities or branches are specified below:

1. *As specified by Ralph Piddington*
   (i) Physical Anthropology
   (ii) Cultural Anthropology
      (a) Pre-historic Archaeology
      (b) Social Anthropology
2. *As specified by E.A. Hoebel*
   (i) Physical Anthropology
      (a) Anthropometry
      (b) Human Biology
   (ii) Archaeology
   (iii) Cultural Anthropology
      (a) Ethnology
      (b) Linguistics
      (b) Social Anthropology
3. *As specified by Ralph Linton*
   (i) Physical Anthropology
      (a) Human Palaeontology
      (b) Somatology
   (ii) Cultural Anthropology
      (a) Archaeology
      (b) Ethnology
      (c) Linguistics

At the outset, we have said that there is no general agreement on the meaning and definition of anthropology. There is much differentiation in the meanings in the European continent, the United States and the Third World countries. In Europe, there is agreement on the two broad branches of anthropology: (i) physical anthropology, that is, biological study of man; and (ii) social-cultural anthropology. In USA, there is physical anthropology and cultural anthropology. Social anthropology or ethnology becomes a part of cultural anthropology. In the Third World countries, however, there is a definite place for physical anthropology and social anthropology. Ethnology in these countries becomes a part of social anthropology. If we make a broader division of anthropology, it consists of the following:

(1) Physical Anthropology
(2) Cultural Anthropology
(3) Ethnology
(4) Social Anthropology

Physical Anthropology

While discussing the understanding of anthropology in the European continent, we have observed that the meaning of the term here is taken by physical anthropology only. A.L. Kroeber at one place has defined it in specific terms:

> Physical anthropology is more immediately 'natural' and less 'humanized' in its concern. Anthropology, therefore, accepts and uses the general principles of biology.

Actually, physical anthropology is more elaborate and detailed than biology. For instance, when a zoologist tries to understand the biology of an animal, he never goes into the details of the length and breath of the skull. Physical anthropology examines the skull in all its details, and the number of degrees two bones are twisted in, and the like. Thus, physical anthropology has a sort of specialization or sharpening of certain aspects of general biology. Still another speciality of physical anthropology is that it is concerned only with limited and restricted study of the human species. It never moves beyond the study of humans.

David Bidney has taken a similar position. Though an American anthropologist, he defined physical anthropology in terms of the origin, evolution and development of man. He stresses on the comparative methodology employed by physical anthropology. For instance, in the classification of human races, comparative physiology has bean employed by all physical anthropologists. Bidney observes:

> Man is the concern of that branch of anthropology known as physical anthropology which takes up such problems as the evolution of man and the comparative anatomy of races.

If we analyze the whole kit of definitions of physical anthropology, we would be able to draw the following characteristics of physical anthropology:

(1) It is a natural science.
(2) Its nature is organic and physical.
(3) It draws from the general principles of biology, zoology and other natural sciences.
(4) It depends on heredity and the doctrines of cell development and evolution.
(5) It utilizes the methods of laboratory and experimental conditions.
(6) It has a limited field of studying only one species, that is, man.
(7) It studies all varieties of men, different races, sexes and ages, and uses predominantly comparative methods.

Cultural Anthropology

A.L. Kroeber, in his celebrated work on anthropology published in the forties, divides anthropology broadly into two divisions: physical anthropology and socio-cultural anthropology. At a later stage, the socio-cultural anthropology got split into cultural anthropology and social anthropology. Even today, this split is not readily accepted all over the world. As a matter of fact, before discussing social anthropology and cultural anthropology, we must reiterate that the meaning of sociology, as we said earlier, varies from continent to continent and in fact, from society to society. The diverse traditions of anthropology in the domain of cultural anthropology and social anthropology are very successfully elaborated by Eriksen. His narration, which is a little lengthy, goes as under:

> Anthropology is a large and diversified subject, which is practised somewhat differently in different countries, although it retains its distinctive character everywhere. Since the Second World War, the core areas have been Great Britain, the US, France and Australia. *British anthropology, which is generally spoken of as social anthropology and which also enjoys a strong position in Scandinavia and India, emphasizes the study of social processes and is thus close to social anthropology.* The British social anthropologist Edmund Leach (1982) once characterized this subject as a *comparative micro-sociology. In the US, we tend instead to speak of cultural anthropology, and in general the sociological underpinning characteristic has bean less dominant there.* Instead, linguistics and pre-history have informed American anthropology in different ways. Several important specializations such as cultural ecology, linguistic anthropology and various approaches in psycho-

logical and interpretive or hermeneutic anthropology were developed in the US.

Eriksen has also discussed the anthropological tradition prevailing in France. There, after the Second World War, cultural anthropology has been replaced by structuralism. This brand of structural anthropology is proposed by Claude Levi-Strauss, Louis Dumont and the distinguished structuralists such as Marxist Maurice Godelier and others. Eriksen further informs that in South America, Italy and the Iberian Peninsula, and partly in Belgium and the Netherlands, the French orientation is strong.

If we elaborate further the anthropological traditions at the regional level in each country and continent, we would identify a number of variations. Actually, the discipline of social-cultural anthropology has emerged out of the local needs and processes. However, for a broader analysis, we put the traditions of anthropology as discussed above in a capsule form below:

Traditions or Culture of Anthropology in Different Countries/Continents

Country/Continent	*Traditional Form*
Great Britain, Scandinavian countries, India and other Asian countries	Social Anthropology
USA	Cultural Anthropology, Linguistics, Cultural Ecology, Psychological and Interpretive Anthropology, Pre-history
France	Structuralism, Structural Marxism
South America, Italy, Iberian Peninsula, Belgium and The Netherlands	Same as in France

It is interesting to note that the orientation to physical anthropology in all parts of the world is the same. However, in social-cultural anthropology different orientations have emerged. In India, which was influenced by British social anthropology, as a part of colonial imperialism cultural, linguistic and ethnic anthropology have not developed. Basically, social-cultural anthropology has three branches: (1) cultural anthropology, (2) ethnology, and (3) social anthropology. The former two constitute the tradition of the USA and France. India and the other South Asian countries have the tradition of social anthropology.

We now dwell on the definition of cultural anthropology as given by the eminent American anthropologists. In USA stress on cultural anthropology is laid with the objective that man is more-than-merely-organic man. He is cultural also. By knowing the culture of the society, we can better understand civilization irrespective of time and place. It is with this purpose in mind that cultural anthropologists study 'other cultures' of the world. The American cultural anthropology also includes archaeology, that is, the science of what is old in the domain of this discipline. Similarly, stress on culture study has also created ethnology—the *science of people*—as a speciality in USA.

Eriksen, in his book *Small Places, Large Issues*, has provided the etymology of the concept of cultural anthropology. According to him, 'culture' originates from the Latin word *colere* which means to cultivate. He defines cultural anthropology as below:

> Cultural anthropology thus means knowledge about 'cultivated humans', that is, knowledge about those aspects of humanity which are not natural, but which are related to that which is acquired.

It must be admitted that the word 'culture' is very complicated. In 1952, Clyde Kluckhohn and Alfred Kroeber presented 161 different definitions of culture. It is not possible to consider the majority of these definitions here. In a broader way, it could be said that anything which is acquired by members of society is culture. And, cultural anthropology is concerned with all these acquired attributes.

Herskovits has defined cultural anthropology in a very precise way. He observes:

> Cultural anthropologists study the ways man has devised to cope with his natural setting and his social milieu; and how bodies of custom are learned, retained, and handed down from one generation to the next.

Herskovits' definition makes a clear differentiation from physical anthropology. Whatever material and non-material things man has devised, constitute the subject matter of cultural anthropology. The works of man as Herskovits argue include traditions, folkways, social institutions and other social networks. Thus, a survey of definitions of cultural anthropology given by American anthropologists indicate that all that is considered as cultural anthropology includes besides cultural orientation, social orientation too. For cultural anthropologists social system is a part of society. Culture cannot emerge without a social system. They are two sides of the same coin. David Bidney has argued this point at a greater length. He says:

> Social anthropology and cultural anthropology are then understood as two branches of a common discipline of anthropology concerned with the study of man and his cultures in society.

For cultural anthropology the subject matter consists both of social institutions and the culture.

Ethnology

The dictionary meaning of ethnology refers to "a group distinguished by common cultural characteristics". It means that a group of people having common cultural characteristics constitutes an ethnic group. For example, in India, the Jat caste has certain common cultural traits---marriage pattern, re-marriage, divorce, agricultural practices and above all a history shared by all. Viewed from this perspective, the Jats form an ethnic group. These days, in the European continent, a nation is considered to be an ethnic organization. Likewise, the Americans are said to be pragmatic, immediately goal-oriented. These characteristics make the American society an ethnic society. Ethnicity is also applied to races. In a broader way, therefore, ethnicity is concerned with shared common traits including the customs, dress and food.

Yet another aspect of ethnicity is the ethnography. The dictionary defines ethnography as "scientific description of the races of the earth". When we discuss ethnology as a branch of anthropology, we consider ethnic and ethnography as parts of the branch. Ethnology, as we understand it, *treats the varieties of the human race in technical terms*. In USA, ethnology is considered to be a part of cultural anthropology. Before we carefully examine the concept of ethnology as an established branch of anthropology, we must discuss the new significance and importance which this branch has recently assumed. At the outset, we must advance a caution that the traditional meaning of ethnology has now undergone a watershed change.

Contemporary Ubiquity of Ethnology

It would be erroneous to think that social anthropology and ethnology are conservative social sciences and have no relevance to the modern, fast changing social life. It must be observed that not only in anthropology but in other social and natural sciences also, a tremendous change has come about in their conceptualization. As a matter of fact, the conceptual tool of social sciences has undergone vast transformation. It we look at the anthropological journals and monographs published during the last five decades, from 1950 to 2000, we would quickly find that a radical change has come in the language of the subject. "The terminology has generally become more influenced by hermeneutics and literary theory than by natural science during this period. Words such as 'function' and 'social structure' have become less common. Those like 'class', 'infrastructure' and 'contradiction' had a brief spell of popularity in the 1970s, while terms such as 'discourse', 'de-construction', 'resistance' and 'symbolic capital' have steadily grown more popular since the early 1980s."

Traditionally, the chapter scheme of ethnology and social anthropology is followed by the description of 'subject matter' and 'scope'. Such concepts are now replaced with 'culture' and 'tradition'. In India, it is fashionable to use the terms 'tribe' and 'weaker sections'. Obviously, such uses have given place to ethnic minorities.

In fact, a new interest has arisen in the discussion of ethnology. Earlier, ethnology was taken up as a theme of cultural description. And, in anthropology, cultural description, that is, ethnology was a theme of queer customs, folkways of the tribal people, etc. That kind of orientation restricted only to the tribals has gone today. A new interest has now emerged for the analysis of ethnological behaviour. Now, the anthropological branch of ethnology has assumed a pervasive importance ranging from local to national and international level. Observing on the newly emerging importance of ethnology, Eriksen very rightly opines:

> For one thing, a term like 'ethnic group' which has largely replaced that of 'tribe' simultaneously expresses that tribal organization is no longer common and that anthropology no longer works from a rigid boundary between 'us' and 'them'. For ethnic groups (and nations) are omnipresent or ubiquitous and exist in the anthropologist's own society as well as elsewhere.
>
> Looking at the political situation in the world at the end of the 20th century, the immediate impression is that most of the serious armed

> conflicts today have an important ethnic dimension. From Panjab to Northern Ireland, from Tibet to Bosnia, from Sri Lanka to the former Soviet Union, there is conflict and competition between different ethnic groups regarding political sovereignty and control over territories. There are also other kinds of conflicts where ethnic groups emerge as corporate groups. Indigenous peoples and immigrant groups may, for example, demand the right to cultural survival and the right to equality with the majority, usually without demanding their own state.

The observations of Eriksen help us to understand the new importance of ethnology in analyzing the situation of the Indian subcontinent. The relations between Pakistan and India revolve round ethnic considerations. Religion and history, which are ethnological in character, determine the relationship between the two countries. The conflict between the Tamils and Sinhalis in Sri Lanka is also based on ethnic conflict. Again, the movement started by the tribals in India for autonomy as well as resettlement are basically ethnic conflicts.

However, ethnology in the present-day world is not concerned necessarily with conflict. It can be expressed in quite undramatic ways through everyday definitions of situations. This can be seen in religions cults and other peaceful phenomena. It can also be identified at different levels of scale---from dyadic interaction to civil war. Eriksen has provided the definition of ethnology in a new context:

> The phenomenon of ethnicity (that is, ethnology) is, in other words, a complex one. In everyday language, the concept of ethnic group is normally used to describe a minority group which is *culturally distinguishable* from the majority, and as such the term encompasses groups in very different situations ranging from New York Jews to the Yanomamo in Brazil. In anthropology, the expression ethnic group may also be used to describe majority groups, and ethnicity concerns the relationship between groups whose members consider each other culturally distinctive.

The way Eriksen has illustrated and described the concept of ethnology makes it clear that this branch of anthropology is cultural at its core. It tries to identify common or shared cultural traits found in a group---minority or majority. These cultural or ethnic traits encourage conflict or cooperation. Ethnology, therefore, can be seen in all kinds of groups including nation, race, caste, class, region or village.

Cultural anthropology in the United States is essentially ethnology. Kroeber considers ethnology as a part of general cultural anthropology. He says that ethnology is the science of peoples and their cultures and life history as groups, irrespective of their degree of advancement. He also makes a differentiation of ethnology from ethnography. Accordingly, ethnography is more descriptive than ethnology, as more theoretically or more historically inclined. As a matter of fact, ethnology and cultural anthropology are two sides of the same coin. Viewed in this way ethnology is the oldest of the sisterhood of sciences. Every savage is a bit of an ethnologist about neighbouring tribes and knows a legend of the origin of mankind. Herodotus, the 'father of history', devoted half of his nine books to pure ethnology. Lucretius, a few centuries later, tried to solve by philosophical deduction and poetical imagination many of the same problems that modern anthropology is cautiously attacking with concrete methods. Until nearly 2,000 years after these ancients, neither in chemistry, nor geology, nor biology was so serious an interest developed as in anthropology.

Evans-Pritchard, who has defined ethnology from the British perspective of social anthropology, observes that despite social anthropology and ethnology having the same subject matter, they differ in their perspective. In the beginning, no distinction was made in Britain between ethnology and social anthropology; however, the two are now considered as separate branches. Evans-Pritchard writes:

> Though in the past no clear distinction was made between ethnology and social anthropology, they are today regarded as separate disciplines.

Having established ethnology and social anthropology as independent social disciplines, Evans-Pritchard spells out the definition of ethnology as under:

> The task of ethnology is to classify peoples on the basis of their social and cultural characteristics and then to explain their distribution at the present time or in the past times, by the movement and mixture of peoples and the diffusion of cultures.

Evans-Pritchard argues that the basic task of ethnology is to make a classification of peoples and cultures. When this is done social anthropology makes comparisons between primitive societies. If we take the Indian situation, we will find that K.S. Singh in his report on the *People of India* (POI) classifies the tribal groups into four social stocks, namely, the Negrito, the Protoaustraloid, the Mongoloid and the Caucasoid. According to him, the Jarawas, the Gonds, the Nagas, and the Gujjars fall into these categories, respectively. This is the work of pure ethnology. Based on this classification, Singh compares the developmental scales of these tribal groups.

The usefulness of ethnology as a branch of anthropology helps us to reconstruct the history of primitive peoples, for whose past historical records are lacking. The ethnologists are compelled to rely on references from circumstantial evidence to reach their conclusions, which in the nature of the case, can never be more than probable reconstruction.

Thus, Indian ethnology, which is a part of social anthropology, in much influenced by British ethnology. K.S. Singh has discussed the development of ethnology in India in his *Tribal Society in India* (1985). He accepts that Rai Bahadur Sarat Chandra Ray was the father of Indian ethnography. He is given this status because of his book *The Mundas and their Country* (1912). Sarat Chandra has written a large number of monographs on the tribals of Bihar. As a matter of fact, ethnology is concerned with three basic things:

(1) classification of groups on the basis of racial types,
(2) narration of culture, and
(3) study of tribals and primitives.

Social Anthropology

A single-sentence definition of social anthropology is of doubtful utility. Nevertheless, anthropology, in general, as we have defined it earlier, is the empirical and scientific study of man in his totality. Social anthropology, as we find it in India, South Africa and elsewhere outside the US, originates from England. Evans-Pritchard has elaborated the origin and development of social anthropology in England. He says that the subject was taught at Oxford since 1885 under the name of anthropology (not social anthropology) or ethnology. It was started at Cambridge and in London in 1900 and 1908, respectively.

But, the first university chair which bore the title of social anthropology was started in 1908. Sir James Frazer was made the honorary professor at Liverpool in 1908. Since then, the subject has received wider recognition and it is now taught under the name of social anthropology in Great Britain.

According to Evans-Pritchard, social anthropology includes the study of all human cultures and societies. The basic idea is that it tries to find out the structure of human societies all over the world. What social anthropology seeks to establish is that all societies notwithstanding any country are an organized whole. It is not just the separate customs or beliefs that are different, but the whole pattern of working, living, marrying, worshipping, organizing politically, keeping order and so on. Everything is different from the way we do things because the structure, the plan and the ideas behind them are different.

Let us take the case of different tribal groups of India. The POI survey has identified 461 tribal groups in the country. In terms of customs, folkways, food habits and rituals no one tribe is similar to another. Despite this diversity all the tribal groups constitute a society which may be called as tribal society. In this tribal society, there are some traits or institutions which bear a close similarity or uniformity. There is a legitimate way of acquiring a mate, some system of succession and some kind of polity. It is here that social anthropology, on one hand, accounts for the social and cultural variations among the different tribal groups, but on the other hand, it also conceptualizes the similarities found between tribal social systems and human relationships. As a matter of fact, when we try to understand the tribal economy as a particular group, say Santhal, we try to find out how this economy is connected with other aspects of the Santhal society. If we are required to define social anthropology in a comprehensive way, we would say that this discipline seeks to find out institutional relations within the society and relations between societies. In other words, we try to find out the social institutions of the Santhals as connected with the tribe and also the relations of these institutions with the institutions of other tribes and the wider non-tribal society or the national society.

The British social anthropology, as Evans-Pritchard observed, is a branch of sociology. He writes:

> When people speak of sociology they generally have in mind studies of particular problems in civilized societies. If we give this sense to the word, then the difference between social anthropology and sociology is a difference of field, but there are also important differences of method between them. The social anthropologist studies primitive societies directly, living among them for month or years, whereas sociological research is usually from documents and is largely statistical.

Evans-Pritchard, by comparing social anthropology with sociology, brings out a clear definition of social anthropology. According to him, "social anthropology has primitive societies as its subject matter. In other words, it is concerned with the affairs of the primitive, indigenous people, hills and forest people, scheduled tribes and other such groups of people". Another part of the definition of social anthropology is the fieldwork. Data in social anthropology are generated in the field and not on the desk of a study room in a library. It is because of this that M.N. Srinivas lived for months together in Rampura village. Similar fieldwork was done by Mackim Marriot in Kishangarhi of Aligarh district.

The definition of social anthropology, as given by Evans-Pritchard is as under:

> It is the relation of this general body of theory to primitive social life which constitutes the subject of social anthropology. In other words, social anthropology studies: (1) primitive societies, and (2) generates data by doing fieldwork.

John Lewis, another British social anthropologist, has also defined social anthropology on the pattern of the definition given by the British social anthropology school. In a very straightforward manner, he says that anthropology is the study of the way of life of primitive people as they can still be found today, or not too much altered by contact with civilization.

Lewis has defined social anthropology in a very conservative style. He argues that social anthropology studies primitives but these primitives are qualified by a statement that they should remain unaffected by social change. In other words, only those primitives according to Lewis need to be studied who remain outside the impact of social and cultural change. Such a study would bring out only those characteristics of the tribal society which are queer and rigid.

For Lewis, anthropology is nothing but the study of other cultures, as advocated by John Beattie. This makes social anthropology a comparative discipline of the study of social institutions. However, despite limiting the field of social anthropology to the study of primitive communities, Lewis suggests for establishing a pattern of indigenous society.

Eriksen puts all emphasis on the study of small places in social anthropology. He argues that social anthropology intensively is concerned with the small places. But these small places relate to large issues. Defining social anthropology in a new perspective, Eriksen writes:

> One may, therefore, say that anthropology asks large questions, while at the same time it draws many of its insights from small places... it has been common to regard social anthropology's traditional focus on small scale non-industrial societies, compared with other subjects dealing with culture and society. However, because of changes in the world and in the discipline itself, this is no longer an accurate description. Practically, any social system can be studied anthropologically and contemporary anthropological research displays an enormous range, empirically as well as thematically.

Eriksen's definition of social anthropology contests Lewis' definition. Lewis says that social anthropology studies primitive people as they can still be found, uninfluenced by social change. Eriksen rejects it, objects to it and says that social anthropology does not remain restricted to primitive people; it studies any social system, the qualification of such a social system is that it is of a small-scale non-industrial kind of society. Thus, according to Eriksen, social anthropology studies:

(1) small-scale society,
(2) non-industrial society, and
(3) small and larger issues of the society.

Early Social Anthropology

The students of sociology generally talk about the founding fathers of the discipline. It is unanimously agreed all over the world that Emile

Durkheim, Max Weber and Karl Marx are the architects of sociology. They have constituted the tradition and culture of sociology. It is argued that historically, early anthropology started sometime during the 18th century. If we are able to identify the thinkers who founded anthropology, we would be able to define the discipline.

According to some historians, the origin of social anthropology is traced to David Hume and Immanuel Kant who were the first philosophers to define social anthropology. Hume was a British empiricist who argued that "experience was the only trustworthy source of valid knowledge". It was through the initiation of Hume that empiricism entered the social sciences including social anthropology. Empiricism literally means "based on experience". Thus, according to Hume, social anthropology studies the society out of empiricism, that is, experience.

Kant contested the empirical approach to social anthropology as given by Hume. He argued that people had certain shared innate faculties, which were assumed to be embedded in their mode of thought. In other words, he held that human beings were born with certain 'formulas' for thinking; from this idea, it follows that people all over the world would think in roughly the same way.

The definitions of anthropology given by Hume and Kant, though quite vague, boil down to the fact that anthropology records the experiences of people. It is not a desk social science. It builds on data coming out of experience. However, the approach taken by Kant is highly philosophical and psychological. He propounds that anthropology should study the universal mental traits of human beings. If a serpent spreads it hood, it frightens a man; and if a locality is gutted, the inhabitants run in panic. Such a behaviour is universal; it is found all over the world and in all societies. According to Kant, anthropology, therefore, identifies the human universal mental traits.

It is also amazing to know that the history of anthropology neither begins with Herodotus nor with any other thinker. It is said that the systematic history of anthropology rightly begins from Henry Maine and Henry Morgan. These two thinkers could be said to be the founding fathers of social anthropology. How did they define social anthropology? For them, social anthropology was the study of social evolution. These thinkers tried to find the origin and development of social institutions, namely, law, marriage, family and society. Let us now turn to the definition of social anthropology in terms of evolution which remained pervasive and dominant all through the 19th century.

The 19th Century Evolutionary Approach

The 19th century social anthropologists were greatly influenced by the findings of Darwin and his associates. The biological evolutionists established that the origin of man has passed through several stages—from *homo sapiens* to apes. Darwinism promoted Social Darwinism. The anthropologists following the logic of Darwinism tried to establish the origin of social institutions. It would not be wrong to say that Social Darwinism prevailed throughout the 19th century and first quarter of the 20th century.

The definition of social anthropology given by Social Darwinists is a landmark in the development of this discipline. The foundations of present anthropology go back to Henry Maine's *Ancient Law* (1861) and Lewis Henry Morgan's books, including *Ancient Society* (1877). "Both of these authors developed theories of primitive society which were to wield influence far into the 20th century. Maine, who had worked in India, proposed a distinction between status and contract societies, a conceptual pair which is reminiscent of many later distinctions between 'modern' and 'traditional' societies. In status-based or traditional societies, Maine argued, kinship was usually crucial in determining one's position in society; in contract-based societies, on the contrary, it would rather be the individual achievements of persons that provided them with their positions."

The contributions by Morgan to early anthropology was, however, a beginning of the theory of social evolution. The theory says that anthropology studies the human society which has passed through the stages of savagery, barbarism and civilization. At the savagery stage human beings had an economy characterized by subsistence. Man earned his livelihood through hunting and food gathering. At the stage of barbarism agriculture and animal husbandry were the sources of living while those societies which reached the stage of civilization, developed literacy, technology, industry and the state.

The theory expounded by Morgan was one; there were other theories too; for instance, Westermark set out the theory of human marriage; Brifault propounded the theory of family. What we intend to conclude here is that there was a team of evolutionists which established theories of culture, including religion and other fields of social anthropology. These evolutionists included W.H.R. Rivers, Tylor, Frazer, William James, A.C. Haddon and Charles Seligman. All these early social anthropologists defined social anthropology as a science of social evolution. In other words, social anthropology studies the origin and evolution of social institutions such as society, religion, marriage, kinship and so on.

Emergence of Modern Social Anthropology

Before discussing the emergence of modern social anthropology we would like to observe that the social anthropology as we teach and research today has to be relevant to the reality of society, if it has to survive. With this current perspective in mind we propose to discuss historically the meaning and definition of sociology as it has come after the arrival of modern anthropology. Franz Boas and Bronislaw Malinowski are often regarded as the first modern anthropologists. Boas belonged to Germany but he came to the US in 1880 to study the American Indians. He conducted field research by himself and founded modern American cultural anthropology. Alfred Kroeber, Ruth Benedict and Margarete Mead were students of Boas. Boas contributed substantially to the field of anthropology. His most important contribution seems to be the doctrine of 'cultural relativism'. It is a concept which argues that each group should be studied according to its own culture. In other words, culture is specific to a group. Even today, Boas' contribution of cultural relativism is consid-

> *Franz Boas* (1859-1941) was born in Germany. Though his initial training was in geography, at a later stage he turned to social anthropology. In his later life he migrated to the US and took its citizenship. Boas is called the founder of Modern American Anthropology. His fields of specialization include ethnology, linguistics, archaeology, and physical anthropology.
>
> Boas has contributed richly to the domain of cultural relativism. He emphasized cultural variation and uniqueness of each culture. He advocated that anthropology should study the indigenous populations. For him, anthropology is a social science of primitives and tribals.

ered to be an indispensable methodological tool of social and cultural anthropology. Thus, Boas defined anthropology as a social science of culture study. This is one aspect of modern anthropology.

Malinowski hailed from Poland who later on emigrated to Britain in 1910. He is known for his work on the Trobrianders living in the islands of New Guinea. He conducted fieldwork among these tribals between 1915 and 1918. This kind of work, where he had close and enduring contact with the local community, contributed a lot to the knowledge kit of social anthropology and sociology. As a matter of fact, the method of functionalism which Robert Merton developed in sociology draws heavily from Malinowski. He emphasized the importance of studying the interrelationships of various aspects of society, and therefore, held that long field studies were absolutely necessary.

According to Malinowski, social anthropology is concerned with the interrelationships of various parts of tribal society. In other words, tribal economy, politics, kin are all interrelated. Social anthropology is interested to study functional relations among the members of tribal society.

Yet another thinker who substantially contributed to British social anthropology and helped to define it was A.R. Radcliffe-Brown. He was profoundly inspired by Durkheim's writings on social integration. Durkheim made important studies about the division of labour in primitive societies and about religion and totemism. Radcliffe-Brown was a functionalist and considered society as an organic whole. He is said to be the founder of structural-functionalism in anthropology. This is a doctrine about the ways in which the various institutions of a society contribute to its stability. Malinowski was no

Alfred Reginald Radcliffe-Brown (1881-1955) is said to be the founder of the British school of anthropology. He was influenced by Durkheim's theory, which he applied and developed in his own empirical analyses. His prominent works include *The Andaman Islanders* (1922) and *The Social Anthropology of Australian Tribes* (1931).

Radcliffe-Brown is known for developing structural functionalism in social anthropology. Through this doctrine, he explains the integration of societies and thus shows the interrelations between social institutions. According to him, social anthropology defines primitive society in terms of its functional interrelations.

structural-functionalist, although he described himself as a functionalist. Radcliffe-Brown and his followers regarded individuals and their actions as 'side-effects' of society, whose deepest meaning constituted in contributing to social integration, Malinowski was instead inclined to argue that society exists to satisfy the needs of the individuals. The contrast between these leading in early modern anthropology can be traced up to this very day: some tend to regard society as an unintended consequence of the actions of individuals, whereas, others regard persons largely as products of their society.

Besides Boas, Malinowski and Radcliffe-Brown, there are also others who have shaped the subject matter and definition of modern social anthropology. These include Marcel Mauss, Levy-Bruhl and Sigmund Freud.

As pointed out earlier, social anthropology, as we find it in India and other Asian countries, is the offspring of British social anthropology. In order to define social anthropology in a scientific and precise way, Evans-Pritchard makes a list of the titles of theses which were awarded degrees. All these titles indicate the kind of work social anthropologists were doing. On the strength of the research work done, it could be said that the students of social anthropology are concerned with the study of political institutions, religious institutions, class distinctions based on colour, sex, or rank, economic institutions, legal or quasi-legal institutions, and marriage, and also of social adaptation, and of the entire social organization or structure, of one or other people. On the basis of the sample of these titles Evans-Pritchard observes:

> Social anthropology, thus, not only covers societies round the globe but also a number of different studies... . Social anthropologists study a primitive society in the same way whether it is in Polynesia, Africa,

E.E. Evans-Pritchard (1902-78) was a student of Malinowski. At a later period he came closer to the structural-functional school which was originated by Radcliffe-Brown. He is well known in social anthropology for his classical monographs on the African tribes—Azande and Nuer. He was also influenced by Mauss and Levy-Bruhl. In his last innings of life he rejected anthropology as a natural science and argued it to be viewed as one of the humanities.

or Lapland; and whatever they are writing about—a kinship system, a religions cult or a political institution it is examined in its relation to the total social structure in which it is contained.

Evans-Pritchard's approach to the understanding of the subject draws only from the earlier modern anthropologists, mainly, Malinowski and Radcliffe-Brown. His definition does not go further: it is the study of the interrelations in a primitive society.

Evans-Pritchard was the product of the forties. During this decade and earlier also, the British colonial empire had wider horizons extending to India and Africa. The prevailing social reality, therefore, inspired Evans-Pritchard and his generation to define social anthropology in terms of the social status of primitive societies. It also brought home the fact that fieldwork in colonial societies was easier to carry out. For instance, in India, the British administrators-turned-anthropologists never had to bear the brunt of the rough and tough life of India's villages. The fieldwork was done by the petty Indian bureaucrats. Evans-Pritchard's approach to social anthropology was quite suitable not only to him but also other British social anthropologists. His definition was, thus, historically conditioned.

Marxian Anthropology: A Move towards Neo-functionalism and Structuralism

Indian social anthropology has been constantly fed by British and Indian functionalists. Whatever works of repute that we have in our country are dominated by the perspectives initiated and developed by Bronislaw Malinowski (1920), E.E. Evans-Pritchard (1940), Henry Maine (1961) and the Indian sociologists like M.N. Srinivas, D.N. Majumdar and G.S. Ghurye. All these have been unidimensional. Their perspective has been the methodology of functionalism. The tribals or primitives studied by them belong to Africa, Australia and Asia.

Commenting on the trend of social anthropology in India, T.N. Madan, though a functionalist himself, has rightly commented that the indigenous tribals have largely been neglected to be studied from the non-functional and historical perspective. Madan observes in his latest book *Pathways* (Oxford, 1994):

Indian sociologists have been the products of western universities or their outposts in India and have remained rootless, being strangers equally to the Indian and the western philosophical traditions. The need for a synthesis of the philosophical presuppositions of 'social science' has been voiced by some scholars, but no significant advances have been made mainly because the questions have not been posed properly: in fact, it is not easy to do so.

There is one more important approach to social anthropology which is neo-functional, structural and Marxian. There are social anthropologists belonging to Europe and the US who have approached the subject from the traditional path of functionalism. They included Maurice Godlier (1971), H.K. Schneider (1970), M. Sahlins (1973), Eliott Skinner (1970) and a few others. These scholars have developed a new methodology which became popular in Europe, and particularly in France. It would not be erroneous to say that the new variant of social anthropology which has come to light is neo-functional and structural. This variant is influenced by French structuralism.

Godlier's Approach

Maurice Godlier, a Marxian anthropologist, has developed a new perspective on social anthropology. He wrote *Perspectives in Marxist Anthropology* in French in 1973. The original French text was translated into English by Robert Brian and has been published by Cambridge University Press, London (1977). During the following year, the book was reprinted twice. It also got published from the United States of America in 1978. The rapid reprints of the book have made Godlier's approach to anthropology quite popular and interesting. Basically, he works on the oft-repeated premise of Marxism. He begins with the question on economics: Is there a hidden logic in economic systems and what constitutes the necessity for their appearance, their reproduction or disappearance during the course of history?

It is with this question related to economics that Godlier comes to history and anthropology. His argument is that there is no true rationality which can explain economic production, distribution, exchange and consumption. Economics can be comprehended by *structural analysis of social relations*. In doing that we will be able to find out the basic causes of modes of production in different social structures. In fact, Godlier's contention is that in each society there are some modes of productions. These modes vary from society to society. Economics tries to find out the causality of modes of production in each society. In reality, what Godlier argues is the old theme of Marxism, the mode of production. What is particular about him is that he tries to detect the structures of social relations which emerge from a particular mode of production. The emphasis on the structural analysis of social relations, at the end of his work, leads him to consider social anthropology as neo-functional and structural. This is obviously a new approach and contests what has been said by Malinowski, Evans-Pritchard and Srinivas. We shall now elaborate the approach and methodology taken by Godlier in his above mentioned book.

Contents and Boundary of Anthropology

Social anthropology does not have any well-defined specific scope or boundary for study. Theoretically, neither does it have any clear-cut premise for scientific inquiry. As a matter of fact, the scope and subject matter of social anthropology has evolved over a long period of history.

History as Part of Anthropology

Godlier has tried to construct the history of the scope of anthropology. Before the emergence of anthropology, history was a dominant discipline in social sciences, and it revolved round the study of production relations. But, with the extension of the net of imperialism and colonialism, history failed to provide any reliable data on the societies which were non-western and characterized by illiteracy and backwardness. For instance, when the Britishers came to India, naturally, they were interested to know the vast masses of the Indian people. There was an Indian history but they did not have any first-hand account of the village people and the illiterate masses. The colonial domination in Africa and Australia also faced such problems. This obliged history to give up its scope to ethnology or rural sociology. In some cases, as in Britain, ancient and modern history gave place to social anthropology and ethnology. Thus, anthropology took to the study of regional or local societies through direct observation and visible enquires. When Hutton wrote about the caste system in India, he generated data through verbal enquiries. So was done by Evans-Pritchard in the study of Nuer, and Malinowski of Argonouts or

Trobriand. In the beginning, when anthropology parted company with history, it studied historically known western societies through the method of observation and verbal enquiries. Godlier observes:

> At the same time, and for the some reasons, entire sections of western history, ancient and modern, were abandoned to ethnology or rural sociology... Anthropology was handed over the study of all aspects of regional or rural life which appeared to be survival of pre-capitalist and pre-industrialist modes of production and social organization or which had very old ethnic and cultural characteristics.

In France, and also the rest of Europe, anthropology was considered not necessarily to be a study of primitive people only. It focused on all groups which did not have written documents and which were cast aside by historians. It is because of this that Hutton and Risley paid little attention to tribes and greater attention to castes. The study of caste was beneficial for the strengthening of British regime. The objective of the study of non-western, pre-capitalist and pre-industrialist man was two-fold: (i) colonial exploitation, and (ii) extension of market.

Evolutionary Approach: Reconstruction of European History

Godlier argues that during the 19th century, evolutionary approach to the origin of social institutions was very popular. History was not interested in evolution. It was restricted to written documents and archaeological evidences. In such a tradition, as we have mentioned earlier, anthropology came into existence to study all aspects of regional or rural life. With anthropology having the goal of generating ethnological material, it became its job to reconstruct the European social history. Europe, by 19th century, had come up with modernization as a consequence of the Industrial Revolution. But, what happened to it before the coming of capitalism and industrialism? It was hypothesized that if the primitive, pre-industrial and pre-capitalist institutions of non-western societies were found, it would help the European society to reconstruct its social history. Obviously, Godlier asserts that anthropology in 19th century took to evolutionary approach. The argument given by Godlier runs as below:

> Furthermore, there was the evolutionist idea, current in the 19th century whereby it was held that European customs were survivals,

relics of former stages of evolution, which could still be found flourishing and preserved among non-western peoples; in this way two fields abandoned by historians were taken over by anthropologists. Only they could provide the missing links by studying European customs and their exotic purchases. Thus, they achieved their theoretical task---considered as a duty—of reconstructing a complete and faithful picture of the first stage of mankind at least from those of its representatives who had left no written record.

As its the tradition with all variants of historians---Marxist or non-Marxist---civilization is the idiom of their analysis. Both the variants consider history as a science and knowledge of civilization. In such a situation, naturally, Godlier looks at the study of non-western societies from the vantage point of mode of production. It is the mode of production which determines the course of change. Godlier, therefore, relates anthropology with mode of production, that is, history. For him, history and anthropology are very closely related. If anthropology studies barbarians, savages or backwards, rural European populations at an inferior stage of civilization, it should try to adopt a method which will help an analysis of structures and discovery of reciprocal laws of compatibility or incompatibility and their concrete, historic effectiveness.

Godlier argues that such a method is found in the works of Karl Marx although in Marxian arguments it is said that mode of production has determined the structure of society and its course of study. And, therefore, when an anthropologist studies a primitive society, he must invariably dwell on the processes—social and cultural—in a society which emerges from mode of production. The linkage between modes of production, in broader way, history and anthropology can hardly be separated. They are one and the same. His thesis runs as follows:

> In order to resolve these problems, a method is required which allows an analysis of structures and the discovery of reciprocal laws... Such a method seems to have been elaborated and applied for the first time by Marx in his efforts to analyze the modes as capitalist production and bourgeois society. Marx's answer to the problem of the differential causality of various instances of social life—in other words, the 'mode of production' of 'material life conditions', in the last analysis the process of social political and intellectual life in gen-

eral—seems to us to be the essential hypothesis to be taken up and systematically explored in order to renew the scientific content of history and anthropology.

Whatever happens among Azande, Nuer and for that matter Gond and Bhil is due to the forces—whatever they may be—of modes of production. Viewed from this perspective, Godlier maintains that there is enough scientific input in history and sociology. It means that the method of anthropology shall have to be borrowed from history. And, the method of history is the mode of production. This means that the approach to anthropology should be the analysis of social processes which are released from the modes of production. However, the modes of production in all the societies are not similar. There exists a wide diversity in modes of production. For instance, the societies studied by anthropologists show that there is very little common in all the societies. Actually, each society has adopted different speeds by processes of change. "We must not forget that since the beginning of the Neolithic Age, the economies and societies of hunter-gatherers have been gradually eliminated and driven back into ecological niches which are unsuitable for farming and herding; today, they are close to complete extinction."

Contradictions among Anthropologists

An anthropologist generates his data from direct observation and verbal enquiries. For him fieldwork is the major method of collecting data. Through data generation he creates ideological fetishes and ambiguities. But, at the same time, an anthropologist is also concerned with the study and reconstruction of his own society as against the traditional one. He finds that on one hand, he studies the primitives characterized by primordial institutions, and on the other, he is committed to study his own society which is changing. For him, therefore, the static nature of society (primitive) and the changing nature of society (civilized) create a contradiction. In such a situation, an anthropologist, as a professional, is concerned with the living history. This differentiates him from the traditional historian who enquires about the history of past things—a past where the outcome is known in advance. But, the present study of primitive society creates problems for his analysis. These primitive societies are fast-changing. As a professional, he is required to justify or criticize the changes happening in primitive societies. Such a contradiction is professional and the anthropologists have to bear it.

Content and Limits of Anthropology

Godlier makes a case for Marxist anthropology. The speciality of this brand of anthropology is that it tries to develop and broaden the analysis of the modes of production of primitive society. What Marxist anthropology has to do is to apply the postulate of modes of production to primitive kinship, politics and religion. Such an application of modes of production would give rise to new theories on kinship and other primitive institutions. If efforts in this direction are made, there would be emergence of neo-functionalism and structuralism. Marxist anthropology also borrows heavily from Claude Levi-Strauss. Levi-Strauss uses the method of materialism. For him, the society is holistic. He also rejects positivism. As a matter of fact, there is much that is common in Marxian anthropology and the structuralism of Levi-Strauss. Both are against positivism, against empiricism and part studies rather than wholes. Discussing the similarities between Levi-Strauss' structuralism and Marxian anthropology, Godlier observes:

> This complex theoretical situation determines the critical relationships which the Marxist approach has with anthropology along with two other trends which attempt to create conditions for a general renewal of this scientific discipline, that is, the neofunctionalism of 'cultural ecology' and the structuralism approach of Claude Levi-Strauss. Both use a materialistic approach. The first studies societies afresh, considering than as parts of larger wholes, different eco-systems of nature. Like Marxism, it pays particular attention to the material bases of society's functioning. The second, again like Marxism, rejects the methods of positivist empiricism and endeavours to take into account the social realities in terms of structure.

Godlier has also given the contents of anthropology. In a broader way, he says that it studies non-western societies, non-literary societies and colonized societies. These societies have a backward mode of production. They are pre-capitalist and pre-industrial. The social organization of all these societies constitutes the contents of anthro-

pology. In short, these contents can be characterized as below:
(i) non-literate,
(ii) uncivilized,
(iii) arrested in development,
(iv) moneyless,
(v) non-industrialized,
(vi) non-urban,
(vii) lacking economic specialization,
(viii) low level of technical achievement,
(ix) traditional, and
(x) small scale.

Godlier has provided a specific approach to the study of non-western societies. But, all non-western societies do not constitute the contents and subject matter of anthropology. He has specified the non-western societies also. Usually, these societies are primitive and do not exhibit the traits of capitalism, industrialism, technology, and absence of surplus production. The basic element, which differentiates Marxist anthropology from the general anthropology, is its stress on modes of production. Second, social anthropology borrows its methodology from history. In short, Godlier's concept of anthropology moves towards methodological, neo-fuctionalism and structuralism. In a precise and broader way, it studies the classless society.

Concluding Observations

In the preceding pages we have tried to define social anthropology and bring out its meaning. It must be admitted that any attempt to define social anthropology at a universal plane in the present situation is very difficult. Social anthropology today is such a melting pot where each coin is trying hard to maintain its identity. In the US, anthropology is essentially a cultural social science; in the European continent it is physical anthropology; in Britain it is social anthropology plus ethnology; and in India and other Asian countries it is social anthropology. In such a diversity and heterogeneity, the definitions and meanings of social anthropology have become society-, nation- or continent-specific. In India, the definition has become all the more complex and confusing. The Indian history, in terms of colonial rule, has defined it in a different way. Right from Sarat Chandra Roy to S.C. Dube and M.N. Srinivas social anthropology has been defined as a study of primitives and tribals.

What is particular about Indian social anthropology is that it is blended with the sociology and cultural anthropology of the US which renders it very difficult to define in precise terms. We have studies of tribals with a perspective of culture, with a perspective of social system and with a smaller dose of physical anthropology. For instance, in the *People of India*, K.S. Singh writes a lengthy introduction on the status of Scheduled Tribes in India. In doing this exercise, willingly or unwillingly, he has become victim of all the three traditions of anthropology, namely, US culturalism, continental physical anthropology, that is, racial composition, and British ethnology. Thus, if one has to define social anthropology in terms of Indian social science, it could be said that social anthropology studies the social system, culture, ethnology and physiology of the tribals and the general weaker segments of society.

Despite the difficulties in defining social anthropology at a universal plane or global horizon one could very safely say that social anthropology makes a holistic study of the primitives, tribals and backward segments of society living in small scale, small size and small places with a comprehensive perspective including culture, ethnology, physiology and social system.

Further Readings

Beattie, John, *Other Cultures*, London, 1964.

Eriksen, Thomas Hylland, *Small Places, Large Issues*, Pluto Press, London, 1995.

Evans-Pritchard, E.E., *Social Anthropology*, Cohen and West Limited, London, 1964 (reprinted).

Godlier, Maurice, *Perspectives in Marxist Anthropology*, Cambridge University Press, Cambridge, London, 1978 (reprinted twice).

Lewis, John, *Anthropology*, Heinemann, London, 1982.

Murdock, G.P., "British Social Anthropology", *American Anthropologists*, III, 1951, p.471.

2

The Scope of Social Anthropology

Anthropology as a social science discipline studies *anthropos* or man and his society and culture. Its subject matter traditionally consists of primitives and tribals. The scope includes two dimensions: the objectives or aims of the discipline; and the subject matter covered by it. The general understanding of social anthropology is that it tries to study human societies all over the world. This meets the objective of studying the society. Secondly, by employing the comparative method, social anthropology finds similarities and differences in diverse societies. Identification of these similarities helps us construct universal anthropological theories which will enable us understand the human society. This objective of social anthropology becomes all the more relevant in the context of the accelerating processes of localization and globalization. In any projection towards the building of a world society, social anthropology has enough to contribute.

At this stage of discussing the scope of social anthropology we must address one question to ourselves: If we accept that social anthropology, notwithstanding India, European continent or the US, studies the primitive peoples and if these primitive peoples become extinct from the social map of world in the context of the all-embracing changes, what would anthropology study? In other words, if there are no tribals in India, what would social anthropologists do? Whom will they study? The question is relevant and is very much concerned with the scope and subject matter of social anthropology today.

Let us take the problem of the scope of social anthropology as is addressed to us. What has become of the peoples first explored by anthropologists during colonialism? Nearly all of them are, to varying degrees, integrated into the wider economic, cultural and political systems. It is reported that the Trobriand islanders, whom Malinowski studied in the first quarter of the 20th century, have now adapted themselves to the process of modernization on their own terms. Modernization has led to changes in political organization: in the economy and in the politics of identity, but both the kinship system and the system of ceremonial exchange still function, even if they do not have the same meaning as before.

In India, the Toda, Gond, Khasi and Bhil tribes have embraced new political and economic systems unleashed by the national government. It appears that the tribals today are not the same as they were fifty years back. The situation is very complex and we have to examine the scope of social anthropology in this new context. Admittedly, social anthropology cannot be 'sold' in the academic market where it is not relevant in understanding the reality of society. It is also in the interest of social anthropology that it does not remain only 'a veiled discipline' closing its eyes to the society's demands and expectations.

At the outset, we would like to observe that the subject matter and scope of social anthropology have never been conservative, not willing to change, quite static and sterile. It has always been changing. In this chapter, we shall discuss the scope of social anthropology with these perspectives in view.

Traditional Scope of Social Anthropology

The traditional scope of social anthropology has to be traced from Radcliffe-Brown and Malinowski as these are the "two men who have shaped social anthropology into what it is in England today". However, British anthropologists are inclined to distinguish social anthropology from ethnology. In India, not much difference is made between scope and subject matter. Customarily, in traditional textbooks in India, a chapter is devoted to scope and subject matter. There is also confusion in scope and subject matter. In practice, what we include under the theme of scope is also taken as a subject matter. This is bewildering. If we seriously look into these two aspects, it could be said that scope focuses on the aim and objective of a particular discipline under discussion. It is the point aimed at. The subject matter, on the other hand, constitutes the theme and topics included in the discipline. The difference, it appears, is of emphasis. When we talk about scope we are concerned with the objectives of the study and when we deal with subject matter it is that which constitutes or forms the contents of discipline. Evans-Pritchard has tried to resolve this confusion. In his lectures delivered in 1945 he prefers to use scope and does not give any place to subject matter. In the book containing his lectures, despite giving an elaborate subject index, he provides no place for subject matter.

A cursory look at the literature on social anthropology makes it obvious that social anthropology studies the primitive peoples. However, the traditional social anthropologists have, theoretically as well as principally, argued that social anthropology goes beyond the study of primitives and studies the contemporary society also. This point of view is made very clear by Evans-Pritchard. He writes:

> While social anthropologists consider that their subject embraces all human cultures and societies, including our own, they have... for the most part given their attention to those of primitive peoples.

In the beginning and till the first quarter of the 20th century, the subject matter of social anthropology consisted of the study of primitive societies. This has been emphasized by D.N. Majumdar and T.N. Madan also in their book *An Introduction to Social Anthropology*. They follow the argument given by Evans-Pritchard and say that in matter of principle, primitive peoples are the subject matter of social anthropology along with the study of contemporary society. In practice, social anthropology for a longer period of history has remained restricted to primitive and tribal peoples only.

Study of Holistic Society

It is said that social anthropology traditionally does not study the primitive society in its different institutional aspects. It believes in holistic study. For instance, if an Indian anthropologist studies the Gond society as M.N. Srinivas has studied the Coorgis, all the institutions of tribe, namely, economy, polity, religion, kin, clan are studied. This is the kind of holistic study anthropologists have been making. This has also been stressed by Evans-Pritchard and others. There is reason for making a holistic study of the primitives. Social anthropologists try to show the linkages among the social institutions and this gives the whole picture of the primitive society. Evans-Pritchard observes:

> With the emergence of functional anthropology it is regarded as the task of social anthropology to study social institutions as interde-

pendent parts of social system, the more it is seen to be an advantage to be able to study those societies which are structurally so simple and culturally so homogeneous, that they can be directly observed as wholes.

If we conclude the scope and subject matter of social anthropology, as identified by earlier and traditional social anthropologists, it consists of: (i) primitive societies, and (ii) their holistic study. Social anthropology is rich in the study of primitive peoples. The African tribes, viz., Nuer, Tikopia, Santi, Yao, Bantu, Murle and the Indian tribes, viz., Coorgis, Bodo, Naga are examples of holistic tribal studies.

Why Study Primitive or Tribal Peoples?

When social anthropologists study primitive peoples they have a reason for this. It can be argued that during the colonial rule, when the non-tribal peoples had many problems to encounter, why social anthropology kept itself restricted to primitive societies only? As elsewhere, in social sciences also, there is some system of priorities. Perhaps, on the basis of certain priorities, social anthropology focused its attention on primitive peoples. The arguments given for the study of primitive peoples may enumerated below:

(i) Primitive society is simple and small

Social anthropology has a wide scope for the discipline. It wants to study man is his totality. It requires a wide ranging comparison. For such an approach, the study of primitive peoples is quite rewarding. The primitives are small in number. The territory occupied by them does not cover larger spaces and what is most important is that the range of social relations among these peoples is not wider. Besides, it has simple technology, and does not have any systematic art, science or theology. Our empirical generalizations made out of simple societies can be helpful in studying the evolution of larger and bigger societies.

(ii) Primitives live in a state of nature

The primitives had been living in a state of nature before the emergence of civil government. In the 18th century, the philosophers were interested in learning about the state of society and the primitives provided an excellent example. The anthropologists later on realized that for constructing a theory of evolution the tribals were a good laboratory. Evans-Pritchard, hinting at the evolution theory and the study of primitive institutions, argues:

> Later anthropologists were interested in them (primitives) because it was held that they displaced institutions in their simplest forms, and that it is sound method to proceed from examination of the more simple to examination of the more complex, in which what has been learnt from a study of the more simple would be an additional help.

(iii) Emergence of functional anthropology

Yet another reason for the study of primitive peoples has been the emergence of structural-functional analysis propounded by Radcliffe-Brown and Malinowski. It was established in social anthropology by these scholars that a society introduces order and system through the interrelationships of social institutions. For instance, the economy of a people is related to religion and policy. In fact, according to functional anthropology, a society is a web of interrelationships between institutions. According to Claude Levi-Strauss, the rules of marriage and kinship are related to exchange relations. The functional understanding, therefore, promoted the study of simple societies.

(iv) Search for social order

Social anthropology has its prime scope for finding out uniformities and regularities of social life. This search can be fulfilled by the primitive peoples who have a very simple social structure. Evans-Pritchard assets that social order in a society can be better found in primitive societies. He writes:

> Uniformities and regularities of social life, for a society must have some sort or order, or its members could not live together. It is only because people know the kind of behaviour expected of them and what kind of behaviour to expect from others in the various situations of life, and coordinate their activities in submission to rules and under the guidance of values that each and all are able to go about their affairs, and lead their lives in harmony with their fellows.

(v) Primitives have intrinsic human values

Study of primitive peoples contributes much to our knowledge about some of the values of human life. There has been a tendency among the British anthropologists to neglect the role of values in tribal life. The works of Risley, Rivers and Hutton have very callously overlooked the study of values in tribal life. The fact of the matter is that the tribals and the non-literate peoples are not lacking in ethical principles. But, the anthropologists have either forgot the place of values or have underscored these. However, there are some scholars who have very intensively studied the inherent values found in the tribal society.

In a recent study on Badaga—a tribal group in the Nilgiri hills of Tamil Nadu—Paul Hockings has very elaborately discussed the role of values in tribal life. He has analyzed some myths surrounding the Badaga people. He observes:

> The analysis of the various myths surrounding the ancestral figure of *Hette* (it is a ritual related to spirits) shows that they are something more than a handful of brief *justso* stories. Badaga myth is a meta language which permits talking about some very basic facts of life: what it means to be a Badaga, to be distinct from other communities, and how this way of life can be maintained. Ritual is similarly concerned with the lives of real people, and not merely with the presumed requirements of the gods.

From all considerations it could be said that the study of primitive societies have a specific value system. The analysis of values has a bearing on the understanding of modern societies.

(vi) Other cultures are equally superior

Our understanding of western or continental society and also Indian society suffers from some prejudices. These prejudices have made us eurocentric. We assume that European-American ways of living are universal, obviously the only conceivable ones and some-how right. These prejudices make us think that the other cultures are backward, conservative and rudimentary. This is not so in reality. The first thing is that culture can never be compared. We cannot say that Negro music or for that matter tribal music is inferior to classical music. Music is music everywhere. Each music has its own superiority.

The study of primitive peoples would bring out a new world of social life. We find that each society has its own historicity and specificity. In order to better understand the contemporary society, we must make a thorough study of primitive society. The argument is that to understand Indian villages, let us study the Japanese villages. It is this comparative perspective that prompts us to emphasize the study of primitive people.

(vii) Vanishing primitive social system

With the onset of globalization and the subsequent liberalization, the primitive societies are also fast changing. This is one aspect of social change. Social anthropologists have concerned themselves with this accelerating pace of change. But, still, another outcome of social change remains neglected. The indigenous institutional framework, along with its knowledge is fast vanishing. It is found that many of the aspects of tribal animism, witchcraft, and in fact, the total social structure are fast disappearing. If we turn our head towards these vanishing institutions, without any codification and record, the institutions would be lost in oblivion. Anthropological studies, therefore, should take up primitives as early and as urgently as possible. Evans-Pritchard very rightly stresses the importance of the study of vanishing primitive societies when he says:

> Another and very cogent reason for studying primitive societies at the present time is that they are rapidly being transformed and must be studied soon or never. These vanishing social systems are unique structural variations, a study of which aids us very considerably in understanding the nature of human society, because in a comparative study of institutions the number of society studied is less significant than their range of variations.

(viii) Constitutional obligations

To better answer the question of the logic for studying the primitive peoples on priority basis, it could be said that for India the study of primitive peoples is all the more important. We have more than 400 tribal groups that are included in the list of Scheduled Tribes. They suffered considerably economically, socially, culturally and educationally in the past. This situation is now being mitigated through constitutional provisions in the form of protection and development safeguards. We have introduced special development programmes among the tribals. This warrants us to study the primitives. It is constitutionally obligatory for us to study these peoples.

New Dimensions

It was during the forties that the social anthropologists brought out the scope of the discipline. They suggested the study of primitives but theoretically agreed to take up all 'human societies' as their wider scope of study. Actually, the British social anthropologists laid down the study of the entire social structure as the basic scope of social anthropology. The entire social structure of the society is composed of a number of subsidiary structures and systems which may include kinship system, economic system, religious system and political system. Besides this, social anthropology also endeavours to find out uniformities and regularities in the social life of a society on theoretical plane. Keeping in view the perspective of social structure and the new areas of study providing wider dimension to social anthropology, we will now discuss its new aspects that constitute the current scope or tradition of social anthropology in India and abroad.

Study of Village and Tribal Communities

Besides the study of primitive groups, social anthropology now takes to the study of village and peasant societies also. This is a new dimension of social anthropology. Robert Redfield, for the first time, in 1928 studied Tepoztlan, a Mexican village of tribals, intensively. He defined a village in terms of: (1) small size, (2) limited technical knowledge, (3) simple and backward economy, (4) lack of literacy, (5) based on clan, (6) physical isolation, (7) separate dialect, and (8) animistic religion. Besides giving these characteristics of a village community, Redfield also proposed some new concepts, namely, folk culture and peasant culture.

Along with the study of this Mexican village, a few other village studies were also made. Among those who conducted these studies were Arensberg (1937), Embree (1937) and Fie (1939). In our country also, village studies came in a flood, but only in the mid-fifties. Important among then included by S.C. Dube (Shamarpet), D.N. Majumdar (Mohana), G.S. Ghurye (Lonikand), Andre Beteille (Shivpuram) and F.G. Bailey (Bisepada). Thus, the new dimension of social anthropology both in India and outside contained village studies. Hence, in the current perspective, the scope and subject matter of social anthropology includes the study of villages.

Along with rural studies, tribal studies also increased in number. Accounting for the increase in tribal studies as a scope and subject matter of social anthropology, Sachchidananda writes in the *Trend Reports of 1969-1979*:

> This is on account of the fact that a large number of institutions in which social anthropologists work entered the stage of making fruitful contributions to anthropological studies... The largest contribution has been made by the Anthropological Survey of India which has the distinction of employing the largest number of anthropologists in the country. The Tribal Research Institutes, which have come up, have recently produced some significant studies along with the life and culture of Indian tribal communities. The departments of anthropology in various universities not only promoted serious fieldwork by their students but also encouraged writing of doctoral dissertations on subjects bearing on Indian tribes.

The scope of social anthropology also included ethnography besides tribal studies. The new dimension of tribal studies encompassed the study of tribal economy, tribal religion, tribal political structure and the changing scene. What is important about the tribal studies made under the banner of social anthropology is the generation of some concepts. The concepts are several, the important and significant; e.g., little community, dominant caste, village unity, sanskritization, westernization, little and great traditions and parochialization. The generation of a conceptual framework through village studies has enriched the scope and subject matter of social anthropology.

Industrialization and Modernization

We have been arguing that the British social anthropology and ethnology, which traditionally studied primitive and tribal groups, have come much ahead in their scope. Recently, the continental countries and also South Asian countries have taken to modernization and urbanization. Modernization in South Asia does not necessarily cover industrialization, but in these countries primitive peoples have taken up selected cultural traits and behavioural patterns of western societies. In fact, modern western society, business and industrial technology have offered enough to the Asian countries. Modern transportation, radio, newspapers, television are a few of the most obvious items which the tribal villages and urban societies have adopted. These modern cultural means have greatly influenced the urban people. They have thus become the new subject matter and scope of social anthropology.

A strange situation of migration has taken place all over the world. There have been migrations of peoples from the European continent to the US and from Asia to the European continent and the US. These large-scale movements of people have created problems of social and cultural integration. In the case of India, the recent trend of migration is that poverty and unemployment have pushed a large number of people to urban areas. When the village people migrate to cities, their culture undergoes great transformation. The migrant groups live in two cultures—the indigenous culture and the urban culture. The interaction of both the cultures has created a rich field for anthropological studies. By the mid-seventies some sociologists and social anthropologists brought out significant studies of urban communities. Victor D'Souza conducted studies on aspects of inequality and integration in an industrial society. M.S. Gore discussed the problems arising out of organization. Milton Singer and Bernard Cohn edited a big volume on structure and change in Indian society. The contributors to this volume analyzed anthropologically the problems of industrialization and urbanization.

Study of Problem-Specific People Rather than Holistic Communities

It must be emphasized that the current studies, which are coming out in the name of social anthropology and ethnology, are not of a holistic nature. Admittedly, the primitive, tribal, village communities are studied by social anthropologists as they provided new dimensions of scope and subject matter. A significant and new change that has come about is that there is focus on the specific problems of a tribal, primitive, urban or village community. The grip of ethnography in the study of tribals, it appears, has given way to problem-oriented studies. Now economic anthropology and demographic anthropology are emerging as current areas of scope and subject matter in social anthropology.

Recently, Paul Hockings (1999) has made a watershed in the study of Badaga—a Nilgiri tribe of Tamil Nadu—with a perspective of demography. Hockings has studied a moderate size of Badagas distributed in four villages. His findings are quite rewarding. He says that the decline of population among the Badaga tribe is largely due to modernization and transportation. Hockings' study is from all considerations a problem-specific study of a tribal group. In this study, the researcher has combined his knowledge of anthropology, history, demography and linguistics and very pointedly brings out demographic transition and social change over a decade. He also studied Badaga kinship, marriage, household structure and various aspects of contemporary life, including the influence of the mass media, schooling, economy and migration. As a matter of fact, Hockings has studied the nature of the process of modernization among Badagas of north-west Tamil Nadu.

There are a few other studies also which take into consideration urban and industrial societies. The scope of sociology has undergone a vital change in terms of the simple and complex societies. Definitely, the scope has swung in favour of large and big societies. Despite this widening scope, the essential anthropological bias, that is, the study of man in terms of uniformities and similarities remains the same. Social anthropology continues to maintain its status as a comparative study. It is this perspective or emphasis that makes it a distinct and different social science.

Concluding Observations

Writing on the scope of social anthropology, Evans-Pritchard once observed that social anthropology in principle studies all human societies, and not merely primitive societies. For three to four decades primitives and tribal groups constituted the scope and subject matter of the discipline. But, with the coming of democracy and liberty in Third World countries, including Africa and Asia, the social reality pertaining to tribals witnessed a great change. This also brought about a change in the scope and subject matter of social anthropology. This has to be looked upon in terms of theory, data and method. The theory has changed, the data, that is, the tribals have changed but the methodology continues to remain the same. Though Hockings has studied the Badagas in great details, he argues that the tribal kinship system and the social institutions remain the same. Eriksen, in his concluding note on the new scope and subject matter of social anthropology, writes:

> Social and cultural anthropology has the whole of human society as its field of interest and tries to understand the connections between the various aspects of our multiple relationships in existence.

3

Social Anthropology and the Social Sciences

Social anthropology is one of the social sciences. Natural sciences deal with natural phenomena whereas social sciences deal with cultural as well as social data. The scope and subject matter of social sciences consists of social institutions, polity, economy, crime and several other aspects of society. The objective of all the social sciences is to study the different aspects of society. On the basis of this study certain empirical generalizations are made, which in course of time, are formed into social theory. Same is the process with natural sciences. Social scientists have tried to define their subject matter from time to time. In a broad sense, social sciences, namely, economics, political science, history, anthropology, sociology, and others focus on the study of man as a member of a group or society. Thus, the nature of social sciences is essentially mental and cultural.

Efforts have been made to classify the social sciences. There is a tradition of the classification of sciences in general inherited from Plato and Aristotle. According to Comte, "the inorganic physical sciences deal with the most simple and universal phenomena. Next, the biological sciences, which presuppose that the phenomena of the physical sciences, are more particular and complex. Finally, come the social sciences, which presuppose the data of the organic sciences". Spencer has gone a little ahead and distinguishes three levels of phenomena, namely, the inorganic, the organic, and the superorganic or social. Interpreting the classification or hierarchy of social sciences, David Bidney comments:

> Superorganic phenomena were but extensions of organic phenomena into the social sphere, and hence, the former were not intelligible

apart from a knowledge as the kinds of organisms involved in any particular type of superorganic process.

Bidney has attempted to define social sciences considering varying classifications and says that "the social sciences are, as a matter of fact, empirical sciences. There has been a drastic change in our approach to the understanding of social sciences. There has been a breakaway from the old ontological orientation of social sciences". Now, all social sciences are considered to be empirical. These social sciences have their focus on two social aspects: (i) study of interrelationships in the society, and (ii) emphasis on culture.

Admittedly, social sciences deal with different aspects of society. Despite this common character, all the social sciences differ from each other. Each has its autonomous identity. The difference that we can make out is in the degree of emphasis put by each discipline. Secondly, the difference also lies in the methodology adopted. Kroeber has explained the perspective and focus difference among social sciences in the following statement:

> All the so-called social sciences deal with cultural as well as social data. Caesar's reform of calendar was a cultural innovation. His defeat of the senatorial party was a social event, but it led to institutional and, therefore, cultural changes, just as it affected thousands of individual lives for better or worse. When a historian analyzes Caesar's character and motivation, he has, in fact, gone beyond both society and culture and is operating in the field of informal, biographical, individual psychology. In economics, the banking system, the gold standard, commerce by credit or barter are institutions, and hence, cultural phenomena.

Kroeber lays down in detail the scope and subject matter of social sciences in general. He argues that social sciences are highly culture-conscious. They aim to investigate human culture as such. Though his emphasis on culture study may be contested, the fact is that social sciences study all the specializations of a society. When we look at the relationship of social anthropology with other social sciences, we are put to confusion and uncertainty. Before we discuss the relationships of social anthropology with other branches of anthropology—physical anthropology, cultural anthropology, pre-history, linguistics—it is essential that we look at the different traditions of anthropology vis-a-vis other social sciences.

Relationship of Social Anthropology with Other Social Sciences

When we take up the relationship of social anthropology with other social sciences, the immediate question which confronts us is, what do we mean by social anthropology in terms of its tradition. In Britain, social anthropology means ethnology or sociology; in the US it refers to culture, and in France and other countries it means structuralism. The point is that all the branches of anthropology have varying meanings and traditions in different countries. Such a situation cautions us from relating social anthropology with other social sciences keeping in view the specific meaning given by different traditions to social anthropology.

Yet another explanation is necessary. There are two kinds of relationships in anthropology. One is of sister type. For example, anthropology has some important branches, such as social anthropology, cultural anthropology, ethnology, pre-history, linguistics, and physical anthropology. The relationship among these branches is sisterly or collateral. There is another level, for instance, that with economics, politics, history and psychology. These two kinds of relationships are discussed in the following paragraphs:

Sociology and Social Anthropology

Sociology and social anthropology are very closely related. This closeness or proximity is more intensive in Great Britain. In the universities of England social anthropology is considered to be a branch of sociology. Evans-Pritchard, writing about the relations of these two disciplines, states:

> When people speak of sociology they generally have in mind studies of particular problems in civilized societies. If we give this sense to the word, then the difference between social anthropology and sociology is a difference of field, but there are also important differences of method between them. Social anthropology studies primitive societies directly, living among them for months or years, whereas sociological research is usually from documents and largely statistical. The social anthropologist studies society as wholes... The sociologist's work, on the other hand, is usually very specialized, being a study of isolated problems, such as divorce, crime, insanity, labor unrest, and incentives in industry.

Evans-Pritchard agrees that generally both sociology and social anthropology study the society. But they both differ on the following points:

1. *Field differences*: Social anthropology focuses on primitive societies whereas sociology concerns itself with civilized society.
2. *Methodological differences*: Social anthropology employs fieldwork as a dependable source of data generation. Sociology, on the other hand, depends on the collection of documents and generation of statistical data.
3. *Holistic and specific differences*: Social anthropology believes in making holistic studies of the primitive community. Different institutions of the community are functionally interrelated. Quite contrarily, sociology dwells on specific problems of the society.
4. *Philosophical orientation:* Social anthropology makes a general body of information about primitive social life. In anthropological studies theoretical input is relatively less; the sociological approach, on the other hand, has a heavy dose of social philosophy and theoretical approach.

In conclusion, it could be said that both these social sciences have difference of emphasis and perspective. The specialization of social anthropology rests on primitive peoples and methodology of research. Fieldwork method is taken up in small-scale society; it takes a long time to generate data. On the other hand, the theme of study of sociology is larger societies and the fieldwork is through tools such as schedule and questionnaire which usually take lesser time.

In India, the development of social anthropology is conditioned by certain historical factor. Yogendra Singh has discussed the relative situations of sociology and social anthropology in terms of historical and social forces. He observes:

> This social conditioning, however, is historically constituted. To the western pioneers of sociology, major challenges come from the emerging industrial society and its accompanying cultural and epistemological tensions. In the Indian context, the colonial experience, the memory of the past glory and the project for future political and cultural emancipation constituted the major cognitive and moral concerns.

In a later description Yogendra Singh cites illustrations from the British anthropologists and says that they treated caste and tribe as discrete structural and cultural formations. Verrier Elvin developed social anthropology based on the British social anthropology in his earlier writings. Yogendra Singh comments:

> The colonial ethnographers, for instance, took a placid, even a synchronic view of the tribal society. The conceptual framework developed by the British administrators-turned-ethnographers and by anthropologists was inspired by the then prevailing model in anthropology. Tribal communities were treated as isolates, tribals as noble savages and the primitive condition was described as a state of Arcadian simplicity.

If we look at the status of social anthropology during the colonial regime in India, we immediately find that both sociology and social anthropology became vulnerable to colonial forces. This brought social anthropology and sociology closer. Both disciplines had a common theme to study and research about. M.S. Gore was formally a sociologist but he studied tribals in great detail. M.N. Srinivas occupied the chair of the Professor of Sociology, but all through his life he studied tribes, castes and villages. His classic work, *Religion and Society among the Coorgs* and his edited work *India's Villages* are essentially an anthropological output. Similar best are the works of Andre Beteille, S.C. Dube and T.N. Madan. Interestingly enough, the sociological conceptual formulations brought out by sociologists are essentially social-anthropological in nature and content. The Indian social anthropology has firstly borrowed much from the British social anthropology; and then, developed closeness with sociology. In the field of method, theory and data, they are interrelated. Thus, from the viewpoint of theme and method, it is difficult to separate the two in India. What A.L. Kroeber wrote about the relationship of social anthropology and sociology in the US, very rightly applies to Indian situation. Kroeber observes:

> All in all, these are differences only in emphasis. In principle, sociology and social anthropology are hard to keep apart.

Cultural Anthropology and Social Anthropology

Cultural anthropology is one of the branches of anthropology. Both social anthropology and cultural anthropology are sister disciplines, studying the primitive peoples. Both include 'other cultures' as their themes of study. Both have the same methodology dominated by fieldwork. Despite these similarities, there is a fundamental difference in their approach. Cultural anthropology, which is prevalent in the US, has culture as its idiom of study; whereas social anthropology, which is popular and practised in Britain and Asia, has social structure as its guiding perspective. In other words, social anthropology has social relations or social structure as its perspective. In the US, cultural relations are the guidelines for cultural anthropology.

But it will be very simplistic to differentiate social anthropology and cultural anthropology on the basis of these two concepts—cultural and social. In Europe and USA, there is a debate on the relationship between social and cultural. The cultural anthropologists or culturologists consider culture apart from society and as an entity independent of society, and having an objective reality and intelligibility of its own. On the other hand, the social anthropologists argue that they study social relations rather than culture, social institutions and their relations to social systems rather than isolated customs and cultural traits.

David Bidney, who has developed theoretical anthropology, tries to bring these two branches closer. His argument is that there is much closeness between these sister disciplines of anthropology. First, both had a holistic approach to primitive people or other cultures. Both have the same methods of study. And, then to argue that both are antithetical or at best independent disciplines, is erroneous. He suggests that there cannot be a culture without a social structure and vise versa. He observes:

> If, however, one were not to grant the assumption that anthropology need be limited to the study of culture on the ground that such limitation is impractical and unintelligible and were to maintain instead that cultural phenomena and social systems are internally related, then the way would be prepared for a holistic approach which studies human social and cultural phenomena as functional wholes.

It must be admitted that social anthropology and cultural anthropology are two autonomous branches of anthropology. Though there is some overlap in scope and subject-matter, there is a basic difference in their emphasis. We again quote Bidney and say in his words:

Social anthropology and cultural anthropology are then understood as two branches of a common discipline of anthropology concerned with the study of man and his cultures in society.

Ethnology and Social Anthropology

In the words of Evans-Pritchard, "ethnology classifies peoples on the basis of their distribution. This is irrespective of any time scale". In other words, ethnology looks at people from the ethnic point of view at the present time, or in past time by the movement and mixture of people and the diffusion of cultures. There is much similarity in ethnology and social anthropology. Both study the indigenous and modern peoples. In USA cultural anthropology and ethnology are used synonymously. Both are regarded as complementary branches of the more general science of anthropology. It was after the First World War that ethnology parted company with social anthropology. Earlier, under the influence of Durkheim and Rivers, American anthropologists were at first inclined to accept the general position that culture consisted of social facts and that ethnology or cultural anthropology was an autonomous science.

As a matter of fact, ethnology is a science of culture history. It means that an ethnologist seeks to specify cultural and mental laws to explain the processes of culture history. The similarity or close relationship between ethnology and social anthropology is simple. Both study society, that is, man and culture. Ethnology is concerned with the common cultural elements of all the groups, notwithstanding place or time. Despite this affinity, there are some differences between the two disciplines:

(1) *Narrative*: Ethnology is narrative. It describes the cultural traits of a particular group with great elaboration. For instance, the cultural specificity of a Gond and for that matter any tribal group of the country, constitutes the theme of ethnology. Basically, ethnographic accounts are narrative. Risely studied peoples of India; and also their racial composition and their fairs and festivals. But nowhere has he analytically brought out concepts of the kind of dominant caste, caste ranking and the like. Ethnologists are narration-oriented. They describe and their work is done.

(2) *Analytical*: Social anthropology is both descriptive or narrative and analytical. Where ethnology limits itself to culture, social an-

thropology discusses patterns of interrelations. We have a large number of social anthropological studies, such as Andre Beteille's, *Caste, Class and Power* (1965), which bring out analytical constructs which bear value to tasks of development.

(3) *Comparative*: Ethnology works as ethnography and codifies the classificatory characteristics of a cultural group. Comparison has no place in ethnographic accounts. Social anthropology is inherently comparative. It studies the primitive society and compares it with other societies—past and current.

(4) *Empirical*: Ethnology has a historical bias. It codifies customs, traditions, folkways and food habits on a historical basis. It cannot move without historical context. Social anthropology draws heavily from empirical fieldwork. There is a controversy between social anthropology and ethnology. It is said that ethnology depends on history and social anthropology denies history.

History and Social Anthropology

There are many variants of history. It cannot be defined in a single sentence. Most of the scholars define history as a chronological account of the past events. Traditionally, therefore, the emperors, rulers and elites, who make history, constitute the theme of history. Looked at from this perspective, history is like a railway timetable which moves year after year, century after century. In simple words, history is the account of ruling dynasties. The preliterate people do not have anything of this history. There are no records for them. Here is a breaking point between history and social anthropology. Social anthropology writes about prehistoric people and their traditions and institutions. The field of history is the people of society; the field of social anthropology is the society; and the field of social anthropology is the masses of people who are illiterate.

Yet another definition of history is that given by the Indian historian, D.D. Kosambi. He has defined it from the Marxian conceptual framework and argues that history is about the means of production and the property relations developed out of production. On the other hand, yet another approach to history is suggested by Carr who says that the events which involve and affect larger masses of people are historical events. Without entering into the controversies of the definition of history, it must be said that history is a methodology and it should be used as such only. The relationship of history and social anthropology is of a kind of love and hate. There was a time when social anthropology did not employ historical methodology. If we look at anthropological texts, we usually find that these are written in the present context. "Many of the most influential monographs in social anthropology were written half a century ago or more, and in virtually every case the societies they deal with have changed radically since the original fieldwork took place." The social anthropologists all over the world have hated history. They were concerned with detailed narration and, therefore, generated only empirical data. Tracing the relationship of history and social anthropology, Eriksen says that in the past social anthropology did not criticize historical accounts for empirical narrations. He writes:

> Frequently, moreover, fieldwork was carried out during an unusual not a 'typical' historical period. For example, classic African anthropology was developed during the last phase of French and British colonialism, namely, between the First World War and 1960.

It must be stressed that social anthropology has never tried to replace history. Its analyses have traditionally been focused on social and cultural interrelationships at a particular point in time, and until recently, have rarely emphasized the historical processes which have led up to the present. Interestingly, in the British, American and French traditions, the aim is usually to account for the workings of a particular society or culture, not to try to explain how it emerged. As a matter of fact, the founding fathers of social anthropology, namely, Boas in the US and Radcliffe-Brown and Malinowski in England, were all critical of the rather speculative forms of cultural history which preceded modern anthropology. Thus, the older social anthropology was more or less a still or snapshot anthropology. The historical methodology and social anthropology remained averse to each other because of the anthropological thrust of functionalism which dominated the first quarter of the 20th century.

A change has come about in the relationship of social anthropology and history after the 1980s. It became obvious to Third World countries that the situation of primitive peoples can hardly be analyzed without explaining the historical processes which shaped their structure. The status of Nuers in Africa is empirically alright but it is also resultant of the domination of whites over the coloured people.

In India also, the primitive peoples were dominated by the colonial rule. Functionalism as a methodology took an amazing turn in India. Though empiricism all over the world has emerged as a reaction to historicism, in India, empiricism and historicism go together. Here, those who are empiricists are also history-friendly. For instance, M.N. Srinivas explains the status of Coorgs and for that matter the caste hierarchy from a historical perspective also. Explaining the relationship as is currently found between social anthropology and history, Eriksen very interestingly observes:

> Anthropology may be described as the processes whereby one wades into a river and explores it as it flows by, whereas historians are forced to study the dry river bed. One cannot engage in particular observations of the past.

Not only Eriksen who is British but also Kroeber from the US stresses the importance of knowing the history of a society and its contribution to the present. This can be specially rewarding—some would say absolutely necessary—in studies dealing with societies with a written history. Further, the connections between different societies which are often crucial for the understanding of each society, can only be properly investigated historically. It would be impossible to understand, for example, the Industrial Revolution in England properly without prior knowledge of the slave trade and the cotton plantations in the United States.

As a matter of fact, history and social anthropology are not mutually exclusive. Empiricism and history are both integrated. It could be safely said that in the Indian context social anthropology cannot be properly understood without reference to its history. The classical works of social anthropology, such as those of Andre Beteille, S.C. Dube and K.S. Singh, very clearly indicate that historical context is quite useful in understanding tribal ethnography and social anthropology. Despite this relationship, social anthropology earns its own autonomous status. For it there is no bias of time. It studies its subject matter notwithstanding any period boundaries.

Psychology and Social Anthropology

Psychology has two variants—general or individual psychology and social psychology. Both are related to social anthropology. The

American anthropologists were greatly influenced by this relationship. However, Franz Boas, a noted American cultural anthropologist, literally dominated the field of the relationship of social anthropology and psychology. Boas had undoubtedly stressed the importance of the relationship of these two fields of study. In his monumental book, *The Mind of Primitive Man*, he set forth his conviction that there is no fundamental difference between the mind of primitive man and that of civilized man, and that whatever differences exist between the achievements of different races could be accounted for on historical and cultural grounds rather than in terms of innate biological differences. Lewis has also established the role of psychology in understanding the ethnology of primitive peoples. Social psychology, however, is the closest kin of social anthropology. It deals with the mass behaviour of the primitive peoples. If, for example, the tribals are influenced by the Devi movement in south Gujarat, it is a clear case of the relationship of social psychology and social anthropology. However, general psychology interprets the behaviour of man as his individual manifestation.

Regarding the relationship of psychology with social anthropology, it can be said that there are two different realms dealt with by the two disciplines. Psychology is concerned with the behaviour of man and social anthropology focuses on interrelationship among different institutions of the society. There is a basic contradiction regarding the approach adopted by the two disciplines. Psychologists begin by taking the tribal culture for granted, as if it were uniform and universal. With this assumption they study psychic behaviour in a tribe. On the other hand, the same approach is taken by social anthropology. It tends to take human nature for granted, as if it were uniform and studies the diverse cultures of the tribe. In reality, in technical language, we have two variables, viz., mind and culture, and each science, that is, psychology and social anthropology, assumes that it can go ahead by treating the other variable as if it were constant. But researches now undertaken in both the fields have made it clear that such constancy is not actual. But, to deal with two highly complex variables is difficult; and as for specific findings, only beginnings have as yet been made.

W.H.R. Rivers, who conducted his studies among the Todas of South India, has dealt with the relationship of psychology and ethnology or social anthropology. He has argued for the independent science of social anthropology, though ultimately the discipline is related to human behaviour because, as he observes:

> The final aim of the study of society is the explanation of social behaviour in terms psychology.

To simplify the relations between psychology and social anthropology, it could be stated, that the study of interrelationship in a primitive society owes much to the psychological conditioning of the people in that society. This can be illustrated by referring to the situation of Indian tribals. The tribals, historically, have been exploited by the moneylenders and traders. I.P. Desai notes that when there is a meeting of the tribals of Bardoli *taluka*, they simply prohibit the entry of non-tribals. They consider caste Hindus as their enemies. This psychological mindset determines their behaviour. Therefore, in any study of primitive society, the psychology of the primitives constitutes a relevant point. This also explains the relationship between social anthropology and psychology; the former is concerned with a variable of culture and the latter with the mind.

Archaeology and Social Anthropology

Archaeology is a branch of anthropology and is very close to social anthropology and ethnology. In very simple terms, it could be said that archaeology is concerned with the historical reconstruction of human society. It tries to find out artifacts such as wheel, jug, axe, arrow, loin cloth, etc., which are made by humans. These findings are excavated. For instance, the excavations of Harappan culture help us to reconstruct the history of Indian civilization. In America, several of the areas of archaeology are taken over by ethnology. The basic objective of archaeology is, therefore, to find out, as Kroeber says, what is old in society.

Archaeology is basically prehistoric. It is specific to time. Admittedly, it is related to social anthropology but what is social anthropology in Britain is in reality ethnology. It focuses on finding out the old culture by excavation. Discussing the relationship between archaeology and social anthropology or ethnology, Evans-Pritchard writes:

> Prehistoric archaeology is best regarded as a branch of ethnology. It attempts to reconstruct the history of peoples and cultures from hu-

man and cultural relations found by excavation in geological deposits. It also relies on circumstantial evidence and, like ethnology, can tell social anthropologists little about the ideas and institutions, in which they would be interested, of the peoples whose bones and artifacts it discovers and classifies.

What Evans-Pritchard has said boils down to the fact that archaeology learns about the culture of people by excavating the artifacts, and social anthropology links these with the prevalent culture and traditions of the primitive peoples. There is, thus, a reciprocal relationship between these two disciplines. In fact, they are complementary to one another.

Political Science and Social Anthropology

On principle, social anthropology is concerned with the social structure and culture of the primitive peoples. Social anthropology, despite its variants in the US, Europe and Asia, restricts itself to the study of the cultural and social ways of life of the people. On the other hand, quite opposite to the anthropological tradition, politics and for that matter political science is concerned with power and authority. The realms of focus are different; access to society is also different. But there are very close relations between the two disciplines.

The traditional textbooks of social anthropology tread the oft-repeated track of defining a particular discipline, show its subject matter and scope and finally mention the relationship. This does not take into consideration the empirical research position of the relationship of the two disciplines. We have taken a departure from such a tradition.

Sometime back M.J. Swartz observed that "politics is parasitical on other social relationships". If we make an effort to study the role of politics in society, it would soon be evident that all societies have some mechanism to maintain law and order. There are some agencies that exercise constraint on property taxes, torture and genocide. The all-embracing concern of politics is to maintain law and order and implement the rights of citizens, effect conflict resolution and encourage social integration. Thus, political science and social anthropology go hand in hand. This establishes the relationship of these two disciplines.

There is a special branch of anthropology which is known as political anthropology. John Gledhill has brought out a study on the political behaviour of primitives, *Power and its Disguises: Perspectives on Political Anthropology*. A similar study by John Middleton and David Tait deals with the African tribes who do not have rulers and states. Works of this kind very well establish that social and political anthropologies are very close in their perspectives. Both have a common theme of political activities. The only difference is that political science is concerned with the political behaviour of the modern societies, whereas social anthropology studies the political behaviour of primitive peoples. Thus, in the domain of approach and perspective, both the disciplines are quite close. The differences arise when we discuss their perspectives.

One very important thing about politics is that all the primitive societies, which anthropology has studied, do not have political institutions. In modern state societies, it may seem fairly easy to delineate what is politics and what is not. Political science, as we find it today, deals with the formal political institutions; with a legislative assembly, local administration, voting patterns and other aspects of a society recognized as political. The situation of primitive society is altogether different. A few of them do not have any state. Very often, in such stateless societies, kinship and religion are, in practice, indistinguishable from politics.

The basic question raised by political anthropologists in the study of primitives is: when there is no state in these tribal communities, how are they integrated and what keeps them disciplined? Such an enquiry made by political anthropology brings it closer to social anthropology. One very common feature of social anthropology and political science is that they both study power. In short, power as it was defined during the old days by Max Weber, is the ability to enforce one's own will on others' behaviour. It means that power gives the ability to a person or a group to make someone do something they would otherwise not have done. According to Weber, people have power over each other. What is important about the distribution of power is that it is not equally distributed.

Thus, it can be concluded that both these disciplines start on a similar track, but as they go ahead and bring out their empirical generalizations, the differences arise.

Economics and Social Anthropology

Marshall D. Sahlins is a social anthropologist who has worked on the economy of primitive peoples. He has argued that for a modern society money is everything and for a primitive society it is the kinship which is all important. Sahlins' observation explains the relationship and differentiation between social anthropology and economics. The status of economics among primitives can be seen from the theory given by Malinowski. His thesis was that among tribals the economy is an integrated part of social and cultural totality. His observation was that economic systems and actions can only be fully understood if we look into their interrelations with other aspects of culture and society. Admittedly, social anthropology studies the tribal economy, and this brings it closer to the discipline of economics. Despite this inherent relationship between social anthropology and economics, it must be said that each has its own distinct autonomous status. They differ in their perspective and approach.

> *Marshall D. Sahlins* (b. 1930) has worked on the processes of evolution. His study of polynesian social stratification (1958) is quite interesting. It is in this book that he shows the relationship between state formation and kinship organization. He has constructed the conceptual framework of cultural relativism, that is, each society has its own culture. In other words, culture is group-specific. He has also been influenced by Marxism and structuralism. His study of primitive economy very clearly establishes and differentiates the relations between social anthropology and economics.

Recently, a new branch of economic anthropology has emerged in the wider domain of anthropology. This brings economics all the more closer to social anthropology. Now it is being stressed that tribal economy is basically different from the general discipline of economics. To spell out the specificity of the tribal economy, it would be better if we refer to Eriksen. He observes:

> Anthropologists have always wished to call attention to the ways in which the economy is an integrated part of a social and cultural totality, and to reveal that economic systems and actions can only be fully understood if we look into their interrelationships with other aspects of culture and society. Just as politics ought to be seen as part of a

wider system which includes non-political aspects as well, the economy cannot be property studied as an isolated sector.

Thus, the tribal economics as discussed by anthropologists has a functional nature. It is related to other parts of tribal life such as religion, kin, clan and polity. The modern economy is different in its perspective and approach. This economy is rational and is importantly based on market principles. This theoretical difference between social anthropology and economics has been aptly brought out by Douglas and Isherwood, in their book, *The World of Goods*. The authors have given an anthropological answer to the question: why people in modern societies want commodities? "The drive for consumption witnessed in these societies is far from natural, even if it is taken for granted with in academic economics and among lay people. Why is it, for example, that people want to eat food (A) instead of food (B) if it can be shown that both are equally nutritious and even that food (B) is less expensive. The full answer must be sought in an analysis of the cultural categories of the society in question, not in an analysis of "rational choice and maximization of value". S.L. Doshi has elaborately worked on the food habits of the tribals of Rajasthan. He argues that there is culture in food and, therefore, food consumption cannot be analyzed wholly on the principle of economic theory.

The academic economics is quite different from the economy of social anthropology. Modern economy is basically a capitalist economy. It is a newcomer to the world. Its theory and principles are helpful in understanding the general economic behaviour but the tribal economy is essentially different for it stresses ethnicity rather than rationality. The example of gift system, which is prevalent among the Trobriand islanders, fully explains the nature of tribal economy. As a matter of fact, among the tribals, much of the economics is guided by 'gift economy'. In a capitalistic economy, money is the common denominator for what is commonly thought of as an economic activity, and it serves to single out an economic institution in those societies as something apparently separate from the rest of society. If we look at a tribal society there is no single word for economy as an institution separated from social life in general.

What we find in the relationship of economics and social anthropology is that both are concerned with the study of production, distribution, exchange and consumption. But, the understanding of these processes in social anthropology and economics is altogether different. To summarize the relations and differences between social anthropology and economics, we observe:

(1) Social anthropology is empirical whereas general economics is analytical.
(2) Social anthropology is basically micro; economics is importantly macro.
(3) Social anthropology considers economics as a part of the whole society. It cannot be studied separately. Economics, on the other hand, is separate and has a distinct existence in society.
(4) Economy in social anthropology is basically a community economy; general economics is individual centred. A person wants to maximize his benefits through cost benefit calculations.
(5) Social anthropology begins its economic research right from a small, little society. Contrarily, economics concerns itself with the macro level communities.
(6) Social anthropology looks at economic processes from the cultural point of view. General economics is national, it looks at the maximization of benefits.

Social anthropology has by now established itself as an autonomous academic discipline. It has its relations with other social sciences. These relations stem from the fact that as a social science, social anthropology shares some of the common aspects of theory, data and methods of other social sciences. On a broader plane, it could be safely said that social anthropology is different from other social sciences on many counts. However, its distinctness is largely upheld by the study of indigenous people, holistic study and network of interrelationships in the primitive society.

Further Readings

Beattie, John, *Other Cultures*, London, 1964.
Hoebel, E.A., *Man in the Primitive World*, New York, 1988.
Kroeber, A.K., *Anthropology*, London, 1948.

4

Methods of Social Anthropology

Social anthropology, like any social science, tries to learn about social phenomena. This is a scientific endeavour. The objective of science as is now propounded by post-modern social theory is not to know the reality of society, but the so-called truth about the affairs of society. It seeks to develop skills so that human beings can live a better life. To develop skills one has to employ scientific methods so that social and natural phenomena can be properly exploited and harnessed. If there is a science, there is certainly a method. Theory, method and data go together. Social anthropology has a well-developed methodology for learning about society. This methodology has not developed overnight, but has been evolved through several decades.

What distinguishes social anthropology in the realm of social sciences is its fieldwork methodology which is the guiding idiom of this discipline. It is amazing to find that despite methodology being an important ingredient of social anthropology, it does not find any suitable treatment in the textbooks. What is worse, it does not even find a place in the index. As a result, under the theme of methodology, all sources of procedures and techniques are discussed. Method is a logic. When an anthropologist is confronted with a problem, he first devices a logic, that is, he argues: how can the problem be approached logically so that the desired objective is fulfilled. It is this logic which leads to the attainment of the objectives of social research that decides the method. There are several methods of logic to tackle the research problem. The researcher analyzes the merit of the logic and identifies one or more methods. In short, method is the logic of enquiry; it is the rule of accomplishing an end; it is an orderly procedure.

If we make a survey of the tradition of social anthropological research, we find that fieldwork and empirical tradition have been constant characteristics of social anthropology. It cannot survive even for a moment without fieldwork method. Thomas Hylland Eriksen has stressed the importance of fieldwork in social anthropology as a reliable method, that is, logic for generating field data. He observes:

> Anthropology distinguishes itself from the other social sciences through the great emphasis put on fieldwork as the most important source of new knowledge about society and culture. A field study may last between a few months to two years, or longer. And it aims at developing as intimate an understanding as possible of the phenomena investigated. Although there are differences in field methods between different anthropological schools, it is generally agreed that the anthropologist ought to stay in the field long enough for his or her presence to be considered more or less 'natural' by the permanent residents, although he or she will have to some extent remain a stranger.

At a later stage we shall have the opportunity to discuss the fieldwork tradition continued by social anthropologists of the European continent, the US and India The point we want to stress here is that the meaning of 'field' is taken to be "an area of knowledge". This knowledge area is observed by the researcher. As for natural sciences there is a laboratory, so for social anthropology there is fieldwork. Yet another meaning of fieldwork is the scientific survey work done in the field. By conducting survey work the social anthropologist tries to find the patterned or organized whole of the society. He does not look at the primitive tradition, belief system or a ritual as a separate and isolated occurrence. Rather, he looks at the whole society, finding out the pattern of working, living, marrying, worshipping and organizing.

The methodology of social anthropology is mainly fieldwork. In other words, fieldwork is empirical and empirical work is experience. This experience is gained through the sensory system. No fieldwork can be done without empiricism. But empiricism or fieldwork is not the end in itself. It generates data and gives new knowledge about society, but it remains incomplete without interpretation, and the real rub lies in interpretation. This requires other methods like comparative method, historical method and functional method. Case study, observation and administration of schedule are some of the techniques which we employ to make a better interpretation.

Theory versus Fieldwork

In sociology, the controversy regarding the reciprocity between theory and empiricism has almost been settled by Robert K. Merton. He has, of late, established that the relations between theory and empiricism are inseparable. C. Wright Mills reiterates the position taken by Merton when he says:

> Theory without data is empty, but data without theory are blind.

This is how the reciprocity between theory and empiricism goes in sociology. The situation in sociology in different. Here, we find a controversy. Long back, in the 1940s, Evans-Pritchard referred to this debate and said that when anthropologists study primitive people with a theoretical bias, it distorts the account of savage people. As a matter of fact, a practical man goes with no such bias. He brings out an impartial record of the facts as he sees them. This observation of Evans-Pritchard was based on the fact that some five decades back there was a gap in anthropological theory and fieldwork. But, it appears that the current orientation to theory and empiricism has undergone much transformation; they have, in fact, come closer.

Evans-Pritchard makes a compromise between the anthropological theorist and the layman who conducts fieldwork. In fact, both have theories: one variant of the theory is scientific and the other popular. Without theory the empirical fieldwork cannot go ahead. Evans-Pritchard writes:

> The difference between them is really of another kind. The student makes his observations to answer questions arising out of the generalizations of specialized opinion and the layman makes his observations to answer questions arising out of the generalizations of popular opinion. Both have theories—the one systematic and the other popular.

When a social anthropologist conducts his fieldwork he works within a body of theoretical knowledge and he makes his observations to solve problems which derive from it. This emphasis on problems is, of course, a feature of any field of scholarship. Lord Acton, the renowned historian, told his students to study problems and not periods. Collingwood, the noted archaeologist, asked his students to study problems and not sites. The anthropology students should study problems and not peoples. Thus, the method of social anthropology is fieldwork and its theme of study is the peoples.

Fieldwork is not an easy job; it is very demanding, both professionally and in human terms. A researcher has to remain in the field for long periods, say, for months together. He has to bear boredom, illness, personal privations, disappointments and frustration. It is only for a few anthropologists that fieldwork is an exciting job. Besides, one often has to face the risk of suspicion and hostility. Despite all the hardships that a social anthropologist faces in the field, there is no escape from this work. It is considered to be an authentic source of generating data.

Fieldwork

Social anthropology has a rich tradition of conducting fieldwork. The nature of fieldwork has changed from time to time. There are large number of social anthropologists who have conducted protracted fieldwork among the tribals. Evans-Pritchard has lived several months among the Azande tribals of southern Sudan. He also worked among the Nuers of South Africa. Paul Bohannan worked for a long period among the Tiv tribals of eastern Nigeria. The Tiv tribals are traditionally farmers who have just been introduced to money as a medium of exchange. In India, S.C. Dube has conducted fieldwork in a village called Shamerpet of Andhra Pradesh. M.N. Srinivas has worked for about two years in Rampura village of southern India. Andre Beteille remained for a protracted period in his study of caste, class and power in Sripuram village. Thus, we have enough instances to support the point that anthropologists have lived in their respective fields of study for months together. Recently, we have a study by Paul Hockings who studied the Badaga people for months together. Thus, it is obvious that fieldwork is a dependable source for generating data and, therefore, a dependable method of social anthropology. It is the tradition and culture of anthropological methodology.

Nature of Anthropological Studies

If an attempt is made to review the earlier studies conducted by social anthropologists we find that most of these studies have been narrative and descriptive. These studies in the beginning did not attempt any systematic analysis, though they made pseudo-historical speculations.

Their main objective was to present a socio-economic survey of the primitive community. They studied environment, racial characteristics, demography, vital statistics, technology, economy, social organization, law, religion, magic, mythology, folklore, pastimes, etc.

However, there is a marked change in the recent fieldwork reports. Modern fieldwork monographs are generally intended to give more than merely a description of the social life of a people with interpretations of the more popular kind which any description of one culture in terms of another necessarily entails. They aim at an analytical and integrative description which will bring out those features of the social life which are significant for the understanding of its structure and also for general theory.

Earlier accounts of primitive life were mainly given by travellers and missionaries who found the customs of the primitive people unique and strange. Similar was the case with the Christian missionaries. In their objective of conversion of the primitives to Christianity they found very strange religious ways which they reported to the civilized world as anthropological monographs. During the middle of the 18th and 19th centuries, the European colonization of America had been widely expanded; British rule had been established in India, Australia and New Zealand, and many parts of Africa had been settled by European emigrants. The character of ethnographic description of the peoples of these regions began to change from traveller's tales to detailed studies by missionaries and administrators who not only had better opportunities to observe, but were also men of greater culture than the gentlemen of fortune of earlier times.

It must be said that whatever data were generated by the missionaries and administrators they were very useful for theory building by the later anthropologists. The new information generated in this way was sufficient in bulk and quality for Morgan, Mclennan, Tylor and others. There was also a sufficient body of knowledge for speculation to be tested and for new hypotheses to be put forward on a solid basis of ethnographic facts.

Field Methods

Systematic and scientific fieldwork was pioneered by Radcliffe-Brown who was a student of Rivers and Haddon. His study of the Andaman islanders, conducted from 1906 to 1908, was the first attempt by a social anthropologist to investigate sociological theories in a primitive society and describe the social life of a people in such a way as to bring out clearly what was significant in it for those theories. Even today, sociologists like Robert K. Merton and Talcott Parsons borrow from the conceptual framework developed by Radcliffe-Brown. Later on, Malinowski joined Radcliffe-Brown to establish and strengthen the fieldwork tradition. Malinowski was a pupil of Hobhouse, Westermark and Seligman. "If Radcliffe-Brown has always had a wider knowledge of general social anthropology and has proved himself the abler thinker, Malinowski was the more thorough fieldworker. He not only spent a larger period than any anthropologist before him, and also after him, in a single study of a primitive people, the Trobriand islanders of Melanesia between 1914 and 1918, but he was also the first anthropologist to conduct his research through the native language, as he was the first to live throughout his work in the centre of native life." Under these favourable circumstances, Malinowski came to know the Trobriand islanders well, and he described their social life in a number of bulky, and some shorter monographs up to the time of his death.

The tradition of conducting fieldwork as is done today draws directly or indirectly from Malinowski, for he insisted that the social life of a primitive people can only be understood if it is studied intensively, and that it is a necessary part of a social anthropologist's training to carry out at least one such intensive study of a primitive society.

It was at the inspiration provided by Radcliffe-Brown and Malinowski that fieldwork method become a popular source of generating data from the primitive societies. By the beginning of the 20th century a flood of researches on primitive people came from India and Africa. By then fieldwork had been established as a dependable anthropological method. In Africa, there were thousands of groups which claimed political autonomy. Study of these political groups were conducted exclusively by fieldwork methodology. The first study of this kind was done by Mrs. Seligmen in 1909-10. It was followed by the study of Evans-Pritchard who concentrated on the intensive study of Azande tribe of Sudan. This study began in 1927. "Since then most intensive studies of primitive peoples have been made in Africa, and political institutions have received the attention they require." For instance, Schapera studied Bechuana, Forbes gave an account of the Tallensi of the Gold Coast, Nadel brought out a monograph on the Nupe of Nigeria, Kuper provided an account of Swazi, and Evans-Pritchard gave a lucid description of the Nuer. Coming to India the tradition of fieldwork came at a later stage, after the Second World War. H.S. Risley, J.H. Hutton, W.V. Grigson, W.W. Hunter and others admittedly prepared ethnographic accounts of the tribals but they did not have any fieldwork tradition. It was just desk work done by them by collecting information from their loyal 'servants'. The real and authentic fieldwork is of recent innovation in India's social anthropology. On the classical fieldwork done by Indian anthropologists, mention may be made of Iravati Karve, Verrier Elvin, M.N. Srinivas, Andre Beteille and others.

Meaning of Fieldwork

Fieldwork is the practical work done by a researcher in a specific area of knowledge. Eriksen has defined fieldwork in the specific context of social anthropological methods. He observes:

> A principal requirement in fieldwork consists of trying to take part in local life as much as possible. Anthropologists also use a variety of specified formal techniques for the collection of data. Depending on the kind of fieldwork one is engaged in structural interviews, statistical sampling and other techniques may be required to varying degrees. Most anthropologists depend on a combination of formal techniques and unstructured participant observation in their fieldwork.

In defining the fieldwork method, Eriksen links fieldwork with field methods. The researcher resides in the field and also generates data through the administration of structured schedule and observation. It must be observed at this level that administration of schedule does not seem to be relevant in the case where the primitives are not sophisticated in education and social and cultural life. Generally, fieldwork means to live in the field and identify with the people. Yet another requirement of fieldwork is a prolonged stay. According to British tradition, it is expected from a researcher to live in the field for at least two years. This period could extend up to one year more. In India, M.N. Srinivas says that the researcher should reside in the field for about a year. Thus, the first need for a researcher is to identify himself with the local people, and second, reside in the field for a prolonged period.

Attributes of Fieldwork

There are several ways of undertaking fieldwork and it is impossible to provide a clear recipe to carry it out. For one thing, the anthropologist himself is the most important 'scientific instrument' used, investing a great deal of his own personality in the process. In other words, the social anthropologist himself is a variable in the research. Another source of variation is the field situation and the topic of research. For instance, the field situation of a desert village is altogether different from that of a village situated in the plains. There is also structural and cultural variation between a tribal village and a caste village. In both these situations, the nature of fieldwork would differ. As a matter of fact, research method, that is, fieldwork must be tailored to fit the requirements of the settings and the subject.

Evans-Pritchard once recalled his first attempts to learn about fieldwork in the early 1920s. He has asked a number of renowned anthropologists how to do it. And he had received various answers. First he asked the famous Finnish anthropologist Westermarck, who said: "Don't converse with an informant for more than 20 minutes because if you aren't bored by that time he will be." Evans-Pritchard comments: "Very good advice, if somewhat inadequate." Alfred Haddon said that "it was really all quite simple; one should always behave as a gentleman". Evans-Pritchards' teacher Charles Seligman, "told me to take 10 grams of quinine every night and to keep off women". Finally, Malinowski himself told the novice, "not to be a bloody fool". Evans-Pritchard himself emphasizes later in the same account, that facts are themselves meaningless; in other words, "one must know precisely what one wants to know". And "then fashion a suitable methodology from the available techniques". There is alas no simple recipe for fieldwork. It is a method where the researcher's most important 'scientific instrument' is himself or herself.

In this section, we have tried to list some of the attributes which characterize excellent fieldwork. These are presented below:

(i) Knowledge of local language

One of the essential rules for good fieldwork is the familiarity with the language which the local people speak. Language is nothing but an arrangement of signs and symbols. These signs and symbols hint about the structure of a society. The new structuralism which draws heavily from Saussare argues that a society can be perfectly understood through symbols of a language. For perfect communication, therefore, the researcher should speak in the language of the people. The earlier professional fieldworkers were always in a great hurry. Their quick visits to native peoples sometimes lasted only a few days, and seldom more than a few weeks. They did not come face to face with the real life of the people. Local language needs to be learnt before going out to the field.

(ii) Familiarity with people's culture and social life

Morris Carstairs, who conducted his studies among the Bhil tribe of southern Rajasthan, has narrated his experiences with this tribe: During the 1940s, the Bhils of this region had a tradition not to allow any stranger to sit on the cot where the tribal couple slept. Not aware of this tradition, Carstairs occupied one of the corners of the cot. It meant for the tribal people to have sex relations with the wife. He was immediately assaulted by the husband and was not only turned out of the house but was also made to flee the village at the earliest. Fieldwork, therefore, requires that the researcher should have familiarity with the culture and traditions of the region. We have similar instances which show that a minor flaw on the part of researcher has resulted in bitter experiences. Andre Beteille made his first approach in Sripuram village among untouchables. In the latter part of his fieldwork acceptance by the high caste Hindus became very difficult. In any fieldwork, the first objective of the researcher should be to understand the people and establish a rapport with them.

(iii) No ethnocentric bias: Stress on cultural relations

The idiom of any fieldwork is to understand the society on its own terms. Each society has its cultural and social milieu. It has its history. In such a situation, the researcher should not apply his own cultural scale in the evaluation of the primitive society. Admittedly, there is a macro scale of evaluation. But, there cannot be any shared universal scale. For instance, a scale pertaining to gross national product (GNP), democratic rights, literacy rates, which bear longevity, should not be adopted to the study of tribals. Whenever in African studies, European scales were applied, the results were disastrous. In India, the national scales of norms and values, or input-output, if applied to tribals, would draw a blank.

(iv) Study society from insight

Each society has its own understanding. The perceptions of the society are conditioned by historical and socio-cultural forces. What we call the good life might not apply to a tribal society. As a matter of fact, a social anthropologist cannot provide an answer to a question like---which society is better than others—simply because the discipline does not ask it. If asked---what is the good life—the social anthropologist will have to answer that every society has its own definition of the good life. What is vital is that the social anthropologist should try to understand the society from inside, that is, how the society evaluates itself.

(v) Cultural relativism as against cultural ethnocentrism

Bias for the superiority of one's own culture is termed ethnocentrism. Such an approach to primitive society has been condemned by social science tradition. What is considered to be useful for understanding of a primitive society is to analyze it through cultural relativism. Sometimes cultural relativism is posited as the opposite of ethnocentrism. A doctrine in social anthropology states that societies or cultures are qualitatively different and have their own unique inner logic, and therefore, it is scientifically absurd to rank them on a scale.

Eriksen has stressed the importance of cultural relativism as a reliable tool of methodology. He observes:

> Cultural relativism is an indispensable and unquestionable theoretical premise and methodological rule of thumb in our attempts to understand alien society in an unprejudiced way as possible. As an ethical principle, however, it is probably impossible in practice, since it seems to indicate that everything is as good as everything else, provided it makes sense in a particular society.

(vi) Rejection of positivism and application of critical enquiry

The new social anthropological researches that we find today reject the constraint of positivism. Positivism means scientificism. If social anthropology attempts to study social reality among the tribals, such a positivistic approach is not helpful. It must be accepted that reality is not unified. It varies from group to group and society to society. In such a situation, what we find is a set of multiple realities, constructed by people in different ontological positions. It is also certain that anthropological field research tries to probe into multiple realities and identify a unified truth. What is meant by social anthropological research is to explore and study each multiple reality. To attain this objective social anthropology has to focus less on positivism and more on the researcher's self-critical capability.

Amita Baviskar, in her study *In the Belly of River*, argues that in the fieldwork pertaining to tribals one must stress on the social realities as the people themselves understand it. It is a question of stress and focus. She observes:

> If the world consists of many contested realities, all of them backed by different groups of people, which version do we privilege?.. I have mainly chosen to ignore the various ways in which the state regards *adivasis*, favouring a view that focuses on the ways in which *adivasis* regard the state.

Baviskar has really stressed on the importance of self-critical inquiry. How does the state perceive the *adivasis*, and contrariwise how do tribals perceive the state? The question is important. The fieldworker must understand that what is important in the research is that what people think of the content of social reality.

(vii) Culture is autonomous

When a social anthropologist goes to the field, he is confronted with a dilemma: on one hand, he has his ideology, and on the other, there is the autonomy of the culture of a group under investigation. Cultures, as we have stressed elsewhere, cannot be compared; each culture has its origin and development. It is conditioned historically. With this assumption we must state that the culture of a society is autonomous. But, the researcher does not go to the field in a vacuum. He has his own ethnocentrism; his own ideology. It is possible that he is a Gandhian, a Marxist or a supporter of capitalism. In such a value-loaded ideology, how would he behave in the fieldwork? The situation is challenging but there is a solution also which is traditional. The common good of the people who are subjected to study is uppermost. The researcher, therefore, is advised to remain neutral as far as possible. But, on the other hand, he should focus on the independent or autonomous status of the group under study.

(viii) Physical proximity

One of the obligations of the social anthropologist is to establish as much physical proximity as possible. He is required to stay in the field. During his stay, he should physically and morally be a part of the community. He should keep his ears and eyes open all the time. It is advised that while doing fieldwork the researcher should observe everything which is of seemingly routine matter also. It is possible that the routine affairs are not published at a later stage, but they may help comprehend the society in some way. Evans-Pritchard, who has been credited to have studied African tribals by conducting intensive fieldwork, advises:

> He must live as far as possible in their villages and camps, where he is, again as far as possible, physically and morally part of the community. He, then, not only sees and hears what goes on in the normal everyday life of the people as well as less common events, such as ceremonies and legal cases, but by taking part in these activities in which he can appropriately engage, he learns through action as well as by ear and eye what goes on around him.

(ix) Role of a learner

It would be wrong to think that a social anthropologist in the field is a catalyst. The missionaries were catalysts, for they wanted to seek conversion of the tribal people; the British administrators-turned-anthropologists very much wanted to consolidate colonial power in India and Africa. A social anthropologist should in no case work among the tribals as an agent of change. He is in the field to understand the people. Someone else might use his data for changing the people. Stressing on the status of a social anthropologist in the field as a learner, Evans-Pritchard writes:

> Unlike the administrator and missionary, he has no authority and status to maintain. And, unlike them, he has a neutral position. He is

not there to change their way of life but as a humble learner of it; and he has no retainers and intermediatries who obtrude between him and the people, No police, interpreters, or catechists to screen him off from them.

(x) Not only familiarity but friendship also

Bohannan, in his study of African tribes, observed at one place that the tribe does not think much of anything which comes from a person who is not himself a Tiv. Kinship is the key aspect of a tribal community. In such a milieu, the social anthropologist is supposed to be a friend and a kin of the community under study. When the researcher finally leaves the village, it should not be a goodbye affair. There should be a marked sorrow of parting in both the sides. In his *Remembered Village*, M.N. Srinivas gives details about his experiences, that is, empiricism of the Rampura village. On the day when Srinivas had to catch the bus for his final return from the field, he was invited for meals not by one but by several families, preceding the farewell. A band music and a procession was arranged by the people to give a pleasant but also painful departure to Srinivas. He had, in fact, become a friend of the people. He also officiated at a number of negotiations in disputes pertaining to civil and marital life.

(xi) Holistic study

Since fieldwork is all-pervasive, covering different aspects of village social life, the researcher should have functional relations of the people in mind. When he observes the functioning of different social institutions of the village, he should always think in terms of holistic study. As a matter of fact, it is impossible to understand clearly and comprehensively any part of a people's social life except in the context of their social life as whole. The fieldwork in all respects should be characterized by wholism.

(xii) Fieldwork diary

The popular portrait of a social anthropologist in the field is that of a man wearing trousers and a long *kurta* with a *jhola* hung on his shoulder. It is in this *jhola* that he keeps his diary wherein he writes all the details that he observes during his visit to the study area. In fact, it records all the happenings of the day in minute details. He is expected to write down even the most commonplace activities, for example, how a cow is milked and how meat is cooked. Also, though he may decide to write the book on a people's law or their religion, or on their economics, describing one aspect of their life and neglecting the rest, he does so always against the background of their entire social activities and in terms of their whole social structure.

Fieldwork is the major tool of data collection for the social anthropologist. It has long been their methodological tradition or culture. It is true that any educated, intelligent and sensitive person can get to know the primitive people well and write an excellent account of their way of life. Perhaps, this non-social anthropologist gets to know primitive people better and writes a better book about them than many professionals do. We have instances which indicate that excellent ethnographic accounts were written long before social anthropology was even heard of. Dubois, who was not a social anthropologist, has written authoritatively on *Hindu Manners, Customs and Ceremonies* in 1816. There are other examples also. But, there is a certain insight in the writings of the professional. Actually, anthropological fieldwork requires, in addition to theoretical knowledge and technical training, a certain kind of character and temperament which is non-existent in a lay writer. As a matter of fact, the social anthropologist identifies himself with the study of primitive people. During the course of the fieldwork, he himself becomes the part of native society. There is no separation between the two. Such an approach to the primitive society distinguishes a professional social anthropologist from other lay writers.

There is no better way to end the discussion of fieldwork in social anthropology than to refer to the statement of Evans-Pritchard:

> The native society has to be in the anthropologist himself and not merely in his note book... to succeed in this feat a man must be able to abandon himself without reserve, and he must also have intuitive powers which not all possess. Most people who know what and how to observe can make a merely competent study of a primitive people, but when one has to estimate whether a man will make the study which will be on the deeper level of understanding one looks for more than intellectual ability and technical training, for these qualities will not in themselves make a good anthropologist any more than they will make a good historian.

Translation, Interpretation and Observation

Related to fieldwork are the tasks of translation and interpretation. Here translation does not mean rendering into another language. But, whatever a social anthropologist observes in the field is translated into the meaning which the people give to an event or a phenomenon. It is expected of a researcher to provide an authentic version of the practices as they occur. And, in doing so, no evaluation should be made in accordance with the standards and values of his own society. In other words, it becomes a central challenge to the researcher to honestly put the events as they are understood by the people.

Translation

There is really a paradox in the task of translation. On one hand, we have to understand the society and culture of the other people in their own terms, and on the other hand, we have to employ the social anthropological concepts for explaining the field situation. It is possible that at some points, we might find the existing conceptual framework inadequate. If such a situation we shall have to formulate new concepts. This has happened in the field of social anthropology in India. The concepts of dominant caste, sanskritization and parochialization have emerged out of the social and cultural life of the simple societies.

There are some questions which are related to the problem of translation: How can we translate an alien way of experiencing the world into our own mode of thought? How can we be certain that we do not misinterpret or distort the society when we try to describe it in our own terms? And, how can we be entirely certain that we understand the alien society and culture at all, imbued as we are with our own cultural background, concepts and values? These interrelated problems are fundamental to anthropology.

Within the discipline of anthropology, it is necessary to use abstract terms such as kinship, social organization, social control, religion and so on. These terms are necessary for the discipline to be comparative in its scope. How could it be possible to compare, say the kinship system of the Trobrianders with that of the Yanomamo, if we did not have a general concept of kinship? However, the abstract, technical terms used by anthropologists exist only rarely in the societies we study. They form a part of our world, not their's. How can then we justify according to an alien society in terms which are demonstrably not its own, if the aim of anthropology is to understand societies and cultures from within. The fact of the matter is that all efforts should be made by social anthropologists to provide an honest description of the state of affairs of the alien society.

Interpretation

Traditionally, fieldwork monographs are poor in their interpretation. Historically, the ethnographic data are presented in the form of narration. For instance, Risely talked about different races and castes of India. His work is wholly descriptive. He could hardly give concepts like sanskritization and parochialization. These concepts emerged only during the 1950s. The monographs resulting from fieldwork today have a stronger input of interpretation. What is important is that the researcher should understand the difference between description and interpretation. The descriptive aspect of an anthropological account is usually close to the native conceptualization of the world. When describing a social and cultural life-world, the anthropologist will often resort to direct annotations from information, to give an account of the world as it appears from within. The analysis, on the other hand, will try to connect the society at a theoretical level, to other societies by describing it in comparative terms of anthropology.

Observation

Fieldwork is done through the method of observation. When the researcher goes to the field he must observe all that he encounters. Participant observation defined as a research technique may serve as a convenient blanket term to conceal both ethical and methodological shortcomings in the actual research process. One problem could, perhaps, be the fact that one develops an antagonistic attitude towards the people one studies.

It must be admitted that the method of fieldwork essentially goes with the technique of participant observation. Participant observation is both capital-intensive and labour-intensive. The researcher is required to stay in the field for a protracted period. And this involves money as well as time. Observation in the field is essential, for he has to see the world as the locals see it. Even if this kind of prolonged observation is not possible for a variety of reasons, the anthropologist must do his best to participate in the affairs of the people.

We have mentioned in the beginning of the chapter that social anthropology, quite like other social sciences, has a methodology. Right from the times of Spencer, Tylor and Durkheim, social anthropology has tried to agree to a methodology which is acceptable to all the practitioners of the discipline. There is even today as much disagreement among them as there was in the past. It is doubtful that we will ever have a wholly agreed upon method. But, it appears that there is a broad consensus on some of the methods which can be fruitfully utilized in social anthropological research. The Trend Reports on the Survey of Research in Sociology and Social Anthropology since 1959 to the present day sponsored by ICSSR very clearly show that the most favoured methods of social anthropology today are: (1) fieldwork including observation, (2) comparison, (3) historical, and (4) functional. We have already discussed above the fieldwork method. The other three methods are discussed below in the remaining part of the chapter.

Comparative Method

Andre Beteille, in one of his articles published in the *Economic and Political Weekly* (October 6, 1990), writes: "It is a fact that our deepest insights into society and culture are reached in and through comparison. We have to improvise and exercise our judgement as well as imagination and beyond that we can only hope that our comparisons as well as our contrasts will be illuminating and fruitful. At any rate, it will be futile to suspend our comparisons until the perfect classification or the perfect typology of human societies is placed within our grasp."

After all, what does social anthropology do? It studies man in his totality. In other words, we assume that whatever may be the kind of society, it surely has some order, some organization. Social anthropology tries to find out what is common to all societies and at the same time what is different in all societies. The identification of the common, that is, universal would enable us understand human society. Such an objective of social anthropology has become important all the more and immediate in the wake of the present process of globalization. This can be achieved only through a comparative study.

It would be interesting to mention a meeting of the authors with a Japanese social anthropologist. We wondered why she had come to study an Indian village when there were hundreds of villages in Japan too. Her reply was prompt: I can understand Japanese villages better only when I understand Indian villages. This clearly shows that social institutions of a particular culture can be understood better by comparison to other cultures. This stresses the need to employ comparative method in social anthropology.

Historically, it should be mentioned that during the 19th century extensive comparisons were attempted by social anthropologists. These pertained to the whole society and also to particular institutions and practices such as kinship systems, marriage practices, techniques of agriculture and pottery, magical practices, religious beliefs and so on. The central place assigned to comparison was signalled by Durkheim when he wrote: "Comparative sociology is not a special branch of a sociology."

Thus, the methods of social anthropology and sociology are common not only in India but all through the Third World. Ravindra K. Jain, writing on the methods of social anthropology, says that "the distinction between social anthropology and sociology at the level of theory and method is extremely tenuous, particularly in the context of 'third world' countries. And yet, precisely for the reason that the distinctive disciplinary traditions of the two subjects are obliterated in our practice..." In the same vein, Andre Beteille also observes that in India comparison is the methodology of social anthropology as well as sociology.

It is noteworthy that the ICSSR, which is the apex body of social science in the country, has also combined social anthropology with sociology. All the trend reports published by it include both sociology and social anthropology in the title. In fact, the aim of social anthropology as it has emerged in the west, according to Ravindra K. Jain, "is the holistic comparative understanding of societies, cultures and civilizations that are primarily of the non-modern types". The notions of holism and comparison can be explicated only with reference to the theory and method of the discipline. Holism in current anthropological theory and practice means the study of the total society in all its parts. This holistic study is usually compared with other societies.

Methods

When a social anthropologist makes a comparative study, he has three levels of comparison. First, he compares a single society with other societies; second, he compares one or two institutions of a society with similar institutions of other societies; and third, he compares the institutions within a single society.

Ravindra K. Jain mentions that in India anthropological holism is combined with comparative perspective. He refers to the statement of Gopalasarana who advocates the analyzing of social and cultural aspects from a comparative perspective. He mentions two justifications for anthropology being called a comparative discipline:

> One of the two justifications is the following: By convention and established tradition of doing fieldwork in a culture other than one's own, the anthropologist uses a comparative framework in his study. In other words, there is much implicit comparison both in data gathering and data processing... the second justification for anthropology being a comparative discipline is for work in the library rather than in the field. From the days of unilinear evolution anthropologists have utilized the available ethnographic materials to serve many different ends. There are marked differences in the ways these ends have been attained. The common feature of all these ventures is the fact that with very few exceptions they all involve inter-cultural or cross-cultural explicit comparison.

Whatever Gopalasarana observes boils down to three things:

(1) Social anthropology accepts unquestionably comparison while generating data. This assumption relies entirely on comparison as the main purpose of fieldwork. He calls it implicit design of comparative process.
(2) In the analysis which is made on the desk and not in the field, comparison is very clearly or distinctly accepted as a mode of interpretation. This is obviously explicit comparison.
(3) In the method of comparison two things are done: within a society inter-cultural approach is taken and outside the society cross-cultural access is adopted.

Thus, social anthropology in India generates and analyzes data implicitly, and finally, makes both intra-cultural and inter-cultural analyses.

Objectives

The history of the use of comparison as a method of study in social anthropology goes back to the 19th century. It was a period strongly influenced by evolution. The use of comparison begins from Durkheim to Evans-Pritchard in British social anthropology. The early researchers had the following objects in employing comparison as a dependable method for data generation:

(1) It is through this method that social anthropologists reconstruct the past and discover the laws which govern social processes. As a matter of fact, comparison of particular features of social life for the purpose of historical reconstruction has great value. Actually, such a kind of exercise helps explore the varieties or forms of social life as a basis for the theoretical study of human social phenomena. This objective has been greatly stressed by Radcliffe-Brown.

(2) It is through this that we make classification of the social systems in different categories such as caste, class and groups. Radcliffe-Brown observed in his famous Chicago seminar of 1937:

> I would suggest that an examination of the other science immediately suggests that the first step in social science will be to undertake the task of taxonomy and classification, and in the first instance, the classification of social systems themselves. I propose that no scientific study of societies can get very far until we have made some progress towards a classification of social systems into whatever types, groups of classes suggest themselves as expedient, that is, likely to lead to valid generalizations with respect to all societies.

Thus, the comparative method is employed for discovering the laws of social processes; and to classify the social systems of all the societies of the world as well. If these two things are attained through comparison, social anthropology would be able to reconstruct the past and classify different societies into specific types.

From Durkheim to the Present

More than a hundred years have passed since Emile Durkheim introduced comparison as a reliable method of data generation. In his classical work, *The Rules of Sociological Method* (1895), for the first time, Durkheim explained the significance of the comparative method. Actually, in the 19th century, the principal attraction of the comparative method lay in the belief that it could be used for discovering scientific laws about human society and culture. The strong advocates of the comparative method believed in the possibility of a natural science of society that would establish regularities of co-existence and succession among the forms of social life by means of systematic comparisons.

When Durkheim's book on methodology was published, there appeared an essay by Franz Boas entitled, "The Limitations of the Comparative Method of Anthropology". Boas contested the arguments of Durkheim that the latter had made only sweeping generalizations. Despite this criticism, Boas did not, at least in principle, declare himself against the comparative method. After Durkheim Radcliffe-Brown pleaded the usefulness of the comparative method in social anthropology. In his Huxley Memorial Lecture of 1955 he argued that comparative method was highly useful in reconstructing human social history. When anthropologists make comparisons, they find both similarities and differences in human society. At a later stage, Evans-Pritchard took up the theme of comparative method at his Hob House Lecture in 1963. He argued that despite all its scientific pretensions, the comparative method as used by Radcliffe-Brown and many others was little more than the illustrative method.

Now, a question arises: If social anthropology tries to find out similarities and differences in comparative studies, what has it gained for a hundred years since the days of Boas and Haddon to Radcliffe-Brown and Evans-Pritchard? This question was also asked in the Chicago seminar of 1937. The findings of the seminar suggest that nothing substantial has been gained by social anthropology by way of the comparative method. No uniformities or differences in human society have come out, which suggests the hollowness of the comparative method.

Enthusiasts and Sceptics

In the 19th century and the middle of 20th century, there were different attitudes of social anthropologists towards comparative method. It is true that, by and large, all social anthropologists rely on comparative method. But this is not all. There are those who are very enthusiastic towards the use of comparison; and there are also sceptics who plead for limited use of this method. Among the enthusiasts are included Spencer, Tylor, Durkheim and Radcliffe-Brown. Those who constitute the group of sceptics are Boas, Golden Weiser and Evans-

Pritchard. In the old guard, Durkheim and Radcliffe-Brown strongly advocate this method, and among the opponents are included Evans-Pritchard and Boas.

Indian Scene

Indian anthropologists have conducted inter-cultural or cross-cultural comparative studies. Among these are included D.N. Majumdar, N.K. Bose and Irawati Karve. These have chosen to study societies and cultures which were unfamiliar to them. While doing this they had some implicit assumptions about comparison. Ravindra K. Jain, explaining the comparative method employed by these first-generation researchers, observes:

> They undertook explicit comparison, combining the results of their own field studies with library resources. Thus, we have Majumdar's general comparative writings on primitive tribes; Bose's comparative treatment of Indian tribes, the peasantry and of urbanization processes in Bengal and Orissa; and Karve's classic *Kinship Organization in India,* first published in 1953. The fact that comparisons such as those undertaken by Bose and Karve were all situated in India and were, moreover, attempted within the framework of Indian cultural history, did elicit a protest from latter-day structuralists.

At a later stage, with the coming of Dumont and Pocock, the comparative method fell to disrepute. In the tradition of Levi-Strauss and Evans-Pritchard, Dumont is reluctant to accept the comparative perspective. Instead, he has adopted the structuralist approach. As a matter of fact, Dumont, in his *Homo Hierarchicus* (1970), has taken ideology as his major perspective for studying the Indian society. He compares Indian ideology which is holistic and hierarchical with the western individualistic and egalitarian ideology.

We have, in India, a large number of village studies. These are, in fact, holistic studies. But, the researchers of these studies should have employed the comparative method. From all considerations, today, it appears that the sociology in India has given up comparison as the dominant method of enquiry.

Historical Method

There is a clear mark of history as a method in anthropological monographs. The 19th century was a period of evolutionary studies in Europe, including Britain. If we study the employment of history as a method of study, we find two classical streams. One use of history is non-chronological which is actually social history. This kind of history as a method has been used by evolutionary anthropologists. Simultaneously, there is the second stream of history which is Marxian.

The evolutionary tradition in social anthropology was used at the instance of Darwinism. As Darwin tried to find out the history of the origin of mankind, similar attempt was made in social anthropology by Spencer, Hobhouse and others. These have tried to reconstruct history by tracing the origin of social institutions such as family, marriage, kin, polity and economics. For instance, Westermarck has given a history of human marriage. In yet another study, Oppenheimer has traced the history of the state in an evolutionary fashion.

After the first generation of Spencer, Hobhouse and Comte, Max Weber used history to learn about the evolution of capitalism, bureaucracy and religion. He studied the six great religions of world (however, he could study only five) through the historical method. In the present anthropology Raymond Aron and C. Wright Mills have applied this method at great length to analyze a series of social institutions.

As a matter of fact, the historical method goes hand in hand with comparative method. The Marxist social anthropologists have used new categories to analyze different aspects of the social system. These include production relations and production forces. The analysis of capitalism by Karl Marx is a classical example of historical analysis. His theory of conflict and social change owes much to historical forces. His classical observation that all the history of communities is a history of class struggle quite importantly stresses the importance of historical method.

In India, the historical method, both evolutionary and Marxian, has been used by social anthropologists. Iravati Karve's analysis of India's kinship organization borrows much from Sanskrit textbooks. Similarly, G.S. Ghurye's interpretation of the origin of caste in India is highly historical. He also draws his data from historical documents. When they took to the study of civilizations, historical methodology became all the more important. M.N. Srinivas completed his study on the *Religion and Society among the Coorgs of South India* (1952) under the supervision of G.S. Ghurye. In this classical study he has established the interrelation of religion and society. His method of study was historical; at a later stage, however, when he revised his work, he analyzed the material from a functional point of view.

There are some Indian studies which are oriented to Marxian history. D.P. Mukherji took up the issue of the dialectic between tradition and modernity. In this analysis he is effectively oriented towards Marxism, but he has turned heavily on the particularistic model of Indian sociology with its emphasis on tradition and history. His notion of dialectics, which he recommends as an important analytic device, never takes on the universalistic meaning which it has in popular interpretations of Marxist theory.

History has been very widely used as a method by both Marxist sociologists and anthropologists. These scholars have made modes of production their centre of analysis. Though there is a long history of Marxian method of sociology in India, it appears that this method has been applied only recently in in-depth empirical studies. History, which has been a prime method of enquiry, has been fruitfully utilized by D.N. Dhanagare, Kathleen Gough, A.R. Desai, Ramkrishna Mukherjee and others. Dhanagare has analyzed agrarian social movement from Marxian perspective. Gough has studied Thanjavur villages purely from Marxian historical categories. She has started from the traditional Marxist premises of the succession of the 'Asiatic', 'feudal' and 'capitalist' modes of production in India within the overarching system of colonialism. This is indeed an exemplary use of the historical method in an analysis of social stratification.

The Marxian historical method has also been gainfully employed by social anthropologists such as Daniel Thorner, Gail Omvedt, Jan Breman and others. A.R. Desai has used it in analyzing the macro structures of Indian society.

If must be observed that history as a method was very popular among social anthropologists who worked on the evolution of social institutions. With the emergence of functionalism, evolutionary historicism suffered a serious setback in the European continent and in India. However, we shall soon find that the variant of functionalism in India has taken to the historical method quite unlike the social anthropology of the European continent and the US. Despite this lesser input of historical method, the Marxist anthropologists and sociologists continue to use history as a method of analysis.

Functional Method

Functionalism, as a method of study in social anthropology, has come as a revolt against the historical method. Increasingly, the evolutionary historicism came into disrepute owing to the emergence of empiricism. Empiricism is experience. When the social anthropologists took to holistic studies through empiricism, functionalism came to be known as a new idiom of methodology. The functionalists advocate the holistic study of society through fieldwork. In fact, holism, functionalism and empiricism go together as a method of social anthropology. In the first volume of ICSSR trend reports (1959-1969) T.N. Madan has analyzed the methodology of social anthropology in India. He concludes by saying that the overwhelming method of study, both for sociology and social anthropology, has been functionalism. Functionalism has come through the works of Radcliffe-Brown (1881-1955) and Malinowski (1884-1942). They are regarded as the first functional methodologists of modern anthropology. Malinowski's functionalism has emerged out of his classical study in the Trobriand islands of New Guinea. His fieldwork lasted for more than two years between 1915 and 1918. There, he came in close contact with the local community. He emphasized the importance of studying the interrelationships of varying aspects of society, and therefore, held that long field study was absolutely necessary.

Radcliffe-Brown, a contemporary of Malinowski, was influenced by Durkheim. He studied the Andaman islanders (1922) and social organization of Australian tribes (1931). He has established through fuctionalism that societies are integrated. Robert K. Merton has developed sociological functionalism after improving the anthropological functionalism propounded by Radcliffe-Brown and Malinowski. Merton has given three major postulates of anthropological functionalism as under:

(i) Functional Unity of Society

According to this, the society is held together by the functions performed by different institutions of the society. Each society has its systems of family, kin, clan, politics, economy, etc. These parts of society fulfil the social needs which are required by the members. The contributions of these different institutions make up the functional unity of society. Radcliffe-Brown, while explaining the functional unity of society, argues that a social system "has a certain kind of unity, which we may speak of as a functional unity. We may define it as a condition in which all parts of the social system work together with a sufficient degree of harmony or internal consistency that is without producing persistent conflicts which can neither be resolved nor regulated."

In short, functional unity of society means: (i) each part of society has its functions; (ii) these functions work together to establish consensus in society; and (iii) the result is some kind of unity.

(ii) Universal Functionalism

Radcliffe-Brown further argues that each society has its social or cultural forms which are standardized; these are accepted by all. This aspect of functionalism is also advocated by Malinowski. In his words:

> The functional view of culture insists, therefore, upon the principle that in every type of civilization, every custom, material object, idea and belief fulfils some vital function.

What Malinowski wants to stress is that there is some functional view or utility for all surviving forms of culture. In other words, no culture forms survive unless they constitute responses which are adjustive or adaptive in some sense. Actually, the idea of universal functionalism gains importance because of the fact that the social and cultural forms of a society have survived because they have some positive functions to perform.

(iii) Indispensability

This is the third characteristic of anthropological functionalism. Explaining this part of functional indispensability, Malinowski says:

> In every type of civilization, every custom, material object, idea and belief fulfils some vital function, has some task to accomplish, represents an indispensable part within a working whole.

What Radcliffe-Brown and Malinowski believe is that there are certain functions which are indispensable in the sense that unless they are performed, the society will not persist.

The anthropological functionalism, as presented by Radcliffe-

Brown and Malinowski, has been drawn out of the study of simple societies. It argues that a society is holistic in its structure. It fulfils the needs of the people. One part of society is related to other parts through functional analysis. In fact, functionalism is a method which studies one part with reference to other parts of the society and the whole society.

Concluding Observations

Quite like any other social science, social anthropology has its own kit of methodology. The European-British variant of social anthropology considers social structure as a focus of its study. The focus of the US anthropology is the analysis of culture. Both these variants of social anthropology consider fieldwork, comparison, functionalism and historicism as the methods of study. All these methods have one common objective—to frame certain general laws which help us understand the society from a holistic point of view.

Further Readings

Bose, Pradip Kumar, *Research Methodology*, ICSSR, New Delhi, 1995.

Madan, T.N., "Research Methods in India", Delhi, ICSSR, *Trend Report*, 1970.

Majumdar, D.N. and Madan, T.N., *An Introduction to Social Anthropology*, Bombay.

Radcliffe-Brown, A.R. (ed. by M.N. Srinivas), *Methods in Social Anthropology*, Bombay, 1970.

5

Races of Man and Racism

Frankly, writing about the living races of mankind is not the subject matter of social anthropology. Neither is it its scope. Even then it was included in our discussion because today we hardly understand the meaning of race and much discrimination has crept into our relations with other groups. In scientific paraphrase, race is a valid biological concept. "It is a group united by heredity: a bread or genetic strain or sub-species. It is not a valid socio-cultural concept." As a matter of fact, the meaning of race is ambiguous and is used in socio-cultural situations. It is a tragedy of mankind that a biological and zoological concept is used in ethnic and social connotations. It is this erroneous use of race which has obliged us to discuss it in social anthropology. Thus, when we talk of race, we talk about physical anthropology, and when we talk about racism, racial prejudices, biases and discrimination, we talk about social anthropology.

This can be further explained by an example. When we say that Caucasians or whites have wavy texture of hair, narrow head, fair skin colour and a tall stature, we are explaining the group by its racial characteristics. But when we say that the whites or Caucasians are the only civilized people in the world, it is a prejudicial statement. There are Negros who are perhaps better civilized than the Caucasians. Obviously, civilization is something which is acquired by a group through its achievements. In short, racial characteristics, such as, texture of hair, cephalic index, length and breadth of nose, eye colour, skin colour, etc., are acquired by birth. But socio-cultural characteristics, occupational achievement, poverty or affluence are attained by adaptation. Thus, physical characteristics are hereditary; ethnic and social characteristics are acquired or achieved. Social anthropology analyzes the acquired characteristics.

Race and Caste

In India, we have no consciousness about white or black race. We had some consciousness about whites in the pre-independent period. During the colonial rule we saw and felt that the whites (in this case, the Britishers) had a superior culture. In Africa, there was a long struggle between the white and black peoples. And, the world very well knows the notorious statement made by Hitler during the world war that only the Aryans had pure blood. Much discrimination and conflicts have taken place between the two world wars in Europe, Africa and South Asia.

Caste is a different social institution. Its membership is determined by birth. One who is born as a Brahmin, belongs to the Brahmin caste. Quite in the same way, one who is born as a Negroid is a member of the Negro race. So, birth determines membership of race and caste. But, the difference emerges when we talk about physical characteristics. When a person is born as a Caucasian, he is born with some genetic traits such as stature or bodily height, cephalic index, that is, ratio of the length and the breadth of head, nasal index, prognathism and a certain texture of the hair. On the other hand, when a person is born in the Brahmin caste, he does not inherit any caste or racial traits like the whites. There is no physical difference between a Brahmin, a Rajput and for that matter a Chamar. On the other hand, it is reported by Briggs that the Chamar women all over the country excel their counterparts of other castes in certain activities.

The caste and race, therefore, though determined by birth, belong to different categories. Most of the castes in India trace their origin to the primary stock of Caucasoid or its sub-species. The differences among the castes are thus not racial ones. They are ethnic and socio-cultural. Despite the fundamental differences between race and caste, these two groups have created a war-like situation in the world. If racial prejudices or discriminations have created problems in Europe, USA and Africa, caste has created problems in south and east Asia. In our country, quite like the racial war of black and white in other parts of the world, castes have created a large number of problems. Reservations for castes and politicization of casteism are actually caste-generated problems. There is nothing new about these problems—they are age-old. In the *Mahabharata*, when Karna—born of a *sut* (carpenter)—stood in competition against the Pandavas, it was objected because a carpenter could never compete with the mighty Rajput. This was a disability of the carpenter caste. Karna argued: "Whether I am a *sut* or anyone else, god gave me birth in a family but the competitive skill which I possess is my own achievement." The discourse which took place between Karna and Pandavas is actually a debate on the achievement of man. No discrimination should take place on the basis of heredity or genetic traits: this is what we learn from the *Mahabharata*.

Here we wish to state that a discussion on racial stocks is a part of physical anthropology: when we talk about caste, we are truly analyzing the role of socio-cultural factors in society. It is, therefore, the subject matter of social anthropology. Among the major existing or living races of the world, we only outline here three ones: (1) Caucasoid or 'white', (2) Mongoloid or 'yellow', and (3) Negroid or 'black'. Physical anthropologists have brought out a few other racial stocks which fall in the category of 'doubtful races'. In this category Australoid, Veddoid, Polynesian and Ainu are included. It must also be said that the three major racial stocks are further classified into several sub-species. For instance, Caucasians have sub-species of Nordic, Alpine, Mediterranean and Hindu. The Mongoloid sub-species are Mongolian, Malaysian and American Indian. The third stock of Negroid includes Negro, Melanesian, Pygmy Black and Bushman. It must be noted that it is very difficult to put these races into pure categories because of inter-racial marriages and mutation.

What is Race?

Melville Herskovits states:

> A race is a principal division of mankind, marked by physical characteristics that breed true. In this sense, the word is a biological term, restricted to the bodily characteristics that distinguish one group of human beings from another. This, in turn, sets off the concept of the emphasis on the inborn as against the learned aspects of human behaviour.

Herskovits has stressed on the physical characteristics or traits which make a particular group a race. Actually, the biological definition of race also mentions the acquired or learned practices of behaviour. Stature or body height is a physical trait but the music is a learned trait of human behaviour. Thus, according to Herskovits, the concept of race takes into consideration at least implicitly, both innate and acquired traits.

Kroeber has framed the definition of race in precise and pointed words which we have referred to at the very beginning. We repeat it:

> A race is a valid biological concept. It is a group united by heredity: a breed or genetic strain or sub-species. It is not a valid socio-cultural concept...

Kroeber is an American authority on physical and cultural anthropology. His basic postulate of race is that it is biological, that is, hereditary. It has no socio-cultural meaning.

John Lewis, a British social anthropologist, also stresses only the biological meaning of race. He says:

> Race is a major division of mankind, with distinctive hereditarily transmissible physical characteristics, e.g., the Negroid, Mongoloid, Caucasoid races.

According to Lewis, the idiom of race is a group of hereditary traits which include bodily height, blood group, prognathism, etc. Lewis, however, does not consider socio-cultural aspects as the resultant of racial characteristics.

Perhaps, the definition of race as given by a group of physical anthropologists and geneticists, called together under the auspices of the United Nations Educational Scientific and Cultural Organization (UNESCO) in Paris in June 1951, appears to be the most appropriate. It runs as below:

> In its anthropological sense, the word 'race' should be reserved for groups of mankind possessing well-developed and primarily inheritable physical differences from other groups.

The UNESCO team has underlined the importance of the concept of race in the analysis of the differences between human aggregates. It has also been emphasized that the concept is meaningful when we look at the zoological framework of racial stock. From the definition of race given by UNESCO and physical anthropologists, it is clear that a race has the following characteristics:

(1) It is a biological and zoological concept.
(2) It is united by heredity and, therefore, consists of several genetic strains.
(3) It has certain characteristics which differentiate one group from other groups.
(4) Its usefulness lies in finding out the biological and physical differences in mankind.

Racial Classification

The task of the classification of races is very difficult. This is because of the different connotations made by a single race; for instance, we cannot define perfectly only one single race because of: (i) genetic mutation, (ii) natural selection, (iii) genetic drift, and (iv) population mixture. If we keep aside all these demographic and physical processes, we can safely say that there are three major races existing in the world. These are classified on the basis of some biological and zoological traits. As every human being has a large number of physical features or traits, what we are required is to determine how much weight is attached to these traits. We give below some of the basic traits which are employed for race classification:

(i) Stature or Bodily Height

Each race has its minimum, maximum or average height. Experience has shown that stature has relatively lesser value for classification. Except for a few groups which are numerically insignificant, there is no human race that averages less than 4 feet 11 inches in height for men. There is none that averages taller than 5 feet 10 inches. This means that practically the whole range of human variability in height falls within a foot.

It is also said that stature is much influenced by environment. Each of us is a fraction of an inch taller in the morning than when he goes to bed at night. The standard of living also affects stature. Better-off classes are taller than the poorer classes.

(ii) Cephalic Index

This is expressed in terms of the ratio of the length of the head to its breadth. It has certain practical advantages. First, the head measurements are easily made with accuracy. Second, the cephalic index is nearly the same on the living head and on the dead skull. Third, the index makes it possible to compare present and past generations. Fourth, it is the same for men, women, children and adults. And finally, it is little affected by environment. However, for racial classification, the index does not yield any broad results. It is often useful in distinguishing sub-types, nation from nation or tribe from tribe; but it is not uniform for the primary races. In other words, there is no typical cephalic index for the Caucasoid race.

(iii) Nasal Index

This gives the percentage relation of breadth and length of nose. It runs constant in all the three races. In other words, all Negroids are broad-nosed. Practically, all Caucasoids are narrow-nosed; and the majority of Mongolians have a medium nose. Nasal index varies according to the age of the person; it is utterly different in a living individual and a skull. It is because of this that lesser importance is attached to this index.

(iv) Prognathism

This is the degree of the protrusion of the jaws. It is the conspicuous feature of human beings. It indicates the historical and primitive importance of men. It has a general correlation with the fundamental social types. For instance, all the Negroes are prognathous, Mongolians are moderately so and Caucasians slightly so. What is important is that prognathism is difficult to measure or specify in figures.

(v) Capacity of the Skull

This is not a dependable trait for racial classification. There is much overlapping between races in the realm of cranial capacity. Furthermore, the measurement obviously cannot be taken on the living, except by computation estimates based on diameters. In spite of its interest, the usefulness of cranial capacity is of restricted value in distinguishing races.

(vi) Texture of the Hair

For racial classification this feature is perhaps most significant. Hair is distinguished as wooly in the Negro, straight in Mongolian and wavy or intermediate in the Caucasion. Hair texture seems to run rather strongly along the hereditary racial lines. It is not influenced by age, sex, climate or nourishment.

(vii) Hairiness

Physical anthropologists consider hairiness of the body to be a reliable source of determining race. The baldness or fullness of the head and the degree of development of the chin which covers beards and the body are the most striking manifestation of a race. Caucasians are definitely a hairy race, whereas Mongoloids and most Negroids are smooth-skinned. It is largely on the basis of their hairiness and hair texture that the races like the Australoids have been separated from the Negroids, and the Ainus from the Japanese. It is strange to find that baldness occurs most frequently in association which heavy beards and body hair, in line with which fact women are rarely bald.

(viii) Colour

Colour is another dependable trait of race determination. It includes the complexion of the skin, the colour of the hair, and the colour of the eyes. All of these are due to varying amounts of the same pigment called melanin. It is found that the environment affects skin colour markedly. A day's exposure to the sun may darken an individual's complexion by several shades. In spite of these drawbacks, however, complexion remains sufficiently important to warrant consideration in every classification.

However, it must be said that hair colour and eye colour are practically immune against direct change by environment. They are without doubt excellent hereditary criteria, although they offer much the same resistance to measurement as does complexion. The utility of these two traits in race determination is limited by another factor. Blue eyes and blond hair are racially characteristics of only a single major sub-race, that from Northern Europe. Outside of the Caucasian stock, virtually, black hair and black eyes are the universal norms for human races.

(ix) Lip Formation

There are some other minor characteristics or traits which help us identify a race. Among these are included lips, ears and other such things. Physical anthropologists interestingly associate lip with primitiveness. For instance, it is said that the Apes have thin lips. However, Negroes have the least Ape-like lips. Similarly, the Causasoids and Negroids also do not have thin lips. Ears are also not considered as dependable indicators of a race.

(x) Blood Groups

There are four types of blood: A, B, AB, and O (and many sub-divisions of these). These provide emphatic confirmation of the unity of mankind. "It is an erroneous conception that blood is the factor that distinguishes one race from another. It was Hitler who said that only the Aryans have the pure blood. In reality blood is so similar that transfusions can take place between compatible blood groups in different races and lives can be saved, provided, the type taken from the donor is compatible with that of the recipient.

It must be stressed here that blood groups are no criteria for race classification. It is the creation of some anthropologists with vested interests. As a matter of fact, in the Caucasoid and Mongoloid races, we find an almost equal correlation of blood types. For instance, on a proportionate basis, there are very few people in each race who have blood group O. The same can be said about the other three major blood groups.

Difficulties in Racial Differentiation

As stated above, there are three major racial stocks in the world. Besides, there are some races which do not fall clearly within a specific race category. These races constitute doubtful classification. But, when we strictly examine a particular race, there arises a problem. It would be wrong to say that there is any pure race. There has been so much of inter-mixture that we do not find any pure type. There also exist some hybrid races. In the case of caste, in India, we have a similar concept of *varnashankar*, according to which if a Brahmin marries a Sudra woman, the offspring of the two falls in the category of *varnashankar*, that is, a mixture of two castes. Thus, there are some difficulties in the racial classification. These are described as below:

(i) Gene Mutation

The contemporary advances in medical science are characterized by genetic engineering. According to this, if the genes are changed, the human body, that is, its whole physiology, would undergo changes. Racial composition or characters undergo change by gene mutation. This is a change in the gene structure of the reproductive cell that influences bodily development.

(ii) Natural Selection

Darwin has explained evolution natural selection. In order to survive in a particular environment, the human body adapts itself to the circumstances. This brings out a change in racial composition. Precisely, genes that produce variations and have survival value in a particular environment, will rapidly establish themselves. Thus, albinism offers no advantage and is rare, but heavy skin pigmentation is advantageous in the tropics and spreads quickly.

(iii) Genetic Drift

If a migrant group by chance bears characters unlike those of the larger group from which it separates, then in the course of time, specially, if further splitting occurs, a population different from the ancestral population would emerge. The American Indians have almost certainly lost some of the traits of their Mongoloid ancestors in this way.

(iv) Population Mixture

Today, it is common to find racially distinct populations migrate from one place to another. This results in population mixture. It may also be called inter-breeding. Most existing racial groups today are of this kind.

Racial Situation in India

Work on Indian races has been done by both Indian and foreign researchers. Mention in this connection may be made of H.H. Risely, A.C. Haddon, J.H. Hutton, B.S. Guha and D.N. Majumdar. Efforts have been made to identify racial elements in two broader sections of society, namely, caste Hindus and tribals. Just like in other parts of the world, there are no 'pure' races, in India too. However, there are three major races in India. Writing about these racial types, D.N. Majumdar observes:

> H.H. Risely recognized three principal types in India, viz., the Dravidian, the Indo-Aryan and the Mongolian. The first two were mixed, in varying proportions in the different provinces (now states), with each other and with the Mongolian elements while the third was confined to the north-east frontier and Assam. Risley's 'Dravidian' like the 'Aryan' is a linguistic group and not racial and at least three races have been found to constitute it.

If Majumdar's comments on Risley's racial types are analyzed, it means that India has Dravidian and Indo-Aryan strains in all the states except north-east including Assam. In this part of the country the Mongolian racial type is found. In practice, these racial strains are linguistic strains. Majumdar further analyzes the race elements in the country and refers to A.C. Haddon.

Challenging Risley's racial classification Haddon says that in the country we had various pre-Dravidian jungle tribes. Accordingly, it could be said that "the Dravidians may have been the original inhabitants of the valley of the Ganges in western Bengal... after many wanderings, apparently across India, they settled mainly in Chhota Nagpur." Thus, according to Haddon, the tribal groups who lived in India were Dravidians.

The second racial wave come through the Aryan-speaking people. They migrated into India in the second millennium BC. Their infiltration was slow and gradual and probably extended over several centuries. "They first occupied the fertile lands of the Punjab, their progress towards south-east being barred by the deserts of Rajputana." They could not move towards the east. There were dense forests in the north-east and Assam. Thus, the people having Aryan racial elements remained restricted to the valleys of the Yamuna and the Ganges. It appears that in the south the Dravidians occupied a major portion of the land.

After Risley and Haddon, J.H. Hutton made a significant study of the racial composition of India. According to him, the earliest occupants of India were probably the people who belonged to the Negrito race. There are, however, little traces of the Negrito type in India. The second wave that came to India was from the Mediterranean region.

They spoke an agglutinative tongue from which the present Austro-Asiatic languages are derived. At a later stage, a new wave of migrants arrived in India. They were probably connected with the Indus Valley Civilization.

It is really very difficult to trace racial elements in Indian population. It is said that the basic sub-stratum in India is of the Negrito people. They have been replaced or supplanted by the proto-Australoids. It appears that the Negrito is domiciled in southern Asia. But, judging from the tribal populations in India today, there is certainly no weighty evidence in support of a Negrito racial stock in India. However, Majumdar says that Negroid features are found particularly among the Bhils of Ratanpur in Rajpipla district of Gujarat. Here, a colony of Negroes has been domiciled for centuries, mixing with the Bhils and other tribal elements.

When we discuss the racial types in India, there are some special historical and geographical factors which must be kept in mind. India is such a subcontinent which has received waves of migrants from the West as well as from the East. There might have been some Negritos in the part of the country but the fact remains that India has broadly Dravidian, Indo-Aryan and Mongolian strains among its people. The identity of these racial types is based on their racial characteristics.

Origin of Race

A pertinent question that one could raise is: How did the three major races of world arise? In other words, we would like to know the origin of the earliest man to whom various racial characteristics can be traced back. It is said that there was a single species named as *homo sapiens.* In the latter part of the Old Stone Age, at a time "perhaps twenty-five to eighteen thousand years ago we commence to encounter remains of the Cro-Magnon Man which foreshadow the modern races—and are believed to have entered into the composition of several populations of world today."

John Lewis has conducted an elaborate exercise to find out the origin of existing races. He says:

> If in seeking man's ancestry, we are looking for the least specialized, and are, therefore, rejecting both the modern monkey and the anthropoids in tracing the development from the first man, we must regard *homo erectus* and Neanderthal not as primitive but as relatively

> late and highly specialized forms developing *away* from modern man. We must look for our ancestors among the less specialized forms, and these will be really primitive types.

On this view, then, modern man takes his origin from a source quite separate from that of *homo erectus* and the Neanderthalers, even though in the remote pliocene they probably had a common ancestery. That source had left few representative fossils other than Swanscombe man. The opposing views regards *homo erectus* as the true ancestor of *homo sapiens*.

If we consider *homo erectus* as the real ancestor of human beings, the question is what caused them to differentiate and on which parts of earth's surface each took on its peculiarities and how the differentiating races may have reblended. On these problems we do not have yet complete answer. Partly, though, the questions have been answered by gene mutation, genetic drift, natural selection and population mixture.

Racism

In the preceding pages we have provided a scientific definition and analysis of race. The criteria or indicators lay down some physical features which help us define race. The whole approach is supported by physical anthropologists and UNESCO experts. Logically, it all goes very well. The matter concerns the field of physical anthropology. Racism, on the other hand, falls in the realm of social anthropology. And, it is with this that we are concerned. In fact, though race is characterized by physical features, racism is related to culture, language and religion. The physical types of races influence the culture of the society. Or, in other words, culture influences the race. Commenting on the relations of the culture and physical types of race, Herskovits observes:

> The scientific truth of the matter is that culture influences physical type far more than physical type influences culture. Full recognition of this is all the more cogent since so much of the discussion concerning the relation between race and culture sees the problem as the determination of the degree to which race is the instrumental in shaping the culture of a people and does not consider at all the influence

of culture on physical type. Thus, we meet with the first of the several determinisms of which we take account in studying culture.

Herskovits argues at length the problem of racism. In fact, according to him, there is politicization of racism. In its extreme form racism is observed in the racial doctrines of Nazism, which maintained the existence of a so-called 'Aryan race', a kind of mystic grouping superior to all others, and, for political reasons, another presumed 'racial' entity, the Jews, who were singled out for special indignities.

In scientific terms, neither the word 'Aryan' nor the term 'Jew' has any scientific validity as a racial designation. Aryan is the name of the language from which most European tongues have been derived. Supporting this point F. Muller, who himself was a philologist, observed:

> There is no more an Aryan race than there is a dolichocephalic (long-headed) dictionary. As for the term Jew, its meaning, except when it is applied as a name symbol for a group called Jews, who possess in common a certain historic continuity, is extremely tenuous. No traits have been distinguished that characterize the Jews as such everywhere they are found. A rich store of evidence, on the other hand, demonstrates that the Jews of a given region resemble the general population of the region they inhabit. The difference between the Jews of Germany and France, for example, is about that between the other elements in these two countries.

If we take into consideration the observations of Herskovits and Muller, it would be clear that there is no causal relationship between race and culture. Racism, according to these authors, is the workmanship of politicians. In empirical terms no race is superior to other races. Despite these observations, Kroeber very rightly says that there is a definite relationship between biological and cultural factors. Further, he very categorically says that "the performance of group in any field of life is the product of two sets of factors, biological and cultural, both of which are variable and usually not readily separable". Kroeber has yet another explanation for racism. Besides being political, racism is also derived from emotions. These emotions are justified by reasons.

There are some races in the world which have established the superiority of one race over the other. It is argued that a particular race has some physical traits which put it higher than other races. Kroeber has made a strong intellectual argument to resolve the relationship between race and racism. Actually, at this stage of our discussion it is difficult to speak of one race as doing superior to other. We cannot state that the physical characteristics of a race endow it with superior cultural traits. Kroeber writes:

> It is doubtful whether as yet it is valid to speak of one race as physically higher or more advanced, or less human and less brutish, than another. This is not an outright denial of the possibility of such differential ratings: it is a denial only of the belief that such differentials have been established.

After the First World War, the theory of racism developed in Europe and the US. The arguments which constitute the doctrine of racism are as under:

(1) Racism is the distorted form of racial characteristics.
(2) It is the politicization and emotionalization of the members of a particular race.
(3) The doctrine of racism is explained by historical method.
(4) The instances and data provided by the advocates of racism are untrue and false.
(5) Racism argues that some races are superior to others.
(6) The origin of the doctrine of racism goes back to European feudalism and colonialism. The feudal lords argued that they were created by God to rule over others. This doctrine was supported by colonial rulers. They argued as in the case of India and South Africa that they were meant for subordinating the people. Since they were the rulers, their race was also superior. In short, racism gets its validity from feudalism and colonial regime. The apartheid policy practised by the whites in South Africa is a good illustration of racial domination. The Britishers in India echoed the same argument that it is only the English who know how to rule. It is in their blood.

Actually, racism is nothing but a distortion of scientific truth for ulterior ends. To fulfil the interests of a nation, a wrong correlation has been established by saying that inherited genetic differences are a major factor in producing the differences between the cultures and cultural achievements of different peoples and groups. It does indicate, on the contrary, that a major factor in explaining such differences is the cultural experience which each group has undergone.

The UNESCO expert team, constituted in 1951, made the following recommendations with regard to races and racism:

(1) All human beings are created out of *homo sapiens*. Their ancestors are one and one only.
(2) The physical differences that we find in human beings are essentially hereditary. These differences are basically genetic. These are observable due to processes of mutation, natural selection, genetic drift and population mixture.
(3) Race is nothing but a method of human classification.
(4) Nation, religion, culture, language are not races. They are aspects of our culture bank.
(5) Intelligence is not the creation of a race. It is achieved.
(6) No race is superior or inferior.
(7) No race today is pure. A lot of admixture has taken place.
(8) All human beings are equal and they have equal access to law.

Casteism in India

In the beginning we have stated that race and racism are in no way problematic. They are the problems of the western civilization and also of South Africa. Here our problems of social and cultural level relate to caste. Caste is a hereditary group. However, as stated earlier, there are no physical features which differentiate one caste from another. But, there are social and cultural privileges and disabilities among different castes. Actually, there is a fixed caste ranking which Dumont calls *Homo hierarchicus*. There is caste endogamy. All these differences rest on caste superiority and inferiority. Quite like racism, casteism has also distorted the hereditary characteristics of a particular caste. As there are race wars, so we have in our country caste wars. The doctrine of Mandalization has made the caste war more intense. It is said that the legislation on schedulization has continuously made this war ongoing. In fact, caste continues to remain a hereditary group. It has nothing to do with culture. If a Brahmin can speak Marathi, so can an untouchable also speak Marathi. Brahmin and untouchable are two hereditary groups and language is a culture. It is common to all. In other words, culture is independent of caste.

Language

Recently, the French sociologists have given a new dimension to the concept of structure. Actually, the new structuralism, which has emerged as a tradition of sociology and social anthropology, draws heavily from sociology of language. In the initial development of new structuralism, the influence of Ferdinand de Saussure (1857-1913) is dominant. Basically, Saussure was a philologist. His argument is that quite like the structure of language, there is a structure of society. It is all a culture. Kroeber, a well known cultural anthropologist, tries to explore the relationship between race and speech family. He says that a race does not have its own language. Language is learned. If, for instance, a Muslim is comfortable speaking Urdu or if Pakistan has Urdu as its national language, any Hindu can also speak Urdu. However, the fact is that if one wishes to have complete understanding of a people, one must take its language into consideration.

It is a truism that the faculty of speech is innate. In other words, soon after birth, the child has some speech. But, the language which the child would speak is wholly acquired. Moreover, the environment of which languages are the product is not a natural one; it is geographic and social. It means that someone born in Chennai and speaking in Tamil conveys that there is a geographical area where Tamil language is spoken. The child acquires the habit of speaking Tamil because he is born in a particular geographical and cultural region. The races in this context have their geography. Caucasians are found in Europe and it is this area and cultural milieu which prompts inhabitants to speak any or more number of languages spoken in Europe. Philologists have classified the languages into different linguistic families, and that is how a race has come to be related with a particular linguistic family. Thus, there is a strong association between language and civilization.

Language, Culture and Nationality

Social anthropologists argue that language is a part of culture. It is given by the society to the individual. In fact, language and culture are one. However, for practical purposes, it is generally convenient to keep them distinct and separate. There is no doubt that two people can share in what is substantially the same culture and yet speak fundamentally different idioms and, therefore, feel themselves to be separate nationalities. For instance, the Indians living in England share the same culture with the local people but consider themselves as Indians. This means that the concept of nationality is fundamentally subjective whereas both languages and cultures are objectively alike or unlike, united or distinct. It must be said that nation and state are political concepts whereas nationality is essentially ethnic and anthropological. Kroeber strikes an important conclusive note in this respect:

> All in all, anthropology is more immediately concerned with nationalities than with nations, with ethnic than with political groupings. And, in nationalities and ethnic units, language is always a factor, and often the basic one.

Concluding Observations

Traditional textbook material, both in Hindi and English in India, deals with the existing races of man and the problems of racism. Apartheid policy practised by colonial rulers in South Africa, India and other parts of Asia has been the result of racism. These textbooks usually fail to emphasize the point that races of man constitute the theme of physical anthropology. And, racism which is really social and cultural interpretation or rather distortion of race, forms the subject matter of social anthropology. In academic paraphrase racism is the realm of social anthropology.

There are three major races in the world. The definition of race is based on biological considerations. It is a hereditary group held together by certain physical features. When these biological features are interpreted in social and cultural achievements, the result is disastrous. The world has faced enough discrimination resulting from the erroneous interpretation of a biological concept—race. What social and cultural anthropologists argue is that racism is a distorted form of a biological concept. If this lesson is brought home very well by social anthropology, its objective has been achieved.

Further Readings

Berghe, Pierre, L. Van, Den, *Race and Racism*, New York, 1967.
Bohannan, Paul, *Social Anthropology*, London, 1963.
Hoebel, E.A., *Man in the Primitive world*, New York, 1949.
Kroeber, A.L., *Anthropology*, London, 1948.

6

The Nature of Culture

The Human Development Report (1999) has very critically brought out the culture crisis faced by the people in various parts of the world. The process of globalization has very violently intervened the local culture. The indigenous culture of primitives and villagers is at the verge of extinction. Social anthropology now is required to analyze culture from the wider context of globalization. True, globalization has opened up many opportunities for millions of people around the world. Increased trade, new technologies, foreign investments, expanding media and internet connections are fuelling economic growth and human advance. It is also true that global markets, global technology, global ideas and global solidarity is likely to enrich the lives of people everywhere. But, in this wider process, the tribals face the threat of the extinction of their age-old culture.

Malinowski's Trobrianders are fast taking to modernization. Likewise, the tribal groups, such as the Tiv and the Nuer of South Africa, are increasingly becoming modern. In India, the Gond, Santhal and Bhil tribes are adopting to globalization at the local level. Tribal culture today has become a great casualty of such a global process. Looking at the decay of indigenous culture, Thomas Hylland Eriksen very rightly observes:

> What has become of the peoples first explored by anthropologists during colonialism? Nearly all of them are, to a varying degree, integrated into larger—in the final instance global—economic, cultural and political systems.

As a consequence of global change, the tribal communities, which were isolates and noble savages, have taken to capitalist economy and subordination. Surveying the rural labour distribution and capitalist production in western India, Jan Breman informs that the tribals of south Gujarat have received a serious culture erosion and are fast moving towards progressive economy. The setback received by indigenous culture of primitives at local level is also reported by the *The Human Development Report* (1999). It observes:

> Globalization opens people's lives to culture and all its creativity—and to the flow of ideas and knowledge. But, the new culture carried by expanding global markets is disquieting. As Mahatma Gandhi expressed so eloquently earlier in the century, "I do not want my house to be walled in all sides and my windows to be stuffed. I want the cultures of all the lands to be blown about my house as freely as possible. But I refuse to be blown off my feet by any." Today's flow of culture is unbalanced, heavily weighted in one direction from rich countries to poor.

Amazingly enough, the Government of India has no culture policy of its own and the global culture is encroaching upon the local people. The consequences of the cultural onslaught are serious indeed. It is argued that at this juncture we should very seriously study the status of culture among the tribals, villagers, and other subaltern people. It is because of globalization that the indigeneous people have not only lost their cultural nerve, but their insecurity has also increased. They are suffering the loss of their environment. It has been degraded. Deforestation has increased; there has been land erosion, water scarcity and fuel inadequacy. What is worse is that the biodiversity has been reduced to the lowest level. The tribals have lost their folklore; their melodies are no more in existence, and their folkways and foods are increasingly pushed to the margin in this era of 'global village'. Commenting on such a situation of local culture or the culture of the indigeneous people, *The Human Development Report* (1999) says:

> Such onslaughts of foreign culture can put cultural diversity at risk, and make people fear, losing their cultural identity.

A broader analysis of the theme of culture very vividly indicates that we shall have to take an urgent and immediate view of our culture which is characteristic of our civilization. The traditional textbooks that we find in social anthropology admittedly dwell upon the theme of culture. But, the treatment is old fashioned. No effort is made to look at culture from the new perspective of global culture. What we find today in these Hindi and English textbooks is a junk-like stock of irrelevances. No student or teacher can enrich his understanding of culture in this new perspective. Obviously, the global challenges have obliged us to take a departure from the traditional treatment of culture as given in our textbooks.

What is Culture?

Culture has originated from the Latin word *colere*, which means "to cultivate". In social anthropology, the word 'culture' means "knowledge", that is, knowledge about those aspects of humanity which are not natural, but which are related to that which is acquired. In other words, culture refers to "those abilities, notions and forms of behaviour which are acquired by a person as members of society." Eriksen writes that it is very difficult to define the concept of culture as it is a very comprehensive term. This comprehensiveness also carries with it a basic ambiguity. He observes:

> On the one hand, every human is equally cultural; in this sense, the term refers to a basic *similarity* within humanity. On the other hand, people have acquired different abilities, notions, etc., and are thereby *different* because of culture. Culture refers, in other words, both to basic similarity and to systematic differences between humans.

Culture has been defined differently. There are some anthropologists who view it from an evolutionary point of view. For them, culture is super-organic and super-individual. The functionalists, on the other hand, define it from the organic perspective. They argue that culture is like an organism, wherein one part is related to another part. Then, there are anthropologists who look at culture from a dialectical point of view. Recently, Pierre Bourdieu has provided a new vision to the analysis of culture, when he talks about culture with equal emphasis given to counter-culture. We, therefore, are required to define culture from all these varying perspectives.

Perhaps, the oldest definition of culture is that of Edward B. Tylor. It has been often quoted and has thus been classical. Tylor says:

> Culture or civilization is that complex whole which includes knowledge, beliefs, arts, morals, laws, customs and any other capabilities and habits acquired by man as a member of society.

Tylor makes one important qualification of culture and that is "acquiring of culture". Second, it is the capability which forms the content of culture. A similar definition is given by Ralph Linton:

> Culture is social heredity.

In traditional terms, biologically, heredity gives the characteristics of a set of genes to the coming generation. In the case of culture, the social characteristics are acquired by the present generation from the preceding generations. Thus, culture is a social inheritance. Lowie argues that culture is a concrete, historical, universal truth and all particular cultures are abstractions therefrom. His definition of culture runs as below:

> Culture is the whole of social tradition.

All the above three definitions of culture given above refer to *social* and *society*. Kroeber has commented on these two terms and observes: "We can accept this: society and culture, social and cultural, are closely related concepts. There can obviously be no culture without a society---much as there can be no society without individuals. The converse---no society without culture---holds for man: no cultureless human society is known; it would even be hard to imagine."

Kroeber further says that there is a correlation between society and culture. Another important thing is the term 'acquire'. Without it, culture cannot have its continuum. Amalgamating the definitions of Tylor, Linton and Lowie, Kroeber defines culture as under:

> Roughly, then, we can approximate what culture is by saying it is that which the human species has and other social species lack. This would include speech, knowledge, beliefs, customs, arts, technologies, ideals and rules. That, in short, is what we learn from other men, from our elders or the past, plus what we may add to it.

Actually, Kroeber has constructed his definition from Tylor, who spoke about capabilities and habits acquired by man which Kroeber has taken as a process of learning from the past and from other man. As a matter of fact, Kroeber's definition of culture is a combination of the definitions given by Tylor, Linton and Lowie. In any definition of culture, what is important is the social inheritance or tradition. And, tradition includes speech, language, knowledge and the like.

The functionalists have defined culture in a slightly different way. They have a holistic approach to the understanding of culture. Malinowski stressed the fact that the elements of a culture are closely interrelated and has drawn attention to the dangers of meddling with its functional pattern of interdependent institutions. In his general axioms of functionalism, he states:

> Culture is an integral in which the various elements are interdependent. Cultures are functionally integrated in the sense that all their elements serve as means to the satisfaction of psychological needs and the institutions of a culture are interdependent ... Each culture owes its completeness and self-sufficiency to the fact that it satisfies the whole range of basic, instrumental and integrative needs.

The evolutionary anthropologists have defined culture in terms of its super-organic and super-individual terms. The term 'super-organic' does not mean non-organic, or free of organic influence and causation; nor does it mean that culture is an entity independent of organic life in the sense that some theologians might assert that there is a soul which is or can become independent of the living body. Here, when we say super-organic, we mean simply that when we consider culture we are dealing with something that is organic, but which must also be viewed as something more than organic if it is to be fully intelligible to us.

The term 'super-individual' means that culture is above the individual. For instance, the food habits are determined by the society, quite the same way as rituals are determined by the society. These are super-individual—above the individual. The evolutionary anthropologists, thus, have defined culture in terms of super-organic and super-individual.

In a very textual and simplified way John Lewis has defined culture as below:

> All that is socially transmitted in a society, including artistic, social, ideological and religious patterns of behaviour and the techniques for mastering the environment, constitute culture.

In Lewis' terms culture is social transmission which is prevalent is in all walks of social life. Lewis, however, does not stress on the acquired aspects of culture. He only talks about transmission from the preceding generations to the coming generation.

Bourdieu looks at culture from a new perspective. He is a neo-structuralist and a post-modernist French sociologist. Speaking about the importance of culture in society, Bourdieu argues that there are two variants of culture: (i) official or establishment culture, and (ii) counter-culture. Establishment culture is promoted and practised by men of power. This variant of culture, Bourdieu says, is characterized by economism. According to it, "all social phenomena and more specially the phenomena of exchange are reduced by intellectuals for their profit." Bourdieu further says that "there is a thing as cultural capital and this capital secures direct profits, first on the educational market, of course, but elsewhere too also secures profits of distinction strangely neglected by the marginalist economies". To simplify Bourdieu, it could be said that the official or establishment culture keeps the capitalist and bourgeois away from the common man. The bourgeois benefit from this culture and give it the status of distinction.

The counter-culture, though difficult to define, is marginal or outside the establishment or official culture. The culture of the poorer masses of people is, in Bourdieu's paraphrase, a counter-culture. Thus, from all accounts, the view of culture, according to new structuralists, is a process which benefits the elite groups of the society. Counter-culture naturally belongs to the common man. It is also the theme of social anthropology as it concerns the primitives and subaltern groups.

We have reached a stage of discussion in our effort of defining culture when we can safely say that culture and society go together. There cannot be a culture without society and the vice versa. Culture consists of everything which is learned by the members of a generation from the past. The new generation is also a creator of culture. Then, culture is super-organic and super-individual. It is holistic in nature, it is integral. But this culture cannot be acquired without being a member of the society. There are some aspects of culture which bear basic similarities and then there are culture patterns which show symbolic differences between human beings. In any study of culture, our effort should be to bring out similarities and differences among people in the realm of culture.

Characteristics of Culture

If we carefully examine the tradition of sociology and anthropology, we find that culture has remained, all through the last hundred years, a major theme of discussion. The emergence of ethnology, as a new branch of social science, establishes that culture is super-organic in all its manifestations. However, approach to culture has two distinct methods. For culturology or ethnology, culture is the ultimate reality *sui generis* and society is the vehicle of culture---a necessary but not sufficient condition of culture. For sociology, on the contrary, society is the ultimate reality which renders intelligible the nature of man and of the social institutions by which he is governed. Actually, sociologists consider society as the creator of culture whereas anthropologists think that it is culture which keeps the organization of a society going. David Bidney observes:

> Both sociologists and ethnologists (anthropologists) agreed that culture is the product of social intercourse and independent of psychology; they differed only as regards the metaphysical or metascientific issue of the ontological priority of society and culture.

Bidney's explanation of the different approaches made by anthropologists and sociologists has been further clarified by Kroeber when he says:

> Sociology tends to be concerned with society, anthropology with *anthropos*, man and his specially human product, culture. All in all, these are differences only in emphasis. In principle, sociology and anthropology are hard to keep apart.

The reality is that both the disciplines consider culture as a core theme though their methods of interpretation differ. Our argument is that traditionally anthropologists have brought out certain characteristics of culture. One very essential characteristic of culture is that it is related to society. There cannot be culture without society; neither there can be society without culture. We shall discuss below some of the characteristics of culture:

(i) Culture is a process

Culture of any society is not sterile; it is a process. Traditions change; new traditions emerge. In other word, the structure of culture goes from one generation to another and each generation adds or substracts from inherited culture. This continuity and change shows that it is a process.

(ii) Culture is a social heritage

Whatever we get in culture is transmitted and communicated. The individual is thought of as being born into a man-made world of artifacts, symbols and social institutions which he acquires from his ancestors. The culture moulds the individual to conform to the prevailing cultural patterns.

Among the tribals and villagers of our country there are some well-known cultural practices which constitute the heritage of the people. Each village and for that matter each tribal group has its own local deities. When we talk about India, we very often say that our country has great social heritage. This heritage is manifest in festivals, fairs and rituals.

(iii) Culture is super-organic and super-individual

Most of the social anthropologists consider that culture is above society. It is a tradition which is inherited. This view of culture goes with another characteristic which is called super-individual. This interpretation of culture in terms of super-individual shows that quite like Durkheim's social fact culture is also above the individual. It is a readymade thing borrowed from preceding generations.

(iv) It is an abstraction

Kroeber and Kluckhohn, in their discussion of culture, have concluded that culture is an abstraction of the study of behaviour and behavioural products. But, what is interesting in the statements of these two anthropologists is that they do not consider concrete behaviour as culture. Culture, as we know it, is an abstraction of concrete behaviour; for instance, if India as a nation pays its respect to the national flag, the flag itself is not culture. The abstraction is that a nation has some symbols which indicate its nationalism. Kroeber writes:

> ... but culture is not behaviour nor the investigation of behaviour in all its concrete completeness.

For Kroeber, culture is an emergent, autonomous reality. In fact, it is the logical construct of human behaviour. Bidney supports both Kroeber and Kluckhohn, and says that culture from all considerations is a logical construct of patterns or forms.

(v) Culture is integral

Functionalists, despite their variability in approach, have a consensus that culture is all-inclusive; it contains all aspects of human society including beliefs, law, art, literature, norms, values, traditions, etc. This holistic view of culture has been popularized by functionalists and evolutionists. In simpler terms, culture can be analyzed only with reference to the total social system. It is this integral aspect of culture which is advocated by anthropologists.

(vi) Culture is tradition

True, culture is integral. It is comprehensive. It is holistic. But, in all this, tradition is its dominant part. Each tribal group has its traditions which die a very slow death. Indian traditions are a good example of our culture. Tribal traditions have a great hold over their practitioners.

(vii) Culture is acquired

Kroeber analyzes a large number of definitions on culture. He says that whatever may be the definition, what is important is that culture is characteristically *acquired*. When Tylor defined culture, he talked about "capabilities and habits acquired by man". Thus, culture gives away its survival if it is not acquired. The wider meaning of 'acquired' includes inheritance. Most of the definitions of culture talk about inheritance. When Lowie says that culture is 'social tradition' he means that there is social inheritance of culture. In simple words, culture does not discuss much about what it consists of, but it emphasizes on how it is acquired. Yet another meaning of 'acquired' is learning. One can say that culture is learned.

(viii) Culture is two-faceted

Eriksen stresses yet another aspect of culture. According to him, culture has two sides. There are some aspects of culture which are basic to all the cultures; e.g., marriage, kin, family and polity. A Gond, for instance, has some system, some rule of acquiring a match, and similarly a Tiv has some method of getting a wife. Thus, culture has one aspect which is similar in all the human societies. But, there are also some aspects of culture which are different from others. Social anthropology tries to bring out both similarities and differences in the cultures of various societies.

(ix) Language as part of culture

Kroeber presents a very interesting account of anthropology, in which he emphasizes on language. He says that the culture of a society is manifest in its language. He even goes to the extent of classifying the races in terms of linguistic families. D.N. Majumdar has also done a similar exercise in identifying race elements in India. When he talks about Dravidian people, actually he uses Dravidian language family as a criterion of race classification. In any discussion of culture race occupies a decisive place. Further, the caste composition in our country partly is explained in terms of language family.

(x) Culture is cumulative

Culture is never constructed overnight. It evolves over a period of time. Because of its evolutionary nature it has a tendency of accumulation. Indian culture is a product of hundreds of years of evolution. It is this cumulative nature which provides continuity to culture.

(xi) Distinctness of culture

Culture is conditioned by several factors. It is this aspect of culture which gives it an undifferentiated identity. If we look at the world's civilizations, we find that these civilizations have been the products of certain geographical, ecological, political and historical conditions. Arnold Toynbee, in his classical work, *A Study of History*, has discussed the comparative development of civilization. He propounds a theory of the development of culture and says that it is the challenge given by physical, social and cultural factors which shape the nature of civilization.

(xii) Culture as a standard of society

Each culture provides some standards of behaviour to its people. These standards constitute norms and values and the members of the society are expected to take these standards as their ideals. However, the standards are never rigid. They keep changing.

In conclusion, we observe that openness is one of the general characteristics of culture. The culture of today is largely received from yesterday: that is what tradition or transmission means; it is a passing or sending along, a 'handing through' from one generation to another. Even in times of the most radical change and innovation, there are probably several times as many items of culture being transmitted from the past as there are being newly devised.

Yet another common and general characteristic of culture is its organic diversity and cultural hybridity. Culture is organic in the sense that it is influenced by individuals. Indian culture has been influenced by several spiritual and national leaders. Besides, there is so much intermixing of varying cultures that it is difficult to find a pure culture of a particular group. This is what we call 'cultural hybridity'. In the present era of globalization where there is interaction between global culture and local culture, there has emerged cultural hybridity.

We have also discussed at length the continuity in every culture. Continuity is an inherent part of any culture and the survival of a culture depends on its continuity. The receptivity and assimilativeness of a culture makes the totality of culture a continuum. The parts merge into each other without definite breaks. It is generally assumed that all life is also a continuum; but the continuity of life is traceable only by going back in its history and then accessing other branches.

Culture Structure

Much has already been written on the structure of culture. Culture is a very comprehensive term. It includes everything. It is very complex. Anthropologists have discussed the different structural parts of culture, among them, perhaps, Herskovits' description on cultural structure and cultural dynamics is very illuminating and interesting. When we study culture we find that its unity is made up of several components. In considering any individual way of life, we must see it as a whole, that is, more than the sum of its parts, but when we analyze human social behaviour, we may isolate form or pattern from meaning, and action from sanction. We may describe in minute detail the structure of a building, tell how it is made, by whom, and of what materials, and thus have an assemblage of traits whose distribution can be traced without the slightest reference to their functioning.

The structure of culture can be seen in its various parts—traits, complexes, patterns and culture area. Whatever may be the culture—whether of a tribal group or a group residing in a metropolitan city—it always has got some structure, some composition. The parts of the culture are always identifiable. Their functioning is such that they make the whole culture workable. An analysis of the various parts of the culture helps the researcher to arrive at a conclusion about the organization of a society. These cultural units are discussed as below:

Culture Trait

This is the smallest part of culture which cannot be further divided. Herskovits has defined culture trait very precisely as under:

> It is the smallest unit in a given culture. It is identifiable.

Thus, according to Herskovits, there are two essentials of a culture trait: (i) it has some form, and (ii) this form is structured. Besides, he also lays down some standards of evaluation. Whether an element in a culture is a trait or not can be judged by experts. He observes:

> When a trait is to be regarded as constituting such a minimum, it involves evaluation of two kinds. The decision in a given instance must be the result of an expert's study of the problem, taking into account the unconsidered view of the individuals who live by the conventions of the culture being studied, and realizing that even such an ascribed unity may shift in terms of the larger whole of which it is a part. The form a trait assumes at a given time will thus be determined by its context, rather than by any quality inherent in it.

Thus, a trait is the smallest unit of a culture; it has a context and its own structure.

Kroeber has discussed the importance of culture traits. According to him: "A trait is a minimal definable element of culture." For Kroeber culture is the smallest unit and it cannot be further divided. And, if some division is made, the trait would lose its significance. In a machine, for instance, the iron bolt is a trait. If the bolt is further divided, it would only be an ore. The significance of bolt is that it carries its identity and functional autonomy. In social behaviour, the term 'good night' or 'sorry' are traits as they are identifiable and cannot be further divided.

Let us cite an example of the culture trait. We have our house. Among the material elements in the house are rooms, the stairs, various kinds of furnishings and appliances used for the preparation of food. These material traits are one aspect of the structure of culture. The non-material traits include the attitudes of the members of the household towards themselves, each other and the world outside. Now, let us analyze the structure of our household in terms of traits. The table placed in a room has a unity of its own. It is a physical whole which can be identified as such. And, therefore, we call it a culture trait. But, this is not the only explanation. The chair has no meaning as it is a part of the dining table. It gains importance only when it becomes a part of all the four, six or eight chairs of the dining table. Thus, the culture unit is identifiable only in a context. Therefore, when we identify a trait, as a culture trait we shall have to take into account the entire context of the object of study.

It is interesting to note at this stage of our discussion that British social anthropologists reject the concept of culture trait. They argue that culture trait does not help us explain the appropriate status of culture. On the contrary, the US anthropologists consider culture trait to be quite useful in analyzing culture. Despite this disagreement culture trait has been studied by several eminent social anthropologists. Tylor has analyzed different cultures from the point of view of the development of social institution. Boas has investigated how mythology reflects the mode of life.

Culture Complex

Culture complex has an integrative element which makes it united. Efforts have been made to study culture complex in folk tales too. In a folk tale one can observe settings wherein the incidents take place. For illustration we may refer to the incident of *Devi* possession in southern Gujarat which has been referred to by David Hardiman. He reports that in early November 1922 a large number of *adivasi* peasants from several villages assembled at a place in southern Gujarat to listen to the teachings of a goddess *Mata* or *Devi* known as Salahbai.

The *Devi*, who was not generally represented by any image, was supposed to have come out of the mountains and expressed her demands through spirits. While most of the *adivasis* listened to *Devi*, a number of them went into a state of trance. These men would shake their heads violently and begin to utter what were believed to be the *Devi*'s commands. The principal commands were to abstain from eating flesh or drinking liquor or toddy, to take a bath daily, to use water rather than a leaf to clean up after defecation, to keep their houses clean, to release or sell goats and chicken, and to boycott Parsi liquor dealers and landlords.

Social anthropology can identify the culture complex in the whole episode of *adivasis* of southern Gujarat. The possession of the *Devi* is attained by different rituals, which include shaking of heads and beating the bare back of the possessed with iron chains. All these culture complexes include a large number of traits. These traits, if put together, constitute the *Devi* possession. Yet another example of culture complex is that of *halma* practised by the Bhils of western India. It is a cooperative endeavour. When a peasant wants to harvest his maize crop, he invites all the peasants of the village to help him in harvesting. In a day or two, the process is over. *Halma* involves a large number of activities. The host peasant has to provide simple meals, tea and often *bidi* for smoking. No wage payment, however, is made. All the culture traits observed during *halma* jointly make a culture complex.

Difference between Culture Trait and Culture Complex

Trait is the minimum identifiable culture item, while complex is a combined form of various traits. What is common to both is that they help us analyze culture. Both the concepts are, therefore, methodological devices. However, there are some differences between the two. Trait is an abstraction of reality, whereas complex is a unity of several traits. Stressing the difference and oneness of both these concepts, Herskovits writes:

> Here perhaps lies the principal difference between the culture trait and culture complex. Both are useful devices in furthering the objective, scientific study of culture. But insofar as culture has meaning, and meaning gives to culture its reality, the trait is far more abstraction drawn by the students than the complex.

Culture Pattern

Ruth Benedict has written extensively on culture patterns. Social anthropology takes two meanings of pattern: first, it is a form and second, it is a set of patterned behaviour and sanctioned responses. For instance, when we see the Red Fort at Delhi, we immediately say that it has Mughal architectural design. Similarly, when we look at the south Indian temples, we find in them the Dravidian pattern of architecture. It is the form which constitutes a pattern. Writing about the pattern of culture, Herskovits observes:

> In considering the pattern phenomenon, we are confronted with two differing aspects of it that, though they have given rise to much controversy, are in actuality, complementary rather than contradictory. The first meaning of pattern is the form that the institutions of a culture characteristically take... The second meaning is psychological.

Herskovits has defined the culture pattern with precision:

> When we think of cultural patterns as the designs taken by the elements of a culture which, as consensuses of the individual behavioural patterns, manifest by the members of a society, give to this way of life coherence, continuity and distinctive form.

Besides a form, a pattern assumes consensus of behaviour that characterizes culture. For example, let us take the pattern of mating as we find among Hindus. In Hindu marriage, the choice of mate is imposed by kinship members. Another element in the marriage pattern is its ritual character. Marriages among Hindus are solemnized in the presence of a fire. The ceremony is officiated by a Brahmin. Seven rounds of the fire solemnize the marriage. Marriage, thus, is a ritual. This is a consensus. It is legitimized both by religion and the court of law. It has a definite form or pattern. In practise, pattern gives coherence, continuity and distinctness to a culture. Historically, the pattern emerges out of the form and the consensus.

Among tribals there are patterns of behaviour in terms of varied social institutions. These include family, caste, tribe, village and city. What is important in the pattern is that because of its coherence and legitimacy there is an aspect of continuity in culture. The Indian civilization has innumerable culture patterns which have kept it alive.

Culture Area

Let us begin with an example. The people who reside in Punjab belong to different states of the country. But, for their day-to-day work, they all speak Punjabi. Similar is the situation of Tamil Nadu. There are a large number of Marwadi doing their business in Chennai. They hail from different parts of Rajasthan but conduct their business in the Tamil language. The lesson is that Punjab and Tamil Nadu are cultural areas. People of these areas speak the language of the area, accept the food habits of the area and conduct their ceremonies more or less according to the folk traditions of the area. The culture area has similar, if not uniform, ways of doing things. In a culture area, there are traits, complexes and patterns which the people follow. The process is simple: people who live close together have greater opportunities to borrow from each other rather than from people who are at a distance.

The idea of culture area derives from the fundamental principle that since culture is learned, any element in it can be taken over by any individual or group of individuals exposed to different ways of doing and thinking. It is striking but true that the population structure of Mumbai consists largely of Marathi and Gujarati speaking people. Gujarati women who are married to Marathis speak both Gujarati and Marathi. Such a situation of bilingualism exists because the culture traits of a particular culture area have been adopted by the newcomers to that area. Herskovits has defined culture area in a very precise way as under:

> The area in which similar cultures are found is called a culture area.

The concept of culture area as developed by Herskovits says that in a particular area there might be a limited cultural heterogeneity but the varying cultures found in the area have more or less a similarity. In a systematic and scientific way the concept of culture area was developed by C. Wissler. He worked on American Indian cultures. His definition, though it has been since sharpened, is still useful:

> The natives of the new world could be grouped according to culture traits.

Thus, a culture area, according to Wissler, is an area which has similar culture traits. These traits include food areas, textile areas, ceramic areas, etc. If, however, we take all traits into simultaneous consideration and shift our point of view to the social or tribal units, we are able to form fairly definite groups. This will give us culture areas, or a classifications of social groups according to their culture traits.

Boas, an American anthropologist, has creditably worked on culture. He has brought out culture areas among the North American Indians. In doing so he has taken folk tales and myths as bases of culture area classification. He argues that a culture area has definitely material cultural traits common to all the people. He has also constructed a map of culture areas in North America, South America and Africa.

Kroeber, another American anthropologist, has critically examined the culture area maps constructed by Boas and Wissler. He, however, could not make any effective change in the number of culture divisions, but he did bring out some major changes in the cultural map. It is reported that Kroeber prepared a revised cultural map on the strength of the map created by Wissler. The important thing is the determination of the criteria for marking a particular geographical area as a culture area. Boas took two criteria for identifying specific culture areas—ecology and cultural manifestation. Changes in the culture area come when we change the criteria.

Classification of Culture Areas

In our country some researches have been attempted to identify the cultural areas inhabited by the tribals. For instance, K.S. Singh in *People of India* says that the tribals are found in all states except Delhi, Punjab and Haryana and in all union territories except Chandigarh and Pondicherry. The major tribal culture areas have been identified by him as the north-east part of the country and the tribal heartland.

Besides the tribal culture areas the rest of the country has also been classified into different culture areas. For instance, Iravati Karve has very elaborately worked on the classification of culture areas at the national level. In her classical work, *Kinship Organization in India*, she has taken kinship, marriage, family and language as criteria for preparing a cultural map of India. According to her, the country consists of four distinct culture areas: (1) north, (2) south, (3) central, and (4) north-east. Her approach of enquiry was both historical and fieldwork. Material from the *Vedas, Upanishadas*, epics and myths have been widely used by her as source material. She concludes that there are distinct characteristics for all the four culture areas.

The special traits of the southern culture area consist of matriarchal system, *sapind* marriage and cross-cousin marriage. The distinctness of northern culture area is characterized by taboo on *sapind* marriage and cross-cousin marriage. In north India, there is almost a general practice of village exogamy which is not rigidly adhered to in the south. Yet another difference between the two culture areas is that in the north there are different kinship terms for both blood and marital kin, whereas in the south there is a single terminology for both the kin. In the field of language also, the south Indian languages, viz., Malayali, Kannada, Tamil and Telugu belong to the Dravidian family, whereas the north Indian languages fall within the Indo-Aryan family. Similar differences are also found in the north-eastern and central culture zones.

Besides Karve, a few other notable social anthropologists have also worked on the theme of culture areas. A.C. Mayer has identified central culture area on the criteria of caste and kin. Kathleen Gough and Louis Dumont have also worked to generate culture area classification. On the strength of data, these anthropologists have also identified certain culture areas in central and southern India.

To conclude, it could be said that language and kinship have been used as the major criteria for culture area classification by social anthropologists. The geographers, however, have employed ecology and geography as the bases for such a classification. At this stage, it would also be pertinent to mention that in a single culture area, there also exist sub-culture areas. We propose to write a small note on sub-culture areas.

Sub-culture Areas

Kroeber has used sub-cultures and part cultures as aspects of culture as a whole. We have mentioned earlier that Bourdieu has also used the concept of counter-culture which is outside the official or establishment culture. In the field of culture areas, the idea of sub-culture is of recent origin. The sub-culture areas are differentiated in part from the bigger culture areas. For instance, the south Indian culture area falls into four sub-culture areas: (1) Malayalam, (2) Kannada, (3) Telugu and (4) Tamil. In the culture area of Gujarat there is Kathiawadi or Saurashtra, central Gujarat or *Charottar*, and south Gujarat sub-culture areas. The fact is that each culture area in course of time gives rise to some other sub-culture areas which basically belong to the main culture area.

Universality of Culture

Perhaps, Malinowski was the earliest social anthropologist who talked about universals or similar traits in human culture. He says that there are some basic needs of human needs notwithstanding time and place. The human beings on their part give cultural responses to these needs. The explanation given for the cultural survivals by Malinowski is as under:

Malinowski's Explanation for Universals in Culture

Basic Needs		*Cultural Responses*	
1.	Metabolism	1.	Commissariat
2.	Reproduction	2.	Kinship
3.	Bodily comforts	3.	Shelter
4.	Safety	4.	Protection
5.	Movement	5.	Activities
6.	Growth	6.	Training
7.	Health	7.	Hygiene

In fact, there are some basic needs of men all over the world. In order to survive the man has to produce some consumer goods. This basic need or imperative has given birth to the institution of economics; it is natural for man is to fulfil his needs without a care for others. This has given rise to social institutions, particularly politics, for social control. Yet another need of the man is to train and educate the people for future survival. Education is the institutional response to this basic need. And, finally, it is the need of man to provide some measures for protection. In other words, there should be an institution equipped with power and authority. This basic need ends up in the creation of political organization. Thus, it is clear that the universals of culture are nothing but the institutional response of the people. These responses are the aspects of culture.

Aspects of Culture

Herskovits, in his *Cultural Anthropology*, has discussed some major aspects of culture. After his discussion of the structure of culture he talks about its patterning and integration. He says that there are several traits, complexes and areas of culture but all these are integrated. When he discusses the patterns of culture he analyzes the cultural aspects also. All human ways of life all over the world are basically similar. These ways are manifest in dance, drama, folk music, food habits, etc. While describing the basic aspects of culture, Herskovits refers to the works of Spencer and Tylor. His contention is that despite the diversity in culture there are, however, some universals. These universals are termed as "psychic unity of mankind". The human beings have similar capacities and these capacities give rise to certain universals. Herskovits' argument runs as below:

> One of the earliest postulates of anthropological science was that the ends achieved by all human ways of life, or cultures, are basically similar. This universality in the general outlines of cultures supported the theory advanced by such early anthropologists as Herbert Spencer and E.B. Tylor, which held that the similarities to be found in the institutions of different cultures are to be accounted for by the similar capacities of all men.

Herskovits' introduction to the aspects of culture shows that the capacities of man are found in different institutions. There is yet another explanation. The similarity is also due to biological traits. Biologically, all men instinctively respond to a situation in a similar way. All men are in search of bodily comforts, shelter, protection, reproduction, and so on and so forth. Whether a man is from America or India his response to a threat would be protection. It is because of this biological instinct that there are cultural similarities or universals at the global plane. It is this biological instinct which creates a psychological unity among the human beings. Wissler explains this in a precise manner as under:

> Man builds cultures because he cannot help it; there is a *drive* in his protoplasm that carries him forward even against his will.

Social anthropologists have further elaborated the concept of culture aspects. Literally 'aspect' means a look, glance or an appearance of a particular object. Culture has certain forms or appearances. The aspect of a physical man is his facial make up, body colour, stature and so on. In the same way, the culture of a society is apparent from the social and economic life of its people.

As stated earlier, man is born with certain basic needs which include food, shelter and clothing. To these needs now are added education and health. The basic human needs are universal. Besides, there are some derived needs, which owe their origin to the fulfilment of human needs and are achieved through culture. This, in the end, gives rise to social and cultural institutions. The economic, educational and political institutions supply potentialities to fulfil the derived needs which satisfy the basic human needs. Aspects of a culture are, therefore, manifestation of both human needs and derived needs. Herskovits has defined the aspects of culture as below:

> Basic human needs, manifest in the cultural activities of men, in turn set up a series of 'derived needs', which means that "culture supplies man with derived potentialities, abilities and powers". From the derived needs come a series of 'cultural imperatives' which give form to the institutions of a culture that go to make up those broadest divisions that we shall here term 'aspects'.

The description of culture aspects is also given by Malinowski. He explains derived needs and provides cultural responses. For instance, there are derived needs of consumer goods, shelter and clothing. To fulfil these needs there are economic institutions. For authority and power, there is political organization. Malinowski includes a large number of institutions which are instrumental in fulfilling the derived needs. Among these are included family, clan, local community and tribe. Herskovits, in his *Cultural Anthropology*, has provided a full section on the aspects of culture. These include universals of culture, technology and the utilization of natural resources, economics, social organization, political system, religion, folklore, drama, music and language.

There are some anthropological studies too which have enquired into the several aspects of culture. One such study is that of Shamerpet village conducted by S.C. Dube. Dube has included all the political, economic and social institutions of the village in his study. This is an excellent monograph on the aspects of culture. *Religion and Society among the Coorgs of South India* by M.N. Srinivas is another study dwelling on the study of aspects. Srinivas has studied the family, kin and community of the Coorgs, besides religion. Actually, Coorgs have been studied from a holistic perspective, in which all the vital aspects of their culture are included.

Perhaps, the best example of the basic culture aspects of an Indian village is the one found in a Telugu proverb:

> Settle down in a village
> where you find a moneylender, a medicine
> man, a river flowing unbroken
> and a Brahmin.
> Enter not that village devoid
> of these four essentials.
>
> Sumati Satakam, in a Telugu book, *Practical Wisdom*

If one asks, what are the principle aspects of Indian village culture?, the answer is provided in the above book. According to it, culture aspects of a village are: a *moneylender*, a *physician*, a *source of potable water* and a *priest*. These four aspects of culture fulfil the major derived needs of man.

Kroeber has further elaborated the aspects of culture. He mentions that rural and urban communities are nothing but the manifestations of culture. In the same spirit he says that the institutions of class, caste, tribe and nomadic communities are also broad aspects of culture which are under the process of transformation. Mike Featherstone, in his *Global Culture* (1990), discusses the status of culture aspects in the context of global culture. He argues that the local culture and its aspects are in a state of crisis due to the extending frontiers of globalization. It must be stressed here that though aspects of culture are under strain, and occasionally on the verge of extinction, the basic human needs remain the same. The derived needs may undergo change in the form of social and cultural institutions, but this, however, should not threaten us.

Further Readings

Beattie, John, *Other Cultures*, London, 1964.

Benedict, Ruth, *Patterns of Culture*, Boston, 1934.

Bohannan, Paul, *Social Anthropology*, London, 1963.

Human Development Report, 1999, Oxford, New York, 1999.

Kroeber, A.L., *Anthropology*, G.G. Harrap & Co., Bombay, 1948.

Mead, Margaret, *The Changing Culture of an Indian Tribe*, New York, 1932.

Melville, J. Herskovits, *Cultural Anthropology*, Oxford and IBH, New Delhi, 1969.

7

Culture Processes and Theories of Culture Growth

Culture consists of the acquired or cultivated behaviour and thoughts of individuals within a society, as well as of the intellectual, artistic and social ideals and institutions which the members of the society profess and to which they strive to conform. In other words, culture has a dynamism. It grows and this growth is attained by culture processes. Culture processes and culture change go together. Change cannot be brought about by processes. The cultural growth as we have obtained today is through the medium of processes. Growth does not mean that culture gives away its continuity or persistence. When we talk about Indian culture we to say that the culture here undergoes transformation but it maintains its continuity. Hence, there is continuity and change. Kroeber has defined culture process as under:

> By process of culture we mean those factors which operate either toward the stabilization and preservation of cultures and their parts or toward growth and change. Changes, in turn, may consist either of increments, such as new developments, inventions and learned traits acquired from outside; or of losses and displacements.

What Kroeber calls social processes actually means direction of culture change. There are obviously two directions: one of stabilization and preservation and the other of change and growth. When there is preservation of culture it keeps the continuity of culture, and when there is change, new traits, complexes and patterns enter into the body of culture configuration. It is also possible that the persistences and changes in culture give rise to a new blend of culture. Culture processes take place when one generation handsover its culture to the new generation. While discussing processes we must assume that culture is acquired; it is learned. It is in this acquirement and learning that the culture grows. We shall here, first, discuss some major culture processes and then deal with the theories of culture growth.

Culture Processes

Enculturation

We have observed that culture and society are companion processes. Culture is the way of life of a people while society is an organized, interacting, aggregate of individuals who follow a given way of life. In other words, a society is composed of people, and the way people behave is culture. For instance, the husband and wife meet together and talk about household affairs. This is interaction, or in other words, society. The household affairs are a part of division of labour which is culture. Thus, society and culture are interwoven; however, for analytical purposes, both can be separated. It is in the society that we have social institutions, and economic and political organizations. These organizations provide continuity to society, which is maintained by enculturation. Soon after birth, the child learns the culture traits and complexes of his society. It is through the process of socialization that the whole body of traditions----economic, social, technological, religious, aesthetic and linguistic----is learnt by the child. In short, enculturation is a long process of learning.

The process of enculturation in social anthropology is what we call socialization in sociology. Socialization is a process by means of which men adjust to their fellows in society. It is through the process of learning that men become members of society. Herskovits, in his cultural anthropology, has defined enculturation as below:

> The aspects of the learning experience that mark off man from other creatures, and by means of which he achieves competence in his culture may be called enculturation.

Herskovits brings out the fact of conscious and unconscious conditioning. When a student meets his teacher in the market he expresses his respects by greeting him, which is an unconscious behaviour. Similarly, when a man starts eating, he does not decide it consciously that he would eat with his right hand. The behaviour here also is unconscious. But, in a rally, when a participant raises slogans, he does it consciously. We see that a person adopts the ways of the society both consciously and unconsciously. From the adaptation or adjustment to traditions and ways of life, he becomes a member of the society. Every human being goes through a process of enculturation, for without it he cannot live as a member of that society.

Herskovits argues that the process of enculturation is a process of adaptation. This process does not terminate at the close of infancy. As an individual continues through childhood through adolescence to adult status, he is continuously exposed to this process of learning, which can be said to end only with his death. He writes:

> The difference between the nature of the enculturative experience in the early years of life and later is that the range of conscious acceptance or rejections by an individual continuously increases as he grows older.

The fact is that with the increase in age, the man gradually becomes mature. In other words, on serious matters, he starts thinking consciously and accepts or rejects any aspect of society's culture. It is interesting to note that "the enculturation of the individual in the early years of his life is the prime mechanism making for cultural stability, while the process, as it operates on more mature folk, is highly important in inducing change". What is important is that human beings learn their cultures so well that most behaviours rarely rise to the level of consciousness. During childhood, everything that is referred to the child is unconsciously learnt by him or her. All this is below the level of conscious thought.

Culture is transmitted from generation to generation. The family norms are handedover from one generation to the next. Thus, in the process of culture transmission, enculturation is a basic process. In the present era of information technology (IT) enculturation has assumed new dimensions. The process has become intense and complex.

Acculturation

Kroeber has defined acculturation as below:

> Acculturation comprises those changes produced in a culture by the influence of another culture which result in an increased similarity of

the two. The influencing may be reciprocal or overwhelmingly one way. The resultant assimilation may proceed so far as the extinction of one culture by absorption. In the other, or other factors may intervene to counterbalance the assimilation and keep the cultures separate. The process of acculturation tends to be gradual rather than abrupt.

Herskovits considers acculturation as the strongest mechanism of culture change. Culture diffusion is also possible through acculturation. Sometimes students confuse diffusion as acculturation. In fact, both these processes are supplementary, as Herskovits observes:

> Diffusion is the study of achieved cultural transmission, while acculturation is the study of cultural transmission in process.

We shall take up the definition of diffusion a little later, suffice it to say at this stage that in all respects acculturation is a social process. Though acculturation tends to investigate historic facts, in the study of behaviour it remains restricted to the facts pertaining to the contemporary period only.

Perhaps, an authentic definition of acculturation is given by a committee formulated by the American Anthropological Association and consisted of Redfield, Herskovits and Linton. The definition reads as under:

> Acculturation comprehends those phenomena which result when groups of individuals having different cultures come into continuous first-hand contact, with subsequent changes in the original culture patterns of either or both groups.

The committee has not only defined acculturation, but also distinguished acculturation from cultural change. In fact, acculturation is only one aspect of culture change. The definition given by the committee is further interpreted by Kroeber. He says that the acculturation process has an effect on other cultures. This means that acculturation also affects the society which carries the culture. Kroeber further says:

> Viewed in this way it is evident that acculturation takes in a lot of meaning. It has, no doubt, been operative since there have been separate human cultures. Ninety-nine per cent of all acculturation must

lie in the past; and it involves the nature, the processes, and the patterns of culture as well as its changes.

Thus, the definitions of acculturation, as given by Herskovits and the American Anthropological Association, boil down to the fact that acculturation is the process through which modification in one culture is made by another culture. In the British social anthropology context, it could be said that acculturation processes are studied by ethnology. For instance, Rivers studied the Todas of Nilgiri hills of Tamil Nadu. In course of time, the Toda culture, and for that matter, the culture of any Indian or African tribe has been influenced by western civilization.

Acculturation has certain characteristic features. A few are noted below:

1. According to Linton, a very special aspect of acculturation is that it is always the impact of a dominant prestige-laden society which influences the backward people. Thus, acculturation studies the influence of a dominant culture on the subordinate culture. However, at least theoretically, it is not true. In practice, the culture of backward people could also influence the dominant groups.
2. Acculturation studies the changes which are almost invariably not spontaneous and automatic, but purposively directed or controlled, at least in part, by the superior society through political domination or market domination.
3. Acculturation has been studied as it is intended to work; namely, to result in ultimate disappearance of the minority, in its cultural and social fusion.

Some of the features of acculturation as stated above are drawn mainly from the studies undertaken during the last few decades, but in theory the process in neutral. It is more or less reciprocal. Kroeber, in this respect, observes:

> Each group of people is also likely to be developing new peculiarities even while it is taking over culture from the others. This is perhaps the most common form of acculturation: across a frontier that remains a frontier, although not a closed one.

Acculturation is a social process. It helps us to understand social change. Historically, it was started in 1935 by cultural anthropologists. Both historical and empirical facts are obtained through this process. It is found useful also in the fields of psychology and education. In the developing countries, acculturation studies are quite popular.

There have come about a large number of acculturation studies, which are for the most part, culture change studies. Jan Breman's study of tribals of South Gujarat, S.L. Doshi's study of Bhils, and Beteille's study of Sripuram village are examples of acculturation studies. These studies held out an exciting promise of showing how the wheels of culture change go round. One can see what people have been, what they were and what they are turning into, and why. It has been like catching the dynamics of culture change in the act, almost like setting up a laboratory. This is more or less true.

Culture Diffusion

Diffusion is a very popular process of social change. It is also defined as external change. When the culture of a society evolves some new inventions, a custom, or a trait and it is passed on to another culture, it is called diffusion. In diffusion there is bombardment of one culture on the other culture. The Britishers came to India as a colonial power. They had their culture. During the course of time, parts of their culture such as English language, steam power, dress patterns, etc., were passed on to the Indian culture. Some of the British culture traits were accepted, a few were rejected, and yet others were modified. This is culture diffusion. In another situation, the tribal society in India received culture traits, say, the mode of worship of the tribal society. This is another instance of culture diffusion. Basically, in culture diffusion, traits of one culture are transferred to another culture. There is inter-societal transformation. Diffusion, therefore, is a process which brings inter-societal change. Kroeber has defined diffusion as below:

> When something new has been evolved in a culture, whether a tool or an idea or a custom, there is a tendency for it to be passed on to the culture of another society. This is much like the passing on of culture to the younger generation within the evolving society, except for being foreign-directed instead of domestic. In other words, new culture is transmitted geographically as well as closnologically, in space as well as in time, by contagion as well as by repetition. The spread in area is generally called diffusion, and the internal handing on through time is called tradition.

Kroeber's approach to diffusion is important for the following points it makes:

(1) Culture has a space, i.e., it has geographical meaning.

(2) It has a time cover called chronology.

(3) It is different from tradition. If a custom or an idea is handed-over from one generation to another within a society, it is tradition. But if the custom or idea is given to another culture, that is, outside one's own culture, it is diffusion.

There are several other examples of culture diffusion today. In the present context of globalization, the role of diffusion has assumed a special significance. The *ghaghra* of India has been transmitted to Europe and the US. The transmission is like onslaught of innovations and, therefore, it is culture diffusion. But, an idea or custom that is passed on from one individual to another is not diffusion. Diffusion is always on a large scale. It the idea that is transmitted to masses of people belonging to other cultures, is called diffusion. Explaining the nature of diffusion, Kroeber observes:

> When an invention passes from the inventor to another individual, we call that it's successful cultural acceptance. Diffusion may be viewed as an extension of the process, on *a much larger scale*, by which an invention or innovation—or sometimes even an older culture trait---spreads from the society in which it originated to new societies and becomes established in their cultures.

Following are the characteristics of diffusion:

(1) Diffusion takes place between different societies. It is because of this that we call it inter-societal, or cross-cultural.

(2) Its spread goes to the physical space. In other words, culture diffusion takes into consideration a geographical space. If the dress pattern of the people of the plains is transmitted to the hills, it is called diffusion. Time or space is inherent to diffusion.

(3) Diffusion ends up in transformation. This transformation is observed in the receiving culture. If the Gonds begin to worship Hindu gods and goddesses, their culture experiences a new culture of worship.

It could be said that the conceptual utility of diffusion in the growth of culture was marginal only a few decades back. With the emergence of the global village, diffusion has assumed a special significance. There is a multi-way process in the present globalization context for culture transmission. Such a situation can only be explained by culture diffusion. The total part played by this process in human culture is almost incredibly great. This is quite corollary to what has been said before to the effect that all cultures are largely hybrid composites of material that once entered them from outside. Naively, human beings do not realize this to any great extent. It is of no advantage to a society, ordinarily, to have its members aware of the foreign source of most of their culture; nor is it a satisfaction to most individuals to be reminded of this debt to aliens. So, the fact tends to be forgotten perhaps more rapidly even than most events of history.

Integration

Integration became more relevant when after the Second World War several newly emerged Asian countries began to engage in nation-building exercises. These countries, for example, China, India, Japan and Indonesia, directed all their efforts to attain the status of a nation after their liberation. The task of nation-building could not have been fulfilled without going through the process of integration. The process also became important in India when the recommendations of the States Reorganization Commission were implemented. Let us look at the conceptual meaning of integration.

If we look at the structure of culture, we see that it is automatically integrated. At a superficial level culture appears to be haphazard. Historically, the origin of integration is what Lowie calls a "thing of shreds and patches" or a "planless hodge-podge". However, there is some kind of organic unity in a culture. Culture has a power of persistence. It always changes, but slowly, to suit the reformer. Every nation or tribe has its conservative party, whether it is so labelled or not.

Theoretically, culture has a great speciality. In a culture there are different culture traits. These traits maintain their identity and autonomy. But, functionally, they contribute their share to the attainment of the society's aims and objectives. Thus, each culture has its functional purposes and these are fulfilled by the culture traits. According to Herskovits, integration has two approaches: functional and configurational. The functional approach relates to the interrelationship among various elements in a culture. The configurational approach represents the psychological approach to cultural integration. Explaining these two approaches of culture, Herskovits writes:

> For the moment, we need to bear in mind that the problem of cultural integration presents two faces. One, the *functional* view attempts to study the interrelation between the various elements of a culture; the other, the *configurational* view represents the psychological approach to cultural integration, and seeks to discover the thread of aim, of satisfactions that give to the institutional unity the particular quality, the special 'feel' that everyone senses when he compares one culture with another.

Assimilation

When the social processes reach a high degree of integration, it takes the form of assimilation. It is something like the biological system of food assimilation in which complex food materials are broken into simpler substances and assimilated in the body. At the stage of integration, the culture traits, quite like food materials, maintain their identity but finally in assimilation, lose their identity. This is a very complex process and hardly any society reaches the stage of perfect assimilation. In assimilation, the people and their culture do not maintain their individual identities.

It was in the fifties that the US society was near assimilation. But soon it became clear that each linguistic group and nationality maintained its separate identity. In our country too, in view of multi-ethnicities, multi-languages, multi-regions and multi-identities, integration can be attained only in a limited way. We can maintain our ethnic identities and at the same time identify ourselves with secularism, socialism, democracy and scientific ethics. We could also follow a common economic system and mode of administration. In this kind of integration, on one hand, the different aspects of culture maintain their identity and autonomy and on the other hand, fall into the national mainstream.

Obviously, assimilation is a higher social process of integration. This is a stage which is very difficult to attain. Social anthropologists have talked about tribal assimilation. G.S. Ghurye in his book, *The Scheduled Tribes* argues that some Indian tribes have taken the path of assimilation. Accordingly, some aspects of tribal life have been assimilated in the caste Hindu culture. Ghurye has devoted two full chapters to tribal assimilation in the Hindu culture. In the same way, N.K.

Bose in his book *The Structure of Hindu Society* (1975) maintains that there is a specific method of Hindu culture to absorb the tribals within its fold. Generally, however, it has been observed that the process of assimilation is very complex and perfect assimilation seems almost impossible.

Invention

Kroeber has given a prominent place to invention and discovery in his analysis of cultural change. He says that though both these aspects of culture bring change in a society, they are different in their approach. Discovery is limited to the unpremeditated finding of something new, whereas invention might be defined as purposeful discovery. Discovery is accidental, the culture trait already exists and it is by chance that we find it. Invention is altogether different. We set out to find and something and that something is found out. This is invention. Differentiating discovery and invention, Herskovits writes:

> Although the casual discovery of a new food or material may lead to its use, if the foods already utilized are insufficient and there is a need for new sources of supply, a powerful spur is added to curiosity, and purposeful search is likely to ensue. Necessity is indeed often the mother of invention and is likewise the parent of discovery as well. With the strengthening of this factor of need we pass more and more definitely into the sphere of invention, in which the need is met not by the appropriation to use of hitherto unused thing, but by the creation of something new and fundamentally better.

Herskovits relies more on invention as the process of cultural change. The inventor is a person who invents a new machine, a new mechanical process and a new technology. This results in a new economic system; it devises a new political scheme, or works out a new conception of the universe. The inventor in this sense is a theorist, a philosopher, a visionary, or, with less complimentary connotation, a revolutionist.

Invention has a functional role also. Ethnologists have devised the method of counting descent on one side of the family, or have developed classificatory systems of relationship terminology. Some cultural anthropologists have explained the role of invention in the spread of culture traits. From all considerations, invention stimulates cultural change. Ogburn, in his theory of culture lag, has brought out a large number of culture traits resulting from invention of a technology.

Theories of Culture Growth

Candidly it must be said that social anthropology is not rich in its theoretical content. In this respect, sociology has done much better in the field of theory building. There are social anthropologists who have brought out some conceptual constructs. In the case of India, nothing substantial has been done as far theory is concerned. Even the former Lucknow School of Anthropology, headed by D.N. Majumdar, has not been able to give any substantial concepts. Social anthropology in India is actually ethnology. Most of the social anthropologists have done ethnology. And amazingly enough the 'rich' ethnography has increasingly become irrelevant in the wake of modernization taking place among the tribals. The American cultural anthropologists also have not been able to contribute much to the theoretical stock of anthropology.

Whatever little theoretical contribution that we find in anthropology is through the development of theories on culture growth. There are several theories which explain the diffusion and spread of culture traits. Culture, as we find it today, has not grown or developed overnight. It has taken thousands of years. From cro-magnon man to the present man millions of years have passed. Each generation has contributed something to the stock of culture. Culture processes, all through history, have contributed to the development of culture.

Systematic investigation of the problem of cultural transmission or cultural borrowing dates from about the beginning of the 20th century. In other words, the culture growth theories have taken about hundred years in their construction. Before that only ethnographic data were generated. Whatever theories of culture growth we find today may be divided into three classes as under:

(1) Pan-Egyptian or Heliolithic Theory
(2) German-Austrian Culture Historical Theory
(3) Functional Theory

We now proceed to these theories in some details. The idiom of these theories is diffusion. In other words, culture growth all over the world has been explained with reference to culture diffusion.

Pan-Egyptian or Heliolithic Theory

The 19th century in Europe has been a century of evolution studies. It was in 1817 that Lewis H. Morgan's book, *Ancient Society*, got published. It is said to be a classical work on social evolution. The book starts with these words:

> The great antiquity of mankind on earth has been conclusively established... mankind are now known to have existed in Europe in the glacial period... and even back of its commencement, with every probability of their origination in a prior geological age.

Tracing the origin of mankind, Morgan establishes that man passed through three stages of evolution: (1) savage, (2) barbarian, and (3) civilized. He further informs that "it can now be asserted upon convincing evidence that savagery preceded barbarism in all the tribes of mankind, as barbarism is known to have preceded civilization. The history of the human race is one in source, one in experience, and one in progress".

Besides Morgan there are other social anthropologists also who took a similar position. In their writings they have conveyed in categorical terms that evolution has moved through lower to higher stages of development in obtaining the present state. It is on the basis of such data that we discuss the evolutionary theory of mankind. There first came a group of evolutionists who developed their theory on the basis of culture diffusion. In culture diffusion, as stated earlier, there is inter-societal or inter-cultural change. This group of evolutionists is called pan-Egyptian or the heliolithic school which consisted of G.E. Smith, W.J. Perry, and their followers. "It was last on the anthropological scene and first off it, and the controversies it engendered, as heated as any in the history of anthropology."

The pan-Egyptian school was founded by Grafton Elliot Smith. Basically, he was an eminent anatomist whose work on the brain, and whose studies in paleoanthropology, brought him great and deserved distinction. He decided to study the brains of Egyptian mummies. Actually he undertook a visit to Egypt, where he was much impressed by the Egyptian civilization. He studied the culture traits of Egypt and extended his study to the Mediterranean Basin, Africa, the Near East and India.

Perry followed Smith. He presented his findings in his book, *The*

Children of the Sun. He established on the strength of his data that culture traits diffused from Egypt to the Mediterranean Basin, Africa and India. The people of Egypt are thus the children of the sun. What Smith, Perry and other evolutionary social anthropologists have established is that culture change has come through borrowings. In other words, the culture traits of Egypt have been diffused into other parts of Asia. This school argues that there has not been multiple origins and diffusions of culture traits. Everything has been borrowed from Egypt. It is because of this hypothesis that this British school is also called pan-Egyptian school.

The findings of the pan-Egyptian school are not without controversy. True, a large number of culture traits from Egypt have travelled or diffused to other countries but this does not mean that mankind invents as little and copies as much as this extreme diffusionist position would hold. Commenting on the limited use of the findings of the diffusion school, Herskovits writes:

> Conversely, because we accept the phenomenon of borrowing, this does not mean that it must be regarded as the sole mechanism whereby culture change is effected. It was a neglect to take into account the inventiveness of man, no less than the failure to recognize factors of time and space the worldwide diffusion of Egyptian culture...

The pan-Egyptian theory, in short, establishes that the culture the world over has been diffused from Egypt. There has always been culture borrowing from this great civilization. Such a theory could not stay to the test of time, and soon it fell into disrepute.

German-Austrian Culture Historical Theory

The German-Austrian Cultural Historical school argues that culture has spread in a historical way. This school was founded by F. Graebner and E. Foy, who published their research articles in the Austrian journal *Anthropos*, under the leadership of Pater W. Schmidt and his associates, W. Koppers and M. Gusinde. The school has become one of the leading schools of anthropological thought in the continent of Europe, but has never achieved any degree of acceptance in the English-speaking anthropological circles.

The point of view of the German-Austrian school is quite sophisticated. "Its carefully drawn criteria for judging the value of assumed borrowings, its insistence on caution in the use of source materials, the care with which its definitions are drawn and the wealth of its documentation are fully in accord with the demands of scholarship." For these reasons, this school received wide acceptance. The culture historical theory is based on a mystical view of nature of life and human experience. It employs a terminology which differs fundamentally from rationality. It uses a vocabulary of common anthropological thought. Schmidt, methodologically, divides all cultures and explains their identity through diffusion. "Like all ethnographers Schmidt recognizes the need to understand the meaning of primitive life to those who live it and, more importantly, to those who in past ages lived it. This we do, he tells us, by recourse to the psychological principle of empathy, whereby one projects himself into the psychic state of the person with whom he is in relation."

Graebner is another scholar belonging to this school. He has adopted a methodology to study culture growth by which he argues that historically the cultural traits have diffused from one culture to another. The cultural historical school, quite like the pan-Egyptian school, has also been criticized. It is alleged that the school has employed a mystical approach to the fundamentals of human cultural experiences. Its hypothesis are extremely untenable. However, the criteria for assessing culture contacts make the contributions to the school quite significant. Besides, the school laid an emphasis on diffusion. It was a healthy reaction to the earlier evolution and sociological approaches to the study of culture. It should also be said that Graebner, Schmidt and Koppers carried out rich field studies.

Functional Theory

Herskovits says that the functional theory should not be termed as functional. It is, in reality, a historical approach, coupled with field research. It tried to reconstruct culture history on a world level. It is often associated with F. Boas. Besides Boas, his students Kroeber, Lowie, Colden Weiser, Spier and others also conducted field studies. This school is composed of anti-diffusianist functionalists. Normally, it is identified with Malinowski. The interest of the functionalists is in culture integration. Functionalists are fundamentally concerned only with the understanding of how each aspects of a culture is related to every other aspect.

Concluding Observations

As we said at the outset, culture is acquired; it is handedover from one generation to the other. It is an ongoing process. The dynamics of culture are kept alive by several processes such as exclusion, acculturation, diffusion, integration and assimilation. The social processes provide opportunities to a culture to add innovations within its folds. Then, a few aspects of that culture become oblivious. The wheel of culture, therefore, continues to move from one generation to another. The answer to the question as to how culture grew and spread has been given by several authors. These answers mainly fall into the evolutionary school, culture historical school and functional school. These schools include a large number of social anthropologists. All these attempts are in operation right from the 19th century. There has always been borrowing and diffusion of culture. Today, at the beginning of 21st century, it is difficult indeed to present a precise and clear position of culture growth and spread. This has been very pointedly put by Herskovits:

> In summary, the search for 'pure' cultures, 'uncontaminated' by outer contact, has been almost entirely given over, while the hypothetical nature of reconstruction of unrecorded history has come to be clearly understood as an exercise in probability. The use of historical documents and the field study of peoples whose cultures are changing under contact have, above all, demonstrated that culture change is a single problem, whether studied in process or through the analysis of accomplished cultural facts in terms of the distribution of variant forms of the same element.

Further Readings

Herskovits, Melville, *Cultural Anthropology*, Oxford and IBH Publishing Co., New Delhi, 1955.

Kroeber, A.L., *Anthropology*, London, 1948.

8

Social Structure and Structuralism

Social Structure

E.E. Evans-Pritchard, the doyen of social anthropology, once observed:

> The people who live in any society may be unaware, or only dimly aware, that it has a structure. It is the task of the social anthropologist to reveal it.

Evans-Pritchard was a British anthropologist. His social anthropology was mainly concerned with the study of social structure. On the other hand, G.P. Murdock, an american anthropologists who titled his classical book as *Social Structure*, discussed everything but social structure. His concern was culture, and not social structure. Social anthropology is very rich in ethnographic data. If we look into social anthropology in India, we find that whatever material we have concerning the tribals is ethnography. In a broad way, it could be said in a limited sense, social social anthropology in India is essentially ethnography, out of which social anthropology or social structure is made.

Indian sociology is far ahead of social anthropology so far as the delineation of social structure is concerned. In sociology much has been done to construct formulations about social structure and social system. In anthropology, perhaps for the first time, an effort was made by S.F. Nadel to build a theory of social structure. Nadel very rightly observes in the preliminaries of his book, *The Theory of Social Structure* that he wanted to call this book *Towards a Theory of Social Structure*. Such an observation clearly shows that building of social structure as a theory was made only in the 1950s.

Meaning of Social Structure

Compared to sociology it is easy in social anthropology to bring out the meaning and definition of social structure. There are reasons for this. First, social anthropology stresses on studies of small-scale localities. It is easy methodologically to manage smaller units. These units can be studied by field observations. In a village or a tribal society, most inhabitants know each other personally; they participate in, and reproduce, forming a social structure characterized by face-to-face contact. In this kind of setting, it is possible for the anthropologists to become acquainted with most of the locality's inhabitants in the course of their fieldwork. Second, the local society may be studied as though it were self-sustaining. Most of the activities of the inhabitants take place locally, many of their needs are satisfied locally, and the local community is being reproduced and maintained over a period of time. It is thereby possible to use the methodological tools of anthropology for studying the interrelationship among different social institutions within the framework of local communities.

It must, however, be said that local communities or small-scale societies always remain self-sustaining and unchanging. Though in the wake of directed development programmes, accelerating markets and globalization, these societies are also changing, the core aspect of these societies resists change. And, it is this nature of simple societies that provides continuity. It is this aspect of continuity and change which prompts the social anthropologists to construct the theory of social structure.

Several attempts have been made to define the concept of social structure. Thomas Hylland Eriksen, while taking into consideration the definitions given by Radcliffe-Brown, Raymond Firth, S.F. Nadel and others, gives a tentative definition of social structure. This will provide us a clue to go back and explore the meaning and definition of social structure. He defines the concept as under:

> Social structure may thus, be perceived as the matrix of society, emptied of humans; the totality of duties, rights, division of labour, norms, social control, etc., abstracted from ongoing social life.

It seems that Eriksen's definition of social structure draws heavily on the definition given by Radcliffe-Brown which runs as below:

> The actual relations of Tom, Dick and Harry or the behaviour of Jack and Jill may go down in our field notebooks and may provide illustrations for a general description. But what we need for scientific purposes is an account for the form of the structure.

Social structure does not stand for names, places and other particularities. It is independent of individuals. On the basis of these empirical realities abstractions are made which, in turn, go towards the making of a social structure. M.N. Srinivas, in his book, *The Remembered Village*, quite particular accounts about his stay in Rampur village. All these helped him develop concepts about village life. His study of the religion among Coorgs also helped him build the concept of sanskritization. Sanskritization is not social structure, but an aspect of social structure. Our emphasis is that in the construction of social structure we remove the names of the persons and events, and make an abstraction. This abstraction helps us construct social structure. It is on this strategy of the construction of social structure that Radcliffe-Brown talks about the form of the social structure. Eriksen, therefore, says that social structure is abstracted from ongoing social life. It is to be noted that in the framing of social structure unnecessary details about the functioning of society are deleted. Social structure consists of the abstractions of empirical reality that are used for comparative analysis. Thus, in view of the definitions given above, we can infer that:

1. Social structure is an abstraction.
2. It does not give details of particularities.
3. It is used for wider comparisons.

Raymond Firth's definition of social structure has emerged out of the empirical reality of African tribes. Making a differentiation between social structure and social organization, he says:

> There is distinction between social structure and social organization. The structure is the established pattern of rules, customs, statuses and social institutions. Social organization, on the other hand, is defined as the dynamic aspect of structure, in other words, what people actually do, their decisions and patterns of action within the framework of the structure.

Firth argues that social structure consists of the standards of behaviour. These standards are actually patterns. Patterns and standards do not often change; they are normally invariant. The social organization is always changing. Nadel comes closer to Firth and Radcliff-Brown when he says that the concept of social structure should not be used as a blanket term. Its meaning is technical and specific. He has defined social structure as a precise concept of social anthropology.

Accordingly, the society is a whole. It has sub-divisions. These sub-divisions are the parts of society and these parts are interrelated. In other words, the arrangement of the interrelations of parts is the social structure. Taking into consideration the whole society and the interrelationship of the parts, Nadel defines social structure in the following way:

> Structure indicates an ordered arrangement of parts, which can be treated as transposable, being relatively invariant, while the parts themselves are variable.

Nadel's definition brings out the following features of a social structure:

1. Social structure is an arrangement of the different parts of the society.
2. The interrelations among the parts are invariant, though the parts themselves may vary.

Functionalists have defined social structure in a different way. They relate structure with function. It would be quite interesting to discuss the structural functional analysis as mentioned by Talcott Parsons. Parsons views structure differently. He says that the parts of structure, namely, economy, education, polity, and the like, function in such a way that they maintain the whole system. They keep the system going. Instead of social structure, the sociologists, therefore, use the term 'social system'. Social system may be defined as "a set of social relations which are regularly actualized and thus reproduced as a system through interaction". The difference between social system and social structure is of degree of emphasis. Social anthropologists stress on parts and say that the parts have arrangement of interrelations. They further argue that the parts are more or less invariants. But sociologists do not focus on parts. Instead they concentrate on the functions of the parts in terms of the maintenance of the system.

Social anthropologists look at social structure as providing continuity to the society. It is because of this that they talk about the *form* of social structure. Radcliffe-Brown provides a full chapter on social structure in his book, *Structure and Function in Primitive Society* (1964). In it he argues that social structure is concerned with persistent social groups, such as nations, tribes and clans, which retain their continuity, their identity as individual groups, in spite of changes in their membership. To make the observations of Radcliffe-Brown clear, we would say that in a social structure there are different forms of social relations. There are kinship relations between father and son, or sister and brother, or uncle and his nephew. In a social structure, what is important is the form, which constitutes the structure.

In the process of social change there is change in the actual structure, but the general structural form remains relatively constant over a longer or shorter period of time. Stressing on this general form of social structure, which remains constant, Radcliffe-Brown writes:

> Thus, the actual relations of persons and groups of persons change from year to year, or even from day to day. New members come into a community by birth or immigration; others go out of it by death or emigration. There are marriages and divorces. Friends may become enemies, or enemies may make peace and become friends. But while the actual structure changes in this way, the general structural form may remain relatively constant over a longer or shorter period of time.

Characteristics of Social Structure

We have discussed the meaning and definitions of social structure in the preceding pages. Sociologists have worked on social structure quite elaborately. They prefer to use term 'social system' instead of 'social structure'. However, both sociologists and social anthropologists define social structure in terms of the interrelations between the individuals and functioning of these ordered interrelationships in the maintenance of the society. The definitions given by various social anthropologists help us to bring out certain characteristics of social structure. We enumerate these as under:

(i) Abstraction of empirical reality

Empirical reality has a large number of details about the functioning of society. The construction of social structure removes unnecessary details and brings out abstractions. For instance, there are innumerable caste and tribal groups in India. Each caste has its locus and functioning. The tribes also have their own identity. In the formation of social structure we delete the names and specialities of each caste and tribal group. Instead we use the terms 'caste' and 'tribe'. These are abstractions.

(ii) Exists independently of the individuals

In a social structure, individuals do not matter; they come and go. In our country we had Gandhi, Nehru and Vinoba Bhave. They have left this world. Social structure is independent of any individual—big or small. It is concerned with the interactions between statuses. The family or the university is a social structure notwithstanding the persons who are members of these structures. Radcliffe-Brown, as mentioned earlier, very rightly says that Jack and Jill come and go but the structures continue.

(iii) Persistent social group

Milton Singer and Bernard Cohn edited a book on India entitled, *Structure and Change in Indian Society* (1968). The contributors to this rather big volume discuss caste, joint family and language as components of social structure in India. The editors argue that the speciality of the Indian social structure is not only its change but also its continuity. Thus, when we talk of social structure, we mean persistent social interactions of varying statuses.

(iv) Retains continuity

Throughout their discussions Radcliffe-Brown, Firth and Nadel insist that there may be a change in social structure but there is an "ordered arrangements of parts" which are relatively invariant. Interestingly, the parts themselves are variable but the nature of the social structure is invariable. This invariability of the parts of ordered arrangements gives continuity to social structure. The members of a society are free to have social interactions as they like. There are a wide range of choices. But, the established institutionalized norms change little. They are invariant.

(v) Matrix (Origin) of society

Eriksen has defined social structure rather elaborately. He says that social structure is the origin of society. It is the matrix of society. It is the sum total of all the statuses of society. It contains norms, values, social control, polity, etc. There is difference in social structure and social organization. Social organization is the society in function, it is an ongoing life. Social structure is the abstraction of society. Man may come and go but the structure remains the same.

(vi) Not concerned with the particular or unique

One very important aspect of social structure is that it does not relate to the unusual or unique. The mythological story of *Mahabharata* says that Kansa, who was Krishna's mother's brother, killed his own sister's children. But, the general status of mother's brother is not that of Kansa. Social structure is concerned, therefore, with the usual or general and not specific or particular.

(vii) Having spatial dimensions

Social structure is invariant and continuous. But it has its spatial aspects also; it is related to place. Social structure is not the same all over the world. The kind of social structure that we find in India is different from that in the US. Each space has its particularity, its own history, its own experiences. Therefore, the nature of social structure varies from one locality to another.

(viii) Connected with social personality

Radcliffe-Brown mentions the connections of social structure with social personality. "Every human being living in society is two things: he is an individual and also a person. As an individual, he is a biological organism, a collection of a vast number of molecules organized in a complex structure, within which as long as it persists, there occur physiological and psychological actions and reactions, processes and changes. Human beings as individuals are objects of study for physiologists and psychologists. The human being as a person is a complex of social relationships. As a person, the human being is the object of study for the social anthropologists. We cannot study persons except in terms of social structure, nor can we study social structure, except in terms of the persons who are the units of which it is composed." In other words, there is a close nexus between individual and social structure.

Thus, social structure has almost occupied a place of theory in social anthropology. It includes various institutions of society such as family, marriage, kinship, religion, custom and law, primitive economy, politics, etc. These institutions are based on social organization. Eriksen argues that social organization carries within it the social structure of society. In a broader way it is said that social structure is like an organism which has different parts to maintain the body system. Or, in simple words, it is like a huge building which has different walls, windows, doors and a roof. But such a kind of explanation of a social structure is very naive. As a matter of fact, it is an abstraction of the empirical reality of all these institutions. Social structure dwells on established patterns of rules, customs, statutes, and social institutions. It is the arrangement of different parts of the society whereas social organization is the dynamic aspect of social structure.

Finally, it would be interesting to refer to the question which has been raised by Radcliffe-Brown in his analysis of social structure. He asks: "How do structural systems persist? What are the mechanisms which maintain a network of social relations in existence, and how do they work?" Radcliffe-Brown himself answers the question:

> Morals, law, etiquette, religion, government and education are all parts of the complex mechanism by which a social structure exists and persists. If we take up the structural point of view, we study these things, not in abstraction or isolation, but in their direct and indirect relations to social structure, that is, with reference to the way in which they depend upon, or affect the social relations between persons and groups of persons.

Approaches to the Study of Social Structure

In one of the earlier chapters we have mentioned that social anthropology has different traditions in England, France and USA. These varying traditions have varying approaches to social structure. Here, we shall discuss the concept of social structure as is employed in America, England and France.

America

In America, there is no social anthropology as we understand in India.

In our country, we study social structure with a bias of social structure and social system. Analysis of culture is secondary for us. It is interesting to find that we have in our country a national debate on the form of Indian culture. One group argues for the formulation of a composite culture which could accommodate multiplicity of languages, castes, regions and ethnicities. The other group which consists of right-wing politicians, advocate for one people, one culture, one language theory. When such a debate is heatedly going on in the country, the textbooks of social anthropology do not even mention anything about this controversy. This clearly shows that India's social anthropology has no emphasis to place on culture analysis. We are only involved in the analysis of social structure, that is, caste, primitive tribes and rural life.

The Americans stand for cultural anthropology. G.P. Murdock, in his *Social Structure* (1949), has classified a number of tribal groups on the basis of cultural attributes. In one of his observations Murdock argues that anthropology needs to study the cultural aspects of a primitive group. He concludes that culture can be seen at two levels—generational and spatial. Thus, for Americans, social structure is basically culture structure. We have noticed that Herskovits very often talks about structure of culture.

England

British anthropologists have a strong bias for the study of various components of social structure, namely, caste, class, kinship, marriage and community. They study culture which is the result of social structure. For them, the study of social structure is primary. The theory of social structure developed by British anthropologists is different from that of the Americans. We have discussed Radcliffe-Brown, Nadel and others in this respect. M.N. Srinivas, S.C. Dube and Andre Beteille who have worked in the field of social anthropology have actually dealt with caste, class, village and traditions. The earlier social anthropologists such as Hutton, Risely and O'Malley have also studied social structure within the domain of social anthropology.

France

The concept of social structure as developed in France is altogether different. Among the advocates of social structure in France may be included Sartre, Edmund Husserl, Ferdinand Saussure, Claude Levi-

Strauss and Louis Althusser. Their interpretations draw heavily from linguists who are influenced by the wave of post-modernization. Social structure in France has been developed as a theory of structuralism.

Structuralism

The New Theoretical Aspects of Social Structure

A new French structural school has emerged in the European continent which is dominated by French structuralism. Among its proponents are prominently included Claude Levi-Strauss, Ferdinand Saussure, Ronald Barthes, Maurice Godelier, Louis Althusser and Nicos Paulantzas. The theory of structuralism has come about in Europe as a reaction to Sartre's humanism, especially existentialism of philosophy, and novelist Jean Paul Sart and also Husserl's phenomenology. Social anthropology in Europe means structuralism. The structuralists do not discuss much about social structure; instead, they talk about structure. Structuralism is also in vogue in South America, Italy and the Iberian peninsula, and partly in Belgium and the Netherlands. French structuralism dominates in all these parts of the world. In India, structuralism was initiated by Louis Dumont. He was also French and is known for his structural theory propounded in his classical work on caste system called *Homo Hierarchicus.*

What is Structuralism?

Recently, George Ritzer has published *Postmodern Social Theory* (1997) in which he has defined afresh structuralism in view of the new developments in this theory. He writes:

> At its most general level structuralism can be defined as the effort to uncover the general structures that underlay human activity.

Ritzer has been quite analytical in bringing out the major features of structuralism. The movement for structuralism started some time during the sixties. In a period of about four decades, French structuralism has witnessed two major trends: (i) social structure influenced by Durkheim and Mauss, and (ii) social structure influenced by linguistics. These two varieties borrow much from French linguists, social anthropologists and sociologists. The critics of structuralism allege that the French structuralism is nothing but a philosophical conjecture which has taken different dimensions: (1) Saussure's linguistic structuralism, (2) Levi-Strauss' structuralism, (3) structural Marxism, and (4) above all, Indian structuralism based on caste, ideology and values.

Why Structuralism?

It is logical to ask: What factors in the European continent influenced the emergence of structuralism? To answer this question we should begin with the observation that world sociology as we have find it today, including that of the US, is highly influenced by European sociology. Some of the European social thinkers such as Habermas, Lyotard, Baudrilard, Foucault and Bourdieu have taken a new approach towards the understanding of society. Structuralism is one of the recent efforts to construct a theory. In the following paragraphs, we discuss some of the factors which are responsible for the emergence of structuralism:

(i) Denial of Sartre's Existentialism

Sartre was a French philosopher. In his earlier work he focused on the individual level, especially on individual freedom. He adhered to the view that people are not subject to any social loss. Or, a man cannot justify his actions by reference to anything outside himself. Sartre argued that the individual is free. His existence is defined by and through his own acts. In other words, one is what one does. This is the crux of Sartre's existentialism. He attacks the sociologist's view of social structure which is argued to be objective. For him, "people are free, they are responsible for everything they do, they have no excuses, if they do wrong".

Thus, the emergence of structuralism in France is a reaction to the existentialism of Sartre---a denial of it.

(ii) Humanism

Yet another reason for the rise of French structuralism is Sartre's humanism. In his later work, he provided a critique of dialectical reason as he was against Marxism. The Marxists emphasized the role of power in social structure. This was not acceptable to Sartre. He contested it. Through the predominance of individual he pleaded for humanism. Structuralism, therefore, has also come about as a revolt against humanism, that is, protecting the freedom of the individual.

Structuralism that we find in various forms, has resulted out of different intellectual and historical conditions which prevailed in Europe. As a matter of fact, social anthropology in Europe since its beginning and particularly after the post-war period was strongly associated with structuralism. The emergence of structuralism is basically against Sartre's existentialism and humanism. In our country admittedly, structuralism came as a reaction and revolt to structural-functional analysis. Functionalism in India first came through the influence of Malinowski and Radcliffe-Brown, that is, British social anthropology; later on it influenced Indian social anthropology through functionalism of Merton and Parsons. This kind of British-American structure functionalism was opposed by structuralism of Louis Dumont.

French structuralism was influenced by phenomenology also. Edmund Husserl, who had a great influence on Derrida, was the leading phenomenologist. Though he does not have any direct influence on structuralism, he created a favourable situation for the development of the structural theory. Husserl was struggling to study the basic structures of human consciousness. He was committed to penetrating the various layers constructed by actors in the real world to get to the essence of the structure of consciousness. His interest has been to find out the pure form of consciousness stripped of all biographical and cultural content. Ritzer has defined the structure of consciousness as given by Husserl:

> For Husserl, consciousness was not a thing or a place but a process. Consciousness was found not in the head of the actor but in the relationship between the actor and the objects in the world. For him consciousness is always something of some object. Consciousness is found in the relationship: it is not interior to the actor; it is relational.

What Husserl means by consciousness is that is establishes a relationship between the actor and the object. According to him, consciousness is a process that gives meaning to objects. For instance, an actor develops a consciousness that bureaucracy is corrupt. This consciousness is about the object, that is, bureaucracy. Further, the actor develops another consciousness that women are good managers of an industrial concern. This is again a consciousness about the concern as an object. Tomorrow, the consciousness may change and the actor might say that bureaucracy is hard working, it is goal-oriented. Further, he may develop a consciousness that women turn out to be bad managers. Thus, consciousness is a process and relational between actor and object.

Husserl's phenomenology contributed a lot to the formation of structuralism. Husserl was basically a humanist and existentialist but he does talk about the structure of human consciousness which is situated in the structure of society.

Varieties of Structuralism

We have mentioned earlier that French structuralism has some varieties. These can be listed as below:

(1) Saussure's linguistic structuralism
(2) Levi-Strauss' structuralism
(3) Structural Marxism
(4) Louis Dumont's structuralism

In the following paragraph, we will describe the above varieties in some detail:

Saussure's Linguistic Structuralism

Initially social structure was explained with reference to social and cultural anthropology. When the French anthropologists entered the arena of structuralism, there appeared a shift in the whole concept of structuralism. Now language became a method of explaining social structure. The shift from social to linguistic structures is part of what has come to be known as the linguistic turn which dramatically altered the nature of social sciences. A large number of social scientists shifted from social structure or from individual social beings to language or more generally the science of various sorts.

Structuralism emerged from diverse developments in various fields. But, the source of modern structuralism and its strongest bastion to this day is linguistics. The propounder of linguistic structuralism is the Swiss linguist Ferdinand Saussure. For our purposes two aspects of Saussure's work are important. First, he gave a distinction between langue and parole. This distinction is made by saying that langue is the formal grammatical system of language. It is the system of phonic elements. This is, in other words, grammatology. It is the theoretical science of writing. It views language as a general or abstract system.

Saussure defined parole "as a speech which is expressed by word of mouth. It is the way in which speakers, on a day-to-day basis use language to express themselves". A linguist must focus on language, the formal system of language, not on the subjective terms in which it is used by the actor.

Langue, in fact, is used as a system of signs. When a person speaks camel, the word is a sign which indicates an animal. Camel itself is not an animal but it provides a sign, that is, the word 'camel', to explain it. "A sign can be seen as a whole, a structure which is composed as a *signifier*---the sound image that the recipient hears when a word is spoken, and a *signified*---what is sound image is to indicate." For instance, I meet you in the street and say that a camel is going. In this case, *I* is the *signifier* and the word *camel* is *signified*. This gives you the sign image of the camel that is an animal. In other words, the signifier plus signified structure or compose the sign. Viewed from this perspective sign is a structure. Saussure is not only interested in the signifier and the signified but also in their relationship to one another. To repeat the above example, *I*---the signifier and *camel*---the signified are important but still more important is the relationship between *I* and *you*. Saussure was little interested in the referent, the thing being referred to because it was extra-linguistic. For him, the relationship between *you* and *me* is important. Camel is only a reference. Saussure argues that language is a "close system in which all parts are interrelated. Meanings, the mind, and ultimately the social word are shaped by the structure of language". Language serves a model for all aspects of human life.

There are other linguists also who have contributed to the development of structuralism. Jakobson worked on language for two decades from 1920s to 1930s. Quite like Saussure Jakobson also argued that meaning in language is arbitrary and socially defined. According to him, there is no necessary connection between signifier and signified. However, he identified 'binary opposition' in his analysis of language, what has come to be seen as the elementary structure of meaning by many subsequent structuralists.

Louis Dumont has also employed the term 'binary opposition' when he discusses the purity and pollution aspects of caste. According to Jakobson, the hierarchical and dualistic contrast of like with unlike is regarded as the key to hidden semantic structure, in language and in culture generally. "Binary opposition is one of the brain's most basic operations; it is a deep and primeval structuring principle of culture." We give below some binary oppositions, for example:

Male	:	Female
Outside	:	Inside
High	:	Low
Light	:	Dark
Cooked	:	Raw
Grain for eating	:	Grain for saving
That which is fertilizing	:	That which can be fertilized
Weaving-loom wall	:	Door wall

Saussure and Jakobson are considered to be the main architects of linguistic structuralism. In our country, however, no effort has been made so far to apply linguistic structuralism in the study of our primitives.

Levi-Strauss' Structuralism

Claude Levi-Strauss is said to be the father of structuralism. He is the person who has broadened this concept to include all forms of communication within the framework of structuralism. According to him, "structuralism includes a wide range of social phenomena as systems of communication, kinship system and exchange of spouses". He further says:

> The real structure is the model, or perhaps the mind.

> *Claude Levi-Strauss* (b. 1908) is the father of structuralism. His variety of structuralism is based on how the mind works. He is the expounder of the concept of binary oppositions. The mind of man works in such a way that he thinks about binary oppositions. Strauss argues that there are abstract models of thought or formats in the mind of man. He has been criticized for taking such a position in defining social structure in terms of models of thought or formats of thought. Despite this criticism Levi-Strauss comes out as the most influential anthropologist from the period after Malinowski and Radcliffe-Brown, especially in France and other American countries. He has contributed immensely to the explaination of the structures of kinship.

Strauss' definition of structure is simple. He argues that a social structure is not a reality which can directly be seen. But it is a reality that exists beyond the visible reality. The function of the structure constitutes the underlying logic of the system which can be explained by the apparent reality.

Strauss has developed binary oppositions out of the data which he gathered from the field. He asserts that the "man organizes the world in contrasting pairs and develops coherent systems of relationship from such a starting point". The central element in Levi-Strauss' perspective is the idea that "all kinship systems are elaborations on four fundamental kin relationships: brother-sister, husband-wife, father-son and mother's brother-sister's son". He regards this as the elementary social structure.

Structuralism, other than linguistic structuralism, is associated with Levi-Strauss. He is credited to have made an original attempt at theoretical synthesis in the 20th century anthropology. His work in elementary and complex structures in kinship is unparalleled. Finally, it must also be said that Strauss was greatly influenced by Malinowski and Radcliffe-Brown.

Structural Marxism

Marx has been reinterpreted by French structuralists. He advocated the theory of social structure. In all his works he has argued that "structure consists of visible relations". The new interpretation of Marxism also accepts social structure but differs in that structure is hidden in relations. It is this hidden logic which differentiates the doctrines of Marxism and structuralism. However, most importantly, both structuralism and structural Marxism reject empiricism and accept a concern for the underlying invisible structures. Pointing to this difference, Godelier writes:

> What both structuralists and Marxists reject are the empiricist definitions of what constitutes a social structure.

Both Marx and Levi-Strauss agree that social structure is not a reality that is directly visible and so directly observable, but a lever of reality that exists beyond the visible relations between men and the functioning of which constitutes the underlying logic of the system.

The apparent social relations are explained through the hidden structure.

Godelier has followed the Marxian approach. In his analysis of structuralism he goes beyond Marxism. He argues that what we see and observe is not the real social structure. It is deeper in the mind and needs to be explored for understanding the social reality. He says:

> What is visible is a reality conceding another, deeper reality which is hidden and the discovery of which is the very purpose of scientific cognition.

It should be mentioned here that structural Marxism did not take to linguistic structuralism. Though there are similarities between general structuralism and Marxian structuralism, there is a conspicuous difference also. Structural Marxism did not participate in the linguistic turn which took place in social sciences. For example, the focal concern continued to be social and economic, not linguistic structures. Moreover, structural Marxism continued to be associated with Marxian theory.

Dumont's Structuralism: Indian Context

In his *Trend Report* (1969-1979), Yogendra Singh discussed the contribution of Louis Dumont in the context of India's social stratification. In India, there was a predominance of structural-functional methodology right after the sixties. During the seventies, after structural-functional analysis, there came the structuralist approach. "The lead in this direction no doubt comes from Louis Dumont, particularly his *Homo Hierarchicus* (1970). The pivotal notions of structuralism, such as ideology, dialectics, transformational relationship and comparison, through which a unity of principles among a variety of societal or civilizational forms is established, have been brought to bear upon the analysis of caste stratification in India." Dumont is basically a structuralist. To him, caste is an aspect of social structure. According to him, to understand caste, it is necessary to view it as an "integrated part of a social and cultural totality. One cannot, therefore, talk of caste in isolation from the particular cultural context from which it has emerged. The presence of 'caste-like systems' in non-Hindu societies is accounted for by the spread of some aspects of the caste institution". To Dumont these imitations of the caste system are found among Chris-

Louis Dumont (1911-1999) taught at the Oxford University for several years, but since 1955 worked in France. He belongs to the French school of structuralism. He started his career in the mid-1930s under Marcel Mauss. In the Second World War he was taken as prisoner of war, and learnt Sanskrit. He came home in 1945. He also took lessons in Hindi and Tamil and studied the ethnography of South India.

Dumont spent the years 1949-50 in Tamil Nadu. He studied here the Pramali Kallar. He was also interested in more general themes of South India. He brought out two important monographs in 1957, namely, *A South Indian Subcaste and Hierarchy* and *Marriage Alliance*, besides an irregular journal called *Contributions to Indian Sociology.* He spent fifteen months in 1957-58 in an eastern UP village. The fieldwork contributed to his interest in comparison and he published research on marriage and kinship. From 1951 onwards Dumont lectured extensively on caste. The fruit of this pedagogic effort was *Homo Hierarchicus* which is the most widely discussed book on the subject.

tians in Kerala, Muslims all over India and in Sri Lanka. Caste system, thus, is influenced by Hindu culture though the Muslims and Christians do not take part in Hinduism. And, therefore, Dumont says that caste is an aspect of Indian culture and has to be studied within a Hindu socio-cultural totality. Dumont's structuralism draws heavily from the European concept of individualism.

T.N. Madan organized a symposium on *Homo Hierarchicus* in 1971. There was a mixed response to Dumont's structuralist theory of stratification. Though his work is universally applauded for its scholarship and brilliance, it is faulted on theoretical and substantive grounds. Madan, while analyzing Dumont, says that "Dumont focused on the notion of ritual purity derived from both the textual tradition and fieldwork, and argued that various aspects of caste system, marriage rules, food taboos, occupational specialization can be derived from it". For Dumont caste was different from other forms of social stratification through the disjunction of ritual status and secular power. Madan, though critical of Dumont, has written enough in his praise. He writes:

> It was Europe that beckoned him now. Hierarchy is a lesson, Dumont said, that India teaches the west, and it is no ordinary lesson.

The individualism of the west and its sub-theme of egalitarianism are best understood in the light of holism and hierarchy.

Dumont was an excellent structuralist. He was in favour of holistic and hierarchical studies though as a French sociologist he pleaded for individualism and egalitarianism. One of Dumont's most important contributions to anthropological theory is his presentation of value hierarchies. His argument is that each society is integrated according to specific values which are expressed at a variety of levels, and that some such values determine—they encompass—other values at lower levels. The highest value of European society is the individual.

A Critique of Structuralism

The French structuralist approach has been criticized on several grounds and the functionalists have decried the school. The emergence of structuralism is a rebellion against humanism, existentialism and holism. Some of the major criticisms made against structuralism are given below:

(1) Richard Jenkins, who has discussed the contributions of Pierre Bourdieu in the series *Key Sociologists* (1992), says that in an important sense there is no such thing as structuralism. They are only varieties of structuralist approaches to culture and social reality.

(2) Jenkins further argues that structuralism draws heavily from individualism. But referring to Bourdieu, Jenkins says that "there is more to social life than the subjective consciousness of the actors who move within it and produce it". There is an objective social reality beyond the immediate interactional sphere and the self-conscious awareness of individuals.

(3) Yet another criticism of structuralism is made by Pierre Bourdieu. His point is about the neglected aspect of objectivity. He says that there is something more to social life than the subjective consciousness of the actors who move within it and produce it. Levi-Strauss explains structuralism only in terms of the format of mind. Bourdieu contests it. He was motivated to move beyond this by a realization that the behaviour, the practice of the people about whom structuralist models were constructed, was at variance with the rules of conduct which those models formulated.

His strong argument is that "structuralism had little or no explanatory or predictive power". Thus, the criticism is that structuralism cannot predict the future course of social reality.

(4) The greatest weak point of structuralism is that it draws heavily from the individual and rejects society. The micro theorists such as Mead, Goffman and others have also relied much on individual, self and mind but there are efforts today to integrate micro and macro theories. Viewed from this perspective, structuralism does not stand the test of general theory.

(5) A general criticism against structuralism is about linguistic structuralism. It is said that the linguistic theory has been borrowed as an analogy for structural explanation. So far so good. But there have been technical advances in linguistics itself and the structural theorists have not kept pace with these advances. Randall Collins raises this point:

> In general, it is peculiar that the structuralist thinkers have borrowed linguistic theory as an analogy, or rather as an inspiration, but they have neither kept up with the technical advances in linguistics itself, nor have they contributed in any important way toward unifying sociological principles with those of linguistics.

(6) The post-modern theorists such as Lacan, Derrida and Foucault have criticized the structuralism of Levi-Strauss. They have developed the concept of post-modern structuralism. This is different from general structuralism and is, interestingly, rejects general structuralism though it draws heavily from it. Commenting on the nature of post-modern structuralism George Ritzer (1997) observes:

> Post-structuralism tends to be more abstract, more philosophical and less political than post-modernism. Darrida's post-structuralism is a good example of post-structural thinking, even though he seems to be post-modernist sometimes.

(7) Ritzer and Derrida call structuralism mere grammatology or a theory of the science of writing.

All said and done, structuralism has certain positive contributions also. It is this theory which provides a valuable distinction between the empirical surplus and the underlying structure. It helps us solve some of the social science problems of explanation in a world which is changing, complex and particular. At a time when prevailing intellectual fashion tends to go in the direction of relativism and idealism, structuralism provides a midway point. To conclude this discussion on structuralism, we can do no better than quote Collins:

> Structuralism programme is still valid, although its substantive results (except perhaps for aspects of Levi-Strauss' theory of kinship) are not. Fortunately, there is a sociology which can fill in the spirit of this programme.

Further Readings

Collins, Randall, *Theoretical Sociology*, Rawat Publications, Jaipur, 1997.

Leach, Edmund, *Levi-Strauss*, Glasgow, Fontana, 1970.

Murdock, G.P., *Social Structure*, New York, 1949.

Nadel, S.F., *The Theory of Social Structure*, Cohen and West Limited, London, 1957.

Radcliffe-Brown, A.R., *Structure and Function in Primitive Society*, Cohen and West Ltd., London, 1964.

Ritzer, George, *Post-Modern Social Theory*, The McGraw Hill Co. Inc., New York, 1997.

9

The Family

Family is an important and primary unit of any social organization. It is both biological and social. The biological aspect of family is simple: two parents are required to produce offspring, and the number of ancestors doubles with each ascending generation. Some societies have institutionalized this fact of bilateral—patriarchal and matriarchal—families. More often, however, descent is counted in accordance with a unilateral pattern, whereby a person belongs to his father's or mother's family. The former is called patrilineal, whereas the latter matrilineal.

The social aspect of family is also very important. Wherever we see a community—rural or urban, primitive or civilized—there is invariably the presence of family. It is the family which rears and upbrings a child. There are some needs which have to be fulfilled by the family. But what is that which determines the family? "It is", says Radcliffe-Brown, "the necessary conditions of existence of the social organism." When the child comes out of the womb of the mother, there is nobody to help it. Among the animals, the moment the calf is born, its stands up and its dependence on the cow is short-lived. In the case of human beings the period of dependence varies from society to society. All of us are the products of family. Whether we like it or not, we identify with our family. Besides, our status also depends on our family. In India, right from birth to death, a person is dependent on his family in one way or the other. The family thus helps us fulfil some necessary conditions of existence.

Currently, the institution of family has become controversial. Though it is a universal social institution and is regarded fundamental, both for the individual and society as a whole, there are new perspectives which question many of the assumptions of the more traditional view. For instance, in India, I.P. Desai made a breakthrough by stating that the Indian family is essentially a joint family. His observation though emerges out of his empirical work from Mahua (Gujarat), it applies to all caste Hindus, tribals and rural and urban communities. In the west, during the late sixties, the Women's Liberation Movement began to shake the foundations of the family by attacking the role of women within it. "This attack was developed by some feminist writers into a condemnation of the family as an institution."

What is Family?

Perhaps, George Peter Murdock's work on family is an authentic document. Murdock examined the institution of the family in a wide range of societies. He took a sample of 250 societies ranging from small hunting and gathering bands to large industrial societies. He claimed that some form of family existed in every society. In his conclusion, he defines the family as follows:

> The family is a social group characterized by common residence, economic cooperation and reproduction. It includes adults of both sexes, at least two of whom maintain a socially approved sexual relationships and one or more children, own or adopted, of the sexually co-habiting adults.

Thus, the family lives together, pools its resources and works together and produces offspring. In other words, according to Murdock, the family has three essentials: (i) common residence, (ii) economic cooperation, and (iii) reproduction. If we examine Murdock's definition of family, it comes close to the definition of joint family given by Iravati Karve and K.M. Kapadia. To the Indian sociologists there are two more elements included in joint family. These are: (i) joint property, and (ii) common religion.

The problem of defining a family becomes complicated when there are cases where legitimate sex relations are allowed but there are no offspring. Neither is there adoption of children. The structure of the family varies from society to society. However, the smallest family unit which is found all over the world is the *nuclear family.* It consists a husband and a wife and their offspring. Units larger than the nuclear family are usually known as *extended family* or *joint family.*

There are other anthropologists also who have defined family.

Though Levi-Strauss has worked in the field of kinship, his definition of family is very interesting. Strauss was a hard fieldworker. While interviewing some tribals in his field study, he had an encounter with a tribal of Brazil who lived in a village. He found the tribal forlorn and quite sorrowful. Though he was young he appeared to be an old man. Strauss asked the reasons for his solitary and painful life. The tribal replied: "I have a house, it is a good house. I live all alone. I an not happy." Further enquiries revealed that the tribal hardly prepared his food. Mostly he depended on the food given by his clan and kinsmen. He was satisfied with this kind of living. Strauss put him a last question: "What is the reason for all this?" The tribal had a simple reply: "I am unmarried."

The response given by the tribal defines the family and its importance. A single man hardly makes a family. He needs to have a spouse and children. If he has no spouse, children would help him to make a family. And, if he has no children, spouse will assist him to compose a family. And, above all, if there is no family, like Strauss' tribal, he is unhappy. According to Strauss, the prime condition of a family is marriage.

John Lewis has defined family according to the tradition of British social anthropology:

> Family, the key institution in society, consists of one or more women living with one or more men and their children. It has socially approved sex relationship. The family is characterized by various rights and obligations.

It should also be mentioned here that there are several variations of family. There is a bilateral family. In this form of family descent is stressed from both parents. There is yet another family form known as the extended family. It consists of a series of close relations along either the male or female line, usually not along both. A woman, her husband, their children and her married daughter also constitute an extended family. We shall have an opportunity to discuss different types of families at a later stage of our discussion. However, here, it must be stressed that almost all over the world, the popular form of family is the *conjugal family*. In India also, the traditional joint family is increasingly being replaced by nuclear or conjugal family. Usually it consists of a man and a woman and their children. Murdock has also come to this conclusion:

> The nuclear family is a universal human social grouping. Either as the sole prevailing form of the family or as the basic unit from which more complex forms are compounded, it exists as a distinct and strongly functional group in every known society.

Varying Perspectives

True, family is a universal social institution. It has been subjected to analyses by anthropologists and sociologists. But, its discussion varies in its perspective. For instance, the functionalists define family from the perspective of its function in the maintenance of the system. There are anthropologists who very critically dwell on the dysfunctions of family. Besides, there are a few other approaches which deal with the family as an arena of politics. To understand and define it properly we should look at the family from all these varying perspectives.

Functionalist Perspective

M. Haralambos, in his book, *Sociology: Themes and Perspectives*, makes a review of the definition of family from the functionalist perspective involving three main questions. Firstly, what are the functions of the family? Answers to this question deal with the contributions made by the family to the maintenance of the social system. It is assumed that society has certain functional prerequisites or basic needs that must be met if it is to survive and operate efficiently. A second and related question asks, what are the functional relationships between the family and other parts of the social system? It is assumed that there must be a certain degree of integration and harmony between the parts of the social system if society has to function efficiently. The third question is connected with the functions performed by an institution or a part of society for the individual. In the case of the family this question considers the functions of the family for its individual members.

Actually, the functional perspective does not consider family in isolation from other institutions of the society. Its structure and functions are related to other parts of the social system. Such an approach to family quite suitably applies to the study of primitive society.

Yet another functional approach to family is suggested by Ezra F. Wogel and Norman W. Bell. Their argument is that functionalists have a limited approach to family. They focus solely on the positive aspects of this institution. These scholars take a departure from this approach. On the strength of data collected from American families they generalized that the family has truly some functions for the society but it disturbs the children. The child is made a scapegoat. He/she is emotionally disturbed by the tense relations of his parents. Wogel and Bell write:

> The child is thus used as an emotional scapegoat by parents to relieve their tension. For example, in one case, a son was criticized by his mother for all the characteristics she disliked in her husband. Clearly, the process of scapegoating is dysfunctional for the child. He becomes "emotionally disturbed".

Clearly, Wogel and Bell bring out the dysfunctional aspects of the family within a functionalist framework. Edmund Leach is yet another functionalist who brings out an anthropological-functional study of small-scale pre-industrial societies. Leach does not study family in isolation. It is an extensive network of social relationship among a large number of kins. It is the family which links the individual with the kinsmen. Leach observes:

> In the past, kinsfolks and neighbours gave the individual continuous moral support throughout his life. Today, the domestic household is isolated, the family looks inward upon itself; there is an intensification of emotional stress between husband and wife and parents and children. The strain is greater than most of us can bear.

Leach, in one respect, is a functionalist-anthropologist. He links family with kin and wider society. On the other hand, he talks about the isolation of family from the surrounding society. His hypothesis is that the more there is industrialization of a community, the greater is the isolation of family. In a metropolitan cities like Mumbai and New Delhi, despite the overwhelming population, the family has broken its relations with the kins, neighborhood and wider society. In industrial society, therefore, the family is reduced to the status of an oasis.

Phenomenological Approach

Generally speaking, the institution of family is studied largely from the perspective of functionalism in social anthropology. And, in doing so we have a bias for the American and European approaches. But, we should be clear that the family is not uniformly studied from a single approach in these continents. Earlier, we have observed that family is approached with functional perspective. In Europe it is also studied with reference to phenomenology. R.B. Laing does not consider functionalism as an appropriate approach to study the family. He presents a radical alternative to functional study of the family. Functionalists always present family as a 'happy family'. True, Laing views the family in terms of sets of interactions. "Individuals form alliances, adopt various strategies and play one or more individuals off against others in a complex tactical game."

What is interesting in the analysis of family according to Laing is that there is always some politics going on in a family. The sisters stand on one side and brothers on the other. It is also possible that brothers form factions and stand against each other. There is a constant 'war' in a family, one individual fighting against another. Laing takes a serious view about the state of affairs of the modern family. His perspective is quite clear when he writes:

> A family can act as gangsters, offering each other mutual protection against each other's violence.

David Cooper is the representative of the phenomenological approach taken in the study of family. He is actually influenced by Marxism. His observation is that it is the family which is responsible for generating the ideology of exploitation and discrimination. Feudalism, for example, continued for a long period because of the feudal ideology perpetuated by the family. Family is the root cause of many of our social evils. Cooper writes:

> The family operates as an ideological conditioning device in an exploitive society—slave society, feudal society and capitalist society.

The Marxian Approach

The idiom of Marxism has been a thorough analysis of class formulation. Its pre-occupation with social class has resulted in the neglect of the structure and role of the family. Friedrich Engels (1884) looked at family with an evolutionary perspective. What he has done is to combine the evolutionary approach with Marxian theory. He argued that with the change in the mode of production the family also changes. During the early stages of human evolution, Engels believed that the forces of production were communally owned and the family as such did not exist. This era of primitive communism was characterized by promiscuity. "There were no rules limiting sexual relationships and society was, in effect, the family."

The position taken by Engels has been in a way supported by Kathleen Gough who is credited to have worked for long period of her career in South India. Her supportive comments argued that man's nearest relatives—the chimpanzees—live in 'promiscuous hordes'. This must also have happened with early man. While tracing the origin of family Engels writes at a later stage: "Family is based on the supremacy of the man, the express purpose being to produce children of undisputed paternity; such paternity is demanded because these children are later to come into their father's property as his natural heirs." At the close of his analysis, Engels says that family in capitalist society developed mainly in the late 1960s and 1970s when several feminist writers employed Marxian concepts in their criticisms of the family.

Family Among Tribals

Recently, it is debated in sociology whether the institution of family is passing through a crucial stage of its development. Some sociologists manifest that in the US and parts of the European continent the family is dying. Several of the functions of family are taken over by the state and other social institutions. Now children are born in the hospital; they are brought up in creches: they are taught in different kinds of primary schools; and finally, it is the state, the public and private sectors which provide job opportunities. Employment in ancestral occupations such as agriculture, craft, business and traditional works has now been taken over by other agencies. The media provide both entertainment and learning. It appears that a large number of functions, which were earlier done by the family, are now the responsibility of a large number of social institutions. In such a situation, it is argued that the new society which is emerging will have little place for family and its multiple roles.

Then, there are several empirical instances which show that in some societies there is relative absence of family. About 4 per cent of Israel's population live in some 240 kibbutzim settlements. Capital and property are collectively owned by kibbutzim members and the main economy is agriculture plus some light industry. The 'family' in the kibbutzim has been shaped by a number of ideological and economic factors. Marriage in these settlements is monogamous, the married couple sharing a single bedroom-cum-living room. Common residence does not extend to their children who live in communal dormitories where they are raised by child care takers or educators. They eat and sleep in the dormitories spending most of the day and all of the night away from parents. They usually see their parents for an hour or two each day, often visiting them in their apartment. Economic cooperation between the married couple hardly exists.

Analyzing the absence of family in the kibbutzim, Haralambos observes:

> In terms of Murdock's definition, the family does not exist in the kibbutzim on two counts. Firstly, family members do not share a common residence. Secondly, their relationship is not characterized by economic cooperation... It can only be concluded in the absence of the economic and educational functions of the typical family, as well as of its characteristic of common residence, that the family does not exist in the kibbutzim.

Despite the availability of some stray incidences, it could be safely said that family is the cornerstone of society and is found in one form or the other in all the communities known to us. The debate on the existence of family or its erosion does not get much support. For one thing we are certain: children are not procreated in a factory—they are the outcome of the conjugal relations of two heterogeneous persons.

Elements of Family

Before we discuss the elements of family, two points should be made clear. One, family is a universal institution and it is created to fulfil some basic needs of mankind. It provides a living place, a shelter; it brings up children; it supplies bread for survival and above all, it is a bond of emotions. These are the universal features of family. Second, each family gets its pattern according to social and physical environment, and a historicity. The primitive family surely bears all the universal elements of family but it gets its pattern by hills and forests, isolated living, a constant encounter with the surrounding challenges. On the other hand, a family among the Hindus is constituted according to the traditions. For example, it has been a prolonged tradition among the Caste Hindu to live in a joint family. O'Malley reports that in the census of 1931 he found a large joint family in Bengal which had about 500 members.

In social anthropology, generally, when we talk about the family, we have to look at it in the context of primitive life. Among the Bhils and Gonds, there has been the tradition of polygyny. There are also polyandrous families found among the Todas of the Nilgiris. On the other hand, there are matrilineal families found among the Khasis of Jayantia hills of Assam. The point which we want to stress is that the elements of family are determined by a large number of environmental, occupational, social, cultural and historical forces. We will discuss some of the major elements found universally and particularly among different societies. A few of the major elements of the family are discussed as follows:

Procreation

Marriage is an institution which gives conjugal rights to the couple in the family. It is this social legitimacy which permits sex relations between husband and wife. This results in the procreation of children. The assumption is that conjugal relations should lead to the birth of children. If it is not done, the continuity of society would cease to exist. Among the Hindus, there is a belief that if no child is born in a family the husband would not be allowed to enter the gates of heaven. It is for this reason that an unmarried person of marriageable age is married to any object—a tree, a stone or a plant—before he is put to pyre. The tribals also make sure that as soon as a boy or a girl attains puberty, he or she is married. Thus, procreation of children is an inbuilt structure of marriage. This is found universally all over the world. However, the women's movement which is getting momentum is the US and the European continent, discourages women from undergoing procreation. This trend, however, is not witnessed in India.

Sex Relations

No society allows promiscuity. Sex is always regulated by a system of marriage. Incest is forbidden in all societies: brother and sister, mother and son, or father and daughter are not allowed to have any sexual relations. All societies have some system of acquiring a mate. This system gives rise to different types of marriages—monogamy, polygyny, polyandry and group marriage. The type of marriage which is prevalent in a particular society enjoys legitimacy of its society or group.

Economic Bond

If we trace the evolution of family, we learn that the family came into existence due to economic needs. There is division of labour which determines the role of family members. There are societies where males work outside the home and the women keep themselves confined to house work. And, there are also families where both husband and wife work outside and mutually share the responsibility of domestic work. The children are facilitated to develop their skills through education and training. Whatever may be the type of family, there is always some economic bond which holds the members together. The primitives do not have a sharp division of family work. For instance, among the Bhils of western India, the woman cleans the cattleshed and the man may grind the corn and fetch water. Thus, the division of labour in the family is usually traditional.

Long-time Group

We have all been members of a family; so have our great grandfathers. In fact, there is continuity in the existence of a family. In the matriarchal family, the daughter provides continuity by inheritance; in the patriarchal family, it is the son who keeps the family line alive. Civilizations rise and collapse, but the family lives forever. Family, therefore, is a long-time group.

Upbringing

In the animal world, there is lesser dependence of the new-borns on mothers. The dependence in all cases is short-lived. In human society, however, the offspring have to depend on their parents for longer period. In India, the dependence extends to the period when the sons and daughters are married and well settled. The idiom of dependence on the family is equally applicable among the tribals and primitives. However, in some tribal groups, the period of dependence could be reduced. For instance, among the Tods or Santhals, a son could be separated from the family as soon as he is married. Thus, it is the prime and essential element of a family to upbring, that is, provide education, employment and family tradition to the children. It is the family which provides socialization to its members through the process of upbringing.

Size of Family

One of the crucial elements of modern family is its size. Size has always been a prominent feature of family. Among the Indian tribes, before the attainment of independence, a larger family was preferred. The head of the family had plenty of land which he cultivated through a large number of hands. The practice of polygyny also resulted in large-sized families. In fact, in all the tribal groups larger family size was bestowed with greater prestige. The trend today in all the groups in the country is to go in for a small family. Even the tribals are obliged to conform to the small family norm.

Emotional Base

In a family, there are two types of kin who live together. Brothers and sisters and also grandparents constitute the blood kin whereas wife or wives belong to marital kin. All these members have an emotional bond which is essentially based on kin relations. The family unity is manifest in such emotional bonds. However, on some occasions, there are outbursts of anger and emotional discharges among the family members. But, these emotional outbursts are managed on the basis of kinship.

Sense of Responsibility

It is the responsibility of all the family members to provide perfect protection and upbringing to the new generation. Both among tribals and other ethnic groups in India, it is the responsibility of the parents to arrange the marriage of physically mature members of the family. The family head considers himself relieved if all the youngsters are married and settled in some occupation. Such a head, in the past, used to plan for a pilgrimage. This reveals a sense of responsibility among the grown-up persons in the family. Even if there has been a division in the family, all the members would make it a point to attend marriages and funerals.

Social Control

The family wields power. It provides facilities for the socialization of the family members. The daughters-in-law who come to the patrilocal place are also socialized in a way that after bearing children, they identify themselves with the family of the husband. If there are deviants in the family, the elders do not spare the rod. Any blame on a member is considered to be a blame on the entire family. It is because of social control that the unity of the family and its traditions are maintained by the members.

Tribal Family

If we review the literature available on the tribals of India, we find that most of these studies focus on the unusual aspects among the people, or the village monographs mostly dwell on the ethnographic aspects of the primitives. The studies made recently have begun to discuss social change among the tribals. On one hand, sociologists have raised the debate on the nuclear and joint family, and on the other, no serious attempt has ever been made to focus on the structure of family and relate it to the family found in caste groups and other non-tribal communities. The pertinent questions are: Does the tribal family resemble the caste Hindu joint or nuclear family? Are the families among tribals changing over to nuclear family? What has happened to tribal polygynous and polyandrous families? These questions are uncomfortable. It appears that not much has been done in the field of family by social anthropologists. Even authors of the status of D.N. Majumdar and T.N. Madan, in their well received book, *Introduction to Social Anthropology*, have not discussed this topic much. The only concern that these authors have shown is to describe the family found among Kharia of Chhotanagpur (Bihar) and the Ho of Bihar.

It must be observed that in the wake of directed social change, when the tribal groups have witnessed tremendous transformations, the family structure would also have changed. But, the bias for the study of Hindu joint family has left the tribal family study untouched. Whatever stray empirical material we get in the tribal monographs clearly indicate that in all probability the tribal family was not a joint family. There was not enough property among the tribals nor was there a well-built house. It could be said that whenever a tribal boy or girl attained maturity, he or she was married. Whether Gond or

Chaudhra, the married son today is allowed to erect his own hut but till the lifetime of the father there was no property division. For one thing we are certain: there is no debate in social anthropology about the structure of tribal family as we find in sociology. There is, however, a fundamental change in the family structure of tribals. Historically, the tribals have been polygynous and matriarchal. We have some evidence to support the view that in contemporary times polygyny is fast becoming extinct. So also with polyandry. The matriarchal system is also dying due to the entry of tribals into government and public sectors. Surely, something serious is happening with the tribal family which needs to be studied and analyzed.

Functions of Family

When there is an institution in existence since the origin of mankind, naturally, the institution fulfils certain needs of society. This, however, is the functional approach to the study of family. One of the postulates of functional analysis is the indispensability of a system. Thus, the family has certain indispensable functions for the society. But, at the same time, it should also be stressed that the institution of family generates certain conflicts too. There is no family which does not have any conflict. History is rich with family feuds among the royal families. During the Mughal rule in India no succession to a throne was complete without the assassination of some of the competing brothers. Family land disputes are present everywhere. Despite this there are some functions or needs which a family fulfils. Some of these are illustrated below:

Upbringing of Children

It is the family which takes care of the young. However, the period of upbringing varies from society to society. In western society the period of dependence of children is shorter compared to that in Indian society. In our country, normally, the caste Hindus show their concern for children till they are occupationally settled and married. Among the tribals, the period of dependence is lesser than caste Hindus. As soon as the son is matured enough to plough the field, the dependence is over and the upbringing is complete. The girls become matured when they can fetch water, go to the forest and can handle the household work.

Biological Functions

Procreation of children is the primary biological function of a family. Children born to a lawfully wedded couple only receive legitimacy from society. Thus, it is the family which ensures the continuity of human race.

Fulfilment of Basic Needs

It is the responsibility of a family to provide basic needs to its members. These include food, shelter, clothing, health and education. The head of the family, whether male or female, is expected to provide these to the members till they attain adulthood. The Hindu marriage makes it obligatory for the husband to provide comforts to his wife. Among the tribals also economic needs along with physical needs are fulfilled by the family.

Psychological Security

One very important function of a family is psychological. It provides security to the members of the family. Among the aged in the primitive societies, psychological support is a very strong factor as it provides strength and a measure of safety. The tribals reside in hills and forests. Such a habitation poses great hazards to them. Mostly, the environment is unfriendly and in such a situation it is only the emotional support which provides succour to the people. Though, these days, the state has come forward to take some measures of security for the older people, the family still does provide psychological protection.

In the changing times the functions of family are fast getting new dimensions. Even the Trobrianders living in isolated islands are taking to modernization. In our country too, the tribals residing in inaccessible areas have been witnessing a transformation. Traditional occupations are changing, and education has given a new worldview to these isolated peoples. In such a situation the family has taken up new challenges and new functions.

Types of Families

Preparing a typology of the family is a difficult task since the institution is a universal phenomenon. Whenever social scientists are required to classify it, they are confronted with the problem of identifying some criteria which could help them do this. And when there is no agreement on a set of criteria, the typology dwindles. However, some classification can be made on some criteria which are generally acceptable: (1) size, (2) residence, (3) descent, (4) inheritance, and (5) marriage. In the following section we shall provide the types of families on the basis of above criteria found in our country.

Size

The size of a family is determined by the number of members in it. Accordingly, we have nuclear family or conjugal family, extended family, and joint family.

(i) Nuclear Family

Talcott Parsons calls the nuclear family an isolated family. It is isolated because "it does not form an integral part of a wider system of kinship relationships. Obviously, there are social relationships between members of nuclear families and their kin but these relationships are more a matter of choice than binding obligations." Parsons argues that there is a functional relationship between the isolated nuclear family and the economic system in industrial society. In particular, the isolated nuclear family is shaped to meet the requirements of the economic system. He observes that because of the isolation of the nuclear family from the wider kinship group, the relationship between husband and wife is strengthened.

Parsons is correct so far as isolated nuclear families of industrial societies are concerned. In India, in any case, the nuclear families are hardly isolated from the kin group. Even, in big cities, the nuclear families are, in one way or the other, on one occasion or the other, always an integral part of the wider kindred. For the tribals, social anthropologists have always argued that their society predominantly consists of the nuclear families only.

(ii) Extended Family

This is a family consisting of a series of close relations along either the male or female line, usually not along both. A woman, her husband, their children and her married daughter, with her husband, would be one form of an extended family. This kind of family is sometimes found in the west and among tribals in South Africa. In our country, the extended form of family is known as joint family.

(iii) Joint Family

The Indian family, in general, is a joint family. However, due to increase in migration and social mobility, we see nuclear families more and more. Iravati Karve defines the joint family as one where: (1) members live under one roof; (2) have a common hearth; (3) share common property; (4) have a common purse; and (5) worship a common deity. K.M. Kapadia and I.P. Desai consider the generation depth yet another characteristic of the joint family. On a broader plane, a joint family is defined as a group of several related conjugal or nuclear families in one household. In this family labour is pooled and all are responsible to the same authority.

Tribals do not have the joint family which is a standard pattern found among the high caste Hindus. Among the tribals residence is generally separate for each nuclear family though economically the family is joint. In our country we have more than 400 tribal groups and among them the north-east tribals are in many ways different from the heartland tribals. These groups have the kind of family which suits to their geography and economy.

Residence

Family types are also identified on the basis of the residence of the female. If the female resides with her husband it is patrilocal. Similarly, when the husband resides or visits his wife or the latter's residence it is called matrilocal. Both these types of families are found among the tribals of India.

(i) Matrilocal Family

It is a family in which the married couple resides with the wife's family or kin group. In such families, the husbands either visit their wives periodically or live permanently with the matrilocal family. The women do not leave their families after marriage to live with their husbands. In communities where the system of matrilocal family prevails, the daughter is greatly valued. She will always remain with the family and will not be lost at marriage, whereas the boys will go to live with the families of their wives. The daughter is a complete fulfilment to the mother. She is her mother's constant companion in joy and sorrow, additional hands and feet for an overburdened body, security in old age, and contributor of children to her clan.

In India, there are some tribal groups which have matrilocal families. The Khasi tribe of Assam who are found in the Jayantia hills have a tradition of matrilocal family. Similar primitive groups are also found in the southern parts of the country.

(ii) Patrilocal Family

This is a kind of family wherein a woman after marriage comes and lives with her husband. In this kind of family the descent is also traced through the male line. Most of the tribal families are patrilocal. Mention may be made in this connection of the Kharia, Ho Bhil and Gond. This is the general pattern of family found all over the country.

Descent

(i) Patrilineal Family

In this type of family the authority rests with the oldest male of the family. The patrilineal family is also patrilocal. This is the general pattern of family found all over the world. Among Hindus and also Muslims in our country the line of descent is reckoned through the male head. Recently, due to the women's movement, the women are also made as the legal guardians of their sons and daughters.

In India, patrilineal families are found in Gond, Santhal, Bhil and Ho tribes. The tribals of north-east also have patrilineal type of family. In this family major decisions are taken by the male head. Successor is also appointed by the male head of family.

(ii) Matrilineal Family

In this family the authority lies with the female head. This kind of family is also matrilocal and descent is traced through the mother. In our country some tribal groups in the south and the Khasis of Assam are matrilineal.

Inheritance

Yet another basis of classification of family is inheritance. Inheritance and descent are different. Descent is reckoned with the male or female line, whereas inheritance is traditional and all the members in the family generally do not get right of inheritance. Inheritance means to get the property of family after the lifetime of the father. Broadly speaking, in patriarchal families, all the male members inherit the family property. After the death of the father, the eldest son is looked upon with respect since he represents his deceased father. Sometimes, the male head may distribute the family property even during his lifetime. This kind of family is usually patrilineal and patrilocal.

In matriachal family the inheritance is through the mother.

Marriage

This type of family is based on the number of spouses the man or woman has. We have three such types: (i) monogamy, (ii) polygyny, and (iii) polyandry.

(i) Monogamous Family

This type of family is the general pattern of family where the husband and wife live together. It is the conjugal family and one husband has one wife only. This is the general pattern found in all societies.

(ii) Polygynous Family

In polygynous family a man has more than one wife. Generally, this type is found among the primitives. Only a wealthy minority can obtain wives and other poorer men are deprived. Sometimes it reflects the inferiority of women in the society, and indicates that wives may be purchased. A man who has many wives has great prestige. In such families women do not object to their husband's taking on additional wives. This practice was popular among some tribals in central India. In the past, a Bhil had a large number of wives. According to a folk song prevalent among the Bhils of western India, a male could have as many as twelve wives. However, there is enough empirical evidence found even today that among the Bhils there has been a strong practice of polygyny. The relation between co-wives is usually friendly but competition for the husband's attention is possible. Sometimes, in polygynous family wives have separate huts and domestic utensils. A wise husband will try to be impartial among his wives, but the potential instability of the system is generally recognized.

(iii) Polyandrous Family

In this type of family a woman has several husbands. Outside India, it is found in Tibet. In South India, the Todas of the Nilgiris practise polyandry. This is due to a shortage of women as a consequence of female infanticide. Generally, in a family with three or four brothers, the brothers live together and share their wife without friction or jealousy. The polyandrous family is increasingly becoming extinct.

Concluding Comments

The basic objective of social anthropology is to study the uniformities and differences in human society. Society is organized through a network of social institutions, and the abstractions of social institutions constitute the social structure. Society, thus, is an organization. It includes family, kin, marriage and clan as its parts, of which the family is the smallest and primary unit of society. The characteristics of family vary with the history and locality of a particular society. Surely, the Gond family of India is different from the Tiv or Nuer family of South Africa. This variation in the structure of family is due to the historical, cultural, environmental and other specific reasons. Despite these differences, there are some elements of family which are universal. It is the family which gives emotional satisfaction to its members, provides economic security, gives shelter and many other things. These are the general characteristics of the family. The type of family is determined by several factors. The needs fulfilled by the family are so vital that this institution is persistent in human society.

Further Readings

Beatti, John, *Other Cultures*, Cohen and West, London, 1964.

Bohannan, Paul, *Social Anthropology*, Holt, Reinhart and Winston, New York, 1963.

Lewis, John, *Anthropology*, Heinemann, London, 1982.

10

Marriage

The institution of marriage, quite like that of the family, is universal. There cannot be a family without marriage. Thomas Hylland Eriksen very rightly says that marriage is essential for human survival. Women are important, because it is they who procreate children; men do not. Similarly, women cannot procreate without alliance with men. The observations made by Eriksen need to be quoted here:

> Seen from a male point of view women are a scarce resource. No matter how male dominated a society is, men need women to ensure its survival. In matrilineal systems, the men's sisters do this; in patrilineal societies, their wives do it; and in cognatic or bilateral societies, sisters and wives each do part of the job. A man can have a nearly unlimited number of children in theory, he can be get several children everyday while a women's capacity is usually limited to one child per year, and moreover, in many societies many children die before they grow up.

Whatever may be the rituals related to marriage, it remains an alliance. This alliance can be for a lifetime, or it may be short-lived. But in all situations there is some alliance, some understanding, some sharing between those who give the daughter or receive a bride. In Indian society we find several marriage alliances established for various purposes between royal families. In medieval India, a treaty was signed or peace was bought by entering into a marriage. The Rajputs gave their daughters in marriage to the Mughals. Marriage, therefore, is an exchange of male and female; it is an alliance, a contract.

What is Marriage?

Eriksen has made an attempt to define marriage. He observes:

> Whether or not persons choose their spouses, marriage is very commonly perceived as a relationship between groups, not primarily between individuals.

Eriksen conducts a stock-taking of the ethnographic atlas of world communities and finds that spouses are chosen between groups, clans and communities. It is more a concern of the group and very little of the individuals. His survey shows that polyandry occurs only four times. It is a rare kind of marriage. So is the case of polygyny. "Comparatively speaking romantic love is rarely seen as an important precondition for a good marriage. Rather, marriage is frequently arranged by kin groups, not by the individuals concerned." Eriksen further argues that the marriage institution almost in all the cases is a concern not of individuals but groups. If Eriksen is taken seriously, it could safely be said that though marriage binds two individuals, it also binds a large number of kin groups in alliance. We accept our daughter-in-law, but we also accept other marital kins. In village India, Iravati Karve informs that the daughter-in-law of a family traditionally becomes the daughter-in-law of the whole village. She is obliged to observe *purdah* when she is at public places. And, when a son-in-law comes to his wife's village, the women observe *purdah*. Thus, marriage in India binds a man not only with the kin of the the in-laws, but also the whole caste and the village.

Westermarck is an authority on marriage. His three-volume work on the history of marriage is an in-depth study of the subject. It has been abridged in a single volume entitled *A Short History of Human Marriage*. He devotes considerable space to Hindu marriage, and it is in this respect that his definition of marriage assumes importance. He writes:

> Marriage is a relation of one or more men and women which is recognized by custom or law and involves certain rights and duties both in the case of the parties entering the union and in the case of children born of it.

What is important in Westermarck's definition is that marriage permits sex relations between husband and wife, and these sex relations are legitimized by the society. It is because of this legitimization that marriage undergoes certain rituals which are performed publicly. Secondly, the objective of marriage is to bear children. The upbringing of children is also the responsibility of a family. From all considerations marriage is an institution which regulates sex relations and condemns promiscuity.

Yet another definition of marriage is given by D.N. Majumdar and T.N. Madan in their book *An Introduction to Social Anthropology*. They write:

> Marriage ensures a biological satisfaction (that of sex) and a psychological satisfaction (that of having children) on the individual plane, and on the wider collective plane, it ensures a two-fold survival, that of the group and its culture.

The definition given by Majumdar and Madan stresses the importance of: (i) sex, (ii) children, and (iii) survival of society at large. The meaning of marriage comes close to the concept of marriage propounded by the Hindu *Shastras*. P.N. Prabhu, who dwells elaborately on Hindu social institutions, says that marriage among Hindus is for: (i) *dharma*, (ii) procreation of children, and (iii) *rati*, that is, sex. It is the duty of a Hindu to enter into marriage. There is no salvation without marriage. Second, a man and woman should bear children, and finally, it is for sex. Hindu *Shashatrakaras*, however, give precedence to religion over procreation and sex.

From all considerations it could be said that marriage is not a personal affair. It is not just an institution only for the fulfilment of biological needs. It is a social alliance *par excellence*. Whatever may be the kind of society it has same inbuilt mechanism for providing legitimacy to the sexual needs. However, the functions that marriage institution performs have different priorities in different societies.

Characteristics of Marriage

On the basis of the definitions of marriage given above, we present some of the major features or characteristics of marriage as under:

(1) The institution of marriage fulfils the biological needs of the individual. Freud argued that the man has two innate needs---sex and hunger. Sex is fulfilled through the institution of marriage. However, this desire is fulfilled according to the priorities fixed by the society. For instance, among the Hindus, sex occupies a third place in the hierarchy of goals set by the *Shashatrakaras*. The

tribals and the western society, on the other hand, give first priority to sexual fulfilment.

(2) Procreation is another feature of marriage. It is in the interest of society that children are born out of marriage. This ensures the survival and continuity of the human race. Among the Gonds of Madhya Pradesh and Bihar the objective of marriage is to produce a large number of children. A large family is said to be a prestigious family. The same ideology holds true among the tribals of Rajasthan. However, under the impact of small family programme, this objective of marriage is increasingly giving way to a change in outlook.

(3) Upbringing of children is also an objective of marriage. It is believed that if children are not socialized properly, the result would be a fractured citizenship. The strength of a nation rests on the capability of the future generations.

(4) It must be stressed that nowhere in any society is there a marriage institution without some form of rules. The marriages solemnized or contracted according to the rules of the society are honoured and legitimized. The marriage which does not conform to the rules of marriage is void.

(5) Marriage is performed according to the tradition of society, and the terms of its dissolution are also governed by social rules. For instance, among the Hindus, marriage is a sacrament and cannot be dissolved easily. Among tribals, however, marriage is a social contract. It can be dissolved at the will of either of the spouses. Among Muslims and Christians also similar rules exist.

(6) In western society a new ideology runs through the new generation. It is argued that marriage should be built on pure love. The ideology of 'pure love' transcends class boundaries. This kind of marriage is termed as "love marriage". Actually the marriage pattern is determined by the ideology which a particular society holds. In some instances, particularly among tribals, environmental and historical factors play an important role in this regard.

Dowry

In both European and Indian societies, dowry has traditionally been an important part of marriage. Sometimes it is described as an Indo-European institution. Eriksen has defined dowry as follows:

Dowry means that the bride brings gifts from her family into the marriage, often household utensils, linen and other things for the home.

Dowry has been interpreted in terms of the nature of a particular society. It has been seen as a compensation to the man's family for undertaking to support the woman economically. There are a few societies which consider the amount of dowry as a burden on the family of the girl. Sometimes, the parents of the daughter are obliged to borrow from moneylenders, friends and kinsmen. The dowry system has also made inroads into the tribal society. It is largely due to the increasing contacts of the tribals with the caste Hindus.

We observe that dowry is not unique to India only. In the US and Europe, it is expected of a bride to bring some gifts in the form of clothes and ornaments to the family of her husband. What is to be noted is that in these countries dowry has not taken a vulgar form as it has in some of the Asian countries, especially India.

Bride-price

Bride-price is also sometimes spoken of as bride-wealth. It is more common than dowry in many societies, particularly in Africa and among tribals in India. Defining the practice Eriksen writes:

> In the bride-price the groom's kin is obliged to transfer resources to the bride's kin in return for his rights to her labour and reproductive powers. The payment of bride-price establishes the rights of the man over the woman and her children. If the bride-price is not paid, the marriage may be void, and disagreement over bride-price payments is traditionally a common cause of feuds among many peoples.

When we study the practice of bride-price found among the tribals, we notice the following features:

(1) It gives a right of the possession of woman to the man. If she goes elsewhere taking another man as her husband, the latter is obliged to pay the amount of bride-price to the first husband.

(2) It reduces the status of woman as she is actually 'purchased' by the husband.

(3) The amount of bride-price which is received by the daughter's parents is distributed among the members of blood group. The distribution is guided by tradition. A large portion of the bride-

price amount in some societies is given to the mother, for she took maximum care in rearing her. The siblings of the family also get some share. Thus, the tradition of bride-price fosters solidarity among the members of the daughter's family.

(4) On the side of the groom, the amount for the bride-price is normally borrowed from the blood kin of the groom's parents. This also brings all of them together.

(5) There are cases wherein the groom who is not economically well off renders services to the parents of the bride. In this case, the amount of bride-price is paid over a longer duration period through bride-service. When the amount is cleared through service, the marriage is arranged. This service also brings solidarity between two uniting families.

Thus, the payment of bride-price creates several kinds of moral bonds between people. It creates a contractual tie between lineages, being a sign of mutual trust. The bride-price tradition has given rise to two other types of marriage: (i) levirate, and (ii) sororate.

(i) Levirate

When a marriage is contracted by the payment of bride-price, and in course of time, if the husband dies, his widow is married to the brother of the deceased (the levir) and in this way the patrilineage retains control over the woman and her children after the husband's death. In this case no bride-price is paid.

(ii) Sororate

In this form of marriage which also results from the tradition of bride-price, a widower marries the sister of the deceased. In most of the cases, it means that the woman's kin group commits itself to replacing the dead woman with a living one.

Both these forms of marriage are found among the Scheduled Castes and Scheduled Tribes.

Therefore, we see that the traditions of dowry and bride-price and any marriage, for that matter, is not an individual or personal affair; it is a contract between the two families, or two groups of kin. Emphasizing the alliance part of marriage, John Lewis writes:

> The payment emphasizes the fact that marriage does not concern the marrying pair alone. Marriage is an alliance between two kin groups

in which the couple concerned is merely the most conspicuous link. The man marriages not only his bride but all her relatives as well.

In any discussion of marriage it should be stated strongly that marriage is an alliance. The bride-price cements the links in the web of kinship, allaying disputes and hostility and imposing a check on the disruptive tendencies of inter-group conflict. It also helps consolidate marriage, for having received the bride-price, her relatives do not want to see her return for they would then have to return the bride-price. So divorce is a rare thing in societies where bride-price is an essential feature of the marriage.

Pre-marital Relations

For the tribals, where marriage is a contract, pre-marital relations are not strictly adhered to, and the concept of virginity is not predominant. The high caste Hindus may also deviate from the ideal of virginity though it may be stressed in theory. In primitive societies on a general plane all over the world pre-marital relations among the young, unmarried persons are sanctioned, and in some cases regulated. This must be related to the sharp divisions between the idea of marriage as an economic institution and for sexual gratification. "Pre-marital intercourse, therefore, is not taken too seriously and among adolescents is an aspect of courting experience, or simply a matter of indifference."

Age at Marriage

Primitive people marry young. An unmarried seventeen or eighteen year-old is likely to be a person in some manner inadequate. The lowlier the economy, the more necessary it is that everyone be married, so as to function effectively in producing work. The young begin to participate in general adult activities at an early age, learning the techniques of ploughing the field, and fetching water. In other words, when the sons and daughters are matured and are able to take over the household and forest activities, they are married. Interestingly enough, the Hindu concept of widowhood is absent among the tribals. The widow is soon remarried and a nominal bride-price has to be paid for her. Thus, the taboo and pain attached to widowhood is absent among the primitives.

Rules of Marriage

If the institution of marriage is universal, there are invariably some rules to regulate and control it. But what is interesting is that these rules are not the same in all societies. They vary from society to society. However, there are some norms which are commonly found in all societies. The main objective of the framing rules for marriage is to see that promiscuity does not occur. We shall discuss here some of the important rules of marriage.

Ban on Incest

The most universally found norm is the taboo on incest. No society permits marriage between brother and sister, or between parents and children. Marriage is prohibited among close relations. Banning incest is a very controversial idea, though it is found in all societies. Lewis has defined incest as:

> Incest is the term applied to any such prohibited union. It is essential to an understanding of this question to realize that prohibition extends to those cousins who are held to be within the family, even though they may be several degrees distant and biologically hardly related at all. For instance, it is almost universally held that a man may not marry the daughter of his mother's sister, who is a parallel cousin, for she is a 'sister', or any second or third cousin only distantly related through his great grand-mother; but he may marry the daughter of his mother's brother, who is a cross cousin.

The prohibition on incest is because the partners are closely related. They need not, however, be blood relations in some societies. At the outset, the parameters of the prohibition seem to be simple—no marriage among close relations. But who are the close relations? On this point there are different observations among the anthropologists:

(i) Tylor and Freud have provided several explanations to incest. They argue on the strength of their data that in all societies sex relations with the close kin are prohibited and there are sanctions against their violations. They further argue that there are some social advantages of the rule. The taboo helps expansion of the group through the inclusion of new members and the forging of alliances across kin boundaries. If there is no prohibition on the sexual relations with close kin, the expansion of the family would stop because there will be in-breeding.

(ii) Another explanation in this regard is that if there is no prohibition on sexual relations with close kin, it would lead to biological degeneration. Eriksen is not satisfied with this kind of explanation. "Notably, it does not explain what it is that makes people reject incest, since they are, in many cases, ignorant of its possible negative effects on the genetic material."

(iii) Yet another clarification given by anthropologists against incestuous relations is that people who have grown up together will scarcely feel mutual erotic attraction. It is because of this that marriage among close kin is prohibited.

(iv) Levi-Strauss, who has propounded the theory of structuralism, says that there are forms of relations in the mind of a man. These forms are binary. The man divides the women surrounding him into two mutually exclusive categories: wives and sisters. By way of reference in Gujarat all the women are divided into two binary groups: (1) *ben*, that is, sister; and (2) wife. This clearly illustrates that those who fall in the category of *ben* cannot be contracted for sexual relations. Strauss holds that the exchange of women between kin groups is when all is said and done, an effect of reciprocity which is a fundamental structure of the human mind, be it conscious or unconscious.

(v) Rodney Needham, another noted anthropologist, is against the use of the term 'incest'. This is because of the fact that the meaning of incest varies from culture to culture. In such a situation, the use of the term would create confusion rather than help understand the rules of marriage.

The controversies are several. But most of the social anthropologists find the concept quite useful. They help us understand the institution of marriage. Despite this importance of prohibition on incest, the question that remains to be answered is that who are the close kin.

Who are close kin?

All those who speak about incest in primitive societies have mentioned about close kin. They have stated that there is taboo between marriage among close kin. The meaning of close kin varies from society to society. For instance, there are societies which prefer marriage relations between a man and his mother's brother's daughter. In some societies such as Muslim, this form of marriage is permitted. The Hindu castes have defined close kin in a rather specific way. It is said that those who come in the direct ancestral line or those who belong to the same *sapinda* are prohibited from having sex relations.

Preferential Marriage

In some societies there is the practice of giving or receiving daughter from groups which are considered socially higher. In all societies there are instances of preferential marriages. Among these may be included: (i) levirate, and (ii) sororate. These two forms of marriage have already been discussed. Here, we would only say that after the death of husband or wife, this proves to be a useful means of maintaining the link between two kin groups that was established through the original marriage.

Exogamy

Exogamy is a general rule of marriage. When a person marries outside a specific social group of which he is a member, it is exogamy. In other words, a marriage outside the lineage group is exogamy. A lineage is a descent group either from the father's or mother's line which traces its origin from a common ancestor. In such a situation it becomes interesting to differentiate between the close kin and the descent or lineage. Certainly, the size of the group of close kin is smaller. Normally, it consists of father, children and siblings. Beyond this small group there is a larger group which consists of descent and lineage groups. According to the rules of exogamy one is not allowed to marry within the lineage and descent group. Marriage outside this group is exogamy.

Among the tribals too there are clans. A clan is a lineage group. A Gond, for instance, is not allowed to marry within his own clan. The Bhils of western India have about forty clans. Normally, a tribal village consists of one or two clans. In this situation all the members of the village are 'brothers' and 'sisters'. Because of this there is the practice of village exogamy according to which a tribal would not prefer to marry within his own village.

Westermarck has provided yet another interpretation for exogamy through an anecdote. Once, when his barber had come to his house, Westermarck enquired from him, "Are you married?" "No", the barber replied. Westermarck suggested that he could have married in his village. There were enough girls. To this the barber commented: "Oh, the girls of my village are good for nothing; I know them all." The statement made by barber shows that it is the instinct of man to look for a girl who generates curiosity. Such a man is considered heroic who brings a girl from from great distances. Such kinds of male attitudes also explain the prevalence of exogamy. Westermarck gives yet another empirical evidence to support the practice of exogamy. In London, there are two schools situated on either the sides of a road. One school has co-education while the other one is exclusively for girls. He found that the boys of the co-education school often went to the girls school in search of love and romance. When they were reminded that there were girls in their own class and they could very well take a fiancee for them, the boys replied: "The girls of our school! We know them all; they are rotten." And hence exogamy.

Endogamy

In endogamy a member is required to marry within his own group. Lewis defines endogamy as follows:

> The rule that requires a person to marry within a specific social group of which he is a member.

In the Indian context, the caste is defined as an endogamous group just as the Gonds are a tribe. The Gonds marry within the Gond tribe. Thus, Gond is an endogamous group. Brahmin would not marry a Rajput. In the same way, a Gond would not marry a Santhal. However, there are cases of inter-caste and inter-tribal marriages, though such marriages are not the rule. Where the society is stratified on class lines, a member would marry within his own class. In this sense membership class is endogamous.

Eriksen writes:

> In a sense, all human groups are both endogamous and exogamous to varying degrees. One is expected to marry "one's" own kind, but not someone classified as a close relative. Who is a close relative and who is not is naturally culturally specified, although the people classified as parents, children and siblings in Europe are virtually everywhere seen as close kin.

Forms of Marriage

All persons normally do get married. Monogamy appears to be a natural form of marriage. But, a person could choose his mate through other forms of marriage also, namely, polygyny and polyandry. Anthropologists have widely discussed the forms of marriage. Sometimes it is termed as acquiring a mate. These forms of marriage are: (i) monogamy, and (ii) polygamy. Polygamy is further divided into (a) polygyny, and (b) polyandry. Some anthropologists have also found traces of group marriage. But this form of márriage is fast on the way to extinction. In this part of chapter we shall discuss the forms of marriage as found in different societies.

Monogamy

All available information on the way of life of peoples of simple food-gathering societies leads to the conclusion that a family composed of one male and one female, who care for the needs of their immature offspring, may afford one of the most efficient ways of keeping down the mortality rate and facilitating community survival. Discussing the importance of monogamy in the earlier parts of human history, Melville Jacobs and Bernhard Stern write:

> When a distinction is made between basic social relationship and relationships that are largely sexual, there is not a society in the world that is other than monogamous as far as the majority of its people go. The people in societies of low-technological level cannot take care of unmarried adults who know only the skills of their own sex and not those of the other sex.

Monogamy seems to be the earliest form of marriage though its evolution has been controversial. Some argue that in the earlier periods of history there was promiscuity, followed by matriarchal and patriarchal forms of marriage. But there is also enough evidence to suggest that before the emergence of agriculture, people of subsistence economy had monogamous marriage. If we do not enter into the debate and look at the present popular form of marriage, it could be safely said that all over the world monogamy is the most favourite form of marriage. Even those who practise polygamy—polygyny and polyandry—are returning to monogamy. The tribals in India are also abandoning polygyny. The classical Hindu joint family is also getting weak in the present context of globalization. If democracy has become a standard mode of government, monogamy has become a standard form of marriage all over the world. In all cases, it consists of husband, wife and unmarried children.

Polygamy

Though popularly polygamy is understood to mean marriage with two or more wives, it properly designates marriage of either a man or a woman with more than one mate. What is commonly reckoned as polygamy is accurately called polygyny, the complementary institution being polyandry. In addition it must be considered as the union of a group of men with a group of women—a custom known as 'group marriage'.

(i) Polygyny

Robert H. Lowie has written authoritatively on primitive society. His book *Primitive Society* is considered to be the second important work after Morgan's *Ancient Society*. While working among tribals, Lowie has found and recorded several cases of polygyny. Introducing this form of marriage Lowie observes:

> Polygyny is one of those dangerous catch words that required careful scrutiny lest there result a total misunderstanding of the conditions it is meant to characterize. In every human society, the number of male

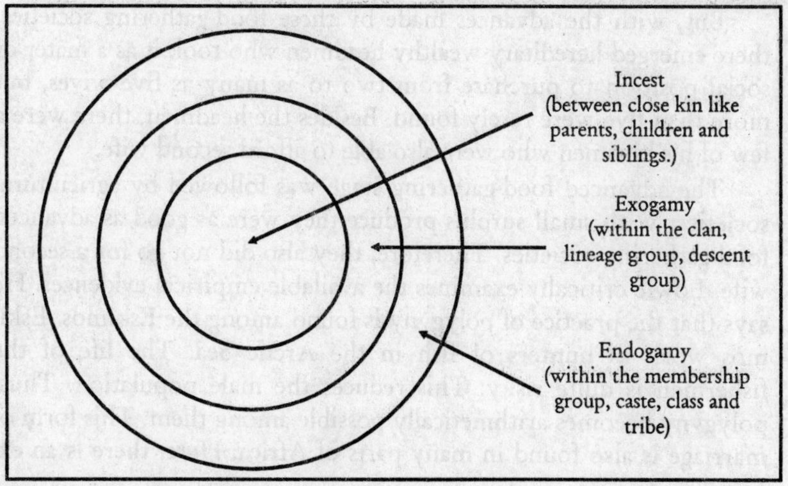

> and of female individuals born is approximately equal. Hence, in order to have either polygyny or polyandry as a fairly common practice, it is obviously necessary that some non-biological factor should disturb the natural ratio.

Lowie has put his argument in a very logical way. He says that nature has ordained human procreation in such a way that the ratio of males and females in a society remains more or less equal. In such a situation, polygyny or polyandry is created not by nature or due to biological reasons. They are the cultural constructs made by society. If some people keep more than one wife, some others will have to go without a wife. Similarly, if the natural equilibrium of male-female ratio is disturbed, there would be two or more men to share one wife. Lowie argues that except monogamy all other forms of marriage are socially and culturally constructed.

The question is: why polygyny? The answer to this question can be sought with reference to history. In simple food-gathering economies polygyny was rare, though it was permissible. Since the sexes were of equal status it was not often that a woman wanted another wife in her home occasionally, however, she asked her husband to take another wife, or she acceded to his wish for another. However, three or more wives were virtually never found in these societies, if for no other reason than because the lowly economy involved so much labour for the husband in fulfilling his portion of the household's productive work.

But, with the advances made by these food-gathering societies, there emerged hereditary wealthy headmen who took it as a mater of social position to purchase from two to as many as five wives, but more than five were rarely found. Besides the headmen, there were a few of his kinsmen who were also able to afford second wife.

The advanced food-gathering stage was followed by agricultural societies. With small surplus produce they were as good as advanced food-gathering societies. Therefore, they also did not go for a second wife. Lowie critically examines the available empirical evidences. He says that the practice of polygyny is found among the Eskimos. Eskimos work as hunters of fish in the Arctic Sea. The life of the fishermen is quite risky. This reduces the male population. Thus, polygyny becomes arithmetically possible among them. This form of marriage is also found in many parts of Africa. Here, there is an extraordinary multiplicity of wives. Lowie says that there have been well-authenticated cases of men with five, ten, twenty and even sixty wives. Lowie thus makes his hypothesis on polygyny clear:

> Unfortunately, none of the authorities I have seen on the subject deigns to furnish us with data as to the relative numbers of the sexes. From remarks incidentally dropped by them it seems certain that only the wealthy and the eminent man have polygynous households.

Lowie has also referred to the polygynous situation of the Kikuyu tribe of East Africa where two or three wives were common, and the rich had six or seven.

The African data also help Lowie to make yet another generalization. He says that in polygyny one is required to pay bride-price. The amount of bride-price is so high that for most of the people it is difficult to go for polygyny. In this situation, polygyny became the luxury of the rich only. On the basis of such empirical evidences from Eskimos as well as from Africa, the following inferences about polygyny can be drawn:

(1) Nature has biologically balanced male-female ratio. This permits only monogamy. Polygyny is socially and culturally constructed.
(2) In some societies males are exposed to serious risks as are the Eskimos, and the male-female ratio is disturbed, giving rise to polygyny.
(3) In food-gathering societies, the status of males and females is almost equal. It naturally does not promote polygyny.
(4) In agricultural societies, where the landholding is large and additional hands are required, polygyny is prevalent.
(5) The bride-price also gives rise to polygyny. Those who can afford it go for polygyny.
(6) Polygyny does not encourage the degradation of women. In most cases it is the first wife who encourages her husband to take on a second wife with the objective of shifting part of her household duties on other shoulders. Like the Kikuyu wife, she would address her husband: "Why have I to do all the work; why do you not buy another wife?"

Considering all the empirical data that are available from tribal societies it could be concluded that polygyny is practised only among the wealthier classes, whose males can afford to buy multiple wives.

These societies, mostly agricultural, were wealthy enough to permit the nobles or monarchs to exceed by far the maximum of five wives found in African tribes. It is said that some of the African monarchs have been reported to have had hundreds of wives.

The Indian scene is not very different from that of African. Here too, tribals who numbered more than 400 groups also practise polygyny. It is a different thing that in the wake of development and modernization polygyny among them is increasingly decreasing. The monarchs or the rulers in our country also had a band of wives in their palaces. In Hindu mythology, Dasharath of *Ramayana* had three wives. The rulers of princely states also had a rich tradition of polygyny. Very clearly, polygyny has been the idiom of the rich class. It was assumed that polygyny gives status to a man.

Our description of polygynous marriage would remain incomplete if we do not mention anything about the patterns of relationship in this kind of family. In Africa, where the number of wives is considerable, each wife occupies a separate hut with her children and manages an independent household. It should also be said that harmony in the polygynous family lies in the definite superiority of the first wife. It is said that all the other wives serve as maids of the first wife.

Today, however, polygyny is on the way to extinction. It must also be observed that its emergence is not due to biological reasons. In all situations it is a form of marriage which is constructed by the society. As Lowie opines:

> But the one fact that it is most important to remember is that while probably a majority of primitive tribes permit polygyny, biological and in some measure social conditions prevent the majority within any one group from availing themselves of their theoretical prerogative.

Here, it should be made clear that in a tribe, which is theoretically polygynous, does not mean that a majority of members practise polygyny. It is empirically the privilege of very few.

(ii) Polyandry

Admittedly, the practice of polyandry has been rare. Claims for its presence suggest that less than 1 per cent of the peoples of the world's

tribes or other politically independent units have permitted it. Moreover, where polyandry was permitted only some of the families were polyandrous while the majority of the persons in such societies lived in monogamous or polygynous family. This form of marriage is that where one woman has many husbands.

John Lewis has provided a definition of polyandry. He says: "It is a marriage in which a woman can have more than one husband at the same time." Polyandry has been found in small number of societies. In simple food-gathering societies, it has been reported, for example, among the Wahuma tribals of East Africa and among the tribal groups of Tibet and Toda (southern India). Among the Wahumas polyandry is an altogether unique phenomenon. Though it is legitimate to practise polyandry, it is not a dominant institution among them. When a man is too poor to buy a wife alone, he is assisted by his brothers, and they share his marital rights until the woman's pregnancy, when they become his exclusive prerogative.

We have also noted earlier that there is prevalence of polygyny among the Eskimos. But there are instances wherein the group also practises polyandry. It should be said that among Eskimos polygyny and polyandry go together. Among certain Eskimo communities the conditions of life are so arduous that female children are considered a burden and are killed frequently after birth, "and thus the polygynous tendency due to the perils of masculine life is more than checked".

There is wide prevalence of polyandry among the Todas of Nilgiris. Why do they practise polyandry? We have some data which indicate that in the past the tribe had marked excess of men over women, coupled with the practice of female infanticide. But this custom has been abandoned and now there is a progressive diminution of male preponderance.

Among the Todas, when a man marries a woman it is understood that she automatically becomes the wife of his brothers, who normally live together. Even a brother born afterwards will be regarded as sharing his elder brother's rights. In such cases of fraternal polyandry no disputes ever arise among the husbands, and the very notion of such a possibility is flouted by the Toda mind. When the wife becomes pregnant, the eldest of her husbands performs a ceremony with a bow and arrow by which legal fatherhood is conventionally established in this tribe, but all the brothers are reckoned to be the child's fathers.

"The situation becomes more complicated when a woman weds several men who are not brothers and who, as may happen, live in different villages. This is non-fraternal polyandry. When the husbands are scattered over several villages, the wife usually lives for a month with each in turn, though there is no absolute rule. In such cases, the determination of fatherhood in a legal sense is extremely interesting. For all social purposes that husband who performs the bow and arrow ceremony during the wife's pregnancy establishes his status as father not only of the first child but of any children born subsequently until one of the other husbands performs the requisite rite. Usually it is agreed that the first two or three children shall belong to the first husband, that at a later pregnancy another shall establish paternal rights, and so forth." Among Todas, thus, biological paternity is completely disregarded, for a man long dead is considered the father of a child provided no other man has performed the essential ceremony.

R.H. Lowie long back (in 1921) took an account of the statistics regarding the incidence of polyandry among the Todas. His conclusions are found relevant even today. He observes:

> What the Todas have done is to cling to polyandry and temper it with polygyny, where formerly three brothers shared a single wife, they now tend to share two. In this way adapting themselves to the excess of women as compared with their former scarcity.

Group Marriage

Another form of marriage called 'group marriage' is also mentioned in the study of primitive marriage systems. The empirical data generated by social anthropologists hardly provide any detail about this form of marriage. Lowie says that the term 'marriage' as we understand it by customary definition, if applied, there is "hardly something of the kind of group marriage". He says that what we term 'group marriage' is actually *sexual communism*. In each society, besides the traditions of monogamy, polygyny and polyandry, there are instances of pre-marital and extra-marital sex relations. These sex relations could be loosely called group marriage. Lowie argues:

> In the first place we must recognize that far-reaching sexual communism may exist side by side with individual marriage. That is to say, one portion of the community may live according to the former

principle, the remainder according to the other. Our own civilization with its connivance at prostitution presents as clear an example as possible. Primitive societies differ mainly in that sexual communism is openly sanctioned within the corresponding limits.

Lowie argues at length referring to a large number of social anthropologists, particularly Rivers, Morgan and others that there has never been a form of marriage called group marriage. He denies the existence of sexual communism in any part of the world. His conclusion runs as follows:

> ...sexual communism as a condition taking the place of the individual family exists *nowhere* at the present time; and the arguments for its former existence must be rejected as unsatisfactory. This conclusion will find confirmation in the phenomena of primitive family life.

Thus, on the basis of the inferences drawn by Lowie and others, it can be said that the popular textbooks of social anthropology are wrong to refer to group marriage as a form of marriage. It has also been stated, in categorical terms, that there has never been and nowhere is there any incidence of group marriage among Indian tribes. We can come to an end by saying that despite the prevalence of polygyny and polyandry in parts of Africa and India, the general form of marriage all over the world remains to be monogamy which has come to stay for all times to come.

Means of Acquiring a Mate

Lowie first used the term "means of acquiring a mate" in his book *Primitive Society*, first published in 1921. Later on, in the book *An Introduction to Social Anthropology* by D.N. Majumdar and T.N. Madan (1957), the same phrase was used. Since then it has become a pattern with the authors to carry forward this phrase. However, Lowie used this terminology only to show the means whereby a mate is secured among the tribals. The legitimacy of the 'means' for acquiring a mate is a suspicious matter. For instance, a Bhil or a Gond may bring his wife by elopement, but the legitimacy given to this means is not of any high respect. Both the husband and wife in this case are considered to be debased.

Generalizations about primitive tribes are dangerous, but few exceptions will be found to the statement that matrimony with them is not so much a sacramental as a civil institution. However, there are two basic and popular forms of matrimony known as marriage by exchange and marriage by purchase. In both, a girl is treated as an asset which her family will not surrender without receiving adequate compensation.

The common means of acquiring a mate is marriage by exchange. Among some tribals of the country a man is not only forbidden to marry his sister and other kin women, but is practically obliged to mate with a particular type of cousin or some more remote relative. With this limitation exchange is commonly practised. It should be mentioned here that compared with exchange marriage purchase has an exceedingly wide distribution. However, there are several varieties of purchase. In some regions, a woman is, to all intents and purposes, a transferable and inheritable 'commodity'; in others, there will be found only the appearance of purchase, since the bride-price offered is balanced by an equivalent gift or dowry. Here, we shall discuss some of the widely prevalent means of acquiring a mate among tribals:

(1) By Probation

This form of marriage is found in some tribes of the heartland of the country, like the Kuki. In this the prospective spouses meet each other before actually entering into the marriage bond. This enables them to get know each other. The Kuki male goes to his beloved, stays there for some time. They are also, by custom, allowed to have sexual relations. If they are agreeable to it, the marriage is contracted. But, if the probation period between the two is not happy, they part company and try elsewhere. However, during the probation period, if the girl conceives, the male is obliged to solemnize the marriage. Hoebel has an interesting observation on this means of acquiring a spouse. Among the tribals bride-price is not so important as the fecundity of the wife to procreate children. If a woman is found to conceive within the least period, she is supposed to be a desirable wife.

(2) By Capture

In a civilized society, marriage by capture is condemned. However, among Nagas, there are some sections who, even today, acquire their mate by capture. One variety of marriage by capture is that prevalent among the Kharia and Birhor tribes. When a man finds a suitable occasion like a fair, a weekly market or a public place, he applies *sindur* on the forehead of the woman he likes. By this gesture, it is understood that the woman has been married publicly by the man. There is yet another variety among the Gonds. Marriage by capture is practised where the parents of the girl approve of it. The same is applicable to the Bhotias, a pastoral tribe living in the foothills of the Himalayas. But this kind of capture is known to the parents of both the girl and the boy in advance.

(3) By Trial

This method of acquiring a mate is actually the trial of the physical strength of the boy. The girls in most of the tribal groups desire to marry boys who are full with vigour and power. This kind of marriage by trial is found among the Bhils of Gujarat, Madhya Pradesh. The Bhils of Rajasthan, however, do not practise marriage by trial.

(4) By Purchase

One very common practice of acquiring a wife is by purchase. We have discussed it earlier. Lowie, in his study of primitive society, has made certain observations. He mentions marriage by purchase being found among the Kirghiz, a turkish tribe of south-western Siberia, the Ho of Bihar, the Ewe tribe of Togo of West Africa, and the Kai of New Guinea. In our country marriage by purchase is known as marriage by paying the bride-price especially among all the major tribal groups such as the Gond, Santhal, Chaudhara and Bhil. Earlier, the amount of bride-price was nominal. But, during the last one decade, it has gone up very high.

(5) By Elopement

It is practised where the arranged marriage is discarded. When one or both the parents object to the love marriage, the partners resort to marriage by elopement. This method is occasionally observed among Gonds, Bhils and Garasias of Rajasthan. However, the bride-price is settled after the elopement when the spouses settle in their life. Among the Garasias of Rajasthan, the bride-price is realized even after a child is born.

(6) By Exchange

There is a practice among the some tribes and even among the lower and intermediate castes to marry by exchange. It is a practice which saves a man from paying the bride-price. According to this, the brother gives his sister in marriage to another man and gets the latter's sister as his wife. In this case, there is no transaction of bride-price. This form of marriage thus saves both the families from any expenditure. In most of the Indian tribes, this means of acquiring a mate is sometimes practised.

(7) By Intrusion

Sometimes a girl forcefully intrudes into the house of the boy for whom she develops a liking. Sometimes gets insulted but continues to stay there till she is accepted as the daughter-in-law by the parents of the boy. This method of intrusion is observed among the Ho, Kamar and Munda tribes. Even the tribals who practise it, do not look upon it with favour and respect.

(8) By Service

This method of acquiring a mate is rare. Evans-Pritchard, in his study of 241 tribal groups, found that only 30 observed it. In our country, the Bhils and Gonds occasionally observe marriage by service. When the parents of the boy cannot afford to pay the bride-price, the boy gives his services to the parents of the girl. Wages for his service are negotiated and the amount accumulated on account of his service is transferred to the amount of bride-price. When there is final adjustment, the marriage is arranged.

Concluding Observations

A man has a hunger for sex. Man or woman, must fulfill this hunger. If promiscuity is allowed there would be anomie in the society. In order to give legitimacy to sex hunger, there is always some institution of marriage. It is through marriage that sex relations are ordered, disciplined. And, when there is marriage the girls should get their husbands, and husbands their wives. When brother and sister or father and daughter or mother and son, that is, close kin can not marry, spouses are drawn from 'other' lineages and descent groups. It is, therefore, that we marry with our enemies, that is, alien clans. The anthropologists whenever talk about marriage, they call it an alliance.

There are rules for marriage. There are forms of marriage. There are ways of acquiring a spouse. Despite all these aspects, there is one specificity of marriage peculiar to primitives. It has been a common notion among all the tribals of the world that some sort of compensation must be yielded in return for the bride. However, there may be some exception in this rule but the study of different forms of marriage, like monogamy, polygyny and polyandry and also of the varying means of acquiring a mate indicates that the core aspect of primitive marriage is the payment of bride-price. It is argued that bride-price has to be paid by the parents of the girl, for they not only gave birth to the girl but also brought her up, nurtured her and in the present context educated her. Bride-price is considered to be valid compensation for such a long period of the rearing girl.

Further Readings

Homans, G.G., and Schneider, D.M., *Marriage, Authority and Final Causes*, Glencoe, 1955.

Lowie, R.H., *Primitive Society*, Routledge and Kegan Paul Ltd., London, 1960 (fifth impression).

Majumdar, D.N. and Madan, T.N., *An Introduction to Social Anthropology*, Asia Publishing House, Bombay, 1957.

Westermarck, E., *The History of Human Marriage*, 3 Vols., London, 1925.

11

Kinship

"Blood is thicker than water" goes an old saying. When we are in distress, we look forward for help to our relatives. Likewise, tribal society is also closely knit by kinship relations. Evans-Pritchard, while working among the Nuers, a tribal group of Africa, found that relatives have an important place in their life. He further says that a Nuer holds a person who is his relative as very close to him. Therefore, if you want to get help from a Nuer, you have to identify yourself as one of their kinsmen. If this kind of identification is convincingly made, the Nuer would accept you as his own man; else you are an enemy.

Iravati Karve, who has conducted intensive fieldwork in different parts of India, says that caste is nothing but an extension of kin. The importance of kinship can hardly be emphasized. In social anthropology much of the literature revolves round the discussion on kinship. Some people think that if kinship is taken out of social anthropology, there nothing left to study. In fact, the study of kinship has been a predominant tradition or culture of social anthropology. Kinship, it appears, is an obsession with the social anthropologists. Eriksen writes about the central place of kinship in social anthropology:

> Generations of anthropologists have been flabbergasted at the intricate kinship systems existing in many 'primitive' societies. Several famous examples of such complicated systems are to be found in the Australian aboriginal population. These peoples traditionally hunters and gatherers have the simplest technology in the world. They lack metals, domesticated animals and writing, and in most cases they do not have even the rudiments of agriculture. Nevertheless, many of these nomadic groups have kinship systems so complex that it may take an outsider years to comprehend them fully... The study of kin-

ship has always been a core topic in anthropology. Towards the end of the 1940s kinship was so central, especially in British social anthropology, that despairing lay people (and students) spoke ironically of the subject as 'kinshipology'. Many known anthropologists have reacted with incomprehension at the great interest in kinship still prevalent in the profession.

Why is kinship so important in social anthropology? Following can be the answers:

(1) It is through kinship that a person earns his livelihood. Traditional occupational knowledge is given through this organization. It is kin who make all efforts for the welfare and of the person.
(2) The career of the individual is planned and executed by kinsmen. It is very common to find in India the Marwaris settled in different parts of country, are running their business through kinship ties. If one member of a kin group goes to Mumbai, the migrant group would grow in big size in a couple of years. The tribals are also drawn through kinship ties to different cities.
(3) It is through kinship that matrimonial arrangements are made. It is common to find the bio-data of the prospective groom and bride contain details about the affinal and agnate kin. This clearly shows the importance of kinship in the settlement of marriage.
(4) On the death of a person the mourning period is observed according to the degree of relationship with the deceased. Birth, marriage and death are the three basic occasions when there is a serious and careful reckoning of kin.
(5) Kinship is related to all the other aspects of society such as economy, celebration of festivals, worship and folkways.
(6) The social organization of a society revolves round kinship. If we examine the organization of a particular society we see that kinship is its integral part.
(7) I.P. Desai, the noted sociologist, has empirically established that the institution of family is nothing but a part of wider social relations. According to him, kinship has its origin in biology but its legitimacy extends to relationship. In the west, on the other hand, some anthropologists such as Schneider have argued that kinship is related to biology and blood ties. However, anthropological research generally analyzes it as cultural classification of people. And, as aspects of group formation.

The importance of kinship is very great in social anthropology. It is the kin group which takes care of one's livelihood, career, marriage, protection and social identity. The importance becomes all the more stronger among the tribals as they reside in unfriendly and inhospitable environment in the hills and forests. We have enough empirical evidence to suggest that the survival of a tribal in poverty and deprivation is almost impossible without the support of the kin group. For instance, on occasion of marriage, among the Bhils, the relatives carry maize bread for the guests; on occasion of death the kinsmen also provide meals to the bereaved family. From cradle to grave, the strength of succour lies in kinship.

What is Kinship?

The central fabric of kinship is biology as stated earlier. It is because of biology that we find kinship in all human societies. But kinship varies from society to society. In a matriarchal society, the mother's brother occupies a pivotal place; on the other hand, in a patriarchal society, the father's brother occupies the important place. Thus, the classification of kin is based on culture. Kinship has now been developed into a full-fledged theory. John Lewis defines it in very simple and general terms:

> Kinship is a social recognition and expression of genealogical relationships. It is not only actual but may be based on supposed ties of blood.

Lewis' approach to kinship is genealogical or based on descent. Descent could be traced from mother or father, or in some cases, both. Lewis also says that kinship relations could also be extended to persons who are treated as being on par with blood or marital kin.

A.R. Brown, who is credited to have conducted fieldwork among three tribes of western Australia (1913), has defined kinship as follows:

> Kinship is genealogical relationship recognized for social purposes and made the basis of the customary relation of social relations.

Brown's thesis is that kinship lies at the root of genealogical relations but its social extensions constitute the meaning of kinship. The importance of kinship, Brown further says, is reckoned on the occasions of various customs observed during births, marriages, deaths and festivals.

Yet another definition of kinship is given by Charles Winick, who observes:

> Kinship system may include socially recognized relationship based on supposed as well as actual geneologicalties.

Quite like others Winick also recognizes both biological or descent kin and socially accepted kin within the kinship system. He stresses on the point that kinship is basically related to social approval. This approval is observable on social and cultural occasions such as phases of life and festivals.

Levi-Strauss is said to be the master figure in developing the theory of kinship. In his classical study titled *The Elementary Structures of Kinship* (1969), he makes an important theoretical contribution. He challenges the descent theory. He does not regard shared descent but rather the development of alliances between two groups through the exchange of women, as the fundamental fact of kinship. Levi-Strauss, in theoretical terms, is a structuralist. He holds the view that the mind organizes the world in contrasting pairs and develops coherent systems of relationship from such a starting point. It is through kinship that there is transmission of cultural values and knowledge between two generations.

Agnate and Affine Relations

All of us belong to a family. Let us take, for example, the Indian joint family. In this family there is one pair—husband and wife. They are affinal kin which means they are united by marital ties. This relationship is also called consanguineal kin. Their bond is that they are permitted to have sexual relations. Another set of relationships is between parents and siblings. The siblings are kin by blood. They are the offsprings of their parents. These relations are called agnate relations, that is, relations tied by blood. If there are grandparents in the family, they are also agnate kin. Similarly, if one of the sons in the family is married, his wife is affine. She is related to her husband and other members of the family through marital relations. Thus, a family consists of agnates and affines. All the members are related to one another by marriage or blood. But this kind of explanation is limited only to family. Kinship extends beyond the family also. There are kin who belong to other families also. For instance, the sister of the family is married to a boy of another family. Relations with such a family are affine relations.

Standard Kinship Symbols and Abbreviations Used in Anthropology

To understand kinship relationship better, let us provide an explanation to some of the kinship symbols used by anthropologists in fieldwork. These symbols are standard and used universally by anthropologists all over the world.

The triangle is the symbol for a man. For our purpose this man is named Rama. The circle denotes a woman, Basanti. The equals sign shows marriage. It indicates that Basanti is married to Rama. A horizontal line connects the siblings. In the following figure, Jaya and Yash are siblings in family 1, and Sushila, Shantu and Ramesh are in family 2. A diagonal line through a symbol indicates that the person in question (here, Rama) is dead. Rama's and Basanti's son Yash is married to Gora's and Shanti's daughter, Sushila.

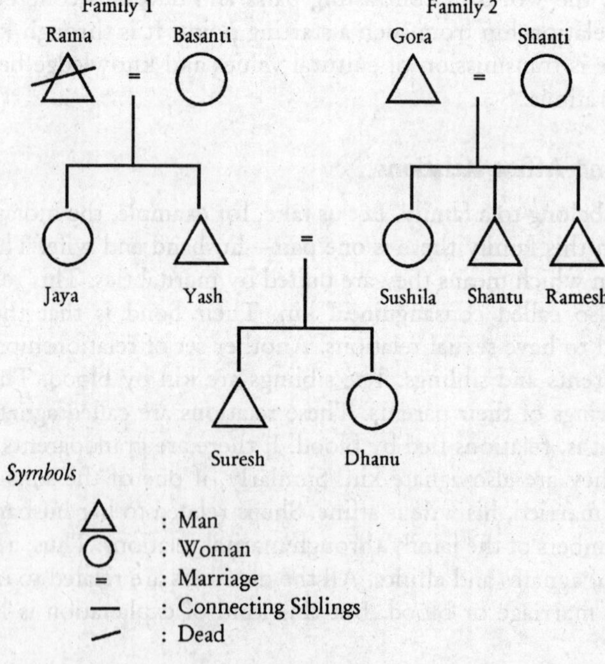

Quite like symbols, the anthropologists also use some standard abbreviations for kinship terms which are given below:

B : Brother
D : Daughter
F : Father
H : Husband
M : Mother
S : Son
W : Wife
Z : Sister

Thus, MBD is mother's brother's daughter. In these abbreviations ego is the reference point.

Kinship Terminology

Kinship is established as a special branch of study in social anthropology. Any study in social anthropology is incomplete without an elaborate description of kinship. However, whatever anthropological studies and monographs pertaining to various tribal groups in India that we have hardly provide any insight into kinship. Interestingly, the eminent social anthropologists who have brought out classical monographs, make only a passing reference to kinship. This is a sad commentary on our achievements. However, Iravati Karve and Kathleen Gough have worked excellently in the field of kinship. Those who study kinship have a kit of conceptual framework which helps them analyze kinship behaviour adequately. We would, therefore, discuss a few of the concepts which are central to the study of kin relations.

Kinship emerges only with reference to a particular person. If we talk about a daughter, it presupposes parents. Daughter originates from parents. Similarly, if we talk of nephew, there is surely some uncle. Thus, there cannot be daughter and nephew without the kin of parents and uncle. Kin are broadly divided into two categories: kin from the side of mother and those from the side of the father. In Europe as well as in our sub-continent both the mother and father's sides are equally important. These relations belong to both the genders.

The kinship terminology or the concepts specific to kinship relations are a few only. We discuss some of these crucial concepts in the following paragraphs:

Descent

Descent traces its origin to persons who were ancestors. These ancestors were real beings. Descent thus is geneological. It links the present generation with the preceding generations. (A) is the ego. His father was (B), his grandfather was (C), his great grandfather was (D), and so on and so forth. Descent, thus, traces a person's origin to the one who created the generation. Anthropologists have defined descent in many ways. According to Meyer Fortes:

> A descent group is an arrangement of persons that serves the attainment of legitimate social and personal ends.

Fortes has defined descent group with reference to his study of African tribes. He stresses on the social functions of the group. He does not take into consideration the biological origin of the members of the descent group.

G.P. Murdock, who is the celebrated expounder of the concept of social structure, says:

> Descent refers solely to a cultural principle whereby an individual is socially allocated to a specific group of consanguineal kinsmen.

A consanguineal group, according to Murdock, is that which is a blood group. And, thus, the members of a descent group essentially are members of a blood group. When the descent membership is traced for generations, the members born out of this group are the members of the descent group. There are some characteristics which are common to a descent group:

(1) Members of a descent group trace their origin to a single ancestor who happened to live in the past.
(2) The ancestor is a living being, a reality.
(3) The ancestor is never mythological or fictitious.
(4) The members of a descent group are united by blood ties.
(5) Marriage and sexual relations are not allowed among the descent group, since they belong to the same ancestor.
(6) Members of a descent group are also related to inheritance and succession.

Anthropologists have found certain types of descent. The following types are generally referred:

(i) Unilateral Descent

The members of this descent group trace their origin to a single ancestor. Most of the societies in the world traditionally give the father's side a certain priority, since the father's surname passes on to the children.

(ii) Bilateral Descent

In some societies descent is traced to two ancestors---male and female. This is called bilateral descent. Bremnes has hinted at the difficulties to base unilineal principle in counting both the descent groups—matrilateral and patrilateral. It is said that the bilateral way of kin reckoning creates problems in the construction of genealogies. "For each generation one moves back in time, the number of kin is doubled. We have two parents, four grandparents, eight great grandparents, sixteen great-great grandparents, and so on. Genealogies, thus, tend to be shallow in this kind of society—most persons are unable to name ancestors more than three or four generations back."

(iii) Patrilineal Descent

The descent in a patrilineal system incudes at least ego's siblings, father father's siblings and the children of the men in the group. Father's sister's children, however, do not belong to ego's group, but to her husband's group.

(iv) Matrilineal Descent

The matrilineal descent includes both female and male relatives of mother, mother's mother and mother's mother's mother. One's father, however, belongs to a different lineage, namely, his own mother's lineage. The matrilineal system is a mirror image of the patrilineal one.

Lineage

Lineage is yet another term which needs to be defined. Its occurrence in kinship terminology is very common. Sometimes lineage is used synonymous with clan. However, they are different terms. Eriksen defines lineage as follows:

> As a general rule, we may say that a lineage consists of persons who can indicate by stating all the intermediate links, common descent from a shared ancestor or ancestress.

Lineage, thus, is a group of people who link themselves to a common ancestor. The members practise strict exogamy. Eriksen has made this differentiation clear: a clan encompasses people who assume shared descent from an ancestor/ancestress without being able to enumerate all of these links. For instance, in medieval Rajasthan, the rulers and *jagirdars* used to have bards or *charans* who maintained the genealogy of the *thikana* family or the royal kin. Bards, thus, were genealogists and they enumerated all the generations which linked the ego to the ancestor. Thus, the genealogists gave the names of the descent group. In such a group enumeration is essential. In the clan only those groups are identified who share common descent from a particular ancestor.

Filial

The kin who are related through father and mother are called filial relations. Among the filial there are agnates and affines. Agnates are also called consanguineal or blood kin. Ego's brother's son is an agnate, and ego's wife's brother is an affine. Both affines and agnates are termed as filial.

Collateral

A person's blood relations from generation to generation are called lineal. For instance, ego's sons, son's son are lineal. But, the parallel cousins are called collaterals. For instance, ego's father's brother's sons are collaterals. These relations are parallel relations, that is, running side by side with the descent group. The collaterals reckon the same ancestor but not in a direct line. Thus, lineal relations are in the same generation up and down but in collateral relations. Those who belong to the parallel line are collaterals.

Corporate Group

The corporate kin consists of all the kin—patrilineal, matrilineal and collaterals. Defining the corporate group Eriksen writes:

> Corporate kin groups tend to be unilineal, which means that new members are recruited on a genealogical principle, either becoming a member of the father's kin group (patrilineal system) or the mother's kin group (matrilineal system).

Thus, the corporate group is very large in size. It includes patriarchal descent group or the matriarchal descent group. Collaterals constitute a part of corporate group.

Reckoning the Kinsmen

Kinship relations are very complicated. Each society has traditions of membership to a particular kin. The resources of one group are transmitted to another through tradition. The reckoning of kin varies from society to society. For instance, in the patriarchal society, the descent group occupies a higher place compared to that occupied by the affinal kin. Eriksen has mentioned six principles of reckoning kin. He observes:

> Formally, there are six possible principles for the transmission of kin group membership and other resources from parents to children. As already noted, the same principle does not have to hold true for succession, inheritance and descent, although the three are frequently lumped together, particularly in patrilineal societies.

Eriksen further says that members of a particular kin are those who are born in the group, that is, who are blood kin and those who are brought into the group by marriage. The first principle, therefore, is that members to a kin group are related by blood and marriage. The second set of kin who are from amongst the first set or group are those to whom resources are transferred. In some cases it is not necessary that to whom resources are transferred are members of the kin group.

There are six possible ways of kin group membership:

1. *Patrilineal*: Transmission of membership and/or resources takes place unilineally through the father's lineage.
2. *Matrilineal*: Transmission of membership and/or resources takes place unilineally through the mother's lineage.
3. *Double*: Some resources are transmitted through the father's line-

age, others through the mother's lineage. The two lineages are kept separate.

4. *Cognatic*: Resources can be transmitted through kin on both mother's and father's sides (bilaterally).
5. *Parallel*: In this, men transmit to their sons and women to their daughters. This is, however, a rare form.
6. *Crossing or alternating*: Another rare variety which represents the opposite of the previous one: men transmit to their daughters and women to their sons.

Of the above, the first two principles are generally applicable, whereas the remaining four are exceptional only. "This simplistic typology should not lead anyone to believe that, for instance, persons in patrilineal societies are not related to their mother's relatives. Practically, all kinship systems organize kin relations on both the mother's and the father's sides, although rights, names and group membership frequently give priority to one side. In a patrilineal society, one's commitment to the father's lineage is, in most situations, stronger than one's commitment to the mother's."

Theoretical Development of Kinship

Normally, social anthropology seems to be weak in its theory building. However, there are some areas which are rich in this regard. These areas include culture, evolution and kinship. Recently, the area of social structure has also been theoretically strengthened. Social structure has reached the status of structuralism. The field of kinship has also witnessed radical changes during the last century. It was Lewis Henry Morgan who took a keen interest in developing an elaborate classificatory kinship system. He was the founding father of kinship terminology. Morgan's theory was discovered by the British anthropologist, W.H.R. Rivers. Acknowledging the contribution of Rivers in properly interpretating kinship Meyer Fortes writes:

> It was a British anthropologist, W.H.R. Rivers, as all student of the subject know, whose rediscovery of Morgan restored him to his rightful place in the mainstream of anthropological scholarship and this was the beginning of a method and theory of research which took deep root in British anthropology.

Morgan's kinship theory was further put to new heights by Levi-

Strauss. We will in this section discuss the contributions of Morgan, Levi-Strauss and others to theoretical development of kinship.

Morgan's Classificatory Theory

Morgan proposed a much controversial theory of kinship. During his lifetime his theory was rejected. It was after his death and particularly after River's interpretation that his theory came into prominence. The structural theory of kinship which Levi-Strauss developed at a later stage borrows heavily from Morgan. It is because of this that Meyer Fortes calls Morgan the founding father of kinship theory of structure and social organization. Morgan's classificatory theory of kinship is found in his *Systems of Consanguinity and Affinity*. Besides being a theorist, Morgan was a first-rate ethnologist. When he propounded his theory of sex promiscuity or communism, he was criticized severely. Among his critics were Radcliffe-Brown and Frazer. He was rejected for making conjectures without any ethnic evidence. His classificatory kinship theory begins with systems of relationships. Morgan does not consider biology as a central point of kinship. For him social relations were highly important in kinship.

> *Lewis Henry Morgan* has been a victim of history. And history as is often said a fickle jade. He was honoured by Americans and was equally condemned. Morgan was, by all accounts, as robust and uncompromising an American of his day as could have been found anywhere in the United States. Along with Henry Maine, Morgan is also considered to be the founder of modern anthropology. His most important contribution to early anthropology was his theory of social evolution. His *Ancient Society* (1877) is said to be a classic piece of work. His other work *Systems of Consanguinity and Affinity* is of equal status.
>
> Morgan worked on social evolution and established that all societies passed through the phases of savagery, barbarism and civilization. His theories include structural theory of kinship and social organization. He also established: (1) the theory of primitive promiscuity, (2) group marriage, and (3) classificatory kinship system. Whatever theories of kinship we have, all stem from Morgan's theory. His contemporaries were Rivers, Boas, Henry Maine and Radcliffe-Brown.

And, therefore, kin need to be classified according to the degree of their social relations.

In his classical theoretical treatise *Systems of Consanguinity and Affinity* Morgan elaborates the classificatory and descriptive systems of kinship. After having analyzed this, he gives his master hypothesis of primitive promiscuity and group marriage. He has defined descriptive and classificatory terms with reference to marital and blood relations. For empirical evidence he has taken Ganowanian, Turanian and Malayan families. In a Malayan family blood relations are never described by a combination of the primary terms. On the contrary, these are arranged in classes or categories upon principles of discrimination peculiar to these families. All the individuals of the same class are admitted into one and the same relationship. The same special term is applied indiscriminately to each and everyone of them.

To explain the classificatory system, Morgan gives an example: My father's brother's son is my brother under the system about to be considered, and I call him by the same term which I use to designate an own brother; the son of this collateral brother (my father's brother's son's son) and the son of my own brother are both my sons. And, I apply to them the same term I would use to designate my own son. In other words, the person first named is admitted into the same relationship as my brothers, and those last named as my sons. The principle of classification is carried to every person in several collateral lines, near and remote, in such a manner as to include them all in the several great classes. Morgan's classificatory system reckons the kin in arbitrary and artificial way, but the results produced by this theory are coherent and systematic.

The descriptive system is defined as the reverse of the classificatory system. In this system each relationship falls in the recognized relationship. The relations are not classified but are addressed only as their description is given. To differentiate descriptive and classificatory system it can be said that in the descriptive system a single special term is applied to each relation, whereas in the classificatory system there is a combination of primary terms.

Meyer Fortes has given an analysis of the legacy of Lewis Henry Morgan in his work *Kinship and the Social Order*. He says that descriptive and classificatory terms of kinship are actually the terms of binary opposition. Later on, Levi-Strauss also developed his theory of elementary and complex kinship relations in structural analysis. The structuralists consider binary opposition as a form of mind. Morgan has followed the binary terms consistently in his work. He works on descent relations. His classificatory system is applied to descent group. The major elements of classificatory system are given below:

(1) It is generic in its connotation. It takes into consideration the descent of kin relations such as mother's brother and sister's son.
(2) It is a method of dividing kin according to socially pre-established categories or types.
(3) It indicates social relations based on affinal (marital) and agnate (blood) ties.
(4) It is an important part of the knowledge system of any society. Knowledge is always related to social organization and power. This is what sociology of knowledge gives us.

Criticism of Morgan's Theory

Morgan has been very uncharitably criticized and condemned throughout. It was after his death that social anthropologists appreciated his work. His critics allege that he did not have any ethnic evidence to support his theory. His theories are, therefore, said to be only conjectural formulations. His contemporaries such as Rivers, Boas, Radcliffe-Brown later on changed their opinion. Leslie, while taking a complete stock of Morgan's contributions, admits that "Morgan's work has been of great theoretical importance."

We summarize the contributions of Morgan as under:

(1) He gave the theory of primitive promiscuity,
(2) He developed the theory of group marriage,
(3) He constructed classificatory kinship system of theory, and
(4) He founded the evolutionary theory which characterized the 19th century in Europe.

Levi-Strauss' Structural Theory

Levi-Strauss has provided two forms of kinship structures—elementary and complex. The elementary form was developed in his work, *The Elementary Structures of Kinship* (1949). The complex form was developed at a later stage. Strauss was a prolific writer known for developing structuralism in France and Europe. It would be interesting to remind ourselves here that when the Indian anthropologist Iravati Karve wrote the preface to her second edition of *Kinship Or-*

ganization in India (1965), she argued that her work should be tested with reference to the kinship theory of Levi-Strauss. Therefore, we see that all over the world Levi-Strauss is considered to be a respected authority on kinship. He was greatly influenced by Emile Durkheim and Marcel Mauss, both of whom were French sociologists. Other linguistic structuralists who influenced him were Ferdinand de Saussure and Roman Jakobson. Strauss has borrowed much from linguistic structuralism. The enormous ethnic data which he had collected were synthesized by him. He is credited to have propounded the elementary and complex structural theories of kinship.

Elementary Structural Theory

Strauss discusses kinship in its different aspects. He says that in all societies of the world there are four fundamental kin relationships:

(1) Brother-sister,
(2) Husband-wife,
(3) Father-son, and
(4) Mother's brother-sister's son.

Before we analyze these four fundamental kin relations, let us very boldly say that Strauss does not regard descent as being central to kinship. Instead, he says that "the development of alliances between groups through the exchange of women, is the fundamental fact of kinship". In other words, Strauss rejects shared descent as a part of kinship relations. For him marriage is central to kinship relation. He makes his point clear when he says:

> The very formation of society occurs when a man gives his sisters away to another man, thereby, creating ties of affinity.

As stated earlier, the descent group consists of the members born in a genealogy. This is the family. The members of this family are the procreation of the family. Strauss says that the society begins to be built when one family makes an alliance by marriage or affinity with another family. Thus, the affinal or marital relations count in the structure of kinship. Strauss' definition of elementary family is based on structures from structural linguistics. Commenting on the elementary structure of kinship, Eriksen observes:

> Levi-Strauss regarded this 'elementary structure', or 'kinship atom', inspired by similar structures from structural linguistics, as funda-

mental to kinship and to human society as such. Some societies are constructed directly on the 'elementary structure', including societies based on classificatory cross-cousin marriage as well as societies based on asymmetrical alliances.

Levi-Strauss' definition of elementary structure of four fundamental kin relations is given in the figure below:

Elementary Structure of Kinship
(Four Fundamental Kin Relations)

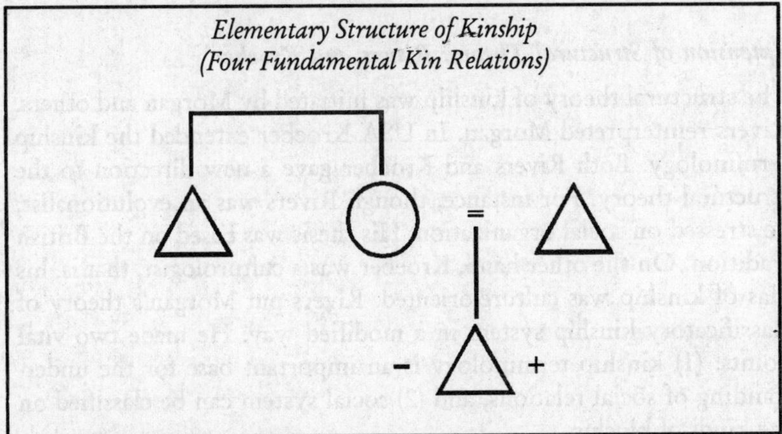

Complex Structural Theory

Elementary structure of kinship remains restricted to a small descent group which is found all over the world. It has been the first and primary structure of relationship and, therefore, it is elementary. The structure becomes complex the day the son or daughter is married. Levi-Strauss has defined complex structure of kinship as under:

> Complex systems add further relationships to the four fundamental ones as determining factors in marriage.

What is particular about the difference between elementary structures and complex structures is that in elementary structures the rules of marriage are positive. They not only specify whom one cannot marry but also whom one can marry. In the complex structures there are negative rules only and are therefore unable to create long-term alliances between kin groups.

The mother's brother is an important character in Levi-Strauss' kinship pattern. Granted the universality of incest prohibition and that men control women, the breeding of children ultimately depends on his willingness to give away his sister. It is because of this that Strauss argues that the relationship between a man and his maternal uncle is crucial. "If the spouses are intimate, the wife will have a distanced relationship with her brother and vice-versa. If one has a close, tender relationship with one's maternal uncle, the father will be a strict and severe person and vice-versa."

Extension of Structural Theory: Rivers and Kroeber

The structural theory of kinship was initiated by Morgan and others. Rivers reinterpreted Morgan. In USA Kroeber extended the kinship terminology. Both Rivers and Kroeber gave a new direction to the structural theory. For instance, though Rivers was an evolutionalist, he stressed on social organization. His thesis was based on the British tradition. On the other hand, Kroeber was a culturologist, that is, his bias of kinship was culture-oriented. Rivers put Morgan's theory of classificatory kinship system in a modified way. He made two vital points: (1) kinship terminology is an important base for the understanding of social relations, and (2) social system can be classified on the kinds of kinship.

Kroeber contested Rivers. He also put forth his argument on two points: (1) classificatory kinship is not a social organization and, therefore, it cannot be made the basis of classifying the societies; and (2) kinship terminology does not refer to social institutions. According to Kroeber, the origin and nature of kinship terminology is basically psychological and it should be used in this context only. In the beginning Rivers contradicted Kroeber but at a later stage his application of genealogical method revealed that kinship terminology is related to social system. Therefore, in any analysis of social organization, kinship should be given an important place.

The debate on kinship which developed between Kroeber and Rivers characterized the beginning of the 20th century. During this part of the century, the American social anthropologists were not interested in kinship studies. In Europe, particularly England, Radcliffe-Brown made a breakthrough in the study of kinship. He come out with a series of lectures on social structure. Though Radcliffe-Brown did not accept the theoretical position taken by Rivers in developing kinship terminology, at a later stage, he developed his theory based on that of Rivers. The basic contribution of Radcliffe-

Brown is that he established a logical relationship between genealogy and kinship relations. He analyzed the descent groups and in doing so he was much influenced by Rivers.

Levi-Strauss and Radcliffe-Brown were poles apart in the development of kinship terminology. The differentials are vital: Levi-Strauss, who was a structuralist, was influenced by linguistic anthropologists. He talked about the forms which were universally found in mankind. Radcliffe-Brown, on the other hand, was a functionalist. He established that in each social structure there are genealogical relations. In other words, the relations between father and son, grandfather and grandson are genealogical. The society gives recognition to these kinship ties on occasions of birth, marriage, death and festivals.

Malinowski has also contributed substantially to the development of kinship terminology. His approach was also oriented to social structure. His speciality is that he looked at the society from the point of view of biology and psychology. Gulckman very rightly criticizes Malinowski on the argument that the latter over-looked the contributions of the individual in the system. System is important, but individual is also equally important.

The functionalists, namely, Radcliffe-Brown and Malinowski, along with their disciples, promoted the kinship theory on the basis of social structure. Among the followers of Radcliffe-Brown and Malinowski, mention may be made of Fred Eggan also. The kinship theory based on social structure was further developed by Kathleen Gough who worked among the Nayars of South India.

The kinship terminology developed by Kroeber, Rivers, Radcliffe-Brown and Malinowski can be summarized into four substantial points:

(1) It takes a long time for a change in kinship system from one stage to another. Despite changes in different directions, the basic aspects of kinship remain the same.
(2) In order to bring about a change in a kinship system, it is essential to manage a change in the nuclear family. This is possible when the nuclear family takes to marriage outside the group of endogamy and affects biological and cultural changes. For instance, kinship terminology would change after sometime if a matriarchal family changes to patriarchal type of family.
(3) Kinship systems do not diffuse among the neighbours. The changes in the system only come through the family. In other

words, it is very difficult to generate change in kinship terminology only by accepting another social system.

(4) When a social system undergoes change due to exogenous factors, after generations, the social structure of the system also changes.

A radical change in the study of kinship system has come about in the US and the European continent. Earlier, social anthropologists normally studied other cultures and societies. For them, the study of other cultures—cultures other than their own—was social anthropology. For instance, if an American studied Indian family, it is social anthropology and if an Indian studied American family it was social anthropology. Such an approach to social anthropology has undergone radical change. Now, anthropologists are also studying their own culture. For instance, Raymond Firth got his fieldwork done though his students in his own society. Again, G.C. Homans, an American social anthropologist, asked his student David M. Schneider to study the industrial community of America. These studies brought out an important finding: When we move from one community to another, there is a change in kinship terminology. The reason for this change is that in America kinship behaviour is influenced by the individual values. For instance, in the US, the elderly people use the first name of the younger people and not the term meant for a particular kin. Homans and Schneider have drawn out several similar changes in the US communities in the development of kinship terminology. However, it must be observed that in the US there is no role of kinship as we have in India in the realm of politics, religion and economy. Schneider, who worked in parts of Chicago, concludes that kinship is nothing but a system of symbols. In collaboration with Raymond Firth he has made a comparative study of the kinship systems of Britain and America.

Today, literature in social anthropology has cropped up in bulk. From Morgan, Levi-Strauss and Rivers to Firth, Homans and Schneider, efforts have been made to comprehend kinship from different perspectives—evolutionary, structural, functional and social organization. During the last five decades, social anthropologists have brought out some classical works in the field of kinship. Besides the anthropologists mentioned above, Evans-Pritchard studied Nuer, Nadel studied the Nupe and Fortes studies the Tallensy. In this connection, it must be stressed that Fortes made a classical study on the kinship system found among the African tribes. We have already mentioned that Indian social set-up has not been studied with any depth except by Iravati Karve, Kathleen Gough and Louis Dumont. Some work, however, has also been done by T.N. Madan and A.C. Mayer.

The Nature of Kinship: Debate on Biological and Social Nature

Interpretation of kinship by anthropologists has been both biological and social-cultural. Ego's son is son because he is born of the parents. This is biological. But when ego does not have any son or daughter and he adopts a boy as his son, the boy is not biologically related to the ego but he is socially and culturally the son of the ego. The society gives legitimacy to the boy as a son. In polyandry, the eldest brother is the father of all the sons produced out of two or three brothers. Among the Todas of Nilgiris, the social father is legitimized both as biological and social father. In social anthropology there has been a debate on the issue regarding who is considered to be a kin—biological or social. Many of the modern societies, largely of Europe and the US, generally see themselves as more closely related to their siblings than to their cousins, as well as to first cousins than to second cousins. Classificatory kinship seems to be more or less absent in this kind of society. However, it transpires that even this kind of society has kin terms which derive from social organization rather than from biological kinship.

In India, biological kin are not that important as the social and cultural ones. Or, in other words, classificatory kin are as important as biological kin. In Gujarat, the males are socially considered to be *bhai* or brother. In the Dravidian family, the elder is *Amma*, *Anna* or *Swami*. In such classificatory terms biological relationship is not important. The addressive terms in all cases are merely social, and not biological.

However, there are some social anthropologists who argue that the biological kin are the real kin. But this kind of argument is rejected. Needham (1962) and Schneider (1984) have maintained that among the primitives, kin are not recognized only as biological facts. They are always social and cultural. Eriksen deals at length with this controversy. He says:

> At least, the examples given here have shown that the kinship system in a society does not follow automatically from biological kin relations. When the descent is important in order to justify claims to

> land, it may be common to manipulate genealogies... Further, many societies have also developed forms of social organization, with political, economic and other dimensions, which are based on kinship. Both religion and daily rules for conduct may in such communities be based on respect for the ancestors and ancestral spirits.

Those scholars who have worked in African tribes have empirically established that biology has a restricted relevance for reckoning relationship. Wider recognition of kin in all cases is social and cultural. The debate whether biology or socio-cultural factors in the recognition of kin has now been weakened. It is being increasingly recognized that in some cases social kin are more important than biological ones. These kin are reckoned on occasions of birth, marriage and death but there are 'other' socially constructed kin or rather fictitious kin who are also equally recognized. Thus, kinship behaviour and relationship are partly biological and party social.

Kinship, Business and Politics

Kinship also has a role in business, bureaucracy and politics. It is said in our country that the bureaucratic bosses and political leaders miss no opportunity to recruit their kinsmen in government and public sector jobs. One who is not related to the powerful persons cannot hope to get employment. In popular terms it is called nepotism. If we look outside our country towards Europe and the US, we find that "the capitalist labour market is ostensibly based on formally voluntary contracts and individual achievement and not on kinship commitments and ascribed identity. It is, therefore, customary to regard the kin-based organization as a contrast, and possible threat, to the bureaucratic organization characteristic of both the labour market and the system of political administration in modern states/societies."

In big business houses such as that of Birlas, Tatas, Ambanis and Godrej, production is supervised by kin-based executives and supervisors. The business houses have a belief that the kinsfolk in industry and trade have loyalty to specific persons. Though these business houses have now become purely economic and professional enterprises, kin-based organizations continue to remain in operation.

Kinship is also tied with politics. Public life in our country is characterized by the kin groups of those who are in power. Very often we talk about the role of dynasties in ruling the country. We also find that cabinet berths are created in consideration of kin relations. Tickets for contesting elections are also given on kinship consideration. As a matter of fact, in our day-to-day activities kinship and organizational functioning are so intertwined that it is difficult to isolated the two. "The relationship between kin-based and bureaucratic organizations must always be explored in empirical context. Then, we will discover that the two principles very often function simultaneously; that they are not mutually exclusive in practice. A person may support both ideals of formal justice and kinship solidarity in different situations."

Yet another area of kinship is related to gender. Social anthropology has witnessed towering anthropologists who have contributed substantially to the development of this discipline. It is interesting to note that none of these scholars has touched the problem of relationship between kinship and gender. In studies of kinship, the male perspective is often taken for granted. "Certainly women have a place in these studies; they sometimes appear as wives, mothers and sisters, but rarely as independently acting persons. They appear as resources which society (that is, men) controls, they are exchanged between groups, are married, are burnt alive, accused of witchcraft and so on. Additionally, classic anthropological studies of kinship have rarely explored how particular kinship systems create particular kinds of gender relations, what sort of ideology justifies men's power over women or even reflected on the fairly obvious fact that a kin relationship is often a gender relationship as well."

Recently, the gender problem, that is, the discrimination of men against women, has become a burning issue both in Europe and India. It was sometime in the beginning of 1930 that Bombay University debarred a woman from appearing for an undergraduate degree simply became she was a woman.

Today, there has emerged a growing literature in sociology and social anthropology which tries to look at social life from a gender neutral perspective or even with an explicit female bias. When there is a strong wave of globalization it is natural to examine the status of woman with respect to that of man. There are differences in power between persons. But these differences should not dwell on gender.

Categories of Kinship

Kinship categories are constructed on the degree of relation. There are some kin who are very close, and there are others who are remote.

Closeness or remoteness is recognized on different occasions. For instance, on the occasion of marriage, right from close kin to the remote kin are invited. However, the recognition depends on the economic status of a person. The kin who have some functions to perform on some specific occasions are considered close kin. For instance, in a patrilineal society, the bride is brought to the marriage *pandal* by her mother's brother, *mama*. It is his responsibility. In his presence, no other person is allowed to do this. Again, in a patriarchal society, it is the father's daughter's son who leads the funeral procession. Thus, there are close kin who have different functions to perform on different occasions. Anthropologists have categorized varying affines and agnates in terms of close kin. These are: (i) primary kin, (ii) secondary kin, and (iii) tertiary kin.

(i) Primary Kin

Primary kin are those who belong to blood or marital group. The relations of these kin are primary. Among these are included brother, sister, and collaterals. Among the marital kin are included mother's brother, mother's sister and mother's parents.

(ii) Secondary Kin

Secondary kin are those who are related as primary kin to an individual. For instance, ego's wife is primary kin to ego but wife's brother who is primary to wife is secondary to ego. Father's brother who is primary to father is secondary to ego.

(iii) Tertiary Kin

Tertiary kin are those who are secondary kin to the ego's primary kin. For instance, brother's son is secondary kin and brother's son's son who is secondary to him is tertiary kin.

Kinship Behaviour

Kinship stems from biology, and goes beyond biology to the social and cultural realms. Thus, when we talk about kinship behaviour, we only intend to say that our behaviour with the kin people is different from the non-kin people. If we are ill and confined to hospital our kinsmen would immediately pay us a visit. In a village, during illness or accident, the kinship behaviour is worth observing. In no time the exogamous kin of the village would flock together and reach the hospital. If someone goes to a city after taking up a job there, all the kinspeople would come to the bus stop and give instructions to the young man on his way to the city. Thus, the behaviour of kin towards their own people is observable on all occasions of importance. Anthropologists have brought out vivid descriptions about standard kinship behaviour. As a matter of fact, expected behaviour is always forthcoming from the kin.

Avoidance

Among some tribal communities face-to-face relations among some kin is avoided. For instance, a daughter-in-law does not directly talk to her father-in-law and her husband's elder brother. Similarly, it is expected of a mother-in-law to avoid direct talk with her son-in-law. Avoidance has been a tradition not only among the tribals but also among low-caste people. However, in urban families, this type of behaviour is fast disappearing.

Joking Relationship

There are some kin relations with whom it is not considered improper to exchange jokes freely. Some tribals are foul mouthed and in jokes they would not hesitate to use vulgar language which would be out of place if the kinsmen around him are not of the right kind.

Teknonymy

When the relatives are addressed through some medium it is called teknonymy. Usually children are used as a medium of teknonymy. For instance, if a tribal has to address his wife he would address her with the name of his son and daughter. Even among caste Hindus the usage of teknonymy is seen. Tylor and Frazer have also referred to the practice of teknonymy.

Avunculate

This kind of kin behaviour is found in the matrilineal society. The status of the mother's brother is quite respectable. Relations with him are both joyful and pleasant. Avunculate behaviour is also found among the primitive groups of Africa and Australia.

Amitate

This behaviour is mainly related to the father's sister. It is peculiar to patriarchal societies. In this behaviour a high status is given to father's sister. Among Todas in India the father's sister officiates at the cremation ceremony.

Couvade

In kinship system couvade is related to the wife's delivery period. When she suffers from the pangs of labour her husband is also expected to exhibit similar pains in a dramatic way. In the Khasi tribe the husband does not wash his clothes or cross a river till the child is born. Couvade indicates the intimate relations between husband and wife.

To conclude, kinship behaviour which has become standardized among the tribals is not seen much any more. The tribal groups like other groups of the country have experienced vital change. They have acquired new values, new lifestyle and new patterns of behaviour. Even the tribals in Africa and Australia have witnessed changes. A large number of them have taken to modernization. After Tylor and Frazer recorded these forms of behaviour, almost a century has gone by and much intervention and modernization have come about in the life of the tribals in all parts of the world.

Kinship in India

Kinship is the central part of human behaviour. When social anthropology claims to understand mankind as a whole, and tries to study the similarities and differences in human societies, the study of kinship in primary. It is easy to bring out differences in human society through kinship behaviour. Social anthropology in India has not explored the field of kinship among the tribals much. Likewise, very little has been done in building theories of kinship behaviour. However, the European including British, and the US social anthropology have done some substantial work in the field of kinship. The notable theoretical contributions in kinship refer to Morgan, Malinowski, Radcliffe-Brown, Levi-Strauss, Rivers, Fortes, Evans-Pritchard and many more anthropologists.

In India, we have a few scholars like Iravati Karve who have done some work in the field of kinship. Her study *Kinship Organization in*

India (1965) is an outstanding contribution, which is both historical and empirical. Besides, she has focused on the whole country.

Besides Karve a few other minor kinship studies have been conducted which are oriented to ethnology. They are not theoretical or empirical in their analysis. They are only narrative. Again, these studies are restricted to the study of village or a part of a region. Here, in this section, we shall first refer to some kinship studies which have contributed towards the understanding of the theme of kin behaviour. Then, findings of these micro studies will be compared with the Karve's macro study.

Louis Dumont

Reviewing the contributions made to Indian sociology by various thinkers, Yogendra Singh says that during the 1950s and 1960s, much literature was generated by social anthropologists, economists and historians. "On family and kinship systems the contributions of Louis Dumont demonstrated the structural similarity between the interregional kinship systems." Dumont picked up some communities from north and south India and studied their kinship systems. He has also made a comparison between the two groups belonging to these regions.

Dumont differs from Iravati Karve. The latter establishes that there is difference in the northern and southern kinship systems. It is the diversity between these two systems that summarizes the contribution of Karve. Dumont, on the other hand, argues that there is a strong homogeneity between the two. He has compared his findings with the findings of Karve in one of his articles published in *The Contributions to Indian Sociology*. Dumont says that despite some differences in the kinship systems of the two regions, there is a strong homogeneity in the valuation, elaboration and ordering or patterning of affinal relationships. There is also similarity in the ceremonial presentations.

Though Dumont has studied kinship systems from the structural perspective, his theoretical contributions do not give us an overall understanding of India's kinship system.

Kathleen Gough

Kathleen Gough has also worked on kinship systems found in South India. Her approach has been Marxian. She relates the linkages of family and kinship with the modes of production. She keeps her study limited to a small area. Her findings also do not provide any base for all-India comparison. However, it must be said that Gough has tried to explore possibilities of studying kinship in a particular conceptual framework.

T.N. Madan

T.N. Madan has conducted his researches on family and kinship among the Kashmiri Brahmins. According to him, primary kin are those who share their food from the same hearth. This group consists of both blood and marital kin. The collaterals have a strong unity because of the common descent. A number of descent groups constitute the *kul*. In the descent group the collaterals constitute the highest place in the hierarchy. Among the Kashmiri Pandits the hearth, *kutumba* and *kul* constitute the descent group. The findings of Madan have relevance for the Kashmiri Pandits only. He has not made any macro comparisons. Nor does he look at the theoretical findings of Karve, Dumont, Levi-Strauss and others. At best, his study could be called a regional study.

A.C. Mayer

In his book *Caste and Kin in Central India*, A.C. Mayer has reported his study of Ramkhedi village of Malwa. He has described the primary and secondary kin of the village families. The primary kin consist of mother, father, brother and sister whereas marital kin such as brother's wife, mother-in-law and others. Mayer's study describes only the kin found in a patriarchal descent group. He does not make any theoretical attempt to compare the Ramkhedi findings to the findings of other anthropologists.

In short, it is obvious that kinship studies in India have been very restricted. What is conspicuous is that no micro or village study has been made of the Indian tribals. The only study which has wider implications is that of Iravati Karve. We, therefore, make a comparative analysis of Karve's generalizations.

In her study, *Kinship Organization in India*, Karve has conducted fieldwork in four regions of the country—northern, central, southern and eastern. In this study she differentiates kinship systems from the perspective of geography and language. It must be said at this stage of our discussion that the kinship organization of India is quite complicated. It is not a monolith system as is found in Europe and the US. There is great dissimilarity. K.S. Singh in his *People of India* has identified as many as 91 eco-cultural zones all over India, 4,635 communities (in other words, castes), 325 languages and 12 different language families. Given such multi-ethnicities, Karve has, in a broad way, studied two basic systems of kinship. These two divisions are inclusive of tribals of southern and eastern parts of India. These divisions also take into consideration both the matriarchal and patriarchal descent groups. Whereas Dumont talks about the homogeneity in structural terms between the northern and southern kinship systems, Karve says that there is a marked diversity between the two. If we examine Dumont it would really be difficult to find homogeneity in the kinship systems of Hindus, Muslims, Parsis, and other ethnic groups. It appears that the findings of Karve are closer to the diverse social reality of the country. We give below the basic differentials found in the northern and southern kinship systems:

(1) In northern India there is a prevalence of the patriarchal kin system. In the south, however, there exist both patriarchal and matriarchal systems of kinship. The matriarchal kinship system is found in Kerala among the Nairs, Moppilas and Teeyyars. Karve also finds matriarchal system in the east among the Garo (Meghalaya) and Khasi tribes. There are no traces of matriarchal kin system in north. However, patriarchal system is also popular among castes of southern parts of India along with matriarchal system.

(2) In the north *sapinda* marriage is prohibited, whereas in the south cross-cousin marriage has the status of a preferential marriage.

(3) Bride-price marriage is not recognized in the north. In the south it is a common practice in marriage.

(4) Normally, village endogamy is not preferred in the north. In the south, on the contrary there is no prohibition against endogamy, that is, one can marry from his own village.

(5) In the north, there is a specific kinship terminology for blood kin and marital kin. In the south, there is no difference in kinship terminology between these two groups.

Kinship terminology depends largely on the language. Karve has studied both the Indo-Aryan language family and the Dravidian language family. It is on the basis of these two language families that she has studied Indian kinship organization. She calls the Dravidian language family the mainstay of kinship organization.

Matriarchal Kin System in India

It would be prejudicious to say that India has only patriarchal kin system. We have enough research which show that there has been a long prevalence of matriarchal kinship system in the south-west part of India, i.e., Kerala. Besides, there are also some islands in the eastern side of the country where matriarchy is practised. Apart from the Nair and Teeyyar there are some Muslim groups such as Moppila who also have a tradition of matriarchal kin. A matriarchal kinship is also found among the Khasi and Garo tribes of Meghalaya and Assam.

It is quite interesting to note that studies on matriarchal kin have long been done since the first quarter of the 20th century. M. Fasset (1915), K.M. Pannikar (1918), L.K.A. Ayyar (1909-12, 1932), A. Ayyapan (1932-34), Kathleen Gough (1952-61), K.R. Unni (1956) and C.J. Fular (1976) have worked on the matriarchal kin system in Kerala. The patriarchy system found among the Namboodaripad Brahmins has also been studied. Some scholars have studied the social transformation among Nairs, Moppilas and others.

It is said that Nairs were the original inhabitants of Kerala. The Brahmins later on joined them. Other groups such as Izhawa and Tiya came to this land sometime during the 3rd and the 4th century. In the earlier periods of history the King Perumal spread Buddhism. It is stated that Jainism also had its hold in Kerala. As we find the social structure of Kerala today, the Namboodari Brahmins occupy the top place in social hierarchy. The Kshatriya rank second, and among the intermediate castes are Nairs and others. At the lowest rung are found untouchables.

One very interesting feature of Kerala's social structure is its Christian population. These Christians are mostly Syrians. The Christians have borrowed some traits of Hindus. On the occasion of marriage they get *tali*—the counterpart of the *mangal sutra*. Besides the caste groups and Christians, there are Muslims, among whom the Moppilas are dominant.

Matriarchal Tradition in Kerala

Among the matriarchal families of Kerala *Tarwad* is well known. The system itself is called *Tarwad*. In Dravidian language family the patriarchal families are called *ellam*. Primarily, *Tarwad* is found among the Nairs and *ellam* among the Namboodaris. In the *Tarwad* system of Nairs there were female ancestors. The descent among them starts with the mother. In a *Tarwad* all the dead and living are enumerated as members. If a *Tarwad* becomes a large one, it is divided in consultation with all the elders. The division is called *Tavji*, which means mother. It includes the mother and her children. Children born of a single *Tarwad*, though belonging to different *Tavji*, cannot marry amongst themselves. In several groups of a *Tarwad* a woman can marry several husbands. The Namboodari Brahmins can also marry Nair women. After marriage the woman resides with her mother and her husband pays her visit at night. The property of a *Tarwad* or a *Tavji* is indivisible and is owned by all the members.

Among the Nairs descent and *kul* (clan) have a single word called *Tarwad*. This term is also used for the ownership of collective property. Thus, in the matriarchal kin group, *kul* is the biggest unit and its members owe their origin to a single female ancestor. The origin of *Tarwad* is from the word *Tara*, which means a raised place on which the house of a Nair is built. The members of a *Tarwad* believe that they are the progeny of a single female ancestor. The name of a *kul* is in the name of the female ancestor. For a Nair the descent has several characteristics such as clan, name of descent tradition, name of the house and above all, the name of the person. It is on this tradition that when a man writes his name, he includes his clan, descent tradition and the name of the family.

Kathleen Gough conducted a study of *Tarwad* during 1950-60. She informed that normally a *Tarwad* consisted of six members, the maximum number being 25-30. During the last few decades, the *Tarwad* matriarchal kin group is witnessing changes. Now, there is a trend towards the patriarchal system. When we look at the two systems on a comparative plane, it should be said that in both, the management of property is in the hands of the males. And, second, all the matters of importance are decided by the males. Despite this change, there is a basic difference in both the systems. In the patriarchal family the property is inherited from a father to son; and in a matriarchal family the property goes from mother to daughter.

Matriarchal Tradition in North-East India

The matriarchal system is also found among the Garo and Khasi tribes

of north-east India. Garos are found in Meghalaya state. Most of the members of this tribal community are concentrated in the Garo hill ranges though a small part of them has migrated to the plains. Towards east of Meghalaya there are Khasis who are concentrated in the Khasi hills. These two tribal groups have matriarchal kinship systems. During the British regime they came under the influence of Christianity. Goswami and Majumdar (1972) and Parmil Chandra Kar (1982) have studied the Garo tribe in some detail. These studies throw light on the kinship organization of the tribe. Besides, the study published by the Law Research Institute of Guwahati, entitled *Customary Laws and Practices of the Garo of Meghalaya* is also important as it gives some details about the Garo kinship system.

The Garo economy is based on shifting cultivation, locally known as *zoom*. The cultivation is characteristic of the agricultural practices found in hilly regions. The head of the family is the owner of the family property. The whole tribe is divided into two exogamous moities. In Garo language moiety is called *chatchi*. The first *chatchi* is known as *sangama* and the second one *marak*. The Garo kinship system revolves round the matriarchy of mother. The matriarchal descent is represented by the families of the daughters. Property is inherited by the daughters and the family offsprings trace their origin from mother and other female ancestors. The Garo family is called *nok*. The *nok* consists of parents and their children. With the extension of family the mother's unmarried brothers and sisters and widowed mother also form the family. The unmarried brother after his marriage goes to his wife's house and the unmarried sister after her marriage resides with the mother. The widowed mother resides with her daughter all through her life.

In a Garo village, according to tradition, the boys are required to reside at a place known as *Nokpante*. They come to this place after the attainment of the age of five or six. They work in the field throughout the day, take their evening meals with the mother and return to *Nokpante* for rest. They spend their night here. Women are not allowed to enter the premises of *Nokpante*. After marriage the sons break relations with the mother. Now they come directly under the influence of their *mama* or mother's brother. According to the Garo rules of marriage, a person cannot marry within his moiety. The rules of marriage indicate that a person can marry his mother's brother's and ego's sister's children. But he cannot marry the sister of his wife.

The kinship terminology of the Garo tribe show that there is difference between the matriarchal descent group and the opposite descent group from where marriage alliance is made. The terminology indicates that all the female members of the matriarchal descent group are treated as mother's sisters, and of males from her side are considered as mother's brothers or equivalent. Thus, there are two kinship terminologies---one for the matriarchal descent group and another for the opposite group from which marital relations are established.

The Khasi tribe is found in the Jayantia hills of Assam. The language of Khasis belongs to Austro-Asiatic language family. The Mundas of Madhya Pradesh also speak a language belonging to this family. The Khasi economy is based on shifting cultivation. We get details about the economy of the tribe from the work of Gurdon (1914). The tribe has a perfect matriarchal system. The tribe practises exogamy but not village exogamy because in a single village several clans reside and this has made possible the village endogamy. The whole tribe is organized under the matriarchal system. The clan among the Khasi is called *kur* of which there are large numbers. Despite the Khasi having several clans, there is cooperation and unity among them. The individual does not have much importance. He is identified by his *kur*. Religious activities revolve around the matriarchal descent and the village occupies a unit in production and consumption of commodities.

If we analyze the kinship system found among the Khasis, it could be said that in the tribe the relationship between mother and daughter is very important. Next is that of sister and mother. In this kinship system, the relationship between husband and wife goes into the background. The property is handed over from the mother to daughter. The clan is important as far as marriage is concerned. One cannot marry within his own clan. Thus, for all consideration, clan is exogamous.

The Changing Scene Among Matriarchal Tribes

We now have empirical evidence to show that there is a crying need for change in the matriarchal system. The crisis has come about because both males and females try to corner as much power as possible. This struggle for power has put the prevailing matriarchal system in crisis. The male Garo and Khasi tend to revolt against the system. It appears that the females were strong enough to face the challenge given by males but now that region is also under the influence of patriarchy and this has weakened the matriarchal system. Besides, the Khasi women have begun to establish marital relations with the non-Khasi or Garo males and this clearly indicates the erosion which has crept into the matriarchal organization.

Concluding Observations

The theory of kinship is developed in a systematic way in social anthropology. It starts with the contributions of Morgan, followed by those of Radcliffe-Brown, Malinowski, Rivers, Levi-Strauss and others. It must be admitted that kinship theory is well developed in European social anthropology including Britain. However, the contributions of Boas, Kroeber and Lowie are equally important. In India, very little has been done in the field of the building of kinship theory in social anthropology. A serious attempt in this direction was made by Iravati Karve. She, for the first time, discussed kinship organization at the level of the country as a whole. Other contributions, though minor, have been made by Louis Dumont, Kathleen Gough, A.C. Mayer and T.N. Madan.

The kinship system, whether patriarchal or matriarchal, is witnessing some changes due to the acceleration of modernization and globalization. There is a change at the structural level and also at the value level. The movement for the liberalization of women has also challenged the age-old established patriarchal system.

Further Readings

Beattie, John, *Other Cultures*, London, 1964.

Eriksen, Thomas Hylland, *Small Places, Large Issues*, Pluto Press, London, 1995.

Fortes, Meyer, *Kinship and the Social Order*, Routledge and Kegan Paul, London, 1970.

Karve, Iravati, *Kinship Organization in India*, Asia Publishing House, Bombay, 1968 (third edition).

Shobhita Jain, *Bharat Main Parivar Vivaha aur Natedari* (Hindi), Rawat Publications, Jaipur, 1996.

12

Clan

Clan is an exogamous group which comes next to family. If the tribe or caste is endogamous, the clan is exogamous. The institution of clan is found in all the primitive societies. It resembles the family but differs from it fundamentally. In British anthropology sib is understood as clan whereas in American anthropology clan is defined as sib. The family is bilateral, either the individual belongs to matriarchal descent or to patriarchal descent. In other words, an individual recognizes his relationship either with a woman as his mother or a man as his father. Thus, clan or sib traces its origin through either parent to the total neglect of the other. If a tribe is organized into mother clans, every child regardless of sex is considered a member of his/her mother's clan and takes the maternal clan name, if there is one. In the same manner, if the tribe is organized into father clans, every child is a member of his/her father's clan and takes the paternal clan name. In the Indian context, the tribal groups follow both the patterns.

The importance of clan can hardly be exaggerated. It is often said that everybody in a tribal group is related by agnatic or descent ties. Viewed from this perspective the members of the clan are members of a wider blood group, constituting a sort of brotherhood. Normally, clans are found in a particular region and more often a single village consists of one or two clans only. It is because of this that a village is an exogamous unit. Village exogamy goes with the clan exogamy. There are several uses of clan in a primitive society. Anthropologists consider clan to be an organization between family and descent. In this chapter, we discuss the origin and meaning of clan and its differentiation from family, lineage and totemism. All these concepts are closely related. They constitute the comprehensive concept of kinship.

What is Clan?

Social anthropologists define clan as a unilinear group. Originally, the meaning of clan was taken from the Latin word *gens*, the literal meaning of which is unilinear group. But in English the meaning of *gens* has come to mean a patrilineal group. It is because of this that the American anthropologists differentiate the terms clan and sib. They use clan for matrilineal groups and *gens* for patrilineal groups. Thus, for them, the clan and *gens* together make a sib.

The meaning of clan runs into debate. American anthropologists prefer to use sib in place of clan in social anthropology. Murdock, for instance, has suggested that clan should be used only for a descent group whereas in the British tradition the meaning of clan is wider and includes both the matriarchal and patriarchal clans. On the other hand, Morgan and others who vouch for evolutionary theory use clan only for the patriarchal descent group. Despite this controversy there is a consensus in social anthropology that clan is an important kin group which determines the life order of the people. It creates integration among the wider descent group.

It must be admitted that there is rich literature on clan in social anthropology. Kroeber has come out with a classical work on clan known as *Zuni Kin and Clan* (1917). Firth has described the kin and clan organization of the Tikopia tribal group of Africa in his book *We, the Tikopia* (1936). Similarly, Fortes has studied the Ashanti tribe along with other African primitive groups. His book, *The Dynamics of Clanship amongst the Tallensi* (1945) very elaborately describes the changing character of clanship. Evans-Pritchard has also analyzed the kinship organization in his classical work, *The Nuer* (1940). All these works assume importance in social anthropology because for the first time primitive clan and kin have been taken for comprehensive analysis. These studies have also conceptually examined the differences in kinship, descent, lineage, totemism and clan.

Different scholars have defined the term 'clan' differently. To begin with, Robert H. Lowie says:

> The sib ('clan' of British anthropologists) is most briefly defined as a unilateral kinship group.

We have already seen that the family is bilateral. We reckon the origin of the family either from the male ancestor or the female ancestor, never both. An individual cannot marry within his own descent group—patriarchal or matriachal. It is in this sense that family is bilateral. On the other hand, the clan is always unilateral.

Likewise, describing the characteristics of clan found among the Ashanti tribal group, Fortes writes:

> There are only eight such clans in Ashanti, and it is noteworthy that the same *small number* of clans bearing the *same or equivalent names* is duplicated among all the Akan-speaking peoples. This is often adduced in confirmation of their *remote common origins.* There is evidence that traditionally each clan had *specific totemic animal avoidance.* These appear to have been associated with the hereditary offices held in the clan, and have largely lapsed in modern times. What now remains distinctive of each clan is the strict recognition of its structural autonomy, founded on the dogma of *common matrilineal descent.*

According to Thomas Hylland Eriksen, people of one clan belong to a common ancestory. This ancestory could be either matriarchal or patriarchal. Thus, according to him, clan is a unilinear descent group. However, the ancestors do not constitute any regular genealogy. His definition runs as under:

> A clan encompasses people who assume shared descent from an ancestor/ancestress without being able to enumerate all of these links.

Finally, the definition given by John Lewis:

> Membership in a clan depends on kinship through one parent. It is often exogamous. It provides mutual security, government, marriage regulations, religion and ceremonies, property regulations and social control. Some authorities require not only a rule of descent but also a definite place of residence or locality and social integration.

Thus, on the basis of above definitions, we can infer some common characteristics of clan as under:

(1) Clan is a unit between family and descent.
(2) It is unilateral, i.e., either from male or female side.
(3) It is exogamous.
(4) It provides rules for marriage, ceremonies, inheritance and social control.

(5) It is found in some specific places.
(6) It also has some authority over an area.
(7) It is totemic.
(8) It traces its descent from some common ancestor.

Clan, Family, Lineage and Totem

A clan is not a tribe. It is only a pattern of unilateral social relationship within the tribe. It is also not a family, neither is it a lineage. As a matter of fact, clan is related to several concepts, the important ones being family, lineage and totem. There are differences in all the three concepts. For a proper understanding of clan we should bring out the differences in these concepts.

Family and Clan

A family is a group of persons wherein the husband and wife have legitimized sexual relations. It is the objective of family to procreate. Thus, the family consists of affines and agnates. At the time of marriage, the genealogy of father and mother is taken into consideration. Viewed from this perspective the family is bilateral. In the patriarchal family, the clan is traced from the father, grandfather, great grandfather and so on. In the matriarchal family, conversely, the clan of mother, grandmother and so on are traced. Thus, the first difference of family and clan is that family is bilateral whereas clan is unilateral.

A family may become extinct because of the lack of a son. Despite the extinction of family, the clan of the family would continue. Therefore, a clan is the combination of a large number of families and descent groups whereas a family consists only of the parents and their children.

If we trace the origin of family and clan, it could be said that there would have been the appearance of family first and clan later on. It is because of this that the family which does not have a long history might not have a clan system. For instance, among the Kadars, there is total absence of clan system though they have family. On the other hand, the tribal groups which have long family history, such as Kamar, Baiga and Bhil, there is a clan system. Thus, the institution of family is universal, a clan is not.

The members of a family reside under the same roof, take their meals from the same hearth and have a common purse, whereas the members of a clan do not have this kind of sharing. The members of a clan are scattered and claim their origin from a common ancestor. Their relationship with the ancestor is largely social and cultural. The only binding force which holds them together is the common ancestor.

Thus, in any analysis of clan system, the descent system of family cannot be neglected. In a broader way, it could be said that in the structure of clan, family is the smallest unit.

Lineage and Clan

The basic difference between a lineage and clan is that the former is actual and real while the latter is fictitious. If we refer to the case of feudal rulers we find that each ruler had his genealogy which was updated by bards. Similarly, the Hindus have their own genealogies which are maintained by the priests. Genealogies thus constitute the record of the previous generations. However, it is difficult to trace the ancestor who gave rise to a clan, therefore, the originator of a clan is lost in oblivion. John Lewis defines lineage as below:

> Lineage is a group resulting from descent reckoned either from the father's or the mother's line. Whereas in a clan relationship it is assumed, in a lineage group it must be demonstrated, that is, the actual relationship must be specific and known.

Lewis makes the differentiation between lineage and clan quite clear: the former is real, whereas the is assumed. It could be said that a clan is composed of a number of lineages. In other words, lineages or family genealogies constitute a clan.

Eriksen considers lineage an important part of kinship. Actually, kinship begins with the family and grows into a lineage. And lineage goes further to make a clan. He observes:

> As a general rule, we may say that a lineage consists of persons who can indicate, by stating all the intermediate links, common descent from a shared ancestor or ancestress. A clan encompasses people who assume shared descent from an ancestor/ancestress without being able to enumerate all of these links.

Though lineage and clan are technically defined as two different concepts, they are normally used as synonyms. For social anthropological purposes, Eriksen argues that lineage traces its origin from a known ancestor who has a name, a place of birth and an identity. The clan, on the other hand, depends on the assumption of the ancestor who started it. Another observation made by Eriksen is that lineage is found in both the matriarchal and patriarchal societies. This applies to the occurrence of clan also.

The definition of lineage given by Jacobs and Stern is very pointed and precise:

> Lineage is a subdivision of a clan composed of *actual* and not *fictitious* kin.

Lowie has analyzed the importance of lineage in the clan in the tribal situation. He says that the status of an individual, for instance, among the Nootka Indians, is nothing without his lineage identity. It is the lineage which gives recognition to a person in the clan. The position given to lineage in the clan system by Lowie is supported by Sapir also. Thus, for Lowie, lineage consists of all the members of a particular genealogical group.

Totem and Clan

Social anthropologists have produced rich literature on totemism. Among the African tribes totems are very widely found. Each clan organization bears the names of animals and plants. This mode of designating a clan is often coupled with beliefs and practices revolving round the eponym. Sometimes, the animal is held sacred and there is a strong sense of kinship with it on the part of the clan. Elsewhere groups are not named after plants or animals but are nevertheless definitely associated with them. Frequently, there is a belief in the descent of the clan from the eponym. All these and similar usages are brought together under the head of totemism and the animal plant or object in question is called a totem.

Totemism has a very wide distribution among the tribals. It is found in America, Australia, Melanesia, Africa and India. "This extensive diffusion deeply impressed the scholars who first investigated the relevant data, and following the theoretical bias of their times, they assumed without further enquiry that all the phenomena labeled totemism represented identical psychological processes and had originated independently in different areas through the psychic unity of mankind." It appears that totemism has developed from the practice of animal nicknames.

Lowie has traced the origin and development of totemism. He says that it was for the first time that Goldenweiser in 1910 approached totemism from a quite different point of view. He was followed by Boas. These anthropologists argued that totemism all over the primitive world is not alike. It differs substantially. For example, in Central Australia, totemism does not focus on animals. It emphasizes ritualistic performances. It helps enhance the magic power of a person. Goldenweiser also borrows from J.G. Frazer. His conclusion is that totemism is not associated with exogamy. Some anthropologists have worked very elaborately on the theme of totemism. For one thing, all agree that totemic ties keep the people of a group united. It is a part of kinship relationship. In family there is a biological and socio-cultural relationship among the members; in lineage there is a linkage with the ancestors; clan consists of lineages and totem keeps the people held together by an object which the people consider as their common and shared identity.

Totemism binds the people on the basis of some animal, plant and tree. The observance of the totemic rules is not based on biological origin. It is social and cultural. In a precise way totem is different from clan but it forms a part of clan. In Indian social anthropology some work has been done in totemism. For instance, among the Kharias, there are about ten exogamous totemic clans. Similarly, among the Kamars, there are a large number of exogamous clans. Each clan has its own totems. Normally, totems are operative only the in the realm of marriage. Clan, on the other hand, has comprehensive social and cultural functions. The Kamars have totems in the name of tiger, serpent, goat, birds, etc.

Totemism in India has come as a tradition of British social anthropology. In Britain and other parts of Europe, totemism developed through Goldenweiser and Frazer. In England, Malinowski and Radcliffe-Brown worked considerably to develop the theme of totemism. For instance, Malinowski has written extensively on totemism which is found in Trobriand Islands. These primitives believed that totemic plants and animals are helpful for the maintenance of society. Radcliffe-Brown developed a more complex view of totemism. Borrowing from Durkheim, he says that totem causes a special relationship between it and the social order and the ultimate function of totemism is to maintain social integration. The totem is, thus, a tangible identity marker for a group. Durkheim himself mentions flag as a kind of totem. Similarly, defining totem, Jacob and Stern write:

> An animal associated with a clan is a totem. Its flesh is tabooed by the clan members. The clan members believe themselves descended from the animal and they conduct rites for it. Some writers give broader definitions allowing for plant or other beings as clan totems, or for any zoomorphic supernatural powers as totems even if unconnected with clans. The beliefs and practices connected with totems are called totemism.

According to John Lewis:

> A totem is an object towards which members of a kinship must have a special mystical relationship and with which the unit's name is associated. The object may be an animal or a plant.

Our discussion here does not relate to the description of totemism. That is secondary for us. What we want to emphasize is that totemism is different from clan, family and lineage. We have argued that totemism creates a group of people who associate themselves with some animal or plant. This association makes them share their common identity. It ends up with the practice of totemic exogamy. On the other hand, the members of a clan associate themselves with a common ancestor who was fictitious. In totemism the association is with animal or plant but never human beings. Thus, technically, totemism and clan are different. But it is the totem which gives its name to a clan. It is an identity mark of the clan.

Clans among Indian Tribes

It is indeed very difficult to find out the origin of clan in each primitive group of the world and for that matter in India. We do not have enough literature on the origin and development of clan in our country. Despite this limitation we refer to some of the clans found among Indian tribes. But, before we do that, let us refer to the clans found among Hindus. The Hindus regulate their marriage according to *gotra*. *Gotra*, as P.N. Prabhu tells us, consists of two Sanskrit words: *go* meaning cow, and *tra* meaning herd. Thus, the Hindu *gotra* is a group of people united by a common ancestor. There are seven *rishis*, namely, Vishvamitra, Jamadgni, Bhardwaj, Gautam, Ari, Vashishtha and Kashyap who gave origin to seven Hindu *gotras*. Generally, the Hindus trace their origin to one of these *rishis*. The progeny of a single *rishi* are brothers and sisters. Brothers and sisters cannot marry among themselves. And, therefore, the Hindu *gotra* is an exogamous group.

Unlike Hindus the tribals do not have such a simple origin of clan. Each tribe has its history, ethnology and therefore, a traditional history for its clan. It is difficult to describe the clans found among more than 400 tribal groups found in the country. We, therefore, mention some of the notable clans of major tribal groups.

The Santhal tribe is found in Bihar and Bengal. It has more than 100 clans that are related to or trace their origin from a tree, plant, animal or some inanimate objects. Similarly, the Ho tribe has about 50 clans. Some of these clans are the same as are found among Santhals. The Munda tribe has 65 clans. The Bhils of western India are reported to have 38 clans. The clans are related to wild animals, trees and plants. Majumdar and Madan have enumerated eight clans in Kharia tribe. These include *Khoren* (a stone), *Myur* (crocodile), *Samad* (deer), *Barliha* (a fruit), *Charad*, *Hansad*, *Mail* and *Tepna* (all birds). Among the Tamarias the clan name is related to a ghost, animal or plant. For example, the origin of a Panduwing *gotra* among these people is traced to a leaf.

If we make an attempt to trace the origin of clan we shall also find several such mythological or traditional stories. Such material forms part of folk literature. Normally, the tribals associate their clan with some unhistorical and unusual incidence. The origin of clan is a theme which constitutes a potential field of enquiry in social anthropology.

Social Structure of Clan

The clan system has an elaborate social structure. In a single village, there are two or three clans. Generally, the clans have their hierarchy in a tribe. R.H. Lowie has made an attempt to establish different orders of clan among the African primitive groups. In western India S.L. Dolin informs that the Mairiya among the Bhils occupy a higher rank. It is followed by Damor. Similar ranking is also found in Gond and Santhal tribes.

Majumdar and Madan in their *Introductory Social Anthropology* have described the social structure of a clan. According to them, the clans are divided into two: (1) phratry, and (2) moiety.

Some anthropologists have called phratry lined clans. Actually, the phratry is a blood related group. It is exogamous. When for some reason, two, three or more clans unite together, the union is called phratry. Sometimes it so happens that in a large tribal group some people having common blood ties establish a separate identity. This autonomous and separate identity is called phratry. The phratries in a tribal group are individually called a moiety. Thus, the moiety is a part of a phratry. In a single tribe there could be phratries and each part of the phratry is a moiety. The phratry, therefore, constitute a dual organization of the tribe. In a phratry, thus, there could be several clans.

In the following figure we give the social structure of clan:

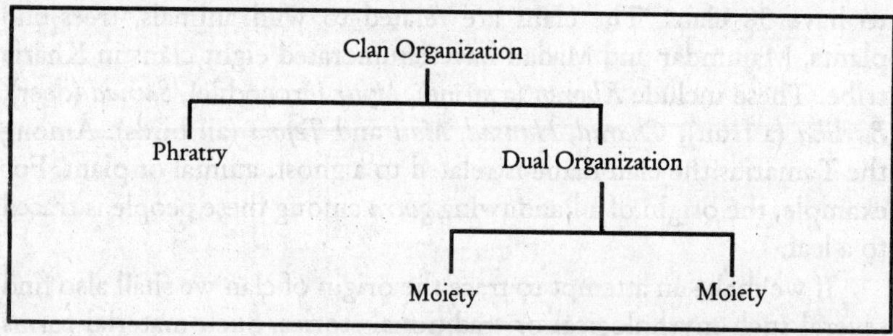

The function of phratry and dual organization is normally to regulate marriages. Empirically, these days, the clan has limited functions. Its identity survives only in implementing the marriage rules. The boundaries of phratries have also become loose. It appears that in the wake of modernization which the tribals are experiencing the hierarchy and status of phratry is fast dwindling. The rights of reservation in terms of safety and security have weakened the dual division of clan. Reservations, is basically concerned with the tribal group and not the clan. This makes phratry irrelevant.

Characteristics of Clan

Social anthropology contains descriptions of various tribal clans pertaining to Africa, Australia and India. On the strength of the empirical data, we give below some of the important features of a clan:

(1) Normally, a clan is an exogamous group. The members of a clan trace their origin to a common ancestor who is normally not real but fictitious. The ancestor could be a tree, plant, animal, bird or an inanimate object.
(2) A clan is unilateral. It links itself either with the mother or father. It is never bilateral.
(3) According to the theory of clan, it is assumed that all the clan members are brothers and sisters. They cannot marry among themselves.
(4) Clan is an independent autonomous unit. That is how it differs from family, lineage and totem.
(5) Ordinarily, the members of a clan reside in a specific territory. Rivers, who has worked among Todas, also informs that the members of a single clan normally reside in a definite territorial area.

Functions of Clan

The primitive peoples all over the world have lived in an unfriendly environment. Though the forests provide them wild game, living within its cover sometimes proves to be very dangerous. The tribals who have taken to agriculture are more often than not victims of floods and droughts. Deprived of most of the facilities of security, they have to depend on their kinsmen and clansmen. We have enough studies to infer that a tribal group can hardly survive without the functioning of clans. It is normal to find a Gond saying: "While hurting the member of my clan, you have actually hurt me." The identification in the name of clan in a tribal group is very strong. Despite this, as mentioned above, under the influence of modernization many of the functions of clan are getting weak or eroded. We, however, give below some of the important functions of clan:

(i) Protection and Help

The insecure environment puts tribals always in constant need of help and protection. The clan members provide them security and help at such times. For instance, if the family is in difficulty, the clan members would come forward to render all material and economic help and when the family is under heavy indebtedness, the clan members would contribute an appropriate amount for redemption. The clan is an exogamous group and therefore it has to give and take daughters and brides in exchange from other clans. This widens the area of assistance for a particular clan. The marriage alliance, therefore, is a source of strength for a particular clan.

(ii) Political Hegemony

In African tribes, as among Indian ones, the clan has a political clout. There are "big men" in a tribal group. These men play an important role to help the tribals integrate themselves in the regional politics. Politics has been defined differently. According to one definition, politics "can be defined as agency; as the establishment of authoritative decisions. Second, politics may be seen as a system in which case the word refers to the circulation of power and authority in a society." In northern Pakistan there is a tribal group of Swat Pathans. They are cereal farmers. A tiny majority of the Pathans---Pakthuns—own virtually all of the land, while the majority of the rest of the population are their tenants. The Pathans are patrilineal and all formal political power is vested with men. Only sons can inherit from their fathers, but all sons have rights of inheritance. In order to expand his fields, a Pakthun needs a large political following, or in other words, he needs many clients. It is for this reason that he gives his land for cultivation to his clansmen. This makes a particular clan politically strong. In our country, the dominant clans get a larger share of political power. In western India, the Maira clan of Bhils has dominance in most of the panchayat samitis.

(iii) Wielding of Sanction

The clan has a right to levy a penalty for non-observance of tribal traditions. It can oblige the clan member to follow a certain course of action. In western India and parts of Madhya Pradesh, if a member of a clan is killed by a member of another clan, the former takes revenge. The loss of a man is the loss of a clan. Therefore, all the clan members make it a point to apply the primitive law---eye for an eye and tooth for a tooth---and annihilate the members of another clan. On the other hand, if the clan member disobeys the tradition of his clan, he is ousted and remains in isolation. The clan can inflict physical injury also on a deviant member.

(iv) Exogamy

All the males and the females of a clan constitute, in a broad way, a common blood group. They are constrained to observe the rules of exogamy. Deviance in the observation of exogamy is penalized severely.

(v) Religion and Customs

Each clan has its deities, ancestors and totems. On occasions of birth, marriage, death and scarcities, the clan deities are worshipped. It is firmly believed by all the members of the clan that only by observing respect for the deities can a crisis be overcome.

The functions of clan are several. However, in the modern context of development, many of these functions have become extinct. Normally, no one comes forward to help the clan members, particularly in the case of financial difficulties. Politics also has become individual-centric. The changes in the functions of clan have made the institution ineffective. Empirically, one could very easily observe that there are conflicts pertaining to land and development benefits. There is much competition to find out opportunities of employment and in this field there are disputes and conflicts in a particular clan. Among Indian tribes, it is really difficult to find any substantial unity among the clan members. However, there is only one function of clan which stands as a high tower and that is the field of exogamy. Normally, one cannot find a person having marriage alliance within his own clan. In this respect, the clan stands as a bedrock.

Further Readings

Evans-Pritchard, E.E., *The Nuer*, Oxford, Clarendon Press, 1940.

Fortes, Meyer, *The Dynamics of Clanship Among Tallensi*, Oxford University Press, African Institute, 1945.

Lewis, John, *Anthropology*, Heinemann, London, 1982.

Lowie, R.H., *Primitive Society*, Routledge and Kegan Paul Ltd., London, 1960.

Majumdar, D.N. and Madan, T.N., *An Introduction to Social Anthropology*, Asia Publishing House, 1957.

13

Gender Issues in Tribal Society

George Orwell, in his popular novel *Animal Story*, makes a conspicuous statement: "All animals are equal but some are more equal than others." In all societies there are differences between persons on the basis of power and resources. No society has all its members on equal footing. Some have privileges, others do not have. Social differentiation and equality are universal phenomena. Biologically, males and females are equal; they have similar vital organs (heart, lungs, kidneys) and metabolism. The differences between them are social and cultural, or say, non-biological—and are constructed by society. Thus, the issues relating to males and females are social, cultural, historical and societal. And, what we call a gender issue is the issue that concerns the social and cultural differences in the discrimination of both the sexes. When women are discriminated against by men, it is a case of gender issue.

Thomas Hylland Eriksen has given an appropriate place to gender issues in his book, *Small Places, Large Issues* (1995). His argument is that if there is a women's movement all over the world, how can social anthropology close it eyes towards the male treatment given to a woman in tribal society. If the modern societies conceptualize differences between men and women in terms of equality, why should we not look at the discrimination meted out to tribal women. Eriksen observes:

> Malinowski, who has often been praised for his ethnographic details, is now said to have neglected important women's institutions completely and exaggerated the contribution of men to the reproduction of Trobriand society. In many other classic studies too, social actors are more or less seen as equivalent to social men.

The British social anthropologists like H.H. Risley, W.H.R. Rivers, R.V. Russel and others have altogether overlooked the problems of tribal women. In India too, those who are called as the founders of social anthropology, such as D.N. Majumdar, S.C. Roy, G.S. Ghurye and K.S. Singh, have either not looked at the issue of the discrimination of women by the men, or even if looked at, not in a proper perspective. It is, therefore, certain that the gender issues in the Indian context, with reference to social anthropology, are overlooked.

What is Sex-Gender System?

The gender problem in India emerged after the seventies. We have in our country a large number of feminists who have advocated the upliftment of women including those residing in rural India. These feminists belong to different disciplines and walks of life, especially social activities. Some of the feminists include Bina Agrawal, Maitriyee Choudhuri, Madhu Kishwar, Janaki Nayyar, Bina Das, Tiplut Nonbri and others. Interestingly enough, the term 'sex-gender system' was coined by an anthropologist Gayle Rubin. This term has recently found wide currency among feminists. It refers to the institutionalized system which allots resources, property and privileges to persons according to culturally defined gender roles. Despite a large number of feminist social scientists, theorists and thinkers in India and elsewhere, the concept of sex-gender system remains not much clear. It is, it appears, in the process of formulation.

Let us begin the analysis of sex-gender system by providing a definition of gender. Though, initially, the concept was introduced by an anthropologist, normally anthropologists in general are critical of feminist tendencies to universalize what are really only culture-specific features of the sex-gender system. It is argued by social anthropologists that the male dominance over females in all the societies is not the same. It varies from culture to culture. The dominance in a nomadic society is lesser compared to a settled society. Stressing this point of variation in gender relations, Sandra Harding observes:

> Of course, the sex-gender system is expressed in differing intensities and forms in different cultures and classes. Men's and women's natures and relative abilities to determine their own social, economic and political lives appear very different if one looks from matrilineal

to patrilineal societies, from pre-capitalist to capitalist formations, from aristocratic to democratic cultures, and of course from wealthy to poverty-level and white to black lives in America today.

Anthropologists differ basically from feminists. The latter argue that women all over the world, notwithstanding their cultural and caste-class belongingness, face discrimination against them. It appears that the anthropological perspective has a wider support from empirical reality. Let us take the example of Hindi novels written by Premchand. It is a common thread in Premchand's novels to find the hero beating his wife. In rural India, generally, disputes are settled by men by beating their women. Even Arundhati Roy, in her Booker Prize winner book *The God of Small Things*, says that normally whenever men return home at night in drunken state, they beat up their women. The anthropologists, are, therefore, justified to say that the intensity and form of sex-gender system is culture-and-society-specific.

The anthropological perspective may further be explained with reference to India. The status of women in a bureaucratic and management society is better. She is respected. She lives in luxury, drives a car, visits beauty parlours and spends money on cosmetics. On the other hand, the discrimination of women in a peasant society is full of injustice. Among the tribals the men often enjoy drinks and make the women toil day in and day out both in the field and the house. Thus, for all considerations, the gender issue has to be analyzed in the context of the containing society. We now take up some of the meanings given to sex-gender system. These meanings are drawn from feminist research, writings and scholarships.

Let us bifurcate the term 'sex-gender' to derive some precise meaning. The term consists of two words: sex and gender. Women, as a sex, are a separate group due to their biological distinctiveness. It is only women who can procreate. Thus, their sex clearly defines them, not as a sub-group or a minority group, but as a half of the whole (population). Men are the only other sex. Obviously, we do not here refer to sexual activity, but to a biological function.

Gender is the cultural definition of behaviour defined as appropriate to the sexes in a given society at a given time. "Gender is a set of cultural roles. It is a costume, a mask, a straitjacket in which men and women dance their unequal dance." Unfortunately, the term 'gender' is used both in academic discourse and in the media as interchangeable with sex. For laymen, sex and gender are synonymous. In fact, its widespread use is probably due to it sounding a bit more 'refined' than the plain word 'sex' with its 'nasty' connotations. Such use is unfortunate, because it hides and mystifies the difference between the biologically given sex and culturally created gender.

Let us make our analysis a little more clear. Whenever in technical terms we talk about sex, we mean biological composition and whenever we talk about gender we attach a cultural meaning. For instance, among Hindus, a woman can wear a *bindi* and apply cosmetics to her face. This aspect of woman explains the gender status of a woman. Again, a woman normally cannot work as a priest or officiate at the nuptial ceremony. She is disqualified for such assignments because she is a woman. Thus, gender is social and cultural and sex is biological. Sex-gender system resembles racism. A race is a valid biological phenomenon but racism is socio-cultural.

Defining sex-gender system in a specific way, we again refer to Harding:

> The size and shape of this newly visible object are becoming clearer. The sex-gender system appears to be a fundamental variable organizing social life throughout most recorded history and in every culture today.

Some Related Concepts

Feminist theorists have always been working to construct some concepts which help us understand the gender issues. In this effort, no integrative approach, however, has been made to give precise meaning to a particular concept. The disagreements are also large. With the emergence of these concepts the gender issues are increasingly getting a shape. There are a few lady social anthropologists who are working at the task of formulating concepts on the strength of empirical data generated by them. Gerda Lerner (*The Creation of Patriarchy*, OUP) has made an attempt to make a precise collection of some common definitions.

(i) Subordination of Women

The phrase 'subordination of women' is used in place of 'oppression of women'. Subordination does not have the connotation of evil intent on the part of the dominant; it allows for the possibility of collusion between him and the subordinate. "It includes the possibility of voluntary acceptance of subordinate status in exchange for protection and privilege—a condition which characterizes so much of the historical experience of women." Subordination of women, thus, means forceful subordination. It has a historical postulation too that women have been subjugated all through the periods of history.

(ii) Feminism

This is the term commonly and quite indiscriminately used. Some of its currently prevalent definitions are: (a) a doctrine advocating social and political rights for women equal to those of men; (b) an organized movement for the attainment of these rights; (c) the assertion of the claims of women as a group and the body of theory women have created; and (d) belief in the necessity of large-scale social change in order to increase the power of women.

(iii) Women's Rights

This indicates a movement—the women's rights movement. It is concerned with winning for women equality with men in all spheres of life and also giving them access to all rights and opportunities enjoyed by men in society. Thus, the women's rights movement is akin to the civil rights movement. The 19th century women's rights and suffrage movement is an example of this kind.

(iv) Women's Emancipation

This implies freedom from oppressive restrictions imposed by sex; it stands for self-determination and autonomy. Freedom from oppressive restrictions imposed by sex means freedom from biological and social restrictions. Self-determination means being free to decide one's own destiny, to define one's social role, and to make decisions concerning one's body. Autonomy means earning one's own status, not being born into it or marrying it; it means financial independence; freedom to choose one's lifestyle and sexual preference—all of which implies a radical transformation of existing institutions, values and theories.

(v) Women's Liberation

This is the most commonly used term. It conjures up political liberation movements of other groups, such as colonials and racial minorities. It implies victimization and a subjective consciousness in a group striving to correct a wrong.

(vi) Gender

The literal meaning of gender is to beget, to generate. In other words, it means social and cultural generation. However, with the emergence of women's studies and the rise of feminist writings and research, it includes both biological as well as social and cultural meanings. Thus, a woman has a biological distinctiveness and also some social-cultural discriminations against men.

(vii) Patriarchy

The word is most commonly used by feminists. In its narrow meaning, patriarchy refers to "the system, historically derived from Greek and Roman laws, in which the male head of the household had absolute legal and economic power over his dependent female and male family members". People using the term that way often imply a limited historicity for it: patriarchy began in classical antiquity and ended in the 19th century with the granting of civil rights to men and married women in particular.

However, in feminist literature, patriarchy is used in its wider meaning. It has its manifestation in the institution of male dominance over women and children in the family and the extension of male dominance over women in society in general. It implies that men hold power in all the important institutions of society and that women are deprived of access to such power. It does not imply that women are either totally powerless or totally deprived of rights, influence and resources. One of the most challenging tasks of women's history is to trace with precision the various forms and modes in which patriarchy appears historically, the shifts and challenges in its structure and functions, and the adaptations it makes to female pressures and demands.

(viii) Sexism

It defines the ideology of male supremacy or superiority and the beliefs that support and sustain it. Sexism and patriarchy mutually reinforce one another.

(ix) Women's Culture

It is the ground upon which women stand in their resistance to patriarchal domination and their assertion and their own creativity in shaping society. "The term implies an assertion of equality and an awareness of sisterhood. Women's culture is never a sub-culture. Women live their social existence within the general culture. Whenever they are confined by patriarchal restraint or segregation into separateness, they transform this restraint into complementarity and redefine it. Thus, women live a duality as members of the general culture and as partakers of women's culture."

(x) Feminist Consciousness

When women gradually become aware of their movement they attain varying degrees of feminist consciousness. It means: (1) the awareness of wrong; (2) the development of a sense of sisterhood; (3) the autonomous definition by women of their goals and strategies for changing their condition; and (4) the development of an alternative vision of the future.

We have tentatively defined some of the currently used concepts in feminist literature. These concepts boil down to the fact that the phenomenon of sex-gender is essentially a system of male dominance made possible by men's control of women's productive and reproductive labour, where reproduction is broadly construed to include sexuality, family life, and kinship formation, as well as the birthing which biologically reproduces the species. All in all, the term 'sex-gender' indicates discrimination against women, that is, their inferiorization and subordination.

Why Study Gender Issues?

There are a large number of social issues which social anthropology and for that matter social sciences should study. In the history of social sciences it has been unhistorical to study the gender issues. True, sociology and social anthropology have studied the position of women through history. These disciplines paid attention to only half of our general population. But, since the sixties, there has been a flood of studies on gender issues. This has partly been explained by A.R. Desai. He says that in post-independent India, the state is obliged constitutionally to transform rural people, Scheduled Castes, Scheduled Tribes and other subaltern groups into more powerful groups. It is a compulsion made by India's Constitution.

Second, it was in the year 1975 that the Declaration of International Women's Year was announced. The year was extended into a decade and this gave rise to women's studies. Women's centres and researches on various aspects of women's problems have been favourably looked upon, attracting many funding agencies, including state and its various agencies. The Constitution of India seems to be the guiding code for a systematic observation of women's status. It would be worthwhile to find out the origin of gender problem in our Constitution. Interestingly, till as recently as 1981, the index of the Constitution does not contain a category of 'women', to which one may refer for understanding the position of women as provided in the Constitution. In the category 'marriage' there is a passing reference, 'family planning' is indexed alongwith 'population control', and not with family or women's welfare. The index maker to this government publication does not find 'women', 'marriage' or 'family' worthy of being referred to in the index of the Constitution.

However, it is in Article 15 on Fundamental Rights, there is a reference to *women as equal citizens.* It lays down that "the state shall not discriminate against any citizen on grounds only of religion, race, caste, sex, place of birth or any of them". Further, in sub-article (3) of the same Article, it is stated that "nothing in this Article shall prevent the state from making any special provision for women and children".

Thus, the Constitution enjoins equal status to women, as citizens, but also takes into consideration some special disabilities, which the state may endeavour to rectify by affirmative action.

Similarly, in Part IV dealing with Directive Principles of State Policy, there are references to the principles to be taken into account wherein concern for women is exhibited. For instance, Articles 39, 42 and 44 refer specifically to certain principles which, though not enforceable in the courts, should provide guidance to the state treating women as equal citizens.

We have discussed some of the indicators of the underlying principles of gender role as perceptible in the Constitution as well as the path of development adopted by the post-independent Indian State.

A.R. Desai, who has been a staunch Marxist, raises some questions regarding gender issues with reference to the Constitution. These questions need to be quoted:

(1) Can a state, which proclaims opposition to discrimination based on sex and other elements, permit religious personal laws, which affect the life of women in a basic manner?
(2) On the grounds of religion, can diverse practices of discrimination in terms of number, choice of partners, control over body and sexual life, residence, inheritance, succession, property rights, adoption, locale and diverse practices discriminatory to women be permitted?
(3) Which of the practices embodied of the personal laws should be called secular and which religious?

Desai has raised some really fundamental problems. Some efforts will have to be made to amend the Constitution for giving a respectable status to women.

Kinds of Discrimination

At the societal level, besides constitutional provisions for avoiding any discrimination against sex, there are some other disabilities also which are inflicted on women for their being of different biological kind. We discuss below a few of such disabilities:

(i) Paternalistic Dominance

Gerda Lerner has studied the causes for the rise of women in the decade of the sixties. She says that for nearly 4,000 years women have shaped their lives and acted under the umbrella of patriarchy, or best described as 'paternalistic dominance'. The term describes the relationship of a dominant group, considered superior to a subordinate group, in which the dominance is mitigated by mutual obligations and reciprocal rights. "The dominated exchange submission for protection, unpaid labour for maintenance. In the patriarchal family, responsibilities and obligations are not equally distributed among those to be protected. The male children's subordination to the father's dominance is temporary; it lasts until they themselves become heads of households. The subordination of female children and of wives is lifelong." There is a Sanskrit *sloka* which says that a woman in her childhood is protected by her father, in adulthood by her husband, and in her old age by her son. This paternalistic protection has made her a commodity.

(ii) A Tool of Sexuality and Reproduction

Human history very comfortably brings out the fact that women have always been a tool of sexuality. She is, therefore, asked to limit her movements within the household. *Purdah* and *burka* are imposed on her, for, she is a possession of some male. Claude Levi-Strauss, to whom we owe the concept of the "exchange of women", speaks of the reification of women, which occurred as its consequence. But it is not women who are reified and commodified, it is women's sexuality and reproductive capacity which is so treated.

(iii) State of Unfreedom

True, women are a source of procreation. But, her power of procreation is controlled by the male. She is vulnerable to the sexuality of man. The decision to cohabit is taken by the male. If she defies it, she is raped. This has put her in a world which does not give her any freedom. Commenting on women's state of unfreedom, Lerner writes:

> But women always and to this day lived in a relatively greater state of unfreedom than did men. Since their sexuality, an aspect of their body, was controlled by others, women were not only actually the disadvantaged by psychologically being restrained in a special way. For women, as for men of subordinate and oppressed groups, history consisted of their struggle for emancipation and freedom from necessity. But women struggled against different from of operation and dominance than did men, and their struggle, up to this time, has lagged behind that of men.

(iv) Stand-by Wife

Right from the early periods of history, to the present day, there is a gender defined role of woman as that of a stand-by wife. The *Rajas* and the *Maharajas* had a large number of wives. The elites and the rich also practised and institutionalized polygyny. Though such women exercised considerable power and privileges, they depended on their attachment to these so-called big men. The gender status of wives thus has been pitiable all through the history.

(v) Sexual Exploitation

Lower class/caste women have always been exploited by the upper class/caste men. This has been obvious from antiquity in feudalism, in bourgeois households and in colonized countries. In fact, in Marxian phraseology, at any given moment in history, each class is constituted of two distinct classes of men and women. "The class position of women became consolidated and actualized through their sexual relationships. It always was expressed within degrees of unfreedom on a spectrum ranging from the slave woman, whose sexual and reproductive capacity was commodified as she herself was; to the slave-concubine, whose sexual performance might elevate her own status or that of her children; then to the 'free' wife whose sexual and reproductive services to one man of the upper classes entitled her to property and legal rights."

On the other hand, the class for men was and is based on their relationship to the means of production: those who owned the means of production could dominate those who did not. The owners of the means of production also acquired the commodity of female sexual services, both from women of their own class and from women of the subordinate classes.

(vi) Economic Oppression

Women are economically dependent on men. Even in village India where the contribution of women in the household earnings is substantially good, they continue to be dependent. Exploitation continues as much on the commodification of female sexuality and the appropriation by men of women's labour power and reproductive power as on the direct economic acquisition of resources and persons.

(vii) Issues Related to Marriage

The history of women's subordination reveals that all through the past, women have been made systematically powerless. They have always suffered at the 'protective' hands of the man. This has resulted in several social and cultural handicaps. The evils of child marriage, dowry and the resultant bride-burnings and suicides indicate that women have been victimized just because of their organic structure. Interestingly, the tribal society that did not practised dowry system in the past has now been experiencing it in the form of bride-price. Obviously, it is the impact of Hindu culture.

(viii) Crimes against Women

The gender problem is complicated further today when we find an acceleration of crime against women. We have enough evidence to infer that many of the crimes against women are because of their biology. She is vulnerable to rape. Several of the cases of rape are committed by those who happen to be close kin or familiar to the women.

The disabilities of women can further be catalogued. Sandra Harding, who has analyzed the gender issues from the Marxian perspective, argues that there is no future for human society as long as women are discriminated against. While concluding the inferiorization of women, Harding writes:

> As long as both men and women regard the subordination of half the human race to the other as 'natural', it is impossible to envision a society in which differences do not connote either dominance or subordination. The feminist critique of the patriarchal edifice of knowledge is laying the ground work for a correct analysis of reality, one which of the very least can distinguish the whole from a part. Women's history, the essential tool in creating feminist consciousness in women, is providing the body of experience against which new theory can be tested and the ground on which women in vision can stand.

Gender Issues in Indian Tribal Society

If the non-tribal society suffers from gender problems, so does the tribal. Generally, the tribals have been studied from the perspective of a few popular problems such as economic backwardness, land alienation, social change, changing stratification and empowerment. During the last five decades, development has also formed a vital part of tribal studies. K.S. Singh very rightly observes in *People of India* that Indian social anthropology has a rich literature on ethnography and development. This is all commendable. But, the gender issues, as mentioned earlier, throughout the post-independent period, have been neglected. It could also be said that with the acceleration of tribal development, the gender issues have become more severe. Earlier, the tribal society was more or less egalitarian. If there was division of labour in the tribal society as is found in all societies, it was based on age and not sex. A Bhil would voluntarily grind the corn and fetch potable water. The women, on the other hand, kept vigil over the crops. It was an egalitarian society. But, with the increase in tribal development, the division of labour turned to gender bais. The gender problem, therefore, is largely due to the new forces of development, social change and modernization. It is urgent for social anthropology to study the gender issues which are manifest in tribal society. In this section, we shall try to throw some light on the tribal problems which result from discrimination of women by men.

Command over Property

Bina Agarwal, a champion of feminist movement, begins her article on gender problems pertaining to right to land with the following quotation, which is actually the comment made by an informant in the field:

> We want land, all the rest is humbug. Please go and ask the *Sarkar* (government) why, when it distributes land, we don't get a title. Are we not peasants? If my husband throws me out what is my security?

The statement made by the landless women in South India raises a basic question: Why do tribal women not have right over land? Agarwal has traced the history of the problems arising out of gender relations in matrilineal and bilateral tribal communities. She says that in some of the South Asian communities, such as Garos, Khasis and Lalvngs (in North-East India) and Nayars, Tiyyars and Mappilas (in South India), women enjoy significant rights over land. The land rights that women enjoyed in matrilineal and bilateral communities fell broadly into three categories: First, among Garos, land was a clan's communal property and could not be inherited either by individuals or by joint family units. All clan members resident in the village had rights in this land as individuals. Second, among Khasis, Nayars, Tiyyars and Moppilas, land is inherited in the female line, and is held as joint family property and women had no individual rights of alienation. Responsibility for land management was vested principally with older men, usually brothers or maternal uncles. Third, in Sri

Lanka, both men and women had individual inheritance rights in land.

If the three categories of land rights enjoyed by women are analyzed, we observe that "the picture of gender relations among these groups is a mixed one. On the positive side women enjoyed considerable social independence and relative equality in marital relations. Indeed, in all the groups, a daughter's rights over land and the fact that she either remained in her natal home after marriage or had inviolable rights to return to it if she so chose, provided her with a strong fallback position within marriage. Women could choose their husband and initiate divorce." It could also be said that women in these societies had considerable freedom of movement and of public interaction.

But, on the negative side, women's property rights in the matrilineal and bilateral communities did not alter the overall gender division of labour: domestic work and child care were still a woman's responsibilities. The range of sexual mores found among these communities indicates that rights in land did not guarantee women the same sexual freedom as men. Formal managerial authority over land in a number of matrilineal communities lay with men. Thus, though rights over land gave certain benefits to women, but their virtual exclusion from property management circumscribed the power they could derive from those rights. The women, therefore, in matrilineal tribes today struggle to get property in land.

In the patrilineal society of tribals women's right in land is altogether denied. The status of tribal women in this regard is on par with that of the caste Hindu women. In North India some movements are reported wherein women demand their right over land. Commenting on the movement in tribal society, Bina Agarwal observes:

> ... today, for women, to gain effective rights in land will require not only removing existing gender inequalities in the law, but also ensuring that the laws are implemented. It will involve strengthening women's ability to claim and retain their rights in land, as well as their ability to exercise effective control over it.

However, in a matrilineal society such as that of Khasi, there is no gender discrimination. The law of inheritance is very simple. Ancestral property is passed from the mother to the daughter, specially the youngest one. In this society men have no inheritance right. The Khasi family assigns a central place to women. However, for protection, the mother's brother is considered very important. Despite the dominance of women in Khasi society man is considered to be quite powerful because of his 'physical strength' and the so-called 'twelve strength' as the saying goes among Khasis. Man has power and he is taken to be the protector and provider. There is one disability of women which is very striking. Tilput Nongbri, who has written authoritatively on Khasi society, informs us: "Although there are no formal laws which prevent Khasi women from holding public office, they are not allowed to attend traditional village and 'state' *durbars* (customary administrative and judicial councils). A woman who dares to voice her opinion on public affairs is regarded as a 'hen that crows'—a freak of nature. Men jealously guard their political prerogatives by defining politics as an arena for mature and physically fit persons." Nongbri further informs that the youngest daughter's position in the religious domain is similar to her position in the economic domain. Women are regarded as the trustees of family rights and traditions as well. The Khasis say: "The woman holds the religion. It is women who have to ensure that family rights are organized in their due course. But they have to seek the assistance of their male kin to actually perform the rituals. Priesthood is a male vocation among the Khasis."

In the matrilineal society there is not much gender discrimination. But, in practice, it is the man who does most of the things. He is the manager of property. He provides protection. But, there is a fear among the women that with the Khasi conversion to Christianity, the matrilineal system is gradually getting weak. Yet another force which weakens the system is modernization.

Gender Inequality and Stratification

Much work has been done in sociology in the field of social stratification. However, the mainstream stratification studies deal adequately with gender inequality. If we make a thorough analysis of Indian village studies we find that women work very hard both at the domestic level and at the level of agricultural operations. But, unfortunately, the labour of the women is not calculated in terms of wage earnings. Even, in the urban and industrial society, the status of a woman is identified with the status of her husband. This denies equal gender status to both the sexes. Recently, the 73rd constitutional amendment has empowered women by giving them reserved status in panchayat raj institutions (PRIs). In this new situation, the identity of woman is recognized by her position in panchayat raj. The Scheduled Tribes have taken the benefit of this.

Rape and the Tribal Response: The Case of Literature

The Scheduled Tribe and Scheduled Caste women are often raped by high caste Hindus. This issue has been taken up by Hindi and regional fiction and story writers in their works. It is argued that the tribal feminism has now become very powerful and it has geared itself to respond to incidences of rape.

Derrida, in his concept of deconstruction, has argued that the post-modernists reject and demystify the macro theories. Something of the kind of deconstruction has come about among the Bengali and Hindi writers. It would be interesting to refer to the work of Mahasweta Devi entitled *Dopadi*. This story revolves round a Santhal Naxalite woman who is not prepared to accept the established patriarchal conceptualization of rape. She struggles and shows resistance to the person who raped her. *Dopadi*—the story runs on the lines of Dopadi of *Mahabharata* but there are significant differences. In the story Dopadi is asked by a *Sainanayaka* to go to gang-rapists. She is raped. Then, she is summoned by *Sainanayaka* in his tent. She stands there with tears in her eyes.

In Mahasweta's story the actions of Dopadi defy the tradition of her namesake Draupadi of the Indian epic *Mahabharata*. When Draupadi was being stripped in public, Krishna intervenes and converts her *sari* into unending yards of cloth. Mahasweta has re-written this episode. Her Dopadi rejects male leadership. She does not want the male to rescue her. Mahasweta's Dopadi dauntlessly asks: "You can strip me but how can you clothe me again." This response given by the Santhal woman shows that when feminism successfully works among tribals, that would mark the end of gender discrimination.

Concluding Observations

Gender issues are not as serious among tribals as among non-tribal groups. However, looking at the widening dimensions of gender problems, it is necessary to look at it in the discipline of social anthropology. Gender constitutes sex plus social and cultural disabilities arising out of sex. The women are discriminated against by the men in their social and cultural life. Crimes against women, dowry, widowhood, participation in public and political life, rape are some of the glaring disabilities with which the women suffer because of their sex. The situation of tribal women is a little better. In *People of India*, K.S. Singh says that tribal women have larger participation in workforce compared to non-tribal women. They are also found to involve themselves in all economic activities, rituals and social functions. The 73rd constitutional amendment has further empowered them, especially in the field of panchayati raj.

Further Readings

Agarwal, Bina, *Gender and Command over Property,* Kali for Women, New Delhi, 1994.

Eriksen, Thomas Hylland, *Small Places, Large Issues*, Pluto Press, London, 1995.

Gilmore, David, *Manhood in the Making*, New Havan, C.T. Yale University Press, 1989.

Harding, Sandra, "Why has the Sex/Gender System become Visible only Now," in *Discovering Reality*, Sandra Harding and Marrill B. Hintikka (eds.), 1983.

Nongbri, Tilput, "Gender and the Khasi Family Structure", *Family, Kinship and Marriage in India*, Patricia Oberoi (ed.), OUP, Delhi, 1993.

—, "Gender Issues and Tribal Development", Rajiv Gandhi Foundation, New Delhi, 1998.

Panjabi, Kavita, "First Syllabus of a New Language", in *Women Heritage and Violence*, Shafali Moitra (ed.), Papyrus, Calcutta, 1996.

14

Religion, Rituals and Magic

Religion has been the core of India's tradition. A Sanskrit *sloka* by Valmiki in the *Ramayana* runs as under:

> There (in the hermitage of Agastya) the *Devas, Yakshas,* the *Nagas*, and the bird-like like community live together, restricting their food habit for the sake of their cultivation of religion.

Religion in India has not only been a tradition of worship, it also controlled the entire community life. Valmiki says that even the tribals were obliged to regulate their food habits along with the prescriptions of their religion. No tribal society could have ever lived without religion. However, one exception has come to the stock of ethnographic data in social anthropology. In 1961, Fredrik Barth reported that among the Basseri pastoral tribal group of South Iran, there was total absence of any interest in religion. The findings of Barth produced waves in anthropology. "His surprise is caused by the fact that religion seems to loom large in the lives of most of the peoples described in classical anthropological studies. This may be a major reason why religion has always been a central field of inquiry in anthropology, even if, as Evans-Pritchard (1962) has pointed out, social scientists have themselves often been indifferent or hostile to religion."

It is difficult to define religion. The difficulty arises because of the fact that everyone who attempts a definition becomes a victim of ethnocentricism. He defines religion from the perspective of his own culture. The result is that there is complete absence non-ethnocentric definitions. Rituals are related to religion. Religion is a belief and rituals are mechanisms through which beliefs are fulfilled. If a community has a belief that floods can be controlled by worshipping evil spirits, the belief is religion and the sacrifice of a goat is a ritual. Again, if it is a belief that the Almighty resides in an idol, the offering of coconut is a ritual. It is through ritual that religion is practised. In the western world, religion was misunderstood as superstition and paganism. The concept of paganism was associated with non-Christian religions and, in particular, their practices of public rituals which expressed aspects of the content of the religion. The concept of superstition was largely reserved for descriptions of invisible interrelationships in the world which neither science authorized religion nor 'commonsense' could account for. From this kind of perspective, Islam and African ancestral cults could be located in the domain of paganism, while, say the Trobriand islanders' belief that they die because of witchcraft and the common notion in the Mediterranean region and elsewhere that some persons are possessed by the evil eye, would be expressions of superstition. Traditionally, in social anthropology, religion has been defined as a form of social belief in supernatural power. This supernatural power is controlled or appeased through rituals.

Indian tribes give a central place to religious beliefs. The traditional tribal religion in our country has experienced the impact of some non-tribal religions also. There has been influence of Christianity on tribal religion apart from. Hinduism is also making its inroads. Whatever we get in the form of tribal religion is influenced by the local religions found in a particular tribal hinterland. The tribes in India have passed through a long process of evolution in their religion.

Religion

Perhaps, one of the oldest definitions of religion is given by E.B. Tylor:

> Religion is the belief in supernatural beings.

The definition is precise and very simple. But it poses a difficult question: After all, what is supernatural?. The answer to this question is related to knowledge. It is the knowledge of the people which helps define religion. Knowledge can be defined so as to include 'facts' which people are reasonably certain of and act upon, and which also have a social origin. If we accept Tylor's definition, it would be difficult for us to answer the question related to supernatural. The definition, therefore, does not satisfy one fully. We can then look at the definition given by Durkheim who is considered to be the father of the sociology of religion. His argument is that what is considered supernatural by the society is supernatural. This means that the society defines the supernatural. It is from this perspective that Durkheim considers society as the god; what is sacred is religion; what is profane is not religion, that is, utilitarian only. Durkheim has distributed all the things of the world in only two categories—sacred and profane. Things which are held in 'respect' are sacred and, therefore, related to supernatural. And, things which are considered to be items of utility are profane and, therefore, related to the worldly activities. Thus, sacred is supernatural and profane worldly. In a famous statement Durkheim claimed that "religion at its most profound level means society's worship of itself".

Durkheim's understanding of religion was basically functional. It was further extended by Radcliffe-Brown and Malinowski, for whom religion was functional for social integration of the society. Malinowski defined religion with reference to the Australian tribes:

> Religion is a mode of action as well as a system of belief and a sociological phenomenon as well as a personal experience.

Obviously, Malinowski takes a functional position. For him, religion is a system which holds together different aspects of tribal life. If we analyze Tylor, Durkheim, Radcliffe-Brown and Malinowski, we find that religion is a functional part of society. Thus, the approach is functional-structural and socially integrative.

Shift in the Approach to Religion

By the end of the 20th century there came about a phenomenal change in the definition of religion. The function-structure and social integration aspects of religion were abandoned. A rather different approach to religion is represented by Clifford Geertz in his essay "Religion as a Cultural System". He defines religion as follows:

> Religion is a (1) system of *symbols* which acts to (2) establish powerful, pervasive, and long lasting *moods and motivation* in men by (3) formulating *conceptions* of a general order of existence and (4) clothing these conceptions with such an *aura of factuality* that (5) the mood and motivations seem uniquely *realistic*.

In the above definition there is a breakthrough in the understanding of religion. Geertz has raised certain questions by defining religion. "He argues that instead of looking at the social functions of religion we ought to explore what religion means to people, how it helps to make sense of the world and how it gives a meaning and direction to human existence. We should study religion itself, not its social causes and the ultimate aim of such an investigation ought to be how the world and human existence appear meaningful to the believer."

Actually, the shift in the approach of religion emerged out of the work done by Evans-Pritchard on Nuer. In this study Evans-Pritchard came out with some conceptual formulations which helped him understand the great religions of Europe, particularly, Christianity. The study also stressed that religion, in fact, is a body of meanings, symbols and social processes.

The new approach promoted by Geertz and other contemporary anthropologists influenced the present social anthropology. Commenting on the shift in the understanding of religion, Eriksen writes:

> The approach advocated by Geertz and foreshadowed by Evans-Pritchard has been very influential in anthropological research on religion in recent decades. This shift in perspective is a part of the general change in anthropological thinking mentioned earlier, whereby the main trends have swung from an interest in functions, structure and social integration which was dominant until the 1960s, to a concern with the interpretation of meaning, symbols and social process... In the study of religion, it is found, among other things, there is a growing interest in relating meaning to experience and in understanding cosmologies.

Elements of Religion

Social anthropologists, particularly the British ones, have generated voluminous data on primitive religion. The data relate to the primitive and tribal people of India, Africa and Australia. The US anthropologists have, however, shown lesser concern on primitive religion. On the strength of the ethnographic data available we present below in this section some of the elements of religion which also characterized religion of several tribal groups:

Ritual

Durkheim has described ritual as an important element of religion. Ritual is a practice of religion, or say, the action part of religion. Conceptually, ritual is different from religious phenomena or beliefs. Beliefs are ideas or thoughts and ritual is their implementation. At the empirical plane of any religion, primitive or otherwise, ritual cannot be separated from religion. Parsons in *Structure of Social Action* has explained the relationship of religion and rituals in the following words:

> The fundamental distinction between religion and ritual is that between two categories of religious phenomena—beliefs and rites—the first is a form of thought, the second of action. But, the two are inseparable, and central to every religion. Without knowing its beliefs the ritual of a religion is incomprehensible. That the two are inseparable does not, however, imply any particular relation of priority, the point is, at present, the distinction. Religious beliefs, then, are beliefs concerning sacred things, their origin, behaviour and significance for man. Rites are actions performed in relation to sacred things.

If a Santhal of Bihar offers a hen to his local deity, it is a ritual in consideration of his belief or thought that the deity has to be appeased to ward off the evils inflicted on the community. Thus, the sacrifice of a hen is ritual and belief in the power of deity is thought. We see that in an empirical situation both belief and ritual work together.

Arousing of Feelings

In order to get consciousness about religion or the existence of belief, some feelings and emotions are also aroused. Fear of God, fear for doing evil things, charity, living a sacred life are all patterns of behaviour which arouse feelings for a religion. Sometimes, however, feelings are also aroused to create terror in the followers.

Beliefs

The edifice of religion stands on the structure of beliefs. The earlier social anthropologists defined religion in terms of beliefs only. Tylor argued that there cannot be any religion without belief. And, what is important about belief is that it cannot be argued; it can not be empirically proved. It is only a matter of understanding.

In recent anthropological literature, the element of belief in religion is severely criticized. It is said that religion has to be understood in sociological and logical terms. Belief has no existence because it does not stand the test of reality.

Organization

In the early history of religion we have evidence to say that there was some organization to regulate the activities of a particular sect. Max Weber, who is said to be the founder of modern sociology, observed that all the great religions of world—Christianity, Judaism, Islam, Hinduism—had some kind of organization. The function of organization was to regulate the activities and functioning of the religion. Christianity has its church which works as a central body to keep the Christians together. Likewise, Hinduism has its four *dhams* where Sankracharyas work as head and regulate the activities of Hindus.

Symbols and Myths

Each religion has its own symbols and myths. For instance, church, temple, mosque, flag and a specific kind of dress and worship are symbols of various religious cults. Similarly, there are mythological stories related to each religion. The tribals who believe in animism have their own totems which are reflected in animals, plants and trees. The origin of the clans is also illustrated by mythological stories.

Taboos

In order to differentiate itself, each religious faith has its own taboos. These taboos are related to food habits and way of living. For instance, Jainism professes that its followers should not take their meals after sunset and that they should be strictly vegetarian. The behaviour patterns of the followers are also determined by religion.

In the above list of the elements of religion, a few more could be added. It must be remembered that these elements undergo change and transformation at the local level. New interpretations are also added to the elements with the functioning of various social and cultural processes. Some new elements also appear.

Forms of Religion: Oral Religions and Religions of the Book

The tribals all over the country have oral religion. The theory and beliefs about religion are not written in any language. The beliefs are, therefore, transmitted by word of mouth and is passed on as tradition from generation to generation. The rituals which accompany the religion are also followed in a traditional form. However, each generation makes some changes in the religious thought and beliefs. For instance, G.S. Ghurye and N.K. Bose have highlighted the changes in tribal religion due to impact of Hinduism. But, the new form of tribal religion continues to remain oral mainly because of illiteracy among the tribals. Though a small percentage of them have taken to formal education---even technical and professional---no effort, however, has been made to bring out their religion in book form. True, there have been tribal religious leaders but they too have not written down the basic tenets of their religion. There have also been tribal movements---religious and ethnic---which have been elaborated by Stephen Fuchs in his *Rebellious Prophets* (1965), but the prophets have maintained silence regarding giving a formal shape to religion. They preached only orally.

However, religions of Hindus and Muslims are written. The tenets of Islam are found in the sacred text of *Koran*. The Hindu religious texts are several, namely, *Vedas*, *Puranas*, *Upanishadas*, *Brahmanas* and *Geeta*. The written forms of religion are called religions of the book by Goody (1986). Bible is found in the written form as the religion of Christians. Such religions including Judaism, Islam, Hinduism and Christianity regard their content as tied to the text and not to a particular cultural context. "Since they are text-bound, these religions can be disseminated throughout the world to peoples who in other regards live very different kinds of lives. Islam, for example, is the main religion in countries as different as Java, Niger, Egypt and Iran; whereas Christianity dominates in countries like the Philippines, Germany and north-east of India. The written religions, and particularly the monotheistic ones with their origins in the Middle East, can also be described as religions of conversion—systems of beliefs to which one can be converted and in which one has to affirm one's faith. Unlike other religions, they tend to be exclusive and not to accept 'syncretism'. Christian missionaries in Africa have, therefore, despaired at the sight of Africans cheerfully worshipping Christ as well as water spirits and ancestral spirits."

Hinduism is partly a religion of the book. But K.S. Singh says that its form is amorphous. Many of its rituals are oral and take different forms in different ethnic groups. Moreover, its doctrines are less fixed and more flexible. Hinduism insists on less obedience to texts than the monotheistic script religions do.

The oral form of religion which is characteristic to tribal religion has been studied by social anthropologists. This form of religion differs considerably from the religions of the book, that is, written religions. The differences are several. First, the oral religions remain confined to smaller places, a locality. No Nuer in his right mind would expect the whole world's population to become followers of his religion's revered spirits or even of their highest God—*Thoth*. The gods are frequently physically associated with revered places in the tribal area. Among Indian tribes there are local deities known as village deities. Second, oral religions tend to be non-conversive. Quite like Christianity, Buddhism and Islam, there is no provision of conversion in oral religion. Third, oral religions appear to be embedded in the social practices of society, whereas written ones are often more detached from other social institutions.

Fourth, "a somewhat related distinction, which was introduced by Robert Redfield (1955), concerns little and great traditions. Redfield argues that different strains and logics of religion and knowledge exist side by side in many societies; they may be radically different, but are often interrelated. The Mediterranean belief in the evil eye, for example, clearly belongs to a little tradition." The individuals who have belief in little traditions simultaneously also believe in the greater traditions. Brahmanic Hinduism is the official great tradition, its beliefs and rituals sanctioned in the ancient *Veda* texts and centuries of monitored ritual practices are the little traditions. Low-caste Hindus, nevertheless, have their own rituals and beliefs, often more reminiscent of oral than written religions, which co-exist with the high or great traditions but are socially segregated from it.

Thus, oral religions are characterized by their local relevance, relative lack of dogma and tight integration with the 'non-religious' domains. The primitive and tribal groups invariably have oral religion. An ethnographic example from India may illustrate the oral character of Bhil religion.

The Bhils are found mostly in western India. They are the second largest group in the country preceded by the Gonds. The Bhils believe in ancestor worship. There is a fixed place in the house for the ancestor. There is no material form of their ancestors. From birth to death there is ancestor worship. On ceremonial days also, the ancestor is worshipped. Next to ancestor is the local deity which resides in a specific part of the village. The marriage procession goes to the village deity. If some sacrifice has to be made, it is made to the village deity. If an epidemic erupts in the village, the deity is appeased. The Bhils have a strong belief in their little traditions. However, due to contact with caste Hindus, they have acquired some familiarity with the great traditions, e.g., Rama and Krishna, Heaven and Hell.

Theories of Religion

Social anthropologists have endeavoured to construct theories of religion which provide an explanation to human behaviour. The religious life of any people is manifested in outward form, in beliefs and in rites. The beliefs are about sacred things and rites addressed to them. Mere beliefs do not constitute religion, it is rites which make religion a living force. The shape of the supernatural power varies from society to society. Some religions believe that the supernatural power is abstract (*nirakar*) and can only be experienced and imagined. On the other hand, there are religions which argue that the supernatural power has a definite shape, a dimension, it is an idol. It is a form, a shape (*sakar*). On the basis of some such notions anthropologists have formed the following explanations about religion:

(1) Animism
(2) Polytheism
(3) Monotheism
(4) Naturalism

Animism

About a century has passed Edward B. Tylor pointed out that all peoples in primitive societies believed in animism. It means there is existence of intangible, non-material or spiritual beings which may be souls, ghosts, ancestral spirits, fauna, flora, ogres or monsters, or simply objects. The origins of beliefs in such spiritual beings are probably multiple, as Tylor believes. The presence of vitality in a living person, which is unquestionably absent from a corpse, results in an animistic interpretation. The persons and things heard, seen or felt in dreams or in temporary hallucinatory experiences as in hot weather or when a person is exhausted, or when he is under the influence of drugs, yield the same result. Additional experiences which bring about or reinforce animistic beliefs are echoes, reflections in quiet pools, or other natural phenomena.

Tylor contended that "once the basic premise of an animistic ideology—belief in the existence of spiritual beings and souls—had been developed, the path was laid for eventual development to later stages of religious ideology. But before the second stage was reached, the original belief in souls and spirits had come to include beliefs in malevolent spirits or demons, and in the spirits of ancestors."

Tylor presumed that the souls, ancestral spirits and other supernatural beings of the first developmental stage tended to change as a second stage into other higher or more grandiose forms of supernatural beings such as nature gods. Neither proof nor disproof is available for such a sequence of stages because the peoples who are of the lowest economic level are not well enough known to indicate that they are largely or exclusively animistic. In fact, other forms of supernatural concepts, such as that of a single deity, also appear along with animistic concepts among such peoples.

Animism thus has passed through several stages of development. And, these stages very from tribe to tribe and country to country. In our country, the form of animism that we find is based on ancestor worship.

Polytheism

Literally, polytheism means belief in more than one great spiritual power. This type of religious belief is found at all socio-economic levels. Defining polytheism John Lewis says that it is "believing in and worshipping in several gods". Polytheism is widely prevalent in advanced agricultural-pastoral socio-economic systems and in cultures like those of ancient Egypt, Mesopotamia, Greece and Rome.

Tylor has tried to establish an evolutionary formulation of religion. In this context, he says that among the tribals, the beginning of religion started with animism. At the second stage of development it took the form of animitism. The concept of animitism holds that a non-material, impersonal, non-individualized spiritual essence pervades all things, manifests itself in inanimate and animate things. This spirit is considered to be a source of great power. It has miraculous efficacy.

The third stage of the evolution of religion is polytheism. This form of religious belief—belief in plural gods—is rarely found. However, when the simple agricultural economy develops, polytheism emerges. In the simple, small-sized societies, there is prevalence of animism and animitism, but polytheism is associated with higher level of development attained by a particular tribal group.

Monotheism

Monotheism means belief in a single deity. Its propitiators believe that the cosmos is a unity, with one god who created and ordered all. Monotheism is the widely held idea that the belief in only one god is of recent development. It has not definitely been proved to be correct. "However, no absolutely pure monotheism has ever developed among peoples in primitive economies and has never characterized any such society. This is known for societies of primitive economy because of available evidence regarding the universality of animistic ideologies among them. Yet, the synchronous occurrence of such animistic ideologies along with a monotheistic-like belief in a high god is certain."

Naturalism

Yet another form of animism is found in naturalism. It is believed that the supernatural power has its manifestation in things of nature. The roaring of clouds, lightening in the clouds and earthquakes are nothing but the expressions of the supernatural power. When there are floods in the rivers, the supernatural power expresses its wrath. The wrath of the power, therefore, has to be propitiated by animal sacrifice.

It is believed, especially by the tribals, that nature has supernatural power which has to be respected. Because of this power there is awe for nature and people worship nature in the form of earth, fire, water, stars, floods, etc.

Primitive Religion in India

D.N. Majumdar has written extensively about tribal religion in India. Since the British period the tribals have been described as animists. According to Majumdar, "animism is that exceedingly crude form of religion in which magic is the predominant element. It conceives of man as passing through a life surrounded by a ghostly company of power, elements, most impersonal in their character, shapeless phantoms of which no image can be made and no definite idea can be formed. Some of these are taken to preside over particular departments of life or spheres of influence."

Majumdar further says that with the process of religious change animism came to be categorized as tribal religion. Hutton has made an observation on tribal religion and says that it is a "surplus material not yet built into the temple of Hinduism". However, in later period, Verrier Elwin pointed out a difference between tribal religion and Hinduism though he says that such an effort at differentiation is meaningless. He observes:

> The tribal people always are willing to worship a few more gods, if by doing so, they can gain some material or social advantage.

David Hardiman, a subaltern historian, has referred to the religious beliefs of tribals of Gujarat. He cites the conviction of the Bhils that when water pitchers are burst in a ceremonial procession famine will be eased.

Ghanshyam Shah has commented on the conversion of Bhils of Dangs (Gujarat) to Christianity. His understanding is that the census enumerators who work in the field are invariably Hindus. Without actually asking the question about religion, they fill in the column assuming that the tribals are Hindus. This has shown that the tribals have taken to Hinduism although it is a fact that the tribals do not hesitate to accept Hindu gods and goddesses, fairs and festivals to improve their material status.

Tribal religion even today revolves round animism. K.S. Singh's *People of India* (POI) project has tried to identify the ethnic and religious status of Indian tribes. He says that "tribes have generally remained outside the *varna* system. Therefore, only 11.8 per cent of them recognized their place in it". Almost all tribal communities have divisions and a notion of hierarchy. This hierarchy is based on ecology, descent, ranking, status and so on. These tribal groups are endogamous. The incidence of inter-community hypergamy and even hypogamy has been reported from 10 and 6 tribal communities respectively, located in central India and other parts. Most of the tribes practise clan exogamy.

The POI data on religion are quite interesting. There are tribal groups that follow only one religion. For example, Hinduism is professed by 59.4 per cent of all the 461 tribal groups; 23.4 per cent practise Christianity, 3 per cent follow Islam; Buddhism is followed by 6.9 per cent, and 45.9 per cent practise animism. There are tribal groups also which follow more than one religion, like Hinduism and animism, Christianity and animism, and Hinduism, Islam and Christianity all at the same time.

On the strength of empirical evidence available K.S. Singh says that admittedly a large number of tribals have taken to Hinduism; some have adopted Christianity but despite all these changes the core of tribal religion continues to remain centred in animism. A Gond, or a Bhil may visit Hindu temples of Rama, Krishna, Kali or Amba; they may celebrate with all gaiety the festivals of Diwali, Holi and Rakhi but simultaneously they will also worship their local village deities, family ancestors and show respect for their tribal priest. In other words, true, tribals have taken to Hindu gods and goddesses but have not looked down upon or discarded their traditional deities. Thus, in conclusion, the observations of Singh, in the POI, may be quoted:

> A major finding in terms of religion has been the continuance of the autonomy of the tribal religious system in spite of the tribes' close interactions with Christianity and Hinduism. The hierarchy of the clan and village deities is intact. There are more sacred specialists among the tribals from their own communities. There are only a small number of sacred specialists from other communities. The calendar of festivals and festivities is also relatively intact.

Rituals

Human beings always have some problems in life. In urban industrial society these problems are solved by knowledgeable people. For instance, if there is illness, the physician is approached; if the problem is related to house construction, the architect is consulted; if there is problem with studies, the respective subject teacher is consulted; and so on and so forth. What does the primitive man do? If he has problems in hunting, domestication of animals or agriculture, he has experienced men around him. But, if there is an illness or some unknown disease, he has to approach people who are specialists and who have access to supernatural powers. When problems of birth or death are not solved local traditional experts are consulted. True, these experts are not always successful in giving prescriptions but there is some articulation towards the solution of the problem. Thus, there is a definite place for rituals in primitive society. In fact, there is no escape from the performance of rituals. Eriksen underlines the importance of rituals in primitive society in the following words:

> This is, in other words, a very complex field, and it is important because the ritual can be seen as a synthesis of several important levels of social reality; the symbolic and the social, the individual and the collective; and it usually brings out, and tries to resolve—at a symbolic level—contradictions in society.

Ritual has been theoretically discussed by Talcott Parsons at great length. Emile Durkheim and Max Weber have also discussed rituals elaborately. They have made their abstract generalization on the basis of empirical facts. Parsons does not differentiate between ritual and rite—both terms are synonymous for him. He defines ritual or rite as below:

> Religious beliefs, then, are beliefs concerning sacred things—their origin, behaviour and significance for man. Rites are actions performed in relation to sacred things.

As a matter of fact, Parsons has drawn his analysis of rituals from Durkheim. He says:

> Religion is an integrated system of beliefs and practices relative to sacred things.

For Durkheim, and in this respect for Parsons also, ritual is a part of religion. It is an ingredient of religion. Therefore, rituals are termed as practices or religious actions. Parsons further adds that rituals are normally irrational. These are actions which appear from the subjective point of view in terms of the relation of means to an end. To the performer these are quite strictly ways of doing things. In other words, the objectives of religion should be fulfilled by means which are recognized by society. Ill-gotten money does not help achieve the religious goals.

Eriksen, on the other hand, stresses the notion of beliefs in the performance of rituals. He writes:

Ritual has been defined as the social aspect of religion. If we may define religion as systems of notion about the supernatural and the sacred, about life after death and so on, then rituals are the social processes which give a concrete expression to these notions. Very generally speaking, we may suggest that rituals are rule-bound public events which in some way or other thematize the relationship between the earthly and spiritual realms.

Characteristics of Rituals

There is enough literature in social anthropology which brings out some basic characteristics of rituals. For instance, Max Gluckman, Roy Rappaport, Edmund Leach and others have worked on rituals among primitive people. In Indian context, M.N. Srinivas has conducted rich fieldwork among the Coorgs of South India. In his analysis of Coorg religion he also discusses rituals. These rituals pertain to Coorg family, kin and community. G.S. Ghurye has shown that the elements of tribal religion are not on empirical but analytical plane. On the basis of these studies we present below some of the basic elements of rituals found among the tribals in our country and elsewhere:

Religious Practice

Religion is philosophy; it is theory, thought, and ideology. Rituals, on the other hand, are not concerned with the theoretical part of religion. They are the practices or empirical actions to achieve the objectives laid down by religion.

Social Aspect

Rituals provide opportunity to the people to enjoy social festivals and ceremonies. On the day of Holi, the tribals organize gatherings which provide opportunities for young men and women to meet and, if possible, run away. Similarly, the rituals of magic man and priest bind the people to regulate their dietary habits. Thus, despite being associated with religion, a ritual is essentially social in nature. It gives rise to a large number of social processes.

Time-bound

There are generally fixed days for the observation of certain rituals.

When the magic man or the priest performs rites to control the supernatural power the days are fixed for it. Normally, these are performed on the dark moon nights. G.S. Ghurye has devoted a long chapter on the spirit world of the primitives. When fasts are observed as a part of ritual performance, the time to observe them is also specified. Thus, the performance of rituals is time-bound; it is conditioned by time, days, months and years.

Symbolic

The nature of ritual is basically symbolic. When the village deity is offered the sacrifice of a hen or a goat, the deity does not in itself consume the flesh; it is distributed among the votaries. The sacrifice is only symbolic. *Mattha tekana*, that is, bowing of the head in respect, is only symbolic which conveys devotion to the deity.

Synthesis of Differential Reality

Reality in society is multifaceted. There is social, economic, political and ethnic reality. All these forms of reality are artificial or superimposed. To balance this reality adequately, rituals are performed. When a society is complex, so are its realities. Thus, the performance of rituals keeps a man in constant touch with the supreme reality.

Articulation of Solution

It is not certain that the performance of rituals will bring forth a solution. But, the rituals are observed with such elaboration that for the common man there is a perfect articulation for solution. The marriage rituals are, therefore, mere articulation of the success of marriage.

Cultural

Geertz argues throughout his analysis of religion that ritual is basically cultural. When we perform a ritual it is always performed in the context of the surrounding culture. The performance of ritual is determined by the culture of the group to which the votary belongs. For example, when a Gond offers worship to Shiva, he offers a coconut and leaves of *billi* tree. These items of ritual performance are items of his culture. On the other hand, when a Kashmiri Pandit worships Shiva, he offers raw meat. Here, it becomes a part of the Kashmiri

Pandit's local culture. Ritual is always culture-specific.

Functions of Rituals

Functionalists have been arguing on the strength of their ethnographic data that the rituals are integrative for the society. The ordinary tribal does not understand the philosophy and thought of religion. He is concerned with the rituals only in his day to day life. He does not know quite well what is the philosophy behind the offering of new crop to the village deity. He only knows that it is the ritual practice of his community to offer the new crop. All others are doing it and so he does it too. But, the integrative function of ritual does not go unchallenged. Edmund Leach has brought out new data from Burma. His book, *Political Systems of Highland Burma*, states that among the Kachins the religious ritual complex in no way functioned in an integrating way. Leach finds that rituals create dissension and imbalance in the community.

Despite the controversy over the functions of rituals there are a few rituals which are beneficial for the people. Some of the important functions are discussed below:

Transformation of Conflicts

Sometimes long-term conflicts of a community are transformed into harmless celebrations. Actually rituals give a new direction to society. Max Gluckman (1956) provides evidence to the effect that in Swazi tribal group of South Africa there are some such rituals. But, at the same time, he cautions that conflicts can be transformed into benefits only if the participants take the rituals seriously.

Turn Down the Customary Rules

Again, to quote Max Gluckman, it may be said that among the South African tribals there are some curious rituals which turn upside down some of the customary rules practised by the tribals. One of the rituals "took place among the Swazi at the coronation of a new king. When this was about to happen every citizen was expected to mock and criticize the king in public, making a grand spectacle of his inadequacy. Similarly, open social criticism was allowed at the medieval carnivals in parts of Europe, but not during the rest of the year."

In India, there are some rituals observed in parts of rural India whereby everyone mouths abuses against one another in public. All foul words are used and dirty songs are sung with the melody of *chang* or *dholak* but no one takes it seriously. It is only a mockery, not a reality. On this day, the general behaviour of the people becomes brash and bawdy. This is an example of a curious kind of function performed by a ritual.

Provide Survival to People

In observing rituals by the community the objectives of the ritual are hardly realized. In most cases, as stated earlier, rituals are symbolic. For example, among the Bhils of southern Rajasthan and Gujarat, there is a ritual performed when the rainfall is inadequate. The Bhils believe that the raingod—Indra—is arrested by the *saukars*, and the God has to be released. For this tribal women carry pitchers full of water on their head in a procession. The Bhils following them pierce the pitchers with their arrows. This ritual is only symbolic. The act cannot bring rains, the Bhils know it very well. But, they observe it just to perform the tradition.

Relationship between the Myths and the Rituals

The rituals are dramatized by the myths. Edmund Leach refers to some myths found among the Kachins of Burma. Leach shows that "the myths and rituals positively encourage a lack of stability, since they offer themselves to conflicting interpretations. Kachin beliefs and rituals nevertheless always function ideologically in the sense of legitimating a particular power structure..."

Use of Symbols

Use of symbols is central to rituals, and this does not involve only the symbols which are used, but also their mutual relationship and their meaning. Among Christians, white symbolizes virtue and purity while black signifies evil and darkness. In India, the Hindus consider white as sacred and green as development. Among all communities in India, as Westermark reports, in the marriage procession of groom rice is broadcast. This is the symbol of prosperity and fertility. The Gonds consider black colour as the symbol of darkness and gloom. Symbols can be of any colour, any size or any material. It can also be an animal or a bird.

Magic

If we make a quick survey of research in sociology and social anthropology, we realize that during the last few decades no empirical study on magic has been made by social anthropologists. Sachchidananda has prepared an elaborate bibliography on rural studies, and to our surprise no study has been conducted on the influence of magic among the Indian tribes. Similarly, the project *Peoples of India* does not mention anything about this. On the other hand, the textbooks on social anthropology invariably carry a chapter on tribal magic. Clearly, there is a wide gap on what we find today and what is given in the textbooks. It is beyond comprehension as to what makes the textbook writers devote many pages to vivid accounts of tribal magic. Perhaps, the fault does not lie with the textbook writers. The responsibility of including magic rests with the framers of the syllabuses.

Magical practices in India go back to medieval and pre-capitalist society. Magic has a specific role in the evolution of our institutions. Malinowski, Evans-Pritchard and Frazer were evolutionalists. It is this evolutionary perspective which led these anthropologists to write about tribal magic. Religion, too, like any other social institution, has evolved through a long process of development. Magic was perhaps the first stage in the evolutionary phase of development of religion. Besides tribals the non-tribal groups who were living in isolation also had firm faith in magic. The allopathic system of treatment had not come into existence then, and people were perennially becoming victims of of varying ailments. They were living in unfriendly environments. There was scarcity, famines, epidemics, and the people had no other alternatives other than resorting to magic.

Malinowski and Frazer who worked among the tribals reported the role of magic in tribal society in middle of the 19th and 20th centuries. Malinowski's Trobrianders and Evans-Pritchard's Azandes have now taken to modernization. All of them have accepted the modern system of medicine.

In India, the 'civilized' castes also took to magical practices and, in some cases, these proved more sophisticated than tribals'. When there was invasion on Somnath temple (Gujarat), the Hindu *Rajas* invited a group of Brahmins to perform magic so that the invasion could be made ineffective. Even today, we see that when political leaders or elites of high status are in a struggle with death, Brahmins and *tantriks* are called to perform *Mratunjaya Jap*—a clear example of belief in superstitions. The point which we want to emphasize here is that magic was not a specific art practised only by the tribals. The whole subcontinent believed in magical practices. If Frazer and Malinowski mentioned tribal magic, they were only discussing the tribal situation which was found during the medieval and pre-capitalist periods, not only of India but the whole of Europe.

What is Magic?

It is a term that denotes a special kind of behaviour, not necessarily religious, which follows from the acceptance of beliefs in one or another type of supernaturalism. If people believe in animism, they may act so as to get certain things done with the help of the spirit beings whom they believe to be present. "If people believe in *mana* or animatism, they may act in a somewhat different way in order to effect desired ends with the help of the impersonal sort of power they presume can be tapped. They also assume that certain things will happen inevitably because the power has always operated in that way. If people believe in a pantheon of deities, one or another of those deities will be propitiated, sacrificed to, or vangled in some way in order to bring about other desired ends. However, the essential characteristic of magic is that its procedures tend to be mechanistic and to function automatically if one knows the proper formula." Religion and magic are alternative techniques. Sometimes, one is supplementary to another.

Anthropologists have defined magic on the strength of their experience in the field, though a few of the definitions are not directly related to empirical observations. However, we would make an attempt here to define magic in a systematic way.

Let us begin with John Lewis. He says:

> Magic is the technique of coercion by making use of belief in supernatural power. Sympathetic or imitative magic supposes that an action committed upon something that stands for a person or a thing will have the desired effect upon the actual person or thing.

Malinowski has defined magic in a very precise way as under:

> Magic is a body of purely practical acts, performed as a means to an end.

According to Herskovits, magic is a substantial part of culture. People often use prayer as a form of worship. A prayer uses words to bring about the favourable intervention of the powers of the universe in the affairs of men. Magic stands in contrast to prayer. This contrast was for the first time attempted by Evans-Pritchard in the discussion of the magic among the Azandes. Herskovits draws his comprehension of magic from Evans-Pritchard and Frazer. His understanding of magic is explained as below:

> The charm and the spell are widely spread devices employed in magic. A specific power, held to reside in a specific object, is set in operation by the pronouncement of a formula that, of itself, can wield power. The magic charm takes innumerable forms. It most often includes some part of the object over which its power is to be exerted, or some element that, because of outer resemblance or inner character, habitually achieves the desired result.

Though the definitions of religion given by the anthropologists vary in their form and content, the basic idea is more or less the same. The tribals believe that there is one supernatural power. None can contest it. It is universal. This supernatural power is endowed with ample power which is positive (white) and negative (black) both. The person who wants to obtain expertise in the art of magic, appeases the supernatural power to make it bestow some power on him. The supernatural thus can be obliged to part with some of its power through certain magical performances. These performances vary from society to society.

Elements of Magic

Magic is an art and has to be acquired. The practitioner has to work hard to develop the skills of magic. Some of the important elements of magic are given below:

(1) Tylor has classified the practices of magic. These practices are scientific. The practitioner works as a scientist. For instance, Tylor says that things which appear similar are put into one category. For example, jaundice bears yellow colour and gold also has the same colour. Magic establishes relationship between these two because of their similar colour. Bohannan does not agree with this

theory. He says that in magical practices no logic of association applies.

(2) Magic is individual-oriented. A person perceives a thing in a particular way; this perception works in his magical practices.

(3) According to Malinowski, there is important role of *mantras*. *Mantras* have the power to imitate the natural voice and, therefore, for successful result of magical practices *mantras* are important. Second, the magician explains the present situation in this language and orders for the fulfilment of his desires. Third, the *mantras* refer to the name of those ancestors who have imparted the magical skills.

(4) While chanting the *mantras* the magician continuously does some activities; for instance, he moves his hands, makes faces and gestures. These physical activities are believed to strengthen the power of magic.

(5) The magician exercises some restrain in terms of diet and sex relations during the days when he engages himself in magical practices.

(6) Magical practices cannot be done at the discretion of the magician. There are some fixed days which are considered to be suitable for this. For instance, the last day of the dark half of month or *amavasya* is most suitable for learning and doing magic. Again, the days of *Dassehra*, particularly *Navratri*, is good for magical practices.

(7) Malinowski says that discipline is most important in the practice of magic. The first thing which is required of a magician is to spell out the objectives of magic. He has to perform them with great caution. A little fault could boomerang on the magician himself. It is because of this that the magician lives a pathetic life in his old age.

(8) In accordance with the objectives of magical practices the magician makes physical gestures to empower his magic.

Frazer and Malinowski have observed interesting instances about the magical practices among the tribals of Australia and Africa. Nadel has also referred to magic in his description of Nupe religion. Evans-Pritchard gives elaborate descriptions about magical practices and its elements among the Azandes.

Theories of Magic

Some anthropologists have developed theories of magic. Tylor has very specifically differentiated magic from religion. He has constructed three basic theories of magic which are as under:

(1) Magic is related to a kind of behaviour which is based on general knowledge.
(2) Whatever is done by nature, can also done by magic. In this situation people do not differentiate between the functioning of nature and magic.
(3) If the magic fails, it is considered due to the faulty chanting of *mantras* or some lapse in the regular life of the practitioner.

Thus, Tylor's theory of magic makes two important points: (i) magic is an ideology, and it has to be relied upon; and (ii) magic is based on logic. If the magical practices are done on these two principles, the results would always be forthcoming. Evans-Pritchard observes that magic and religion are found in all the societies. The presentation of Tylor's theory by Evans-Pritchard is given in the following figure:

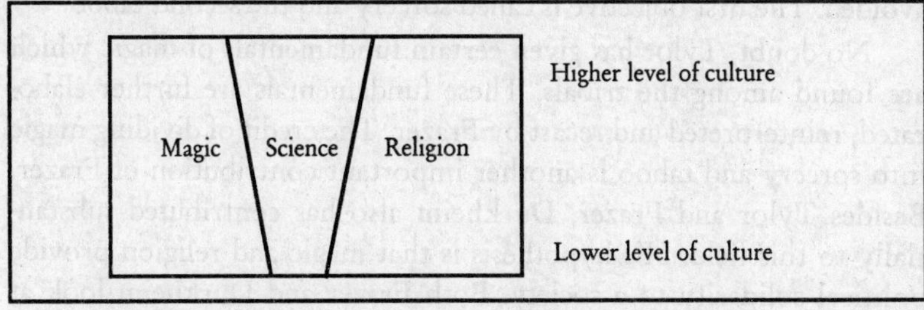

In all the societies, there is the influence of magic, science and religion. But the extent of influence is not similar. For instance, if a society lives at a lower level of culture such as that of tribals and backward classes, the extent of magic and religion would be larger. The members of this society would depend much on magical practices and rituals. However, if the society has a higher level of culture, there would be lesser space for magic and religion; and more space for science. In other words, science has a predominant place in advanced societies whereas the backward societies practise more of magic and religion.

Tylor's theory of magic has been improved upon by Frazer. In the literature on social anthropology, Tylor is very well known for his two classical works: *The Golden Bough*, and *Folklore in the Old Testament*. Whatever Tylor has propounded in the form of theory in these books has been taken up for discussion and analysis by Frazer. While interpreting Tylor, Frazer gives the theory—*the law of sympathy*—which says that the tribal people look at material things in terms of sympathy between the two similar things. Sympathy is of two kinds: (i) on the basis of outward similarity, for instance, between the colour of jaundice and the colour of gold; and (ii) based on contact. It is on the basis of these two sympathies that Frazer has given three theories of magic: (1) theory of sympathy, (2) theory of similarity, and (3) theory of contact.

Frazer's theory of magic believes that when a tribal practises magic, he does it as he has learnt it, and he has nothing to do with the theories of magic—his concern is with the outcome only. It is because of this that Frazer considers magic to be semi-art and semi-science. Magic has two basic objectives: first, through magic certain objectives are achieved, and second, some of the unwanted incidents can be avoided. The first objective is called sorcery and the second taboo.

No doubt, Tylor has given certain fundamentals of magic which are found among the tribals. These fundamentals are further elaborated, reinterpreted and recast by Frazer. The credit of dividing magic into sorcery and taboo is another important contribution of Frazer. Besides Tylor and Frazer, Durkheim also has contributed substantially to this field. His hypothesis is that magic and religion provide political solidarity to a society. Both Frazer and Durkheim look at magic and religion as sources of political solidarity.

Types of Magic

Students of social anthropology often distinguish two kinds of magic. The first kind which is named by Frazer is called imitative or homeopathic magic, whereas the second is called contagious. Describing the two kinds of magic Herskotvits writes:

> Both are held to operate in accordance with a principle of 'like to like' also called a 'principle of sympathy'. 'Contagious' magic is exemplified when a hunter drinks the blood of his kill to acquire its craftiness or its strength. 'Imitative' magic would, let us say, be found

in the performance of a dance in which the simulated killing of an animal was enacted so as to assure success in hunting.

The two kinds of magic as above neither constitute the entire field, nor are they absent from certain practises to which the term 'religious' is customarily given.

Yet another typology of magic is that of 'black' and 'white'. Black magic has some evil intentions. According to it, the victim is inflicted with some injury. The second type, white magic, is beneficent in its intent. In social anthropological literature much emphasis is placed on black magic. "The reason for this is two-fold. There is the challenge to the investigator to uncover what his informants are least willing to divulge. More than this, though, is the dramatic appeal of black magic for the people themselves. Once a willingness to talk about it is established, informants will dwell on the subject with relish and exuberant detail, leaving 'white' magic as something taken for granted."

The horror shows which are presented with different names on television depict several of the practices of black magic. If revenge has to be taken, a magician makes a clay image of the victim and gives it all kinds of pains. These pains, in turn, are experienced by the victim. We have innumerable instances of magic reported from different parts of the world. However, the instances of white magic are very few. This category of magic is also extended to include much of native medicine. Surprisingly, there is prevalence of white and black magic among the literate peoples too. However, with the increase in literacy and education, many of the magical practices are going out of vogue.

Witchcraft

Disease and hardships are common to mankind. To overcome these bodily ailments or social crises people have an inventory of remedies. Premises for the secular practice of medicine, unencumbered by supernaturalism are, therefore, found among all societies. Such knowledge, which of course was empirical and not analyzed in a scientific fashion, was usually available to and utilized by all the people. There were, however, innumerable afflictions which people in primitive societies supposed were caused by factors of a non-material kind. The treatment of such ailments required magical procedures, such as returning a poisonous power injected by an evil *shaman* or magic man into his victim. Individuals who had acquired or inherited or purchased supernatural power and procedures based thereon were asked to help persons supposed to be ill from these non-material causes.

In all societies *shamans* were only part-time workers engaged in curing people or at some ceremonies for which their power also fitted them. The practice of medicine among the peoples in primitive societies is thus everywhere characterized by a few actually useful devices and drugs, but incorrect theories as to causation of more deadly ailments and by resort to the supernatural for treatment of the latter.

Each society has its specialists who treat the diseases by their skills. These are called witch doctor, *shaman*, *ozha* or *bhopa*. The *shamans* or *ozhas* are those who have the power to detect witches and cure a bewitched person. They profess to be able to look into the future, escape harm, transform themselves and accomplish superhuman tasks.

Evans-Pritchard, who has worked among the Azandes of the southern Sudan during 1926-36, has given elaborate information about witchcraft and oracles. In Azande tribe, any misfortune can be, and generally is, attributed to witchcraft. Azandes consider it to be real. The witch despatches what he calls the soul, or spirit, of his witchcraft to cause damage to others. The sufferer consults oracles or a diviner to discover who is injuring him. This may be quite a lengthy and complicated procedure. When the culprit is revealed, he is requested to withdraw his malign influence. If, in a case of sickness, he does not do so and the person dies, the kinsmen of the dead man could, in future, take the affair to the chief and exact vengeance, or they could make, as they do today, a countermagic to destroy the witch.

Among Indian tribals too the practice of witchcraft is found. A witch can injure anyone by a psychic act and gradually bring about his death. This power arises from a certain *substance* in the body of the witch. Witchcraft can explain all unfortunate events. It plays its part is fishing, agricultural pursuits, in the domestic life of the village as well as in communal life. Thus witchcraft plays a prominent role in the total life of the tribal community and forms the background of oracles, magic and countermagic. If, for instance, the maize crop is diseased, it is attributed to witchcraft. If the milch cow dries, it is due to witchcraft.

The occurrence of witchcraft is explained by various causes. Though, there is natural causation, but why did the accident happen just when it did and to that particular man? A man is injured by a bullock. Why this man? and why this bullock? Witchcraft is a causative factor in the production of harmful phenomena in particular places at particular times, and in relation to particular persons. If a tree falls and kills a man, that is natural but why did it fall just as he was passing.

An oracle is consulted to determine whether some individual is bewitching another individual. One of the most popular kinds of oracle is the poison oracle. Fowls are taken into the bush and a small amount of poison is administered to them. If the fowl lives, the man is adjudged to be a witch. The witch doctors are not those magicians who cure the ailments. There are other kinds of specialists who counteract magic. The witch doctor is a diviner who exposes witches and a magician who thwarts them. He also acts as a leech, or doctor.

Magic and Science

Tylor was the first who discussed magic as a science. The question that plagued him and aroused his curiosity was that when scientifically religion has no basis, why do tribals practise it? The question was valid and begged an answer. Tylor noticed that the tribals themselves knew that magic was not true, even then it had a vital place in their life. He contemplated to answer the question:

(1) Magic is related to the commonsense behaviour.
(2) What magic does is actually done by nature also.
(3) Even when the magic fails to perform a certain action, there is no fault with it; there must have been something wrong in the practice of magic.
(4) If magic inflicts some injury, there is always countermagic.
(5) The success stories of magic outweigh its failures.

Tylor argues that the development of magic in a systematic way takes the form of science. The crux of his argument is that magic runs on the principles of nature. Nature is run by positivistic laws, so it is also a science.

Frazer does not accept magic as a pure science. However, he does admit that magic is a semi-science. According to him, magic takes place on the basis of certain logic and rules. Ordinary people do not understand that magic is practised on rules which are similar to science. People only see its applied aspect. They do not think about the principles which guide the magical performances. For a magician, magic is only an art; even he does not understand that these are principles which are solely based on science. In theory magic is based on abstract laws.

Malinowski has worked among the people of the Trobriand islands. He has generated a rich stock of data though he has not raised the question of scientific nature of magic. He takes a functional perspective and says that magic exists in society, people practise it because it has certain functions to be fulfilled. However, he accepts that the methods of magic and science, if not same, are truly similar. Both magic and science work on the logic of cause and effect.

Evans-Pritchard fell in the same line of thinking as Tylor and Frazer. Despite their different approaches all the three agree on the following hypotheses:

(1) There is some supernatural power. This power has two faces. Its one face is benevolent and provides salvation to men. The second face of it is ugly and harmful. Science explores the benevolent face while magic the ugly face. Science and magic are the two aspects of supernatural power.
(2) Ruth Benedict argues that magic is not science. The findings of science are verifiable, whereas the findings of magic are beyond any verification.
(3) There are constant experiments in science. It has made tremendous progress during the last several centuries; instead of registering any progress, magic is increasingly becoming oblivious. Less and less people show their belief in magic.
(4) The basis of science is pure logic whereas the major premise of magic is faulty.

Magic and Religion

What is the relationship between magic and religion? The distinction comes with more or less personified beings, but most religious rites contain examples of magical symbolism, and a good deal of magic includes reference to spirits. In fact, it is not really possible to distinguish clearly between magic and religion.

There is a fundamental differentiation in religion and magic. First, the rituals of a religion are public and collective. They affect the people as a whole, absorbing all its energies for the period of magicoreligious activity. This gathering together of large numbers of people for sowing, harvest feasts and similar celebrations unites the whole community in a mood of happiness and harmony. It gives solemn and collective expression to the social sentiments of an organized community, on which the constitution of a society depends.

The magico-religions rites are not for any celebration but for averting or dislodging the visiting evil. The magical practices relating to hunting have certain rites which help in the easy killing of the animal. Sometimes, the entire hunting performance is done in a ritualistic dance, wearing some part of the animal's skin. It clearly shows that magic is related to religion. There are field reports from Malinowski and Leach which establish that magic is used for successful attainment of goals. For instance, Malinowski reports that when a fisherman sails on the currents of the sea, he applies magic and believes that his boat would not meet any tragedy. The Trobrianders also practise magic to win the heart of their beloved. Durkheim, who is the founder of the sociology of religion, does not see any difference in religion and magic. For him, both the practices are meant to attain certain objectives.

Further Readings

Bohannan, Paul, *Social Anthropology*, Holt, Rinehart and Winston, INC, New York, 1963.

Evans-Pritchard, E.E., *Nuer Religion*, Oxford, 1956.

Frazer, James, *The Golden Bough* (abridged edition), London, Macmillan, 1974.

Goode, W.M.J., *Religion among the Primitives*, Glencoe, Free Press, 1951.

Malinowski, B., *Magic, Science and Religion and Other Essays*, Glencoe (III), 1948.

Nadel, S.F., *Nupe Religion*, London, Routledge, 1954.

15

Primitive Economic System

Social anthropologists have dealt with primitive economy in a very scant way. There is no dearth of literature pertaining to tribal ethnography, particularly by the British anthropologists. But all of them have looked at tribal economy in a very restricted way. They are milestones in the literature on social anthropology, but the economic life of the tribals has been totally ignored.

Indian social anthropologists followed the British pattern. D.N. Majumdar, the doyen of social anthropology, has altogether neglected a separate discussion on tribal economy. Quite like Malinowski and other British counterparts, he links economy with habitat and society. Then, M.N. Srinivas came out with *Religion and Society Among the Coorgs*. He has also not mentioned anything about the economic processes of production and distribution. Srinivas was so much under the spell of British functionalism that his work was considered to be a work of the British tradition. How is it that all these master social anthropologists have overlooked the economic status of the tribal people?

The question needs to be answered in the light of the tradition of British anthropology. How is it that the current social anthropology of India does not pay due attention to the tribal economy in view of the current trends of globalization, liberalization and privatization? Even in the university syllabus there is hardly any mention of tribal economy. Strange enough books on social anthropology continue to project tribal economy in a very crude and primitive form. We would like to mention here that the Azandes and Nuers of Evans-Pritchard, Tallensis of Fortes, Hoes of Majumdar and Coorgs of Srinivas have undergone a sea change in their economy during the last five decades. These tribal groups of Africa and India have attained modernization.

It is tragic that the primitive groups who are now modernized are presented as primitives in our textbooks. Thus, there is an urgent need to look at the economic affairs of tribals in the present context of the capitalist and market economy.

Economy: An Integral Part of Tribal Society

Malinowski made an intensive study of Trobriand islanders, Argonauts, and published it is *Argonauts of the Western Pacific* (1922). The Argonauts are a matrilineal society. They practise horticulture. Malinowski studied the *kula* trade, which was a large-scale trade in shell bracelets and necklaces, constituting the main economy of the Argonauts. Malinowski argues that the trade does not have an independent economic system. It is a part of tribal life itself. He concluded that in a primitive society economics does not occupy a distinct institutional status. It is a part of the tribal social totality. Thomas Hylland Eriksen has discussed the role of money in tribal society with reference to Malinowski. His basic premise is that in present-day society money is everything: money makes the mare go. But, in the primitive society, it is kinship which matters, and not money. Eriksen's comments run as below:

> Anthropologists have always—at least since Malinowski—wished to call attention to the ways in which the economy is an integrated part of a social and cultural totality, and to reveal that economic systems and actions can only be fully understood if we look into their interrelationships with other aspects of culture and society.

Thus, it should be mentioned that the traditional tribal societies did not have any word of the kind of *economy* which might show an independent economic institution.

How do social anthropologists look at a tribal economy? The classical economists discuss economy in terms of rationality, market principles, global market and so no. Actually, the primitive economy is far away from capitalistic economy. In today's world there is hegemony of global capitalist economy. But this kind of rational market economy is not present among the tribals. Marshall Sahlins has not only followed the prescriptions of Malinowski, but he goes a step further. His argument is that among the tribals economy is determined by tribal culture. A man wants to fulfil his material needs. There is a

Marshall D. Sahlins (b.1930) is among the current anthropologists known for reinterpreting social anthropology. His teacher, Leslie White, was well known for his specialization in cultural ecology. Sahlins, therefore, had an abiding interest in culture. Methodologically, he was interested in evolutionary practices. He studied the Polynesian tribes. He argued that the formation of state among these tribals was through kinship. In his later works he had a strong belief in cultural relativism. He was very strongly influenced by Marxist structuralism. He looked at economics from cultural point of view and believed that it is culture which determines economy. Quite unlike Malinowski he advocated that economy pervades the total society but says that it is the culture of society which determines economy. His works include *Culture and Practical Reason* (1976) and *Islands of History* (1985).

process of production. There is also consumption. And in between there is exchange. But Sahlins asserts that all these economic processes are conditioned and determined by culture. For an Indian illustration we refer to a Bhil *Bhagat*. A *Bhagat* is one who has taken to the vegetarian way of life. He is a teetotaler. The Bhil has his consumption pattern. He can easily get a hen for his meals with minimum expenditure. But he will not accept. Instead he would go for the purchase of cereals, which is perhaps costlier for him. The choice of cereal is decided by his cultural commitment to vegetarianism. Thus, Sahlins' argument is very clear. Quite like the capitalist economy the Bhil economy is not guided by cost-benefit analysis. It is not value maximization.

Both Malinowski and Sahlins reject the role of rationality in the tribal economy. Malinowski maintains that economy is diffused in the totality of society and Sahlins stands for relativism. Each group has ethnocentric culture. The economy of the group is conditioned by group ethnocentrism. The role of rational factor in a primitive economy is, therefore, rejected. Quite like culture, economy is symbolic of a group; it is a culture.

Primitive Economic System

Tribal economy is looked at with two different perspectives. One looks at the tribal economy from the point of view of production, distribution and consumption. The second perspective is actor-oriented, which is basically the perspective of classical economics, according to which the actors use the available means to maximize value. The first perspective is normally called the formal perspective, which looks at economics from the perspective of a system. It is, therefore, also called the system-oriented perspective of economy. For instance, Dumont, who has studied the caste system in India, looks at it as an ethnocentric phenomenon. It means, economic activities---production, distribution, exchange and consumption---are dictated by the caste system. If, for instance, the Santhals of Bihar take rice as their staple food, the cultivation of rice is not determined by the actor. It is the Santhal tribe which decides to grow rice as it is their main commodity. Similarly, the people of Karnataka consume *ragi* as their staple cereal. This is determined by the group and, therefore, it is system-oriented. In the study of Swat---an African tribe---Sahlins contests the actor-oriented economy or rational economy and argues that the tribals take their crops on the dictates of the community.

System-oriented or Substantive Economy

Anthropologists who have carried out extensive fieldwork in India and Africa have defined tribal economy in terms of its determination with reference to tribal groups. The individual or the actor has no determining voice in the production process. He has to work according to the needs of the society. Russian peasants do not maximize profits, but instead work just enough to survive and generate an adequate surplus; they are optimizers, not maximizers.

Actor-oriented or Formal Economy

The formal economy is basically the economy of the present market. In this economy, the individuals maximize their value and base their behaviour on cost-benefit, and increase the value of money. This kind of economy is characteristic of a capitalist society. In the tribal society, the unit of production is the group, the village, and in some cases, the region. In this production, the objective is to fulfil the needs of the tribal community at an optimum level. As against this, the formal or actor-oriented economy leaves the task of production to the individual. In simple words, the tribal economy is the economy of the household. The household wants to survive. But, the modern economy is rational and wants to work on the cost-benefit idiom.

Tribal Economy: Godlier's Economic Anthropology

Maurice Godlier has developed economic anthropology from Marxian perspective. His emphasis is on the social relations which emerge out of modes of production. He argues that ultimately anthropology is concerned with the structure of society. The structure comes out of the social processes which emerge from modes of production. Economic anthropology, therefore, is related to the problem of the relationship between economics, society and history. Raymond Firth has intensively studied the Tikopia—a Polynesian tribal group. He has made certain generalizations which have economic bearings on the tribal life. He writes:

> After publishing an account of the social structure, in particular, the kinship structure (*We, the Tikopia*, London, 1936), I analyzed the economic structure of the society, because so many social relationships were made most manifest in their economic content. Indeed, the social structure, in particular, the political structure, was clearly dependent on specific economic relationships arising out of the system of control of resources. With these relationships in turn were linked the religious activities and institutions of the society.

Godlier says that the economic structure of a tribe gives rise to a large number of social relationships. The economic structure is basically a structure resulting from modes of production. It is because of this that Godlier relates economics with society and history. In the case of Firth, state itself was the product of social relationships emerging from economic relationship.

Traditional Definitions of Tribal Economy

The current approaches to tribal economy are based altogether on the traditional approaches. Now, it is increasingly felt that the tribal economy is the part of the tribal social totality. This has been aptly demonstrated by Malinowski and Sahlins. It is spread over all the institutions of tribal life. For example, if a man performs magic for protecting his crop, he has mixed culture for economy. The Trobrianders' rights over women and children has an aspect which the classical economists might call economy. The Bhils get bride-price in view of giving their daughters in marriage. For a rational economy, this is an economic activity. This kind of interpretation does not have relevance to understand the tribal economy. Despite this new approach to tribal economy, a few traditional definitions can be given here. For example, Ralph Piddington writes:

> Economic system designed to satisfy the material wants of the people is to organize production, to control distribution and to determine the rights and claims of ownership within the community.

Obviously, Piddington dwells on production and distribution of commodities. But, the nature of tribal economy does not come under his discussion.

The definition given by Beals and Hoizer is the standard definition of economics given in the textbooks of economics. They observe:

> The economic organization is the pattern of behaving result organization of society relative to production, distribution and consumption of goods and services.

Modern economy, thus, studies all the activities related to production, distribution, exchange and consumption. But, the activities of production and consumption are not in the hands of tribal individuals. This vital aspect of tribal economy remains neglected in the definition.

Bohannan has introduced a few new variables in the analysis of tribal economy. Tribal resources and the indigenous technology constitute part of primitive economy. The author also stresses on the "requirements of human beings" as the motivating factor for economic activities. But he also looks at rational economy in the tribal society.

However, it must he said that whether the economy is determined by the tribal group itself or imposed from the market economy, there is always a need to organize production, distribution and exchange. In other words, if a tribal has surplus production, how would he market it? If there is exchange, what are the indigenous ways of organizing exchange? These are some of the aspects of tribal economy which we propose to deal with below.

Production

We take the position propounded by anthropologists that tribal economics is a part of tribal society. This is true in the sense that it is spread in the totality of society. It is the culture of the tribe which determines the nature of the tribal economy. Though there are production and production factors, but these are traditionally and culturally conditioned. The substantive economy that we find among the tribals is essentially oriented to the tribal system. Such a kind of economy has traditionally been a subsistence economy where tribals organize their production in such a way that it fulfils the needs of the community. The production is optimized and if there is some surplus, these are brought to the markets. It must be noted that the tribals did not produce for the market. The production was only for the consumption in the household. Economists, while discussing production system, also refer to some production factors. These production factors are examined below:

Work

Economists consider work as an activity which is productive. In other words, the production is an economic activity which produces things for the market. Work in the tribal society is not calculated in terms of money. All the work done in the farm by males, females and children is considered to be non-productive labour. But such an approach to the work done in field or forest is something which contributes to the income of the tribal family. The economists now are seriously considering the inclusion of the work done by a household member as productive labour. When a tribal woman works on road construction she gets minimum wages sanctioned by the state. But work of this kind is not taken as productive labour. However, all over tribal belt, men, women and children are engaged in work all through the day without any cash transaction.

Division of Labour

Durkheim, for the first time, systematically worked on division of labour. He advocated the theory that mechanical societies in the process of social change turn into organic societies. The tribal society is a mechanical society. There is no specialization of work. Neither is the work divided on the basis of sex and age. A tribal is the jack of all trades and master of none. He can work on any activity. He hunts wild animals, cuts wood, fetches water, grinds corn, cleans the cattleshed and so on. Similarly, a woman can be a multipurpose worker. There are no specificities of work in the household and field.

Labour Organization

However true it may be that there are no specialists in a tribe, there are some occupations which are hereditary. The members learn the skills from their ancestors. For instance, among the Tongas of Zambia, it is a belief that an artisan who works on different arts, has got the skills from his forefathers. In the same way, the Gonds and Bhils think that hunting, cutting wood and working on stones are something which they have learnt from their forefathers.

Capital

The concept of capital in a tribal economy is different from that we find in a market economy. Fruit trees such as mango, *mahua* and *anwla* are considered to be the property of the family. At the time of the division of family these fruit trees are distributed by the head of the family. A tribal does not have ornaments of gold and silver; nor do they have utensils. The land and the cattle wealth are considered to be the family property. It is here that the tribal system-oriented economy is altogether different from rational and value-oriented formal economy of the developed market.

Exchange

Anthropological literature on economics has received much from Malinowski, who prepared certain classical monographs on the Argonauts of the western Pacific. "One of his monographs is most famous and striking for describing one of the social institutions in the region, namely, the *kula* trade, which is a large-scale trade network in shell bracelets and necklaces. Other aspects of the Trobrianders' economy were subjected to great interest and wonder when Malinowski returned with his material from the islands after the First World War. He showed, contrary to widespread expectations, that 'savages' were by no means driven by lowly material needs in everything they did, that they had a sophisticated religion and that a complex kinship system and a multitude of regulated practises that upheld society and contributed to the fulfilment of far more needs than the purely biological ones. In *Argonauts* Malinowski also argues against those who supposed that 'savages' were extremely 'rational' individuals who acted on pure self-interest."

Malinowski has explained the *kula* method of exchange. There is a cyclical exchange of two kinds of valuables, viz., shell necklaces and shell bracelets. The trade initiated by Argonauts spreads over a large area of south-western Pacific. Eriksen has also provided a description of the *kula* exchange. "The necklaces circulate clockwise and the bracelets anti-clockwise. The *kula* trade takes place both locally, within each island and between the islands. The most valuable objects travel furthest. The people who travel with the shell are agents or partners of powerful men, usually aristocrats, in the various islands."

Exchange of Gifts

Malinowski has also described elaborately about the exchange of gifts which is also found among the Indian tribes. Before we come to Indian tribals, let us look at the gift system found among the Trobrianders. The Trobrianders give yams to their affines, that is, blood kin. In return they do not require any immediate counter-presentation. The yams are classified as gifts. However, it is anticipated that some counter-presentation would definitely come when such an occasion arises.

Among the Gonds, if there is an occasion of marriage, the affines would bring rice or maize as gift. When there is death in the family similar presents are offered. This is quite like the Trobrianders. The Gonds do not expect immediate return but when a similar occasion arises, the presents would be offered by the first receiver.

A gift is a characteristic expression of reciprocity because when one parts with a gift he also expects to receive it. Surely, the gift costs something but it is a token of cultural exchange. Mauce states that in a gift system a large number of institutions are involved—religious, judicial, moral and economic. In the capitalist society, the exchange of wedding rings is, perhaps, the ultimate exchange of gifts.

Technology

It should not be understood that the tribes such as Azande, Argonaut, Tellansi, Tiv, Tikopia, or Gond, Santhal and Bhil are still at the age of subsistence economy. Clifford Geertz has recently declared that the tribals have also crossed the stage of modernity. He very elaborately writes on the post-modernist trends of anthropology in the 1980s and 1990s. He has also strongly influenced the prevailing trends in the study of tribals. His approach to tribals is from the perspective of symbolic systems. He has compared the study of culture with the study of texts, and argues that a cultural system can be 'read' in a manner analogous with the reading of a novel. It is in this context that technology is considered to be information technology (IT). With the coming of money as a medium of exchange, the tribal traditional economy lost its moral character and gradually disengaged itself from the cultural values which had originally constituted it. Pure market principles of supply and demand replaced the rules of right and wrong as well as distinctions between 'high' and 'low' values.

With the monetization in operation among the Bhils of western India, the progressive sections now give cash gifts on occasions of death or marriage. Reciprocity is also experienced in the return of these gifts. Thus, the introduction of money has challenged the traditional value hierarchy among the tribals. Eriksen, commenting on the African tribes, says that "money may be regarded as a form of information technology... money is impersonal and anonymous. It can be accumulated and invested. It makes communication and exchange on a vast scale possible. It is certainly no coincidence that the spread of the monetary economy has usually been concomitant with the spread of state institutions, literacy and quantified liner time, all of which can be seen as standardizing devices accompanying the transition from small-scale to large-scale integration."

Perhaps markets are the most vulnerable places to be covered by information technology. Today, the moment a commodity is launched, it is on the website and informs the audiences at the earliest time possible. Television is the most common and popular mode of information technology. Monetization among tribals has brought them closer to the current market trends. All this is due to information technology.

Meaning and Definition of Technology

There has been some tendency among social anthropologists to deal with technology. They have discussed at length the indigenous knowledge of the tribals in curing ailments, using irrigation facilities and technologically managing animal husbandry issues. Technology, in a very general meaning of the term, consists of the systematized acquired skills and man-made material implements humans reproduce and apply in their dealings with nature. The Gonds and Santhals prepare an umbrella of teak leaves to protect themselves from the rains. In the field of irrigation they make small bunds in of the village *nallah* for irrigating their fields. They have their own herbs which they use for termination of pregnancy. All these are examples of little technologies used by tribals.

Tim Ingold has defined technology as a "corpus of culturally transmitted knowledge, expressed in manufacture and use". He lays stress on its socio-cultural character and links it to the superstructure in a Marxian sense, along with other kinds of culturally transmitted knowledge. It should also be noted that technology literally means "knowledge about techniques" and, therefore, technology is to techniques what... linguistics is to language, for instance, or ethnology to behaviour. In short, technology thus is a theory about technics, or as we might say, techniques.

Among the tribes, technology is considered to be an ordinary way of life. It forms a legacy which is learnt by the younger generations. For instance, according to this view, technical implements are simply made and put to use. It has very little influence on what people think. A Bhil manufactures his own plough. He cannot explain the technology behind preparing a plough. He has learnt to do it and he thinks little about the technology. He simply knows the mode. Similarly, he constructs his own house. He is a novice in constructing a house in terms of archaeology but he knows how to provide ventilators and doors to his house. He has learnt this technology from his forefathers. Thus, technology has come to the tribals through cultural heritage. Viewed from this perspective, techniques are of paramount importance for culture, and social organization as powerful and autonomous agent that dictates the problems of human social and cultural life.

Eriksen has interpreted technology in terms of culture. He says:

> Technologies and techniques are cultural products which form part of ongoing processes in society and can, therefore, not be studied separately from those relationships.

Not only techniques shape our relationships but our relationships also shape techniques. The tractor makes sense as a means of production in very different kinds of society and culture in profound ways. When the tractor is hired by poorer peasants in a village or kinsmen, it establishes a kind of cooperative endeavour. Thus, technology shapes culture or social relationships.

We have no intention to present a portrait of Indian tribes as living isolated from the present trends of globalization, liberalization and privatization. The tribals from the north-east as well as from central India have now accepted money as the state denomination of exchange. Barter and *jajmani* systems no more rule the market. On the other hand, it is the market which determines the exchange processes of tribals. It is the new trend of globalization which opens people's lives to culture and all its creativity and to the flow of ideas and knowledge. But, in this process, there is also a fear, as the *Human Development Report, 1999*, says:

> Poor people and poor countries being pushed to the margin in this proprietary regime controlling the world's knowledge.

Economic System of Indian Tribes

Tribals all over the country are at various stages of development. There are food gatherers, pastorals and agriculturalists. The Bhotias, a tribal group of Himalayan foothills, practise animal husbandry. During the winter season, they climb down to the plains and return when the winter is over. They continue to deal in spices. The women make money by weaving woolen shawls. The Todas of Nilgiri hills place great emphasis on the buffalo. One who owns a large herd of buffaloes, wields a lot of status and power. Besides keeping buffaloes, wherever possible, they practise agriculture also.

The practice of shifting cultivation is now banned all over the country. It was known by different names. At some places it is called *jhoom* agriculture; the Mairyays call it *penda*; it is called *pondu* among Khands and Baigas call it *bewar*. Verrier Elwin calls it axe cultivation. The forest trees are put to axe, and when the fallen trees dry, the tribals set it ablaze. The seed is broadcast, and yields are quite good. It is reported that till 1867 the tribals of Madhya Pradesh practised axe cultivation without any hindrance. But soon after independence the practice was put to an end. However, it is reported that even today among some tribals of the north-east, shifting cultivation is practised.

It seems that the tribals today have not reached any uniform stage of development. Despite variations in the stages of development, the fact remains that the subsistence economy of tribals has now been diversified. They have reservation in governing services. A part of them have taken up a variety of jobs. They are increasingly migrating to the nearby industrial towns and cities. Ranchi has drawn a substantial number of tribals from different parts of Bihar to work in its industries. Tribals here are industry-oriented. The tribals from the neighbourhood of metropolitan cities like Calcutta and Mumbai have also come for jobs. A general trend in the tribal migration is that they flock to cities. They create slums. Smaller cities like Indore, Amedabad, Bhopal and Patna have now become centres of tribal habitations.

K.S. Singh, in *People of India* (POI), has taken stock of the Scheduled Tribes in the country as a whole. According to him, "the tribes are mainly a landholding community. However, the incidence of landlessness is encountered among them, and almost the entire tribal economy is in the vortex of market forces. Whether it is the Nicobarese or the Cholanaickens or the Birhors, all are dependent on the market and the middlemen."

Singh also makes certain broad generalizations about the change coming up in the tribal economy. He says that there is a marked change in the occupational patterns of the tribals. They have taken to new occupations. The findings of POI are also supported by the 1981 census, according to which, more than 87 per cent of the tribal workers are engaged in the primary sector of the economy and of which a majority are cultivators (54.43 per cent), followed by agricultural labourers (32.67 per cent). Of the remaining workers only 2.73 per cent are engaged in livestock, forestry, fishing, hunting, etc.

In a nutshell, the POI project gives its findings as below:

> An interesting finding of our study has been the shift among the tribal communities from the traditional to the new occupations. For instance, the number of communities practising hunting and gathering has declined nearly 24.8 per cent as forests have disappeared and wildlife has diminished. Ecological degradation has severely curtailed the related traditional occupations of the tribal communities. For example, the trapping of birds and animals has declined by 36.84 per cent, pastoral activities by 12.5 per cent and shifting cultivation by 18.14 per cent.

The data given above very clearly indicate that there is a conspicuous fall in the tribal traditional occupations. Mostly, it is due to ecological degradation. But, the POI further reveals that the tribals have taken up certain new occupations like horticulture, terrace cultivation and settled cultivation, which are unconventional for them, but are also allied with their traditional occupations. The POI reports that "there is a sharp rise in the number of tribals employed in government and private services, self-employment, etc. Many of the traditional crafts have disappeared and spinning, in particular, has suffered. Related activities such as weaving, dyeing and printing have similarly suffered. Stone carving has declined. But, the number of tribals employed in mining and masonry has gone up steeply which suggests a new mobility."

Further Readings

Beattie, John, *Other Cultures*, Cohen and West, London, 1964.

Eriksen, T.H., *Small Places, Large Issues*, Pluto Press, London, 1995.

Herskovitz, M., *Economic Anthropology*, New York, 1952.

Singh, K.S., *People of India*, National Series, Vol. III, Oxford University Press, Calcutta, 1997.

16

Primitive Political System

Politics today has become a buzzword all over the world. There are a large number of political ideologies. Earlier, the world was divided into the socialist social order and democratic social order. With the disintegration of Soviet Union, it appears that democracy has become a world social order. Added to it is the capitalist system. It is argued that democracy and capitalism go together. They have come to stay in present-day politics. However, social anthropology is weak in its political analysis. Before the African political system came into existence in social anthropology, it was believed that the primitive people had nothing of the kind of political system as we understand it today.

The third world countries, including that of Asia, Africa and Latin America, which were considered to be less developed in their political systems, have now begun to integrate themselves with the mainstream of national political system. In Africa, the Negroes have very much taken to democracy, so is the case with the people of other third world countries. India is a developing nation, and it is essential for all the minority groups including Scheduled Castes and Scheduled Tribes to integrate themselves with the nation's mainstream. Social and political integration in India has become a catchword. More than 400 tribal groups of the country are required to integrate themselves with the national mainstream. They are persuaded to accept democracy, socialism, secularism and scientific ethics as their new ideology. The civil society of the tribals, therefore, has to merge with the wider framework of citizenship and human rights at the global level. Social anthropology, therefore, is required to study the elements of politics in the tribal society.

Power is a crucial and comprehensive variable in any political analysis. It is, on one hand, linked with political power, and on the other hand, with the wider social relations which people have with others. Though political science discusses power distribution, it is also concerned with the prevention of lawlessness and insecurity. In other words, politics focuses on the maintenance of law and order in society. It is also concerned with conflict resolution and social integration.

Political System is Universal to all Societies

All the societies, whether civilized or tribal, have some kind of political system. However, the nature of the political system differs considerably. In the previous chapter on primitive economic system, we have argued that economics is inbuilt in the primitive social system. It does not have a separate identity. In the same way, the tribals do not have any distinct and identifiable political system, in terms of assembly and parliament. In tribal society power is integral to all other social systems. The comprehension of political system in modern societies is altogether different from that in the primitive societies. For instance, in a Gond or a Bhil society, it is difficult to isolate politics from their kinship and religion. Therefore, politics in tribal societies is inbuilt in their family, kin and religion. Modern societies give a distinct position to the political system in the form of identifiable political institutions. Making a comparative characterization of the political system of modern society and primitive or tribal society, Thomas Hylland Eriksen observes:

> Politics can be identified analytically in all societies, but by no means all societies that anthropologists have studied have political institutions distinct from other societal realms. In modern state societies, it may seem fairly easy to delineate what is politics and what is not. Political science, developed to study politics in such societies, deals with the formal political institutions, with a legislative assembly, local administration, voting patterns and other aspects of society recognized as political. In non-industrial societies, it may be far more difficult to single out politics as something distinct from the ongoing flow of social life.

The social anthropologists who have studied African political systems brought out certain conspicuous data, which have created a stir not only in social anthropology but also in political science. The African studies indicate that there are tribal societies which do not have any state but they have a government. It is argued that the political system is concerned with the analysis of power and not the state. A central problem in African studies during the 1940s to 1960s was to find out as to what extent the stateless societies were integrated. In the absence of any central authority they managed to maintain law and order and resolve conflicts. The findings of these studies have strengthened the content of political anthropology.

In India, we did not have any stateless societies of the kind of those in Africa. The regional rulers in central India brought the tribals within the feudal framework. In such a framework, the tribals often engineered revolt and rebellion. But, by and large, they were domesticated and worked as loyal subjects of the feudal rulers. Indian social anthropologists, who were highly influenced by Malinowski, Evans-Pritchard and Rivers, did not take up the study of political systems among the Indian tribals. Normally, they talked about tribal ethnicity and autonomy. Therefore, there were no tribal political studies in India on the pattern of African studies. As a result of this, political anthropology in India could not make any significant contribution.

Political Anthropology

Power

Political anthropology is comparatively less developed. But wherever social anthropologists have studied primitive political organizations, power has been their central theme of discussion. There cannot be any state or even statelessness without power. Despite many discussions and discourses on power, the definition of power as given by Max Weber continues to remain valid. Weber is the architect of political sociology. According to him, every man has power. He says that "it is the ability to enforce one's own will on others' behaviour. It is the ability to make someone do something they would otherwise not have done". Thus, according to Weber, people have power over each other.

If we simplify the definition of power as given by Weber, it would appear that it is the imposition of the will of actor (A) upon an actor (B), even against B's resistance, so that 'B' is dominated by 'A'. Another implication of the definition of power is that it is a source at the disposal of collectivities and used for their benefits, allowing them to attain their objectives: Power, in this view, is conceptualized as a collective facility. Towney, who has interpreted Weber's definition of power, considers it as "the capacity of an individual or group of individuals, to modify the conduct of other individual or groups in the manner in which he desires, and to prevent his conduct being modified in the manner in which he does not".

Yet another approach to the definition of power is by Karl Marx. The Marxists look at power as a structural phenomenon. According to them, power is found in the division of labour. Maurice Godlier, who has developed Marxian perspective on power, argues that power can be seen in the mode of production—the employer and the employee. According to him, power relations constitute the legislative system and other structural features of society.

Eriksen categorizes the definition of power with reference to perspectives in systemic and structural terms. He says:

> It immediately seems to make sense to talk of 'systemic' or 'structural' power in many contexts: abeyance of norms and implicit rules may easily be seen as a form of structural power—it is not easy to tell *who* it is that forces me to hold the fork in my left hand and the knife in my right. However, if we include any action dictated by cultural convention in our definition, power risks becoming diluted and synonymous with conventions, norms and ultimately culture.

Eriksen further says that systemic or structural power ceases to influence people and, therefore, he follows the definition of power given by Weber. Weber's power is political. It is differentiated from authority. Authority has power but its resource is state, or some institution like family, caste or village.

Powerlessness

This is a situation where people do not have any power. Among such people there is absence of the ability to exert power. For instance, in Indian society, there are Scheduled Castes, Scheduled Tribes, women and other weaker sections who have a negligible power. Even their voting power is decided by the offer of incentives and threat of annihilation. These groups are marginal groups; they are subalterns; they live in a culture of silence. Such groups are powerless groups. When we discuss power in the primitive society, we must always keep in mind the tribals who are lesser tribals and do not get the benefits of development.

Ideology

There is always some ideology in our comprehension of power. There was the divine right theory. And not in the remote past, the princely rulers of India considered themselves to be the kings of their territory. Those who were born of kings, ruled as kings. This is precisely, ideology. There are social anthropologists who have further divided the political system in terms of ascription and achievement. Dumont differentiates Indian caste stratification from European class stratification, the former being characterized by hierarchy. In caste hierarchy, there is ascription. When we compare the primitive political system with the modern political system, the ideology of ascription and achievement, and the role of ideology assume importance.

It is difficult indeed to define ideology in precise terms. It appears that ideology is that aspect of culture which concerns how society ought to be organized; in other words, it concerns politics, rules and the distinction between right and wrong. Actually ideology is a normative kind of knowledge; it may be implicit or explicit, and it may be challenged.

In the Indian context, our ideology about the nature of Indian society has always been changing. It is a democratic, secular society. At a later stage we put the ideology of socialism in defining Indian society. The best way to define Indian society ideologically is to refer to Indian Constitution. There are also some groups in the country who look at society from the ideological perspective of Gandhism and Marxism. What we want to argue is that in any discussion on primitive political system and for that matter on modern political system, the role of ideology can hardly be neglected.

What we call political anthropology is basically enriched by the study of African tribals groups. The studies made by Evans-Pritchard, Fortes, Shapera and others have made a breakthrough in the analysis of power. Traditionally, political scientists have been looking for power in the state institutions of legislature, judiciary and executive. According to modern political science, politics studies power in the state institutions. The African studies have redefined the concept of power. Accordingly, power does not lie only in political institutions, it is also found, for instance, in the family, clan, kin and other traditional institutions. In other words, the African studies have brought a new conceptual framework in stateless societies and those both with territory and government.

State, Law and Justice in Primitive Societies

Modern political science has state as its central theme for discussion. The state has several aspects and political science studies all of them. There are some attributes which characterize a state. These attributes are enlisted below: (i) territory, (ii) legislative, (iii) ecutive, and (iv) judiciary.

It is the state which has a definite territory. It is defined and its integrity is upheld by the political organization. The political organization is a very comprehensive term which essentially includes legislative, executive and judiciary powers. In a broad way, it is called government. Political scientists argue that wherever there is a state, there is always some system of government. The government has power to wage war against enemy. It can levy taxes; it can use force. And, these are the attributes that differentiate the state from other institutions.

Before social anthropologists took to the study of state and government in primitive societies, political science had already made a headway in the study of power and politics. Aristotle had done pioneering work in his book *Politics.* Plato's study *Republic* followed. These works are rated as classical works of political science. However, the fault with these works is that they deal with the ideal form of state and talk very little about the empirical situation of government and state. It was only in the 19th century that the social anthropologists worked on the theme of state and government in the primitive society.

Evolutionary Studies: Morgan

Morgan was a first-rate evolutionary social anthropologist. He has tried to trace the origin of state and government. He argues that the concept of state among the primitives developed in two stages. In the first stage, the state came into existence to fulfil the needs of the people. Morgan calls this kind of state emergence only as a kind of social organization. It is on the strength of data provided by Morgan that some social anthropologists consider social organization in terms of kinship organization. The notion of property came at the second stage of the development of the state. When property was possessed by the people it had to be protected. This gave rise to government. Morgan further says that the government created to protect the property had also some kind of territory, that is, state. Thus, at the second stage of evolution, the state and government became inseparable parts of social organization.

Drawing from the thesis of Morgan some social anthropologists have maintained that there are some societies where there is a state and also a government. Further, it is also found in some societies that there is a government but there is no state. Following the evolutionary trend of studies Maine has propounded that first there were states and the government came into existence at a later stage. On the other hand, Shapera, on the basis of his studies of African tribes, establishes that it is not essential that government is in any way related to kinship organization. He says that there is no such primitive group where kinsmen are controlled by any form of government. His argument is that government and kinship do not have any positive relation. He provides evidence from the Bushman tribe of southern Africa. Bushmen do not have any domesticated animals, neither do they practise agriculture. Wild animals are their game and they move in herds. Each herd has its political identity but they are not related by kin. Thus, government and kinship do not go together; there may be government but it is not essential that people are united by kinship ties.

Thus, right from Morgan to Shapera, social anthropologists have tried to study government and state from the evolutionary perspective. But they were biased in their approach. They had in their mind the political system of Europe, the democratic government of Europe and they tried to search it out among primitive people. Their second fault was similar to the fault of Aristotle and Plato. They argued at length about the kind of government the primitive people should have and dealt with little on the existing governmental situation of the tribals.

African Tribals: The Breakthrough

Perhaps, a watershed in the study of primitive political system came with the flood of studies on African political systems. A classical work by Fortes and Evans-Pritchard, *African Political System* (1940), came to light which created a stir in the study of primitive political system. What is praiseworthy in this volume is that the contributors do not suffer from any bias. They have studied African tribal political systems with an open mind. They have established on the strength of data that there can be a government without a state or a territory. Further, they have strongly argued that government and state are not synonymous. There can be a government without a state, that is, territory. And, to the contrary, there can be a state or territory without having a government. In other words, state is independent of government and government is independent of state.

Thus, Fortes and Evans-Pritchard are credited with bringing the different social anthropologists under the umbrella of their edited work. This has given strength to their argument. Before the publication of this book, Shapera had a thesis which was similar to that of Fortes and Evans-Pritchard. But nobody took him seriously. Dwelling on the theme of African political systems, the contributors to the volume observe that among African tribals governmental functions are fulfilled by three kinds of organizations. First, there were tribal groups which did not have anything of the kind of state. These groups were stateless societies. The second were those which had a state, and in the third category there were groups which had both state and government.

The functions of state and stateless societies were specified. In societies which had state, the functions were performed by kin groups including village and family. But, the groups which did not have a state, the functions were performed by non-kin groups. It would be quite interesting to have a look at the African political system (see figure on next page).

In the figure we have classified primitive political organizations into two categories: (1) society with state, and (2) stateless society. In the first, there is a territory, a fixed area and some form of government either run by the ruler or the army. The social anthropologists who have studied African political systems have found two kinds of such societies:

(i) with a territory and a government which is based on kinship, e.g., Swaziland, and
(ii) without a state as the one in the Ashanti tribe of West Africa and Nuer tribe of Sudan.

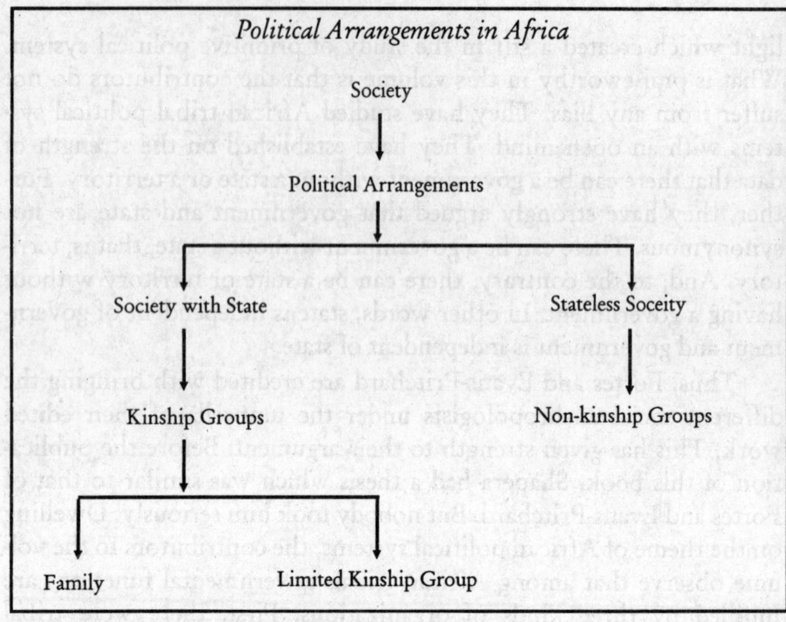

Society with State: Swaziland

In this form of society there is a definite territory and the people are ruled by a few families. The ruling families look after the subjects with paternal love and affection. Swaziland is a small state in South Africa. The people are known as Swazis, who are a tribal group. In this tribe, there is a king who is throned according to traditional rituals. The powers of the ruler are supreme. But other family members also have their share in wielding of power. Even the military force considers the rulers to be the highest authority. Thus, in this society where there is government as well as a state, all the powers are concentrated within the ruler and his family coterie. Coronation follows rules of heredity.

Stateless Society: Ashanti and Nuer

Ashanti is a tribe organized among matriarchal descent groups. The tribe is found in the long track which runs through western Africa. There are eight matriarchal clans among the Ashantis. Each has its ancestor. In a single village, normally, there are plural matriarchal clans. Each matriarchal group sends its representative to the village council. The village council maintains law and order of the village. This is the local government of the Ashantis. Out of all the Ashanti villages, a certain big village is established as the capital.

The government found among the Ashantis is a kind of military administration. Though there is a ruler, his relations with the military are not so strong.

Another classical example of stateless societies is that of the Nuers of southern Sudan. The Nuers have been studied by Evans-Pritchard (1940). They are a nomadic people who mainly subsist on cattle. Although they live in small local communities, every individual has ties of solidarity with other people scattered over an enormous territory. Each Nuer has obligations and commitments towards his or her patrilineal kin; but is also tied to other groups. Actually, a Nuer is a member of an agnatic lineage. Several lineages together form a sub-clan, and several sub-clans form a clan. The Nuer groups thus form a unity in their territory. The total Nuer group thus is a stateless society ruled by non-kinship groups.

State and Government in Indian Tribes

The findings of social anthropologists on the political organization of African tribes indicate that there has been an evolutionary approach to the problem. There are tribal groups which have been without any state but they do have a government---a system of ruler, a kind of judiciary and a pattern of law and justice. On the other hand, there are tribal groups which have a state as well as a government. In both the tribal groups, there has been the existence of some form of government. The government is either run by the kin groups including family and clan or non-kin groups.

Such a situation does not and did not exist in India. Normally, we have two patterns of state formation. First, there are tribal groups which are endogenous, ruled by the tribals themselves. For instance, the Cheros of Bihar, the Gonds of Chattisgarh, the Kolis of Konkan and the Bhils of western India---all of whom had an endogenous system of kinship. Second, there are tribal groups which are exogenous. In this pattern, the non-tribals founded states in the tribal regions extending from Chotanagpur and Orissa (hilly region) to Rajasthan and Gujarat, either in collaboration with the tribes, which was institutionalized in the coronation ceremony, or without it.

Indian social anthropologists have generated enough ethnographic data, mostly on establishments of colonial or feudal rule among primitive peoples, but not on their political system. In the same manner, the historians have also been unkind to tribals. They have elaborately dealt with the chronologies of the princely rulers or the invaders such as Mughals, but tribal political history has always remained outside their purview. The subaltern history, which is a newcomer in the writing of historiography, has not developed to maturity yet. There are some exceptions. Historians like David Hardiman, Gyanendra Pandey and Shahid Amin have dealt with the tribal political system in Gujarat and Bihar. But full length monographic studies are non-existent.

K.S. Singh has made an attempt to study the state formation among Indian tribals. However, he also very strongly feels the lack of political studies about Indian tribes. He observes (1985):

> Study of state formation in tribal society, a relatively uncharted area of anthropo-historical research, is crucial to the understanding of many contemporary processes such as the relationship of tribal and non-tribal communities, development of agriculture, emergence of stratification, interaction of the great and little traditions, and all that has contributed towards the formation of complex regional systems in the exposed zones of tribal India.

Admittedly, much work has been done on the sanskritization of Indian tribes but we have exceptionally insignificant studies on the tribal political system. The *jagirdars* surely kept their documents in the form of *bahis*—state record—but these are limited to the administration of the *jagirdars* only. Despite this shortcoming we have some details about the process of state formation among tribal people. On this basis, it must be said that we did not have stateless tribal groups. The states were either ruled by the tribals (endogenous) or non-tribals (exogenous).

Endogenous Tribal States

K.S. Singh informs that after the downfall of the Gupta empire, the whole of eastern India witnessed the emergence of the rural foci of political power, led by autonomous chieftains who acted as champions of neo-Brahminism. Such communities as Doms, Bhars and Cheros in south Bihar, Kharwars in the Sone-Damodar valley, Gonds and Rakshels in the Chattisgarh region and the Bhumij in Jungle Mahals of

Bengal filled the vacuum in the countryside in the medieval period.

The Doms, Bhars, Cheros and Gonds were either Scheduled Tribes or Scheduled Castes. They were atheists and casteless people. These tribal groups ruled over a substantial part of the country. They had their own territory as well as government. Characteristically, these tribal rulers were against the Hindu castes. There was no participation of caste Hindus in the running of the tribal governments. Coming to western India where we had the Bhil rulers; for example, the princely states of Dungarpur and Banswara in southern Rajasthan and the Panch Mahals of Dohad district in Gujarat. David Hardiman (1977) has studied the Bhils of western India. He gives a vivid description of the political organization of the Bhils. He informs that the Bhils consisted of a large number of localities, i.e., villages, each of which was under a hereditary chief, *Naik*. In this band there was no system of taxation which would have enabled them to accumulate a large surplus and, thus, set themselves apart physically from other fellows. The *Naik*, received occasional offerings from their Bhil fellows. Hardiman observes:

> The principal power of the chief was his ability to call on the Bhils of his area to serve as bowmen under him. This could be either to defend their territory or to carry out a raid on the peasants of the adjoining plains. It was through such raids that the chiefs and their followers made both ends meet, particularly in years of shortage. Some of the more successful chiefs maintained small bands of mercenaries who were paid out of a plunder rather than taxation.

From Hardiman's account, we infer that the tribal endogenous state pattern was not similar all over tribal India. For example, in Gujarat, Bhils had bands, and the chief was not hereditary. It was on his muscle power that he kept the Bhils of his band together. He even did not have right to levy taxes. However, the chief had a territory and a kind of government vested in him.

Conditions for the Formation of State among Indian Tribes

There are certain conditions for the formation of a state. If there is a territory, there needs to be some resources to maintain it and provide some security from outside attacks. If the conditions of forming a state are not fulfilled, there are chances of the collapse of the state and the government. We have seen above that there have been a few tribal states which had their well-defined territory. But, most of the tribal rulers were attacked not only from outside but within their own territory by non-tribal dynasties and the result was that in course of time the tribal rulers were routed out of their lands. This happened with many tribes, viz., Bhil, Gond, Koli and Chero. In a nutshell, there are four conditions which are responsible for the formation of a tribal state:

(1) settled agriculture and organized tribal village community,
(2) acculturation,
(3) emergence of dominant and powerful tribal minority, and
(4) security from exogenous attacks.

Settled Agriculture and Organized Tribal Village Community

Before taking to settled agriculture the tribals lived in hills and forests. At best, they practised shifting cultivation. Their sustenance depended on forest game and forest produce. In course of time, they took to settled agriculture and began to live in villages. The acceptance of agriculture also forced the tribals to take to irrigation. Writing on the preconditions for the formation of states, K.S. Singh observes:

> Settled agriculture and correspondingly organized communities gave rise to state formation. The extension of cultivation through a network of irrigation schemes was necessary for building and sustaining states... the migration of Ahoms to Assam from the east in the 13th century and the subsequent expansion of their rule positively encouraged the extension of *sali* (wet land) cultivation and new transplantation techniques.

Thus, the first condition of any state formation was stability. The tribals having states had to live a settled life and create a viable economy which could maintain the state. The Bhils of western India also experienced similar pattern of life. When the band system was abandoned, the tribe had to settle in plains and provide stability to their government.

Acculturation

Acculturation means borrowing from other groups. The tribals had no experience of agriculture. When they migrated to the neighbourhood of caste peasantry, they borrowed much of the agricultural practices of these people. Besides agriculture there was also borrowing in the realm of culture and social life. The vast network of temples, bearing the imprint of Orissa architecture in the Bhumij region, influenced the tribals. The same is true of Assam where the Bodos learnt *tantrik* practices from Hindus. Likewise, the Gond territory of Andhra and Madhya Pradesh had much of the imprint of Buddhism and Hinduism.

Thus, for a state to be viable socially and culturally, much had to be learnt from other castes. Though, the tribals had been rich in their culture but when placed against Hindus, they had plenty to learn from them. The caste Hindus were taken to be a dominant group and this made the borrowing more significant.

Emergence of Dominant and Powerful Tribal Minority

K.S. Singh, who also happens to be a historian, has amply demonstrated the emergence of some tribal leaders as heads of the tribal states. Without any dominant minority the process of state formation cannot be initiated. "The emergence of the Nagbansis as the head of the *Parha* confederacy, which ultimately developed into a kingdom, is an instance in point. The Ahom ruler Sukapa (1228-68) with the following of eight nobles, subjugated the Nagar and laid the foundation of the kingdom, so did the Cheros in Palamau. The Gond rulers of Garha Mandala probably imitated the Rajput princes who were established in Madhya Pradesh from the seventh century onwards."

There are several instances which show that there has been an establishment of a minority rule in tribal communities. Such minority tribal groups emerged in varying degrees in different parts of the country, including the north-east and central India.

Security from Exogeneous Attacks

The early and middle medieval period was characterized by constant warfare between tribals and non-tribals. The tribal states were required to accumulate money to encounter such outside attacks. The need for economic and human resources constrained the tribal states to take to feudalism. The feudalism could not prolong and weakened in the spate of invasions from outside. The Ahoms were locked in perpetual hostilities with the Kacharis, the Kochs, the Daflas and the

Chutiyas. At a later stage these states were invaded by Muslim armies from Bengal from 1615 to 1662-63. In Madhya Pradesh, the Gond dynasty of Garha Mandala was attacked and conquered by Asaf Khan in 1564, but it survived till the Marathas brought it to an end in 1780.

One can work out a long list to study the fall of tribal dynasties due to exogenous Hindu or Muslim attacks. Thus, the tribal states come into existence and were lost in oblivion in course of time.

Tribal Panchayats

State and territory are altogether different. The state has sovereignty, a territory, a judiciary and above all, physical force and the right to levy taxes. But, it must be stressed that the traditional *panchayats* of the tribals do not carry any elements of state and government. However, these traditional *panchayats* have some legitimacy among the tribals. They control the behaviour of their members by maintaining strict law and order.

If the tribal panchayats are powerful, so are the caste panchayats. In a limited sense both exercise some power. They usually deal with matters pertaining to land disputes, marriage, dissolution of marriage and the defiance of caste/tribe traditions. But, neither uses physical force, levies taxes, nor wages wars. These *panchayats* restrict their working to matters of social and cultural fields. For instance, among the Santhals, the head of the *panchayat* is called *Manzi*. He is elected by the villagers. No village function can be performed in the absence of the *Manzi*. Similarly, among the Oraons, the *panchayat* head is called *Perha*, who deals with local disputes and conflicts regarding land. He also settles disputes regarding marriages. Among the Todas of Nilgiri hills, the traditional *panchayat* consists of five elected members which is called *Naim* and it decides all social disputes.

In a society where there is a state, it is the legislature and parliament which make the law. In primitive societies, however, the traditional laws govern and control the behaviour of people. Normally, the customary laws relate to social matters and civil society. Even today, the civil society takes care of these laws. In a plural society such as our own, there is always a possibility of conflict between customary laws and state laws. In fact, these days, the state and civil society have come into conflict over some areas of life.

It appears that the customary laws regulate the life of the ordinary tribal. The Gonds, Santhals and Chaudharas practise elopement. The traditional *panchayat* settles such cases in its customary manner. However, the laws of the state now are considered to be final. Tribals who are not satisfied with their customary laws, access to state codes. The difficulty with the customary law is that it is implemented through moral authority. It does not have any corporeal punishment, and this has weakened the traditional tribal *panchayat*.

Further Readings

Fortes, M. and Evans-Pritchard, E.E. (eds.) *African Political Systems*, London, 1940.

Leach, E.R., *Political Systems of Highland Burma*, London, 1954.

Mair, Lucy, *Primitive Government*, Harmondsworth, 1962.

Shapera, I., *Government and Politics in Tribal Societies*, London, 1956.

Singh, K.S., *Tribal Society in India*, Manohar, New Delhi, 1985.

17

Social Movements Among Indian Tribes

The tribal situation in India is very strange. There are Munda and Santhal tribes which suffered from the some relative deprivation and exploitation but sought different solutions to their problems during the second half of the 19th century. Even their economy, social structure and culture were more or less similar. The Mundas joined the Sardar movement which was a movement for agrarian reform through constitutional means while the Santhals started the Kherwar movement aimed at religious revitalization. The primary reason for the difference was that for the former the main question was that of land while the latter felt that their culture and solidarity were threatened.

In the case of Jharkhand movement for autonomous state in south Bihar, the problem which the Oraon, Munda and Ho peoples had was that of the exploitative relations between them and the *dikus* or non-tribals (high caste Hindus). The movement, which lasted for more than five decades, has recently come to an end with the formation of new, separate Jharkhand state. On the other hand, the demand for a separate state for south Rajasthan, which was raised by Marxists in 1970, has now almost died. Yet another case is of the tribals of western Madhya Pradesh consisting of Dhar, Jhabua and Ali Rajpur districts where the Bhils and Bhilalas are reduced to the level of sub-human life but they do not resist exploitation. Rather, they are participating in some or the other ethnic/reform movement. Quite opposed to this, the Gonds of Hyderabad (Adilabad) have taken up Naxalism as an ideology to fight against exploitation.

Thus, in some places, the tribals are rebellious while at others, they are possessed by some reform movement or revivalism. How do we explain such a situation? It is the social structure of the tribal community which is responsible for leading the tribals to rebellion or withdrawal.

It was as early as 1950 when Evans-Pritchard made a plea that anthropologists should study problems rather than area or people. Unfortunately, in India, ethnography has still such a grip over the minds of anthropologists that analytical social anthropology has still to make headway. If we are really concerned with the lives of the tribals, we should, as anthropologists, immediately abandon ethnography. If the tribals have an ethnography which is characterized by bride wealth, elopement, magic charms and avoidance of Brahmin in ritual performances; so the caste Hindus have their own ethnography. Ethnography is ethnography whether it is of tribals or caste Hindus. If we make a brief survey of the situation of tribals pertaining to the country as a whole, we would find that only a small number of tribal groups today, out of a total of 461, are engaged in some kind of protest or rebellious movement. Most of the tribals in central India are engaged in movements which are essentially ethnic or reform movements. More and more are becoming teetotalers; engage themselves in *Bhajan Mandalis* and sing songs in god's praise. They are even today victims of exploitation either at the hands of high caste Hindus, political workers, officials or by their own elites who have become new exploiters.

Social anthropologists have hardly paid heed to such a situation. In their analysis of tribal movements they have lumped tribal movements together with peasant or agrarian movements. Condemning such an approach, K.S. Singh writes:

> There has been generally a tendency to link up all tribal movements, no matter how distanced they are in time and to lump peasants and tribes together. Such an approach tends to gloss over the diversities of tribal social formations, of which tribal movements are a part, both being structurally related.

Theoretical Approach

Sociologists and social anthropologists have defined the term 'social movement' variously. But, the crux of the definitions is that a movement involves a larger section of the society to take to some collective action. Normally, a movement intends to reform, reinterprete or oppose the existing order. What is particular about a movement is that it is an ongoing process. The process sometimes takes a very long time. We very often talk about India's freedom movement. It is said that this movement began with the 1857 rebellion and continued to remain in operation for an entire century.

L.K. Mahapatra, who has studied social movements of Oraons, Gonds, Konds and others, has defined tribal social movements as under:

> A social movement occurs when a fairly large number of people or an otherwise identifiable segment of their population deliberately band together for collective action in order to alter, reconstitute, reinterpret, restore, protect, supplant or create some portions of their culture or social order, or to better their life-chances by redistributing the power of control in a society.

M.S.A. Rao, a sociologist, has conducted a review of social movements in India. Obviously, his approach is not limited to tribal movements; rather he refers to movements in general:

> If we consider a social movement to be an organized effort on the part of a section of the population, involving collective mobilization based on an ideology, to bring about changes in the social system, then we have to see the social processes as consisting of interrelated activities...

There are several definitions of social movement. What is common to all such movements is that they continue over a length of time through repeated collective action. On the basis of the characteristics and definitions of social movements, their typologies have also been constructed. The same way, on the basis of differential orientation to the tribal culture and society, there are various types of social movements among the tribals. Movements may be reactionary, conservative, revisionary, or revolutionary. When the movements are organized to bring back the good old days, these are called 'reactionary' by Cameron, but are generally known as 'revivalistic' as Linton calls it. Conservative movements seek to perpetuate the *status quo* and are organized to obstruct the current changes. "Linton would call these 'perpetuative' movements. For Linton, both 'revivalistic' and 'perpetuative' movements are subsumed under nativistic movements."

Revisionary movements are those in which specific changes are desired, and efforts are made to realize them by modifying or supplanting the existing customs. The existing structure as a whole is not to be replaced. "All the movements organized for the 'improvement' or purification of the culture or social order by eliminating 'evil' or 'low' customs, beliefs, or institutions, typically, social mobility movements can be characterized as 'revisionary'." This category may be quite appropriately applied to the social mobility movements among the lower castes in the Hindu society, but not so in the case of a tribal group seeking to achieve a particular status in the local Hindu hierarchy.

In revolutionary movements, the aims are to replace the whole culture or social order with another more suitable, adequate or progressive culture. But this is not to say that actually everything in the contents is replaced, and historically, this has never been the case with any revolution. Moreover, a social movement, objectively and culture-historically considered, may be revolutionary, but may be visualized as purely 'revivalistic' by the participants.

Tribal Movements in India

There is enough literature on tribal movements in India. We have mentioned earlier that in social anthropology tribal movements have been lumped together with peasant movements. This thesis has been contested by K.S. Singh. However, there are social anthropologists and sociologists who do not agree with Singh. For instance, Kathleen Gough and A.R. Desai argue that the tribals today have virtually become peasants. And, therefore, their problems and issues cannot be separated from the general peasantry. Whatever may be the arguments, the fact remains that the tribals have not remained silent all through the periods of history. Their resistance has been quite active. K.S. Singh has edited two volumes on *Tribal Movements in India* (1982-83). He divides the movements into three phases. The first phase was between 1795 and 1860, and coincided with the rise, expansion and establishment of the British empire. The second phase covers the period of colonialism, "during which merchant capital penetrated into tribal economy affecting their relationship with the land and forest". The third phase deals with the period from 1920 till the achievement of independence in 1947. During this phase, the tribals not only began to launch the so-called separatist movement, but at the same time, participated in nationalist and agrarian movements. K.S. Singh classified the tribal movements into: (1) movements for political autonomy; (2) agrarian and forest-based movements; (3) sanskritization movement; and (4) cultural movements based on script and language.

Tribal Struggles in India during the British Rule

When the East India Company was established in India, the British territory which it covered in the beginning included Bengal, Bihar and Orissa. The British had to face popular revolts in both tribal and non-tribal areas. The problem with the British Raj was to maintain law and order in British territory. They had their own perception of tribal problems. For them, they were predatory bandits who used to rob the travellers. They did not want to go into details about the roots of tribal problems. Hutton, however, observed that during the early days of the British rule, the policy of their administration was detrimental to a great extent to the economic conditions of the tribes. Out of sheer ignorance the British neglected their rights and customs. In fact, the British Raj did not distinguish between the tribal society and caste society. Treating both on par, the British did not give any special treatment to the tribals.

Mundas

As a result of this policy, there occurred a series of armed uprisings from 1789 onwards. The Mundas expressed their dissatisfaction from time to time. On several occasions they offered armed resistance to the British which were crushed with the use of force.

In 1899-1900, there was a serious Munda revolt. It was led by Birsa Munda. The movement is known by his name as Birsa movement. Birsa was regarded by Mundas as an incarnation of God. Although the revolt was ruthlessly suppressed by the British, there has always remained a dissatisfaction with the Mundas.

Kols, Hoes and Oraons

Yet another insurrection engineered was by Kols of Chotanagpur. It was then a part of the province of Bengal. The members of the Ho and Oraon tribes also participated in it. The introduction of the permanent settlement by Lord Cornwallis into an underdeveloped tribal area, along with the alienation of tribal *zamindars* and Hinduization, led to general discontent among Bhumijs residing in Jungle Mahal and

Dhalbhum areas of the Midnapur district of Bengal Presidency. In 1832, under the leadership of Ganganarain Singh, they revolted against the British. But, like all other tribal revolts, "it was a hopeless struggle of the weak against the strong, the simple-minded and ill-informed against the concerted resources of a powerful system". According to the British writers efforts to ban the custom of human sacrifice resulted in a revolt by the Konds of Orissa in 1846. It was also easily suppressed by the British.

Santhals

Again, in Bihar and Bengal, the Santhals expressed their resentment against the British. The Santhal rebellion of 1855 was the most serious of all such outbreaks. In the course of the British operations about 10,000 Santhals were killed. Rebellions in 1871 and 1885 by the Santhals were also suppressed ruthlessly by the British.

Gonds

The Gonds of Andhra Pradesh and nearby areas expressed their discontentment against the British from time to time. The loss of their traditional privileges in the forest was one of the main causes of revolt in eastern Mandala. Raghavaiah has described the Rampa rebellion in the regions lying east of Godavari in Andhra Pradesh under Rambhupat. In 1891, the Gonds of Bastar in Madhya Pradesh also revolted against British.

Tribals of Andaman and Nicobar Islands

In 1858, the Andaman and Nicobar islands were reoccupied by the British. From this time onwards the aborigines of the islands constantly troubled the British authorities. As a result of the policy of the British to civilize them, the aboriginal population of the islands dwindled to an alarming extent. The aborigines resisted such attempts. The Onges and Jarawas were the most hostile tribes against the British.

Bhils

In the British territories of Khandesh, the Bhils disturbed the peace of the area. In 1829, the British raised a Bhil corps for establishing peace and order in the region. In Malva, a British administered area, Bhils were a constant source of trouble to authorities. In 1846, an uprising of the Bhils was suppressed.

Thus, in the 19th century, the tribal population of India was dissatisfied to a great extent with the policies of the British. Consequently, there were frequent revolts, uprisings or severe disturbances against the British by the tribals. L.P. Mathur, a historian of modern India (1988) very rightly assesses the British-tribal relations:

> Although the princely states were not directly administered by the British and British promised not to interfere in their internal affairs, they through their political agents virtually directed the princely states to act in accordance with their wishes. The policy towards the tribals residing in the states was also more or less framed by their rulers in accordance with the directions of the British. Consequently, the tribes living in the territories of the princely states also began to express their resentment against the policies followed towards them.

Why Tribal Revolt Against the British?

Tribal revolts in British India and also in princely states were not unconnected with the general popular discontent resulting from their ruthless exploitation. Although the British were not directly responsible for the dissatisfaction and occasional outbursts of anger by the tribals, they altogether cannot be exonerated from the blame.

In the opinion of Raghavaiah enhancement of rent and cesses, eviction from lands by wealthy moneylenders, sufferings caused by wars and harassment by the disbanded soldiery were responsible for dissatisfaction among the tribals, agrarian community and small communities in India. Along with social and cultural causes Stephen Fuchs (1965) has given due importance to the economic factors also. According to him intense dissatisfaction existed among the tribal societies against the social and economic conditions which they were forced to accept. The utter neglect of the area by the British was also responsible for the revolt of Bhumijs under the leadership of Ganganarain Singh.

K.S. Singh considers the land problem as one of the main causes of the rebellion of the Mundas under Birsa in 1899-1900. Due to ignorance about their rights on the land, the British enforced their laws on Mundas. Their areas were also included under the permanent land settlement introduced by Cornwallis. The regulations for the conservation of forest dispossessed the Mundas from their traditional rights. Under these regulations they were prevented from cutting wood free of cost for domestic consumption. They could not graze their cattle in the forests and were not allowed to utilize land in the forests for tilling. In the famines of 1896-97 and 1899-1900 the Mundas suffered heavy loss of lives and cattle. Similarly, the loss of traditional rights in the forests was one of the main causes of the revolts by Gonds in eastern Mandala. In the Andaman islands also, the aboriginal inhabitants opposed the intrusion of the British in the areas of their peaceful co-existence.

Haimendorf Furer has given yet another important reason for the decadence in the position of tribals. The British established a system of law which encouraged the outsiders to enter into the tribal hinterland and exploit their life. Similar was the opinion of Verrier Elwin. The outsiders were prevented from exploiting the tribal people to a great extent. For realizing their debts the moneylenders did not get any support from the government of the area. In order to earn their livelihood they had to depend on the goodwill of the tribals. The establishment of organized government under the British in different areas deprived the tribal communities from this effective safeguard against the attempts of the outsiders to evict them from land by instituting cases in the court. The position of the tribals in south Rajasthan was more or less the same. The attempts of the rulers to enforce law in the areas ruled by them indirectly helped the moneylenders. The immense sufferings caused by the Maratha and Pindari incursions for nearly seventy-five years, increase in cesses and taxes, attempts to prevent the Bhils to collect *bolai* and *rakhwali*, restrictions on cutting of wood from forests for domestic consumption, prohibition on gathering mangoes and flowers and leaves of *mahua* trees, stopping of free distillation of liquor, execution of *begar* (forced labour), exploitation by moneylenders, fresh salt and opium laws, and corruption among the officials were responsible for placing additional economic burden on tribals and depriving them of certain economic rights enjoyed by them for a long period. The pattern of agriculture, which the Bhils were advised to adopt, was unsuited to their habits and traditions. The land under their possession was small in size and unproductive. The Bhils of south Rajasthan, Gujarat and western Madhya Pradesh suffered intensively from frequent natural calamities in the form of scarcities and a famines.

Stephen Fuchs has also analyzed the causes of the revolts engineered by the tribals of central India during the British period. The high caste Hindus ill-treated the tribals. In case of subordination the tribals suffered exploitation. Feelings of nativism, i.e., rejection of alien elements and attempts to restore their pristine culture and religion is also considered as responsible for the rise of messianic movements among the tribals.

Ghanshyam Shah (1990), who has analyzed tribals movements in India, argues that though there are several reasons for tribal movements in India, a few of them are basic, for instance, most of the tribes live in forests. In other words, forests were the main source of tribal livelihood. In order to get the forest products the British government introduced certain regulations and permitted timber merchants and contractors to cut the forests. These regulations not only curtailed the rights of tribals over forest products, but also made them victims of harassment by the forest bureaucracy. The tribals resented this. Verrier Elwin (1945) observed that the "tribals firmly believe that the forests belong to them and that they have a right to do what they will with it. They have been there, they say, for centuries; it is their life and they consider themselves justified in resisting any attempt to deprive them of it".

The Soora tribe of Andhra Pradesh revolted violently against the forest department. "Opposition to the toddi tax was an important issue in the Rampa rebellion in this state. The Kharwar of Palamau (Bihar), participated in the forest *satyagraha* in 1930s demanding restoration of their customary rights to extract timber and collect forest produce for consumption."

Social Movements in the Aftermath of Independence

There have been several tribal revolts which could be included in the category of tribal movements. Raghavaiah, in his analytical study on *Tribal Revolts* (1971), has listed 70 such revolts from 1778 to 1971. In 1976, the Anthropological Survey of India had identified 36 tribal movements in the country. *Man in India*---the Journal of Anthropology---brought out a special issue on tribal rebellions in 1945. The editorial of the issue remarks: "These revolts have been neither numerous nor gravely frequent, yet there is scarcely any major tribe in middle or eastern India which at sometime in the last one hundred and fifty years has not resorted to this gesture of despair." The issue did not cover the tribal revolts in the North-East Frontier Region, now called the North-East.

After the attainment of independence and promulgation of the Constitution, the tribals received a new set of values. Now, it became the policy of the state to integrate them into the national mainstream. Before independence the tribals enjoyed a lot of autonomy. Now, they are required to maintain their identity but at the same time seek to be incorporated in the national mainstream. K.S. Singh, following the categorization of the Anthropological Survey of India, has given a four-fold typology of tribal movements earlier mentioned by us. We will now provide a short description of all these movements.

Movements for Political Autonomy

K.S. Singh examines the movements committed for political autonomy in a historical perspective. He says that at the beginning of the Second World War the Gonds and Bhils demanded the formation of a separate state. The movement was lost in oblivion for the tribals neither specified nor sustained it by any organization. The Kurma Bhimu in Adilabad (Hyderabad) demanded a Gond Raj in 1941. "Then, in a memorandum submitted before the States Reorganization Commission in the 1950s, the Gond leaders demanded the formation of a separate state for the tribals to be carved out of the tribal areas of Chattisgarh and contiguous districts of Rewa region and Vidharbh. A movement consisting of the Gonds of the lower strata led by Hira Singh developed in the late 1950s and reached its peak in 1962-63 before dying down."

I.P. Desai has described the tribal autonomy (*Adivasi Swayat Raj*) movement in Dangs area of south Gujarat in the 1960s. The movement was initiated by the CPI. It could not gather strength for any long time. Districts of south Gujarat, namely, Dangs, Bharuch, Surat and Bulsar were covered by this movement. Tribes which participated in the movement included Vasva, Bhil, Chaudhry, Ghodia and Kunbi. The tribal groups of Gujarat did not form a political party like Jharkhand Mukti Morcha. Only, the Communist Party of India (Marxists) supported this movement. It was argued that the tribals had become agriculturists and their rights as such should have been protected. It is through this movement that the tribals of Gujarat developed class consciousness. Their demand was that the Gujarat government exploited the forests and deprived the tribals from their livelihood and it should be stopped.

Desai has critically examined the demand for an autonomous State in south Gujarat. According to him, the main objective of this movement has been political only and the masses of tribals are not really interested in autonomy. Whatever may be the benefits of an autonomous tribal state, Desai argues, the tribals just have, a desire to integrate themselves into the wider national mainstream.

In the contiguous area of south Rajasthan, western Madhya Pradesh and northern Gujarat, the Bhils have raised their voice for an autonomous state comprising the districts of Dungarpur and Banswara (Rajasthan), Dhar and Jhabua (Madhya Pradesh) and Panch Mahals and Sabarkantha (Gujarat). The whole tribal belt is rich in minerals and it is argued that it should not be consumed by a non-tribal state. Quite like the demand for autonomy in south Rajasthan, the demand of the Bhils of western India, as a whole, also seems to be political.

However, the Jharkhand movement in Bihar was a major movement for the demand for political autonomy. It was a result of the interplay between historical, cultural, economic and political forces which culminated in the emergence of Jharkhand Party in the Chotanagpur division and the Santhal Parganas of Bihar in the late 1940s. Three factors were crucial in the Jharkhand movement:

(1) The administrative unity of the region.
(2) Exploitation of the people and material resources of the region by *dikus*, that is, aliens and outsiders, mainly the non-Biharis.
(3) The ethnic differences between the people of Chotanagpur and Santhal Parganas and the people of north Bihar.

If we look at the history of the movement, we find that before 1940s the Santhal people did not have any political consciousness. It was only at a later stage that they realized that they were being exploited by the *dikus*. The tribal autonomy in the Jharkhand movement comprises the whole of the Chotanagpur plains, some districts of Orissa, Bengal and Madhya Pradesh. The literal meaning of the word 'Jharkhand' is a tract of forest. Chotanagpur, Santhal parganas, and other adjacent districts belonging to the States of Bengal, Orissa and Madhya Pradesh are considered as parts of Jharkhand, by the protagonists of the movement. The formation of the Jharkhand party in 1950 gave a new direction to political and other welfare activities in the Jharkhand region in Bihar.

The history of the Jharkhand movement has passed through at least four phases since independence: (i) 1947 to 1954; (ii) 1955 to 1963; (iii) 1964 to 1969; and (iv) 1970 onwards. During the first phase, the movement was at its climax when Jaipal Singh emerged as the unquestionable leader of the *adivasis.* The Jharkhand Mukti Morcha was formally formed during this period. It contested the 1952 general elections, and emerged as the main opposition in the Bihar Legislative Assembly. The second phase started with the States Reorganization Commission's rejection of the demand for a separate Jharkhand state and ended with the merger of the Jharkhand party with the Congress Party. During the third phase, there emerged factions and cleavages among the Jharkhand cadre. This weakened the movement. After 1970, the movement flourished and recently ended with the formation of a new, independent Jharkhand state.

Agrarian and Forest-Based Movements

Since the tribals have become an agrarian society some of their movements are also included in this category. Essentially, the tribals are forest dwellers. Agrarian and forest-based movements are restricted to only a few regions, such as northern and southern parts of India. In central India, though tribal discontent over various forms of exploitation is widespread, it has been organized into movements only in some places involving a few tribes.

The Gonds in Madhya Pradesh did not have traditions of militant struggles waged in defence of their rights in land and forests. However, from 1940s, instances of the Gonds' resistance to encroachment on their rights in the forests have come to light. Since independence, their territorial and political systems have broken down and their rights over forests and land have been eroded. It appears that forest-based movements have petered out among the Gonds.

There are also instances of agrarian struggles among the tribals of Dhulia of Maharashtra. "There has been large-scale transfer of land from tribals to non-tribals who include moneylenders, rich landlords and traders. As landlessness and poverty, grew the tribals sought employment on low wages. A Sarvodaya worker, Ambar Singh Suratwanti, a Bhil himself, started to organize the *adivasis* in 1967. The Government of Maharashtra issued an ordinance in July 1975 to prohibit alienation of tribal lands and to provide for the restoration of lands alienated in contravention of the law."

Yet another instance of agrarian movement is from the tribal of Chotanagpur in recent years. There, the non-tribals took away the land of the tribals who organized themselves and got their land vacated from the the latter. However, it is not land but forest which has become the focal point of widespread disturbances. More than land, forest is intimately connected with tribal life. It is the abode of the spirit and the place of worship, the seat of lifecycle ceremonies including burial, it is the source of food, and of employment. "Under the law all such customary rights are extinguished in the reserved forests. In practice, tribals have been reclaiming land with the connivance of petty officials, and it is common sight to see patches of cultivation in reserved forests. Of late, the pressure on land has increased, there is demand for more land and, therefore, trees are felled in forest reserves causing loss not only to the national economy but also to the tribal economy in the long run."

A new mass movement, named as Chipko movement, has emerged against the decay of forest and forest laws. However, the participation of tribals such as Bhotiyas is very scant in this movement.

The Naxalite movement has come into existence at the initiation of CPI(ML). The movement mobilizes both tribal and non-tribal peasants against oppression by rich peasants, moneylenders and local officials. "The first phase of the movement was from 1967 to 1972 and the second from 1978 onwards. The movement established bases in north Bengal, the Srikakulam-Adilabad region of Andhra Pradesh, Chotanagpur-Santhal Pargana belt and the Bhil regions of western India. However, it is found that the tribal participation in the leadership structure of the Naxalite movement, as also in its oppression, was marginal."

Sanskritization Movement

Sanskritization has become a significant movement among the tribals, particularly of central India. Bhagat movements have been reported from Madhya Pradesh, Gujarat and Rajasthan. The sanskritization is sometimes also called the Bhagat movement. The tribals find solutions to their problems in the acceptance of the lifestyle, ideas, values and beliefs of the higher castes. Those who convert to this new life are known as Bhagats. David Hardiman argues that religiosity had a profound bearing on the state of consciousness of the *adivasis.* "It provides them with a practical code of political ethics to resist and struggle against their exploitation." Stephen Fuchs informs that "persons of low social status are pleased when they are treated with respect by the people of higher status".

Ghanshyam Shah has reviewed the ethnic movements among the tribals. He observes:

> These movements raised their aspirations and provided a sense of solidarity which enabled them, in some cases, to fight against their exploiters. In some areas like Gujarat and Madhya Pradesh, social reform movements led tribals to participate in the nationalist movement against British rule. In Rajasthan, the Bhagat movement was also aimed at raising the political objective of creating an independent kingdom of the Bhil.

Cultural Movements Based on Script and Language

If a careful study of tribal movements is made, it would be found that many of the things of tribal life are passing through a crisis. The tribals all over the country are essentially a hill and forest people. The forests are decayed and ruined. They no more provide any livelihood and support to the tribals. As the history turns, the tribals have become peasants. Now, they are faced with the problem of land alienation and dispossession. They had their animistic culture which is known as tribal culture. With the tribal identity as forest dweller being oblivious, the tribals are even losing their culture. K.S. Singh says that the tribals have started a new movement whereby they want to evolve their own culture and script. The Gonds have lost their *Gondi* language; the Bhils have lost their *Bhili*. And, thus, if the tribals fail to protect and revive their script and language, they will be deprived of their identity.

The tribals would be Hindus only, Christians only and their nativism or aboriginalism would be forgotten. Introducing the revival of tribal script and language movement, K.S. Singh observes:

> The efforts to evolve a script and build up an indigenous literature in tribal language may be seen as part of an overall movement to define and assert tribal identity.

Singh has reported about such a movement in Chotanagpur area, where the tribals are demanding for the revival of their tribal culture. They also want to recreate many of the cultural symbols of the past.

The movement for revival for language is also found among the tribals of central India and northern Andhra Pradesh. However, the involvement of tribals in such movements is very weak.

Further Readings

Fuchs, Stephen, *Rebellions Prophets*, Asia Publishing House, Bombay, 1965.

Mathur, L.P., *Resistance Movement of Tribals of India*, Himanshu, Udaipur, 1988.

Shah, Ghanshyam, *Social Movements in India*, Sage, New Delhi, 1990.

Sharma, K.L., *Caste, Class and Social Movements*, Rawat Publications, Jaipur, 1986.

Singh, K.S., *Tribal Situation in India*, Indian Institute of Advanced Study, Simla, 1972.

—, *Tribal Movements in India*, Manohar, New Delhi, 1982.

—, *Tribal Society in India*, Manohar, 1985.

18

Tribals: Conceptual Clarification and Their Problems

Tribal insurgency in the north-east, along with the upheaval in the Bastar area of Madhya Pradesh, made it quite clear that we should think over seriously the situation of tribals as a whole. It appeared that there was something wrong in our understanding of the tribals. It is a fact that the non-tribals and especially the caste Hindus suffer from prejudices against the tribals. There has been serious discrimination of tribals by the non-tribals. For long, the non-tribals have been cherishing the notion that the tribals are a savage lot and there is little scope for development among these people.

The need to concentrate on tribals became all the more serious when in 1950 we took to Community Development Programmes. The Constitution of India brought out a new set of values. It emphasized the need for the integration of tribals into the national mainstream. It became clear to all that in independent India if nation-building has to be done in right earnest, there cannot be two futures for one nation. It was not possible to keep the tribals tethered to an inhuman situation and the high caste Hindus raised to a progressive level. The tribals had to be compensated in terms of development via constitutional safeguards and guarantees.

Yet another aspect we must understand is that tribal society is altogether different from non-tribal society. There have been rumblings of discontent and unrest among the tribals resulting from their relations with the non-tribals. The root of the Jharkhand movement is the exploitative relations between the tribals and the *diku* (non-tribals). The insurgency in Nagaland is largely due to the hostile relationship between the Naga society and the state. The Bodos stress their demands in violent action because they find that the non-tribal society of Assam has not historically been friendly with them. Many of our tribal movements stem from the discriminatory relations between the tribal society and the non-tribal society.

It is for the security of the country and also for the development of tribals that social anthropology has to study tribal problems, tribal policy and tribal social change seriously. We should also try to find out the cultural patterns which emerged from the outcome of social change among the tribals. It is largely a matter of structural or value and ideology change.

Historical Backdrop

We talk a lot about caste in India. It would not be wrong to say that a large stock of our researches in sociology and social anthropology belongs to caste study. Sometimes caste and tribe are used synonymously in India. It is to put an end to this myth of putting caste and tribe together that the Constitution of India created a unified Commission for Scheduled Tribes and Scheduled Castes. Theoretically, caste is different; it is a part of the hierarchical caste system. On the other hand, tribe is never a part of caste system. For the 461 tribal groups in the country we cannot prepare any hierarchical scale. For instance, we cannot say that Gonds are at the top of the tribal hierarchy. Each tribal group is endogamous. There is no hierarchy among them.

Actually, the notion of tribe does not have its origin in India. It is, in all respects, a colonial construct. The term 'tribe' is used in a different context in Europe. It is associated with a territory, a language or a common name. Nihar Ranjan Ray (1972), who was a historian of great repute, argues:

> ... with the rise and growth of nationalism in Europe, the term 'tribe' came to be used in denotation of a particular state of socio-political evolution of a community of people within a given territory and language area. Class, tribe, nation, etc., thus came to denote the various successive stages in the progressive march of a people aspiring towards nationhood.

What Ray wants to stress is that in Europe tribals were those who lived in a particular territory with a specific language and had to be brought in the web of European nations. The notion of tribe which the foreign anthropologists had in mind was that of Europe. When Risely, Hutton, Blunt, Russell and O'Malley worked in India, they had the idea of the European tribal situation. They had a feeling that if the British had to settle in India, they had to bring the Indian tribals living in remote corners within the fold of British Raj. In other words, just like the European nations, the British colonial lists in India also had an objective to bring the tribals within their arena or territory. Ray, therefore, compares the Indian and European situations. Thus, what is common to Europe and India is that tribals have to be incorporated in the national mainstream.

One more important point which helps us understand the Indian tribals is that they have to be viewed as a group of people passing through a period of socio-economic evolution. The groups which inhabited the plains went higher in the evolutionary scale. They developed a culture, a particular way of life and above all, a literature. On the other hand, those who lived in the interior parts, lagged behind in the evolutionary ladder. Physical hurdles and an unfriendly environment kept them backward. The tribals, therefore, constitute a type of society which is characterized by a special kind of social-economic evolution. There are, therefore, a large number of factors which impinge on us to study the tribals with all seriousness. We have to pool all our resources to bring the tribals on par with the lifestyle of the average Indian citizen. Second, the historical and ethnic differences between the tribal society and caste society has to be bridged. Third, the tribals have to be adequately compensated for the discrimination, injustices and exploitation which they have suffered in the past.

Origin of the Term 'Tribe'

Let us turn to the origin of the term 'tribe'. Derived from a Latin root, the Middle East term *tribuz*, meaning the three divisions into which the early Romans were grouped, came to evolve into the modern English 'tribe'. Among the Romans, the 'tribe' was a political division while the Greeks seem to have equated it somewhat with their 'fraternities' at times, and with geographical divisions at others. In Irish history, however, the term meant families or communities of persons having the same surname. In certain other areas of the western world and certain periods of history it stood for a division of territory allotted to a family or community. Today, among the anthropologists and sociologists of western origin, the term means, according to the latest edition of the *Oxford Dictionary*:

> A race of people; now applied especially to a primary aggregate of people in a primitive or barbarous condition, under a headman or chief.

It is this meaning, roughly speaking, that most of the western scholars working in India, have been using, but with slight change of emphasis here and there.

The Marxist Approach

Any social science has its universal and particularistic perspectives. Theory normally looks at its universal application. But each concept has its immediate and local perspective which applies only in a restricted area. The natural sciences have achieved a maturity where its concepts have universal application. The chemistry of water is a universal category but the water in a particular village may be hard and thus, lacks the universalistic meaning. But, in third world countries, it has gained a particularistic historical connotation.

Maurice Godlier is a Marxist anthropologist. He emphasizes the meaning of tribe on a universal plane. According to him, when the anthropologists use the term 'tribe' they understand it by a type of society which is different from other societies. In India, for instance, from caste society. Second, when we use the term 'tribe' we have in mind the stage of evolution attained by a particular group of people. Both these characteristics are two kinds of realities. One is that it is a society and second is that it has attained a particular evolutionary stage. Explaining the meaning of the term tribe, Godlier writes:

> Anthropologists, when using the term 'tribe', refer to two realities, two fields of facts which are different, yet linked. Almost everyone uses it to distinguish *a type of society* from others, one specific mode of social organization which can be compared to other modes of organization in society—'bonds', 'states', etc... It also indicates *a stage of evolution* in human society.

What Godlier wishes to emphasize it that tribe indicates a reality. The mode of production determines the social organization of a group, and the mode of production of the tribals is different from that of the non-tribals and, therefore, the tribals constitute a group differentiated from other groups.

Godlier applies the Marxian framework of mode of production in the analysis of the concept of tribe. His observation is that anthropologists today are in a theoretical crisis. The use of the term 'tribe' in the present world context has undergone great change, and is challenged by several anthropologists. It was Edmund Leach who first challenged the meaning of the term 'tribe'. He was followed by Neira who has cried out against the "scandalous imprecision of the concept". The concept is fully vague according to him. Julian Steward, another social anthropologist, who is credited with having worked on evolution, calls the concept of tribe as a 'holdall' concept. It includes everything, and excludes nothing. Swartz, Turner and Toden have systematically chosen to ignore the use of the word. For them, the word is non-existent. But, there are other problems with the concept of tribe. Godlier writes:

> This is only half the trouble; along with these criticisms of a theoretical nature there is real consternation and violent attacks have been made against the ideological use of the concept in its secondary form and the related concept of tribalism.

Godlier is right. The concept of tribe is in a state of crisis, both theoretically and ideologically. In India, there are many people who argue that the safeties and securities given to tribals have created an ideological war between tribe and caste. Referring to the world situation, Godlier says that the existence of tribal organizations in Africa, America, Oceania and Asia appears, in fact, to be the reason for difficulties encountered by young nation-states in their economic and political development and in achieving independence. The continuing presence of pre-colonial tribal organizations appears to have been the cause for insurgency in north-east India.

It could be said that the concept of tribe is nothing but a creation of the colonial period. But even those groups for which continuity with the past could be claimed, have lost so many of their traditional characteristics that in fact, they must be viewed as new entities.

Godlier elaborately explains the dispute and crisis pertaining to the concept of tribe. With all arguments it should be said that if we want to use the concept for the world as a whole, we shall have to develop it as a universal category. He writes:

> Now, there are many anthropologists and politicians who challenge, as theoretically false and politically harmful, the use of concepts such as 'tribes' and 'tribalism' in order to determine modern contradictions found in 'underdeveloped' countries. They see in the contradictions attributed to tribalism not so much a relic of pre-colonial structures (tribal organizations believed to have been destroyed but which flower again, even violently), as a legacy of the colonial period and the new relations involved in neo-colonial domination.

There is thus need to redefine and revisit the concept of tribe. The reasons, according to Godlier, are simple. Our definition of tribe goes back to the period when the containing societies were pre-capitalistic and pre-industrial and the tribals were comparatively at a lower stage of evolution. At his point, Godlier defines a tribe as a social organization, characterized by special mode of production.

Definitions of Tribe

The social anthropologists have made certain attempts to define the concept of tribe. Take, for instance, the evolutionary thinker Morgan (1877). According to him, the tribal forms of social organization are specific. In this respect Morgan's book *Systems of Consanguinity and Affinity of the Human Family* (1871) is very important. He says that in a tribal society kinship relations dominate all forms of relations. In these kinship relations, there is an internal logic and the social anthropologist tries to identify the internal logic. This logic could be discovered by the study of marriage rules and kinship terminologies, customary rules and laws. Morgan says that the concept of tribe thus may be defined as below:

> A tribe is a completely organized society, therefore, a form of social organization capable of reproducing itself.

Morgan further explains his position and says that a tribe is synonymous to clan. Therefore, in a broad way, a tribe is a collection of clans. It is characterized by a social organization having the following traits:

(a) it is not civilized,
(b) it is not a political society,

(c) it is not a state,
(d) it is a collection of clans,
(e) it has a name,
(f) it has a separate dialect, and
(g) it has a government.

Marshall Sahlins, a forward looking contemporary social anthropologist, for the first time in 1961, defined tribe as under:

> A tribe is a type of society within the framework of comparative anthropology as well as a stage of social evolution within a theory of history.

Sahlins argues that a tribe can be properly analyzed if looked at from evolutionary and historical perspectives. According to him, there are four stages of the development of the concept of tribe:
(i) the band,
(ii) the tribe,
(iii) the chiefdom, and
(iv) the state.

In his later work of 1968 he arranged these stages into three and eliminates the chiefdom stage. His definition of tribe now runs as follows:

> A tribe is of the order of a large collection of bands but it is not simply a collection of bands... there is a kingdom also which coordinates economic, social and religious activities and redistributed a large part of the production of local community.

Sahlins differs from Morgan. His thrust of definition is on the collection of bands. For a tribe some government is essential. This government coordinates other activities of the tribe.

Thus, it is clear that the tribe is a collection of clans or bands. It has a name, a dialect, a state, a government and above all it is a kind of society having some specific mode of production. It is at a certain level of development stage. However, our understanding of a tribe is based on the European concept of tribe. Before we shift to India and define tribe, we must stress that in the above definitions we have approached the concept of tribe from a universalistic perspective. We now employ the particularistic approach, that is, Indian approach to the definition of tribe.

The Particularistic Approach: Indian Perspective

Nihar Ranjan Ray had an opportunity to hold a national seminar at the Indian Institute of Advanced Study, Simla in 1969. It is on this occasion that he gave a discourse on the definition of tribe. He says:

> The so-called tribals of India, it is well known, are the indigenous, autocthonous people of the land, in the sense that they had been long settled in different parts of the country before the Aryan-speaking peoples penetrated India to settle down first in the Kabul and Indus valleys and then within a millennium and a half, to spread out over large parts of the country along the plains and river valleys.

Ray explains the term 'tribe' from the historical point of view. He further says that the tribals had an underdeveloped economy; they practised agriculture and animal husbandry. All over the country the tribals tried to possess as much land as possible.

Tribals in India are known by several names: *vanvasi*, *girijan*, *adivasi*, *janjati*, etc. Before the promulgation of the Constitution, social anthropologists in India made an attempt to define Indian tribes. Much literature has come out on tribes and their way of life. Despite this huge mass there are a few anthropologists who have carried out extensive fieldwork among the tribals. Among these may be included Verrier Elwin, G.S. Ghurye, D.N. Majumdar, N.K. Bose and F.G. Bailey. Let us try to understand the concept of tribe as developed by some of these Indian anthropologists.

Elwin was not a professional social anthropologist. He came to India as an intellectual and gradually converted to Indian ways of life and thinking as a result of contact with Mahatma Gandhi, the national movement and tribal India. He was in close touch with Gandhi as well as Nehru, and he studied and lived with several of the country's little-known tribes. He married a Gond girl and made Mandala as his centre for social work. He is considered to be an authority on tribal methods.

It is in 1943 that Elwin come out with a small pamphlet type book, *The Loss of Nerve*. The book was received critically. He has argued that the tribals are the original settlers to this land. They lived with nature and their habits and way of life are conditioned by nature. They have all the excellent characters of human beings. When these tribals come in contact with the non-tribals, they are likely to shed their qualities of life. And, that is their loss of nerve. They should be kept isolated from the mainline of civilization.

The proposition made by Elwin created a debate in India. The Gandhian workers argued that the tribals cannot be kept deprived of the benefits of civilization. Isolation in this case would keep them backward, ignorant, poor and illiterate. At a later stage, Elwin proposed a Public Park Theory. According to this theory, the tribal area should be cordoned off from the main civilization. The tribals will live in the public park. This was his plan for keeping the tribals isolated. However, at the close of his life, Elwin changed his theory and pressed for the integration of tribals on the basis of their genius. Nothing of the modern civilization should be imposed on the tribals. This philosophy was given by him in connection with the study of north-east tribals.

G.S. Ghurye was a typical Maharashtrian Brahmin. He was intensively oriented to the Hindu way of life. He contested the Elwin theory of 'public park' or isolation. His argument was that the tribals are a part of Hindu society. They could be considered as backward caste Hindus. Ghurye was agitated against Elwin and soon after the latter's book, *The Loss of Nerve*, he came out with his own book, *The Aboriginals, So-Called and their Future* in 1943. The book is actually a rejoinder to Elwin. Ghurye's argument is that tribals all over the country are increasingly assimilating themselves into Hindu castes. Actually, he devoted two long chapters on tribal assimilation in this book. It is here that he defines tribals as backward caste Hindus. He further says that the problems of tribals are not specific to tribals only. They are problems of backward caste peasants. Thus, according to him, the tribals are both backward caste Hindus, and peasants.

N.K. Bose, another serious social anthropologist, a Gandhian himself, also attempted to define Indian tribes. He says that the tribals are original inhabitants of this country. But they are increasingly coming within the fold of Hinduism. He has dealt with the matter of tribal integration and says that the Hindus have a method of drawing the tribals within the caste system. Hinduism is very liberal and it can provide a place to tribals. While talking on Hindu method of tribal absorption he also pleads for a secular model for integrating the tribals.

F.G. Bailey has studied the Konds of Orissa. In his earlier work he studied the economic frontier of the castes. In this study he argues that the castes have given a new dimension to the economy. He studies 'tribe', 'caste' and 'nation' and establishes their correlation. It is in this context that he says that the Konds are a tribal group in the sense that they share a common culture and speak a common language. From a linguistic point of view, Bailey says that tribe and caste have separate identities. In the same way, both these structures differ in their political organization. Bailey further argues that the tribal political system is segmentary. Its base is agnatic kinship. On the other hand, the caste political organization draws from social legislation. The Konds have their political relations with the lower castes also. His logic is that there is a continuum from tribe to caste. It is this theme---the tribe, caste and nation—which constitutes the continuum of social change. In course of time the tribals assume the status of a caste and finally the castes lose their entity and integrate themselves in the nation.

In short, Bailey has presented a hypothesis which needs to be verified. He says that the Kond politics is based on agnatic kinship relationship. It is a segmentary system. There are some social anthropologists who argue that the tribals constitute a whole society. Bailey, however, does not subscribe to this view. For him tribal society is a segmentary society moving from its status of tribe to caste and finally nation.

The Official Definition of Tribe

The universalistic definition of tribe is Euro-centric. It has the feudal and colonial background of the 19th century Europe. Its particularistic aspect given on the historical background of our country, whether by Ghurye, Majumdar or Elwin, is not homogeneous and varies from one anthropologist to another. In such a confusing heterogeneity, the Constitution has made a way out. It has laid down a democratic procedure to identify the tribals. The tribals are officially defined as Scheduled Tribes. The official definition of Scheduled Tribe keeps in its view the country's historical experience and tribe-caste relations.

Article 366 (25) of the Constitution of India has defined Scheduled Tribes as "such tribes or tribal communities or parts or groups within such tribes or tribal communities as are deemed under Article 342 to be Scheduled Tribes for the purpose of this Constitution". By the Scheduled Tribes Order, 1950, issued by the President in exercise of the powers conferred by Clause (1) of Article 232 of the Constitution of the India, 312 tribes have been declared to be Scheduled Tribes. Later, by an Act of Parliament, some other groups were also included in the schedule.

In the *People of India* project, K.S. Singh has registered 461 tribal communities in India. Out of the total groups 172 are segments. Many of these are as good as discrete categories. The total population of the Scheduled Tribes in the country stands at 6,77,58,000 (1991 census). They constitute 8.08 per cent of the total population and are spread over all the states except Punjab and Haryana. The largest concentration of tribals is in Madhya Pradesh (23.22%), followed by Orissa (11.46%), Bihar (11.26%) and Maharashtra (11.18%).

The Constitution has provided certain protective and developmental safeguards for the development of these tribal groups. They are provided reservation for a period extending to 2010. The main objective of giving certain benefits to the tribals is to draw these communities of people into the mainstream of life.

Problems of Tribals

Tribal India today is at the crossroads. The tribals are between societal self-awareness and cultural synthesis. On one hand, their problem is to protect their culture from the onslaught of alien cultural forces, and on the other, they are required to integrate themselves in the cultural mainstream. They have become, it is said, victims of 'cultural terrorism'. There are efforts by fundamental Hindu organizations such as Vishwa Hindu Parishad (VHP), Bajrang Dal and others to identify the tribals as Hindus. On the other hand, there are Christian missionaries who convert them into Christianity. To recall the discussions which took place in the Simla seminar of 1969, a Naga participant observed that the country should make it clear as to what it wants to make the tribals in future. The participant, Krieleno Terhuja, said:

> It was often alleged that the Nagas have become anti-national and have not quite come into the mainstream of Indian life because they have become Christian and have been kept isolated. Is the Hindu way of life the mainstream? I believe that this should not be so. But even the Nagas calling themselves Indians are treated differently in the plains of Assam. The Nagas did not come under the influence of any other religion of the world prior to their contact with Christianity around 1880 and in the present circumstances they are not likely to become Hindus. This should not, however, lead to a conclusion that they are off the mainstream.

The problem with the tribals is that they do not know what is meant by national mainstream. Surely, it should not mean Hindu mainstream. If it is secular mainstream determined by the Constitution, what will happen to the civil life of the tribals. They have their customary laws and if they part with it, their very identity is jeopardized. It appears that the tribals have to be integrated into a common whole, where all diverse cultures of the country, along with various populations and geographical regions, are brought together. Besides, the tribals have to be integrated into a common productive organization and finally into a secular and democratic set up provided by the Constitution.

Basically, the problems faced by the tribals are not homogeneous. For instance, the problems of north-east tribals, such as Nagas and Bodos, are different from those of central India. The former are geo-political. These problems are international and related to our neighbouring countries like China. On the other hand, the heartland tribals have problems of land alienation, poverty, illiteracy, exploitation and victimization from former *jagirdars*, *dikus* and high caste Hindus.

Apart from these, there are other issues which have cropped up as a result of social change observed among the tribals. A meeting of anthropologists was held in May 1972 at Vigyan Bhawan in collaboration with the Indian Institute of Advance Study, Simla, and the Indian Council of Social Science Research, New Delhi. This meeting set out to identify the basic problems of tribals along with the problems emerging from social change. We specify some of these problems.

Problems Resulting from Social Change

For long the tribals lived in isolation where they had many problems such as of illiteracy, backwardness and subsistence economy, exploitation and victimization. But, as a result of the implementation of protective and developmental safeguards, they encounter some new problems. These are as under:

(1) Participation in a democratic, secular, socialistic society has affected their village unity and encouraged factionalism on party ideology.
(2) Directed change has created unrest. There is demand for political autonomy.

members of the family have also to be served; some token of liquor is to be given to be neighbours and village kin group and, therefore, it is after a considerable thought that brewing is undertaken, this discourages liquor consumption. Thus, prohibition is a great strain on tribals and needs to be improved.

Displacement

Tribals are displaced or evacuated when big or small dams are constructed. Patrick McCully (1998) takes a serious look at big dams. The human consequences, especially of displacement, are very painful. The tribals who live in the hills and forests are the worst sufferers. McCully writes:

> Evidence from numerous dam projects shows that resettlement kills: sickness and death rates usually increase markedly after displacement, specially among the very young and very old.

If we look at the Narmada Bachao Andolan led by Medha Patkar, it shows that most of the oustees of the river valley are the poor tribals. Arundhati Roy has also made a systematic study of the problems of displacement with the tribals found in the valley of Narmada. She says that the dam construction is not in the interest of the common good of tribals. The tribals have raised a very important slogan: Whose is Mother Narmada? Ours, ours (*Narmada maiya konin chhe? Hamri chhe, Hamri chhe*). The oustees of the dam argue that just as farmers have tilled the land and fishermen have used the river, tribals have been living in self-sufficient harmony with the forest for generations. The government cannot own the resources of the community. The biggest flaw in the Narmada project is the lack of a viable rehabilitation policy for the oustees. Thus, one of the severest problems of tribals is their displacement and the resultant rehabilitation.

Emergence of New Exploiters

Directed social change has given rise to a new class of entrepreneurs, i.e., the neo-rich tribals. Earlier, the exploiters were *dikus* or non-tribals. Today, the exploiters are within the tribals themselves. Nothing can be worse than this. The exploited have now become exploiters.

De-scheduling

When the list of Scheduled Tribes was declared by the President of India, the number of such tribes was 312 only. Within a period of 50 years, this number has gone up to 461. The multiplication is conspicuous. It was expected that with the investment on development the number of Scheduled Tribes would go down. The increase in their size shows that the whole process of scheduling has been politicized. In the case of Rajasthan, for example, P.C. Jain (1999) informs that the socio-cultural and economic status of the Minas—the predominant tribal group of Rajasthan—is much above that of the Bhils. He suggests, why not de-schedule Minas? As a matter of fact, we should have started de-scheduling of some of the tribals who have made substantial improvement in their status. But de-scheduling cannot work as it is highly politicized.

Maintaining Tribal Ethnicity

If the Brahmins, Rajputs and other innumerable high caste Hindus maintain their ethnic identity, so also should the tribals. No group has the right to 'impose' their way of life and ideology on the tribals. If the present trend of drawing tribals into the Hindu or Christian fold continues, there would be no Bhil or Gond or Ho or Naga left in the country.

Integration

Integration is a continuous process. There are some alternatives given by the government and social anthropologists for the smooth integration of tribals. Earlier, in the 1940s, Verrier Elwin suggested the isolation of the tribals. At a later stage, in his *A Philosophy for NEFA*, he argued that the tribals should be persuaded to change but 'no imposition' of non-tribal life should be made on them. D.N. Majumdar talked about 'selective integration' for the tribals. He suggested that the tribals should not be exposed to or their area made 'open' for all aspects of non-tribal life, but some good and beneficial items of civilization should be introduced in their life. G.S. Ghurye, on the other hand, considers tribals to be backward caste Hindus. Their problems should be treated on par with the general peasantry of the country.

The Constitution of India makes tribal integration quite simple and straightforward. It says that the tribals, on one hand, have to integrate themselves in the political and economic life of the nation and simultaneously, on the other hand, they should be allowed to 'live' their ethnic life. Much depends on the tribals themselves. It is they who have to choose out of several alternatives.

Diversified Economy

Traditional tribal economy was forest-centric. Now, since the decay of forest economy, the tribals have taken to capitalist form of agriculture. They are expected to produce more than two crops a year. They are also required to grow commercial crops. On the other hand, a section of them has taken to service profession by way of economic diversification. It must be understood that it is difficult for hill and forest dwellers to adapt to new jobs which require education, professional skills and activities.

Education

Illiteracy is rampant among the tribals. In order to benefit from directed social change they have to accept education as a major step for earning a good income. Women should also be equally encouraged to educate themselves. If the tribals do not accept literacy and education in a massive way, it will continue to hamper their progress and development.

Health

It need not require to emphasize that there are a few diseases among the tribals that have almost reached epidemic. Though the government has implemented programmes to reduce infant mortality and maternal mortality, the problems continue to mar their lives and sap their strength.

The problems of the tribals are innumerable and are likely to remain so for a long time to come. Though some of the problems are specific to tribals, these cannot be viewed in isolation from the wider context of the themes and strategies of national development.

Further Readings

Elwin, Verrier, *The Loss of Nerve*, Oxford University Press, 1943.

Ghurye, G.S. *The Scheduled Tribes*, Popular Prakashan, Bombay, 1943.

Godlier, Maurice, *Perspectives in Marxist Anthropology*, Cambridge University Press, Cambridge, London, 1978.

Jain, P.C., *Planned Development among Tribals*, Rawat, Jaipur, 1999.

McCully, Patrick, *Silenced Rivers*, Orient Longman, 1998.

Ray, Nihar Ranjan, *Tribal Situation in India*, 1972.

Shah, Ghanshyam, *Social Movements in India*, Sage Publications, New Delhi, 1990.

Singh, K.S. (ed.), *Tribal Situation in India*, Indian Institute of Advance Study, Simla, 1972.

19

The Changing Tribal India

The pangs of social change which tribals are experiencing are not new. As aboriginals they lived in this country and have seen the rise and fall of several empires. They have participated in several battles, either supporting the local rulers or resisting them. Social change has become the companion of tribals all over the world. Claude Levi-Strauss observed that "every culture must liberate its creative potential by finding the correct equilibrium between isolation and contact with others". Social change, thus, is not a challenge. What the tribals have to do is find the equilibrium between their indigenous culture and the borrowed culture.

Methodologically, we should be very clear that like other sections of society the tribals also change. It is not possible for the non-tribal world to attain the cyber age and the tribals remaining static. It would be dishonest to portray them as savage and backward. In 1967, Eliott Skinner, an anthropologist and the US ambassador in the Upper Volta in West Africa, wrote:

> It is unfortunate that tribalism with all its connotations of primitivity and traditionalism is the name given for the identity being used by groups competing for power and prestige in contemporary Africa. Some of the names which are now used as symbols for group identity do refer to distinct socio-cultural entities in the past. However, many of the so-called tribal groups were creations of the colonial period. But even those groups for which continuity with the past could be claimed have lost so many of their traditional characteristics that, in fact, they must be viewed as new entities.

In the process of massive social change tribals thus have experienced vast transformation. Malinowski studied the Argenauts of the

Western Pacific in 1922 and declared that these tribals would experience social change very soon. His observations made in the first quarter of the 20th century runs as below:

> Ethnology is in the sadly ludicrous, not to say tragic position, that at the very moment when it begins to put its workshop in order to forge its proper tools, to start ready for work on its appointed task the material of its study melts away with hopeless rapidity. Just now when the methods and aims of scientific field ethnology have taken shape, when men fully ready for the work have begun to travel into savage countries and study their inhabitants, these die away under our very eyes.

K.S. Singh very proudly asserts that Indian ethnology is quite rich in the study of tribals. We grant it. But has this ethnology meted away during the last three or four decades? As a matter of fact, the tribal ethnology of Risely, O'Malley, Hutton, Bose and Majumdar has become outdated today. The tribals have integrated themselves into the regional, state and national societies and finally into global economic, cultural and political systems.

Let us refer again to Malinowski's Trobrianders. These people have largely adopted to processes of modernization on their own terms. Modernization has led to changes in political organization, economy and politics of identity. However, it must be said that despite all these changes, the kinship system and the system of ceremonial exchange among Trobrianders still function, though they do not have the same meaning as before.

Another case is that of Azandes of Africa studied by Evans-Pritchard. These people have taken to wage earning in cotton. The Nuers have also witnessed the some social change.

If Azandes, Argenauts and Nuers have changed considerably, the Indian tribes, e.g., Bhil, Gond and Toda have also experienced social change. It is not that the social anthropologists all over the world were not unaware about the social change which the tribals would encounter in the future. Writing about the wider social change coming in the tribal world, Thomas Hylland Eriksen says:

> Anthropologists have, since the very beginning of the subject, been aware of tendencies towards what we may call cultural entropy—that historical process which is today sometimes described as 'the

global cultural melting-pot', as 'cultural creolization' or, rather inaccurately, as 'westernization'. However, one may wonder if we are not presently at the threshold of a new era in the history of humanity, the global era.

Eriksen is right in his observation. In any corner of the world today—whether tribal or non-tribal—it is not possible to live without regular contact with the world market and the state. The fact is that the tribals today cannot escape from state and its citizenship. The state, on the other hand, is in close relationship with the civil society. Money has become a dominant medium. The subsistence economy of the tribals has taken to capitalistic economy. Tourism, migration and other factors of transport and communication have brought the tribals closer to the wider society. It is in this context that we look at the changing tribal India.

Social Change and Official Tribal Policy

Historically, the Government of India has not been able to resolve the ethnic relations between the tribal society and caste Hindu society. The framers of our Constitution have not entered into this controversy. They have, in a straightforward way, administratively defined Scheduled Tribes for the purpose of governance. If we dig a little deeper into the controversy between the relationship of caste and tribe, we find that it goes back to the Vedic period. Yogendra Singh writes:

> Ethnographers and historians are undecided on the extent to which a relationship existed between the pre-historic Indus valley culture and the traditional vedic culture in India.

Even if we analyze the tribe-caste relations during the British period, we find an uncertain situation. For instance, Hutton maintains that "caste system and many cultural traditions of Hinduism have organic links with the tribal cultures". Ghurye also holds similar views. However, O' Malley and Elwin believe that the tribal and the Hindu traditions are separate. The controversy holds true even today and the government has wriggled out of it by creating a special category called Scheduled Tribes.

Official Policy

The attitude of the government towards tribal problems and social change emerges from the Constitution, tribal development programmes, five year plans and developmental policies enunciated from time to time. The government wants that the tribals should be given benefits of development and protective safeguards. These are necessary because they have suffered enough from exploitation, discrimination and oppression by the rest of society. They remained backward, poor, illiterate and weak because of all this.

Yet another approach to the tribal policy can be seen in the statements made by Pandit Jawahar Lal Nehru in his Foreword to Verrier Elwin's book, *A Philosophy for NEFA*:

> I had no sensation of superiority over them (tribals). My ideas were not clear at all. But I felt that we should avoid two extreme courses: one was to treat them as anthropological specimens for study and the other was to allow them to be engulfed by the masses of Indian humanity.

When Pandit Nehru wrote the Foreword to the second edition of Elwin's book, he laid down five fundamental principles also known as *Panchsheel*. These are as under:

(1) People should develop along the lines of their own genius and we should avoid imposing anything on them. We should try to encourage in every way their own traditional arts and culture.
(2) Tribal rights in land and forests should be respected.
(3) We should try to train and build up a team of their own people to do the work of administration and development. Some technical personnel from outside will, no doubt, be needed, especially in the beginning. But we should avoid introducing too many outsiders into tribal territory.
(4) We should not overadminister these areas or overwhelm them with a multiplicity of schemes; we should rather work through, and not in rivalry to, their own social and cultural institutions.
(5) We should judge results not by statistics or the amount of money spent, but the quality of human character that is evolved.

The *Panchsheel* or five principles of tribal development were given in 1958. How far these principles have been followed in government programmes, is a matter of analysis. But it is clear that we do not want to impose a non-tribal way of life on the tribals. They should develop in accordance with their own traditions. However, when we talk about the integration of tribals, that is, the change of tribals from their primordial way of life to a secular way of life, we have to draw the tribal people into the mainstream of national life.

Social and Cultural Change in Tribal India

In the presidential address to the Indian Sociological Society (1994), Yogendra Singh observed:

> Major occupational and techno-cultural changes have taken place in our society due to the political, social and economic developments. These changes have promoted linkages and interactions among castes, tribes, religious groups and cultural regions. We notice significant magnitude of the spread effect of these cultural changes across regions and ethnic boundaries. These developments have, however, also reinforced people's self-consciousness and narrow cultural identities organized on principles of ethnicity, religion, caste, language and region. The process of cultural integration on a national scale has grown but with simultaneous increase in search for cultural autonomy.

At the empirical level we find that the tribals have become conscious of the fact that their ethnic identity is invaded by Christianity and Hinduism. Fundamentalists of both these religious cults are active in the field. We notice this not only as manifested in their political demands, but also in their movements, such as "return to tribal religion" despite their religion of conversion. Whether trials or non-tribals, cultural pluralism is rooted in our folk culture and civil society. The cultural nationalism, as propounded by some political parties and cultural organizations, does not suit the ethnic structure of our country.

With these introductory observations we give below some of the social and cultural changes observed among the tribals over the years.

(i) Changing Social Stratification: From Tribe to Class

Enough literature is present in social anthropology which indicates that tribals have attained the status of a class from that of ethnicity. S.D. Badgaiyan informs that tribal stratification has become complex in Chotanagpur. For instance, the Mundas of this area have formed themselves into classes. Similarly, Ghanshyam Shah (1977) writes that the differences in material possessions create sharply differing patterns of consumption in food, dress, housing, etc., and also parallel differences in, for instance, the level of education, religious orientation and preferences in political life.

Reporting about the tribal situation of south Gujarat, Jan Breman observes that there is today a class stratification among the Chaudhri tribe. Though the class formation among the tribals in this part of the country has developed to the level of Marxian class consciousness, there has definitely emerged an "agrarian under class, which today comprises 60 per cent of the members of tribal castes which lag behind economically, socially and politically". Breman continues:

> As we have already stated, this process of cumulative inequality has not yet crystallized into a rigid class stratification. This does not alter the fact that to an increasing degree the separate strata are beginning to distinguish themselves from each other by their lifestyles and living conditions.

(ii) Depeasantization

The tribals took to agriculture sometime during the first quarter of the 20th century. At that time they had enough land in their possession. Increasingly, the caste Hindus made their entry into the tribal hinterland and since then the tribal land slipped into the hands of these non-tribals. On one hand, with the rise in population, the land-man ratio increased, and on the other hand, the tribals experienced land alienation. As a result, a section of the tribals in Orissa, Bihar and Madhya Pradesh have migrated from their parent villages. This has made them job workers instead of peasants. This taking up of non-agricultural occupations is called depeasantization.

Breman finds a new trend among the Halpatis and Chaudhras of Bardoli *taluka* of Surat. He says that the tribals have not only been depeasantized, they have also become proletarianized. The fall is serious. Breman writes:

> I would interpret the foregoing as indeed signifying the operation of a process of proletarianization of the peasantry, or depeasantization: one that is complex, but as yet particle in its impact. The new 'technology' has produced conditions in which by a variety of means, the

poor peasantry has lost an increasing share of the operated area to rich peasants. Not only that but the poor peasantry is, in different ways, being transformed more and more into a rural proletariat.

(iii) New Ethnic Dimensions

K.S. Singh, Stephen Fuch and P.K. Bose have very elaborately established that there has appeared an ethnic stratification among all the tribals of the country. The north-east tribals have accepted Christianity as their major faith; it is also found among the tribals of Gujarat, Madhya Pradesh, Orissa and Bihar. The indigenous tribal religion has split into several reform movements. Fuchs reports about the messainic movements among the tribals of central India. Bhagatism is the new form of religion accepted by the tribals. This has created an ethnic stratification among these indigenous people.

(iv) Migration

Traditionally, social anthropologists have defined tribals as an immobile stock of people. They hardly move beyond their village. But the search for employment has pushed them to work in big cities and the Gulf countries. Today, these tribals are working as migrant groups outside their parent village. Government jobs have also encouraged them to move from one posting to another in a state or outside the state. Migration thus has emerged as a powerful factor for the transformation of tribals.

(v) Political Socialization

Rajni Kothari has analyzed the political forces which work among Indian tribes. He says that the universal right for voting, party functioning, social activism have all initiated a strong process of political socialization among the tribals. They have become shrewd enough to make compromises and alliances at the regional, state and central levels.

(vi) Diversified Economy

The tribal subsistence economy now has become diversified. Their traditional occupation was related to forest and forest produce. They have been experts in wood-cutting. Along the coastal belt, they are adept in fishing. But they do not have any hereditary occupations on the pattern of caste Hindu system. This has enabled them to take to any occupation they may find suitable at a given point in time.

(vii) From Local to Global

Eriksen considers social anthropology as a study of small places and large issues. According to him, in the present era of globalization, the tribals cannot be kept in isolation. There are linkages. The small places, that is, the tribal homelands are linked with the region, state, nation and the world. The world problems, for instance, environment, endemics of malaria, cancer and AIDS have become the larger problems of a tribal village also. It was during the 1960s that the media theorist Marshall Mcluhan introduced the concept of 'global village'. This notion was intended to account for the new cultural situation in the world, following the spread of modern mass media. The world had become one place.

The tribals are no longer an encapsulated mass of people restricted to hills and forests. They have become a part of the larger process of globalization. The process is a vigorous and continuous one, and the tribals have to decide which direction they have to march in. The future of the tribals rests on their own rational and cultural decision.

Further Readings

Breman, Jan, *Of Peasants, Migrants and Paupers*, Oxford, 1985.

Doshi, S.L., *Tribal Ethnicity, Class and Integration,* Rawat Publications, Jaipur, 1990.

Eriksen, T.H, *Small Places, Large Issues*, Pluto Press, London, 1955.

Featherstone, Mike (ed.), *Global Culture: Nationalism, Globalization and Modernity*, Sage, London, 1990.

Friedman, Jonathan, *Cultural Identity and Global Process*, Sage, London, 1994.

Sharma, K.L., *Social Stratification in India,* Manohar, 1986.

Index